Further Praise for
Join the Club

"   ıy weaving together riveting stories across many domains,
f   he downfall of dictators and the alleviation of poverty to spiri-
tu   evelopment, Tina Rosenberg mounts a compelling case for the
po   r of social change fueled by positive peer pressure. Her justly cel-
eb   d gift for unraveling knotty social and political issues with
lu   rose is wonderfully on display, together with genuine inspira-
ti   nd insight."   —Thomas Carothers,
Carnegie Endowment for International Peace

"ı   Rosenberg ranges widely as she explores the strategies that
ha   succeeded in changing personal behavior in ways that have
lim   d the spread of AIDS in South Africa, allowed severely abused
wo   en in rural India to transform their lives, enabled young people
to   d in ousting a tyrant in the Balkans, sharply improved the
pe   rmance in mathematics of minority students in Texas, and in
m   other circumstances have helped people overcome seemingly
im   sible challenges. Her reporting is meticulous, her writing is
flu   nd her insights are penetrating. This is a path-breaking book."
—Aryeh Neier, president, Open Society Institute

"V   an exhilarating book. Tina Rosenberg has found an extraor-
di   y key to solving problems as diverse as the misery of Indian
Untouchables, the dictatorship of Slobodan Milošević, dangerous sexual behavior in AIDS-ridden South Africa, the anomie of

American suburbs. It is organized pressure from peers. And she doesn't just philosophize. She has been to the crisis points, all over the world, and she tells us the stories of wonderful human beings."

—Anthony Lewis, author of *Gideon's Trumpet*

"Parents quickly learn to their chagrin that their children's friends often have more power over them than anyone else. But thanks to Tina Rosenberg's compelling and path-breaking book we now know that peer pressure can be a force for good, not just for American children but for huge social improvements around the world. I'm feeling better already!"   —Jonathan Alter, author of

The Promise: President Obama, Year One

Also by Tina Rosenberg

Children of Cain:
Violence and the Violent in Latin America

The Haunted Land:
Facing Europe's Ghosts After Communism

TINA ROSENBERG

WINNER OF THE PULITZER PRIZE

JOIN THE CLUB

HOW PEER PRESSURE CAN
TRANSFORM THE WORLD

ICON BOOKS

Published in the UK in 2011 by
Icon Books Ltd, Omnibus Business Centre,
39–41 North Road, London N7 9DP
email: info@iconbooks.co.uk
www.iconbooks.co.uk

First published in the USA in 2011 by
W. W. Norton & Company, Inc.
500 Fifth Avenue, New York, N.Y. 10110
www.wwnorton.com

Sold in the UK, Europe, South Africa and Asia
by Faber & Faber Ltd, Bloomsbury House,
74–77 Great Russell Street,
London WC1B 3DA or their agents

Distributed in the UK, Europe, South Africa and Asia
by TBS Ltd, TBS Distribution Centre, Colchester Road,
Frating Green, Colchester CO7 7DW

Published in Australia in 2010
by Allen & Unwin Pty Ltd,
PO Box 8500, 83 Alexander Street,
Crows Nest, NSW 2065

ISBN: 978-184831-300-2

Book design by Lovedog Studio

Printed and bound by CPI Mackays, Chatham ME5 8TD

To Rob

Contents

INTRODUCTION: Join the Club xi

ONE Turning Positive 1

TWO The Empire of Irrationality 21

THREE Righteous Rebels 43

FOUR Corporate Tools 63

FIVE The Calculus Club 97

SIX Angels of Change 125

SEVEN A Problem That Has No Name 159

EIGHT The Party 211

NINE   The Judo of Fear   249

TEN   Next   283

ACKNOWLEDGMENTS   353

NOTES   355

BIBLIOGRAPHY   371

INDEX   381

Join the Club

THE MIST WAS STILL RISING FROM THE FIELDS ON A COLD Sunday morning in early May. In a subdivision of brick-and-beige Tudor-style connected houses in Algonquin, Illinois, a far suburb of Chicago, three men in sweatpants jogged up to the house of Ryan Boldt. His family still asleep, Boldt stepped out the door and into the street. It was just before 6 a.m.

Boldt is an area pastor for Willow Creek Community Church, a megachurch with some 18,000 people at services every weekend, a church repeatedly named the most influential in America. The men—Doug Yonamine, Tim Auch, and Matt Lossau—all live in the neighborhood. The Lossau family even moved here in part to be near Doug and his wife, Jen.

For them, this Sunday-morning run is church. The men run through the subdivision and onto a road alongside a field. They run slowly, talking the whole time. "Some of my most intense spiritual conversations have been on the bike paths," Doug said. He is a kind, earnest, serious, and highly organized man of Japanese ethnicity, then forty-three years old, who works in the legal department at the Willow Creek Association. The men aim to run every Sunday, Tuesday, and Thursday morning at six—the hour dictated by Doug's promise to Jen to be back in the house before their three children wake up.

Doug, Tim, and Matt do more than jog together. The men and their families, along with two other families, make up a Table group, one of Willow Creek's neighborhood-based small groups. They do most of the things typical American suburban families do—but they do them together. They eat dinner together once or twice a week. They exercise together. They take one another's kids to and from Girl Scout meetings, church activities, and school sports. They meet to talk about the Bible and religious issues. When they have problems with their kids, struggles with their jobs or money or personal challenges, they bring them to the group. The meetings, formal and informal, are church too, a concept embraced by Willow Creek and the families who make up this small group.

There is some irony in the notion that Willow Creek would be encouraging its members to form the upper-middle-class, minivan-and-riding-mower version of, well, a commune. Willow Creek was built in the 1970s on the values of anonymity and isolation, constructed so people could meet God without having to bump into other humans along the way. Back then, Bill Hybels, the church's founder and still its senior pastor, sought to construct a church that would reach out to the person he called "Unchurched Harry." Harry, the Willow Creek mythology held, was wary of church, so Hybels built a Sunday service to make him comfortable, one that didn't push him and demanded nothing. Unchurched Harry, loath to be pressured or even approached, could simply sit and watch.

But Hybels soon realized that more mature believers needed more community. Like nearly every other large church in America of any denomination, Willow Creek began in the 1980s to place its members in small groups, the idea being that moving nearer to God is best done in close relationship with other people on the same mission.

Willow Creek's small groups used to be very similar to those in widespread use. Eight or ten people who shared some basic characteristic would get together every two weeks in someone's living room to discuss the Bible, talk about a particular reading, or simply discuss how to respond to daily challenges in a Christ-centered way.

In the early 1990s, when he was still single, Doug Yonamine joined one. He signed up to be in a small group with four other single men who lived all over the Chicago suburbs. The group chose parts of the Bible to read and discuss or followed a small-group study guide.

Since they had not forged real connections, the members didn't see each other after the group formally ended. When Doug once ran into the group's leader, he was startled; Doug had thought the man had moved to California.

The group had not satisfied him. He did not feel it was helping him grow in his relationship with God. The meetings were too far away, too infrequent, too superficial. As he put it, "How do you get someone to become a fully devoted follower of Christ in six hours a month?"

Doug Yonamine's feelings were reflected by many others in the congregation. Willow Creek was beginning to realize that conventional small groups were failing many of its members. They could not provide the intimacy and community that people needed for their spiritual growth. A congregational survey in 2004 confirmed what Doug Yonamine felt: many of the church's most mature believers felt spiritually stalled in their small groups.

So, two years later, Willow Creek redesigned its small groups. Gone were the forty-five-minute drives, the contact limited to twice a month. Now Willow Creek held that the path to God was found in "doing life" with next-door neighbors.

This was what was occurring on Sundays at 6 a.m. in Algonquin. The members of this Table group—so named because its centerpiece is a communal dinner—are neighbors. They still have formal gatherings twice a month, over dinner at the house of Tim and Michele Auch. But because they are neighbors, a lot of life is going on between the formal meetings. That's what creates the real intimacy. The men now jog together instead of going their separate ways at a health club. Several of the couples were already going to Willow Creek services on Saturday night at 5:30. So they decided to eat dinner afterward in the food court downstairs, as a group. The Auch family shared a back fence with the Moss family and their children treated both houses as their own. In this sprawl of anonymous Chicago suburb, the Table group has created a small town.

Over time, the members of the Algonquin Table found that the intimacy brought results. They started to take risks, to talk about deeper issues, more personal struggles. In the years before the Table group started, Michele Auch had had a strong disagreement with God and decided she didn't want to talk to Him. "I'd say to Tim, 'OK, I'm ready to try again. I should pray,'" she said.

"But I never did. And I never did. And I never did. I didn't climb out of it until the Table group. I didn't actually start trying until I was entwined in other people's lives again."

Across the world lies Jawalke, a place so different from Algonquin, Illinois, that it is hard to believe the two communities share a planet. Jawalke is a village about an eight-hour drive east of Mumbai, India. Here are people who by accident of birth dwell at the very bottom of the earth's hierarchy: women from the Untouchable caste, a group so oppressed and reviled that traditionally they have to walk with a little broom to erase their footprints as they go, lest they contaminate someone of higher caste. Yet these women have something in common with Doug Yonamine and Michele Auch: they are transforming their lives and their communities by joining a new peer group, one so strong and close-knit and persuasive that they have begun to think of themselves in a different way.

Babai Sathe spent her childhood, such as it was, caring for eight younger siblings. She did not attend a single day of school. Instead, she did farm labor for higher-caste families and often was paid in bread and vegetables instead of money. She was married at the age of ten.

Babai's husband was eighteen at their wedding, and had not wanted a ten-year-old wife. So he took a second one, and Babai went to live in her mother-in-law's house with her husband and his other wife. There she settled into the traditional role of a daughter-in-law: servant. Her job was to take care of the goats and cows and to carry the milk into the city of Jamkhed to sell it, a five-mile walk. She was given only stale bread and chiles to eat. Her husband and her mother-in-law beat her, sometimes with a stick; she still bears scars on her foot and her lower leg. One day the beating was particularly bad—she couldn't walk the next day. When her mother-in-law was out of the house, Babai ran away.

This was the life that women in rural India expected, especially Untouchable women. Babai was sure the rest of her life would be more of the same. "I thought about suicide," she recalled. "I had no support from anyone, no education, no money." The usual consolation for a woman in her situation is that if she has sons, someday she too will become a mother-in-law, able to reduce her daughter-in-law to chattel. But Babai has no children.

She has, however, found other solace. Today Babai Sathe is a respected and influential person, one of Jawalke's village doctors. She provides prenatal care, delivers babies, weighs newborns, takes blood pressure, and treats diabetes and pneumonia and skin infections. She teaches women in Jawalke how to cook nutritious food for their children, disinfect water, and avoid disease. She has organized campaigns to plant trees and vegetable gardens and to build toilets, and she has helped women to obtain small-business loans. In a swift and dramatic shift that is reversing centuries of oppression, women in Jawalke are now starting their own businesses and participating in village-improvement projects, and Untouchables no longer face the same discrimination. This is in part due to Babai. And in 2005, Babai Sathe—still impoverished, able to read and write only enough to find the right bus and keep her logbooks—was elected mayor of Jawalke.

What happened was this: Babai became a member of a sisterhood of women recruited and trained to become health workers in their village. The Comprehensive Rural Health Project (CRHP), founded by a husband-and-wife team of Indian doctors in 1970, is based in the nearby city of Jamkhed. The program asks villages to recommend potential health workers from among their most oppressed citizens, on the theory that it is these women who will care most about the health of the poorest. About half are Untouchables. Some have hands gnarled by leprosy. The model has grown to transform hundreds of villages, and it is being taught to tens of thousands of people who visit Jamkhed from all over the world.

The first step for the women is to go to Jamkhed for two weeks of training. There they learn about the diseases most common in rural India and how to treat and prevent them. They learn to deliver babies safely. Most important, they learn how to teach others in their villages about these practices, as the new ideas usually conflict with cherished beliefs.

Teaching the women these skills is not as difficult, or as important, as teaching them confidence—encouraging the women, especially the Untouchables, to feel that they can speak up and have something to teach. Shobha Arole, a doctor who is the daughter of the program's founders and now runs it, said that some women at first would not say their names or lift their gaze from the floor. They are so deeply entrenched in the caste system that some have difficulty accepting that women of different castes can cook for each other or sleep in the same room.

But they encourage each other to change. After a few days, they make food for each other. They learn to sleep under one huge blanket. After the initial two weeks, each one spends a week in the village of a more experienced health worker. There the trainee can watch her work and, most important, gain confidence that she, too, will someday be listened to and respected.

Then the trainees go back to their own villages, reinforced by a team of doctors, nurses, and social workers who visit each village about once a week. The women go to Jamkhed every Tuesday to stay overnight. Each week they study a new health issue—but just as important is the strengthening of their bonds with their sister village health workers.

Each of these women began with not a scintilla of hope yet acquired a new identity. "First we change, then we go to work in the village," said Lalenbai Kadam, one of the oldest active health workers. Each woman is now more prosperous. Although the program does not pay them for their work, they receive training and loans to start their own small businesses. Each is now respected by her fellow villagers. They have the satisfaction of improving the lives of the people with whom they grew up. "We tell each other our troubles," one health worker said. They also tell each other their successes.

Babai still lives in a windowless hut, sleeps on a mat on the floor, and cooks outside over a twig fire, but the program has made her rich in other ways. "When I came to Jamkhed, I was like a stone with no soul," said Babai. "They gave me shape and life, courage and boldness. I became a human being."

THIS BOOK IS THE STORY of a tremendously powerful kind of social change, one that has accomplished astounding missions. It has drawn oppressed and destitute women in India like Babai Sathe out of misery and passivity, women who have in turn transformed the people around them. It has brought worshippers like Doug Yonamine into a closer relationship with God. It has persuaded teenagers to demand safe sex. It has prompted black and Latino students to excel in college-level math and science classes that minority students, even well-prepared ones, often fail. It has helped cure tuberculosis in hundreds of millions of people around the globe. It has enabled generals to have confidence that their troops would emerge from their foxholes to face enemy fire. It has spurred millions to quit drinking and drugs. It has led teens to rebel against cigarettes, in the process enfeebling a tobacco-company advertising campaign of $35 million per day. It has organized a passive and fatalistic citizenry subjugated by a dictator into the nonviolent army that overthrew him. I call this phenomenon *the social cure*.

I stumbled on the social cure by accident. As a writer, I have specialized in highlighting seemingly intractable problems. I had written a book about political violence in Latin America, and one on the moral and political conundrums of dealing with the past in post-Communist Europe. I had written magazine articles about human rights, poverty, and public health. Problems were in endless supply. But it was starting to seem more interesting and valuable to write about solutions—to find the places where these problems were being solved.

In 2007, a friend asked me what I was working on. I related to her the story of Ivan Marović. A few years earlier, Marović had been a student in Belgrade, Yugoslavia, one of the leaders of the student group called *Otpor* ("Resistance" in Serbian), which sparked the popular movement that overthrew Slobodan Milošević in 2000. Marović then began to travel the world, working with several other Otpor leaders to teach the methods the group had used to bring about nonviolent change.

What made Otpor different from every other democracy movement I had ever seen was that it focused on stripping away the fear, fatalism, and passivity that keep a dictator's subjects under oppression. Otpor turned passivity into action by making it easy—even cool—to become a revolutionary. The movement branded itself with hip slogans and graphics and rock music. Instead of long speeches, Otpor relied on humor and street theater that mocked the regime.

Serbia's youth saw life as bleak and hopeless. They thought of themselves only as passive victims of dictatorship. But now this group everyone was talking about offered them a way to do something important. Each of them could be a part of something, a protagonist, someone who could actually make history. Otpor turned fear inside out—the movement was appealing *because* of the risks. A teenage boy with no future—and very little present—could be assigned a cell phone and memorize passwords and hide from the police at midnight. He could be James Bond. If he was arrested, he became a rock star, and the next day all the girls wanted his phone number.

Traditional democracy activists create political parties. Otpor created a party. People joined the movement for the same reasons they go to the hot bar of the moment. "Our product is a lifestyle," Marović said. "The movement isn't about the issues—it's about my identity. It's about being cool. We're trying to make politics sexy."

While explaining to my friend my fascination with Otpor and its methods, it struck me that I had already written this story—the year before, in a very different context. South Africa has a teen AIDS-prevention program—from the available data, an effective one—called loveLife. It is to the classic public-health approach what Otpor is to the typical political party. It doesn't focus on providing information about AIDS—South Africa's teenagers already know about AIDS and how to avoid catching it. Fatalism and denial, however, keep them from applying that information to themselves.

LoveLife doesn't try to scare teenagers. It doesn't lecture. Instead, it aims to create an "aspirational life-style brand for young South

Africans," as its literature says. It was initially modeled on a Sprite campaign. LoveLife uses celebrity gossip, music, fashion, school sports, relationship advice, and media comprehensible only to teenagers to create a club that teens want to join. In that club, a girl can hear from another girl—from a similarly bleak and dusty township—why and how she rejected a boyfriend who demanded sex without a condom. And she will start to think about doing the same.

THE TYPICAL ATTEMPT TO SOLVE a social ill focuses on giving people information, or it tries to motivate people through fear. But these strategies tend to fail exactly when the issue becomes most salient and emotionally fraught. The more important and deeply rooted the behavior, the less impact information has and the more people close their minds to messages that scare them.

This book tells the story of people who have successfully used a different way, one based on changing behavior by helping people obtain what they most care about: the respect of their peers. Otpor was a student-led, antigovernment democracy movement in Serbia; loveLife is a government-financed public-health program in South Africa. Willow Creek's Table groups are designed to motivate some of the world's most comfortable people to take psychological risks in order to deepen their religious commitment; Jamkhed's village-health-worker program encourages some of the world's least fortunate people to take social risks to bring better health to their villages and break down caste and sex discrimination.

Although these campaigns differ in almost every conceivable way, they are in essence all the same campaign. They accomplish what countless efforts throughout the centuries have failed to do: persuade people to take action that is crucial to their long-term well-being but appears unpleasant, dangerous, or psychologically difficult today. They get people to join the demonstration or confront their inner demons or avoid risky sex or trespass on long-held concepts of proper behavior *not* by lecturing them about that long-term interest or, indeed, talking about anything rational at all. Instead, they aim at what people want now: to belong, to be part of the in crowd, to be loved and admired and respected. These programs change personal behavior through social pressure. They offer people a new and desirable club to join—a peer group so strong and persuasive that the individual adopts a new identity.

"When I ask young people what made them change, they never say, 'You gave us information,'" said David Harrison, the former executive director of loveLife. "They say, 'I feel an identity with a new way of life. I can be like my friend whose life has changed.'"

No one would dispute the power of peer pressure to modify behavior. Along with genetics, peer pressure is probably the most important influence on who we are. The conventional wisdom used to be that the way parents raise their children is what is key. Certainly parents like to think so. But this notion was effectively destroyed by Judith Rich Harris in her book *The Nurture Assumption*. She argued that once parents have passed along the genes, they have very little influence over their children—except to choose their child's peer group. That peer group is what shapes us.

Harris marshaled the scientific arguments, but it is likely that she did not have to go far to convince most readers of the importance of peers. It seems intuitively correct. One does not have to accept Harris's idea that parental nurture matters practically not at all to comprehend the overwhelming influence of peers. Our parents may be our first language teachers, but after we acquire peers, we learn how to talk from them—not only what language to speak but also how to pronounce words, which ones to choose, how loudly to say them. Peers control what we wear, what culture we consume, what we buy. The social norms set by our peers dominate our choices about what we value and what we expect in life.

What is surprising is not the importance of peers but how little use most of us have made of this extremely significant fact. When I would tell someone I was working on a book about peer pressure, invariably my questioner would assume I was talking about bad behavior. The term *peer pressure* usually carries negative connotations. People associate it with teens trying drugs and seemingly grown-up families falling into debt to keep up with the Joneses. The purpose of this book is to argue that peer pressure can be equally powerful when employed for good, and to show how it is done.

Identification with a new peer group can change people's behavior where strategies based on information or fear have failed. The social cure does this in a wide variety of situations. It works stunningly well with teenagers—the group most likely to be taking the kind of behavioral risks that cry out for help and, not coincidentally, the group most responsive to peer pressure. But it also works with adults. It is applicable in many different spheres of life, at all different levels of class and economic development. The social cure is a natural solution to help people take care of their own health—to encourage them to accomplish the difficult tasks of avoiding risky sex; abstaining from cigarettes, alcohol, and drugs; losing weight; getting exercise and following doctors' orders. But it also has been successfully applied to problems in fields as diverse as political change, university education, organized religion, criminal justice, poor-country economic development, and the art of war.

While many of the stories in this book are relatively recent, emerging even in the past decade, the phenomenon is hardly new. The best-known example of the social cure is Alcoholics Anonymous (AA), which works by regularly gathering a small number of people with the common goal of sobriety. They reinforce in each other a new pattern of behavior and a new identity, while holding each other accountable for failure.

AA was born in the 1930s, but the social cure as an idea is much, much older. It has surely existed as long as war has. Armies run on unit cohesion. For a young man with his life before him, leaving the relative safety of the foxhole to charge into enemy fire—often in the service of a cause he does not consider his own—is unnatural behavior. He does it for his buddies, and because his buddies' esteem reinforces his own identity as a brave soldier.

Every good military commander exploits this phenomenon. Shakespeare's King Henry V uses it to rally his troops to the Battle of Agincourt on Saint Crispin's Day in 1415. In the play, Henry's men are outnumbered five-to-one by the French. When his cousin Westmoreland wishes for ten thousand more men, Henry stills him with a speech ending in these words:

We few, we happy few, we band of brothers;
For he to-day that sheds his blood with me
Shall be my brother; be he ne'er so vile
This day shall gentle his condition:
And gentlemen in England now a-bed
Shall think themselves accurs'd they were not here,
And hold their manhoods cheap whiles any speaks
That fought with us upon Saint Crispin's day.

This is probably the most famous passage in all of Shakespeare's history plays, and it is an example of the social cure.

For centuries, organized religions have relied on the idea that your relationship with God is deepened when you are also in relationship with others. Hence Jesus's fellowship with his disciples and the Jewish law that at least ten men are needed for public worship. Randy Frazee, a pastor who is the guru of neighborhood-based small groups and presided over the formation of Willow Creek's Table groups, likes to say that the Table-group concept is simply a return to what Jesus did.

The social cure has been employed by big organizations purposefully searching for a new way to solve an obstinate problem. South Africa's loveLife and Florida's revolutionary antismoking campaign for teens were government-financed programs created by committee, spearheaded by people who simply believed in getting inside teenagers' heads and reaching them with the messages to which they will respond. Although these are both examples from the field of public health, the people who came up with these strategies were—tellingly—not public-health specialists but marketers and advertisers by instinct.

Willow Creek, also a large bureaucracy, adopted an idea from Frazee, an outsider who was considered rather eccentric. But eccentric is sometimes just another word for pioneering. Many examples of the social cure come from one innovator or a small team of them. Ivan Marović was one of eleven students at Belgrade University who met in the city's cafés. They smoked, drank coffee, and hatched the unlikely idea that, armed with the sensibilities of Monty Python's Flying Circus and some really great black T-shirts, they could topple Slobodan Milošević, who by the time of his fall had more blood on his hands than anyone in Europe since Stalin.

Babai Sathe was brought into the sorority of village health workers by a program founded by Raj and Mabelle Arole. The Aroles had graduated top in their class at Vellore Medical School—"an education that would make you a good doctor in France or Germany," Raj Arole said. But it was not what was needed in rural India. They set out on their own to create a new way to promote health among India's poor.

Uri Treisman, in the 1970s a mathematics graduate student at the University of California at Berkeley, adapted the social cure to the teaching of calculus in American universities. Treisman was trying to solve a problem widely seen in college math departments: black and Latino students often did poorly in calculus. This was true even when they reached college well prepared and with high test scores. It was true even when they had taken calculus successfully in high school. Treisman was not willing to accept the usual conjecture about the reasons for this. What he came up with instead has revolutionized the teaching of math—to minorities, but not just to minorities—and upended the conventional wisdom about why people succeed or fail in college.

In all these examples, the people who employed the social cure bushwhacked their own route. They possessed no map. They had to grope in the dark to formulate their ideas and make them work. They had to fight off the armies of conventional wisdom to defend them. Their stories, which form the basis of this book, show how the social cure's various creators invented it and fought for it, how they applied it and defended it against challenges, and how the social cure might work on other problems.

Because of these entrepreneurs, those who are wrestling with large and important social challenges that have proven resistant to conventional attacks can now take a fresh look at these problems. We can draw on an accumulating store of join-the-club models for guidance and encouragement. Perhaps most important, these stories compel us to look at people anew. They reveal novel answers to the questions of what moves us, what we want and need, and why we do the things we do. The innovators described in this book have reimagined fields as diverse as public health, poverty alleviation, education, spiritual development, and political change. But they are also part of an even broader struggle—to reimagine social change, to introduce into common parlance a new strategy based on the most powerful of human motivations: our longing for connection with one another.

Join the Club

Chapter One

Turning
Positive

IF AIDS EVER FINALLY VANISHES FROM THE EARTH,
humankind will likely look back on one aspect of the epidemic as the most damaging and also the most puzzling:
our near-complete failure to stop sexual transmission of the
disease. There are very few people who do *not* know how
AIDS is transmitted. A good number of the people most
at risk for AIDS have watched friends or family members
waste away and die from the disease. Yet they continue to
have sex unprotected by monogamy or even condoms.

At the turn of the twenty-first century, AIDS was a crisis of biblical proportions in South Africa. In 1990, only 1
percent of South African adults had been infected; by the
end of the decade, the number was closer to 15 percent. In
1998, a fifteen-year-old in South Africa had a better than
even chance of dying of AIDS.

The government's response was minimal. Until 1994,
when the apartheid regime fell and Nelson Mandela

became the country's first black president, AIDS had been ignored. It was largely a black disease, which meant the white government wasn't interested—indeed, a plague that selectively killed black people was welcomed by some hard-core apartheid supporters.

After 1994, AIDS was still not a priority in a country where the needs were endless and the government's to-do list infinite. South Africa's AIDS-prevention campaign was perfunctory, consisting mainly of bill-boards featuring the iconic AIDS red ribbon. Then the health minister spent a fifth of her AIDS budget to produce a play about AIDS called *Sarafina II*. The resulting scandal paralyzed the government's efforts to fight the disease.

Nonetheless, even if South Africa had done what other countries were doing in the 1990s, it is unlikely that would have helped to reduce the scope of AIDS. Then, as now, transmission of HIV, the virus that causes AIDS, happened largely among young people. Other countries were trying to reach teenagers through talks in schools, churches, and community groups and through advertisements in the mass media. They were telling teenagers what AIDS is and how it is spread, advising them to use condoms and limit their partners, and warning them about the threat of early death.

None of it was working. Rates of new infections among young people were going up, in some places soaring. Public-health experts believed that if teenagers understood what was at stake and were taught how to protect themselves, they would surely do it. But in country after country, teenagers proved them wrong.

South Africa ended up trying something very different, a strategy designed not only by public-health experts—those usual suspects—but also by psychologists, advertising executives, marketing gurus, and teens themselves. They designed what eventually became South Africa's largest AIDS-prevention campaign. It used no appeals to fear, and its information about AIDS arrived wrapped in a coating of the frothy stuff teenagers love—pop stars, fashion, love advice, teen slang, and gossip. The AIDS-prevention campaign concentrated on teens' need for belonging and connection. It tried to make an HIV-free lifestyle fun and cool. Rather than resort to finger-wagging, it helped young people change their lives by putting them in the company of peers who had changed theirs.

THIS STRATEGY WAS BORN because in 1997, people concerned about AIDS in South Africa recognized that something new was needed. "The challenge was how to get through to younger people, who were articulating feelings of AIDS fatigue, and no sense of relationship to the red ribbon and traditional symbols," said Michael Sinclair, a South African who is now senior vice president of the Kaiser Family Foundation, a health charity based in California. Kaiser decided that if South Africans could decide what was needed to prevent the spread of AIDS in young people, the foundation would pay for the campaign.

Kaiser staffers met with AIDS groups and government officials. Together, they decided that the campaign needed to target teenagers from twelve to seventeen. Research showed that most were still HIV-negative at fourteen, and by eighteen it was already too late. The group also decided to hire Judi Nwokedi to conceptualize the program. Nwokedi was forty-one at the time, a charismatic whirlwind who had recently returned from exile in Thailand and Australia, where she had worked as a psychologist with sexually abused children.

South Africa at the time was a particularly difficult environment for beginning a serious AIDS-prevention campaign. So many people had the virus that any sexual partner had a one-in-six chance of carrying infection. This was Russian roulette, odds that permitted no slip-ups.

No one is sure why the AIDS rate was and is higher in South Africa and its nearest neighbors than in the rest of the world. South Africans do not have more sexual partners than people in other countries. Nor is poverty the answer. Even though South Africa and its neighbors—Botswana, Lesotho, and Swaziland—have had the world's highest AIDS rates, some of them are the richest countries in Africa.

There are several theories about what makes South Africa different. South African men are unlikely to be circumcised, and circumcision, as we have learned in the last few years, helps to protect men from catching HIV. Another factor may have been apartheid—a political system that segregated living areas by race and thus forced many male workers to live in hostels near their jobs, away from their families. Separating families leads to a pattern of simultaneous relationships— one woman in town, one in the countryside. Concurrent relationships help to explode the AIDS epidemic, as the amount of virus in a person's body spikes right after infection; HIV is most contagious when freshly caught. Apartheid is gone, but southern African countries still depend heavily on mining, an industry that continues to separate men from their wives, and the tradition of conducting several simultaneous relationships continues.

South Africans, moreover, did not talk much about AIDS, and largely did not talk about sex. In contrast to America, where gay members of organizations such as ACT UP were so vocal that they forced AIDS into the news, AIDS in South Africa was smothered by a curtain of silence. In 2003, when 600 South Africans were dying of the disease every day, President Thabo Mbeki told the *Washington Post* he didn't know anyone who had died of AIDS.

People with AIDS were stigmatized to the point where the social reaction could be as dangerous as the disease. A small, soft-spoken woman named Gugu Dlamini was stoned to death by her neighbors in December 1998, three weeks after she announced at an AIDS-awareness gathering that she had the virus. Her attackers then threatened to kill her family. Nelson Mandela often said that when he told traditional chiefs that he planned to speak out about AIDS and sex, they told him he would lose their support. He did not give a speech on AIDS in South Africa until late 1998, four years into his presidency. Parents usually limited their conversations about sex with their daughters to "don't run around with boys," and with their sons to nothing at all.

One of the first things Nwokedi did was to commission surveys of South Africa's teenagers. It turned out that teenagers were completely turned off by the traditional prevention campaigns—"the message was coming from Mars," she said—and were most receptive to an AIDS campaign that was about more than just AIDS. "They were saying, 'Don't isolate HIV and make it everything that I'm about as a young person. Engage with me on the level of my excitement and confusion as

a young person—sex, parents, friends, drugs, school, rural vs. city,'"
she said. "They were completely turned off by the red ribbon. And they
didn't want to be threatened."

So the message to teenagers had to change. The next question was
how to reach them. "The normal way of AIDS or any peer education
with young people was to pack them into the church hall, or the school
hall," Nwokedi said. "They would have to sit there while someone
would stand up there and talk at them, unconscious of whether people
were listening. And whatever they told you, you went out and did the
exact opposite because you were so angry that they kept you there for
five hours. I wanted HIV education to have another dimension—it had
to be interactive, engaging, question-and-answer, vibrant debate."

Under apartheid, young people had identified with collective political
action. Now they were tired of politics, tired of "we." An expansion of
electrical service was bringing television to many neighborhoods that
had never had it before. Young people were tuning into the global popular culture they saw on TV, with a very high level of brand awareness.

Nwokedi convened a panel of advisers—including teenagers as well
as advertising executives who designed messages. The working title
for the campaign had been the National Adolescent Sexual Health
Initiative. Nwokedi and her advisers nixed that. "You're dead before
you can even go out to young people," she said. "They'd call it NASHI
as an acronym—that was *soooo* public health!" The AIDS-prevention
program had to be a brand.

The relevant model, they decided, was not any previous public-health
campaign, but rather a recent relaunch of the soft drink Sprite. "Sprite
took the brand off the shelf and into the communities," Nwokedi said.
"They did basketball, fun activities. They sponsored concerts, sent cool
kids onto campus, talked up Sprite in Internet chat rooms. It was very
driven by celebrities in the community creating the hype. I was looking at what is tactile about your brand, what experiences you create."

Instead of a fear-driven, preachy, stodgy NASHI, the AIDS-
prevention campaign became loveLife—positive, hip, and fun.

WHEN I VISITED LOVELIFE in 2006, the "aspirational lifestyle brand" was ubiquitous, one of the ten best-known brands in the country. South Africa was dotted with loveLife's 1,200 billboards. Radio call-in shows reached three million young listeners a week. LoveLife had TV spots and TV reality shows that sent attractive young people into the wilderness to compete in AIDS-related games, such as using the other sex's tools of seduction. A hotline dispensing advice or just a friendly voice received more than a million calls a year. A Web site and magazines featured not only graphic information about AIDS but also fashion, gossip, and relationship advice. (The fashion tips were not those found in *Vogue*—one issue of the magazine was promoting a contest for clothing constructed of found objects, costing no money at all.)

The most controversial part of loveLife's media campaign—because it was the most visible to adults—was the billboards. Adults overwhelmingly hated them. "What does this have to do with AIDS?" they asked. Indeed, the connection of slogans like "Get Attitude!" to AIDS is distant. But the grown-ups missed the point: the billboards were not designed to impart information. The billboards were there to get people talking and get young people in the door of loveLife's programs. Enigmatic coolness can help. It reinforces the message that this is a *teen* thing—it told teenagers, "It's for you, not them."

LoveLife's research shows that the media campaign by itself is not associated with behavior change in young people, but it brings them in to the face-to-face programs that are. "The logic of the brand is to create something larger than life, a sense of belonging," said David Harrison, the tall, lanky physician who was the director of loveLife from 2000 to 2009. "That creates participation in clinics, schools—people go because they like to be a part of loveLife."

That is crucial, because young people already have information. The problem was to get them to internalize it. South Africa's health surveys showed that young people knew that when *other people* had unprotected sex, they could catch the AIDS virus. But they didn't see themselves in the same position. There was no correlation between information and the internalization of risk. The most chilling statistic was that two-thirds of young people who tested HIV-positive—in anonymous surveys, so they didn't know it—did not consider themselves at risk for AIDS.

Later researchers found that this had changed, had morphed into a phenomenon in its own way equally terrifying. The study of HIV-positive people has not been repeated, but other studies asked young people about their behaviors and their perception of their own risk. The kids who were in fact having unprotected sex with lots of partners did accurately report that they were at high risk for catching HIV. But they had no problem living with that high risk. It had become normal, part of the background noise of life. AIDS information was ubiquitous, and teenagers internalized the message of risk. They didn't care.

Especially for teenagers, the psychology of sexual behavior seems to reside in some deep and mysterious place, apparently shielded, as if by a lead curtain, from the reach of traditional public-health messages.

So loveLife used new strategies to help the message penetrate the teenage mind. As Sprite did, loveLife employed kids to recruit their peers. Almost all its programs are run by people the organization calls groundBREAKERS. They are between the ages of eighteen and twenty-five, trained in counseling and sexual health. Along with thousands of younger teens called *mpintshis*, or friends, they run radio stations and computer workshops and school sports competitions (South Africa's only public-school sports in most of the country). They teach debate and talk about sex, AIDS, and relationships. When I visited in 2006, loveLife was recruiting 1,300 new groundBREAKERS each year.

In Orange Farm, a bleak and often violent township southwest of Johannesburg, the loveLife center was a complex of buildings that drew kids in with a basketball court, radio production facility, and computer workshop, but anyone who wanted to take computer classes first had to complete AIDS training. LoveLife seemed to be Orange Farm's only after-school entertainment, aside from drinking, gangs, and sex. After school, it was always filled with kids.

The quality of the groundBREAKERS' programs varied with the local environment and the skills of the young people who ran them. Some groundBREAKERS, especially in remote rural areas, seemed unlikely to motivate anyone. They ran groups of kids through the usual repeat-after-me rote memorization of facts that was the hallmark of education in South Africa.

Some of the groundBREAKERS, however, were admirable. At Serokolo High School, in a mining town in the northern province of Limpopo, twenty-three-year-old Tebatso Klass Leswifi conducted a quiz on HIV, with plenty of discussion that ranged from whether girls get pregnant because of the government's $30-a-month child grant to why you would want to know your HIV status. It was raucous. Leswifi also worked at the local health clinic, helping teenagers feel comfortable going in to get information and treatment. He also ran a league with ten basketball teams. The high school's aerobics team— also coached in part by Leswifi—put on a show to the music of Laura Branigan's "Gloria." A seventeen-year-old named Princess said she called Leswifi every day for some words of wisdom to motivate her to stay in school.

Leswifi seemed to be trying to save Serokolo High School's students from AIDS singlehandedly. He said loveLife saved him, crediting the organization with getting him off drugs: "They gave me a motivation manual that was like a mirror of myself."

In many ways, loveLife resembles a cult. This is a good thing. Many young people said that loveLife had saved them in big or little ways, and they were on a mission to pass that along to others.

In 2006, loveLife contained a large dollop of the same public-health gospel that NASHI would have used: here's what AIDS is, here's how you catch it, now please abstain from sex, or be faithful, or use a condom. This has become known as ABC—Abstain, Be faithful, use a Condom. But the ABC message is received very differently if it comes during a five-hour lecture in the church hall or wrapped in a powerfully motivating message from Sibu Sibaca. This was the groundBREAK-ERS' secret weapon and loveLife's most important strategy: it teaches young people to motivate others by sharing their own personal history. When a teenage girl hears about ABC from a public-health expert in a church hall, it's in a language she doesn't speak. When it comes from Sibaca, it is urgently and immediately about her life.

Sibaca knows, because that's what happened to her. She is a petite, enthusiastic, energetic woman from Langa, a township outside of Cape Town. In 2006, she was twenty-two, a corporate social investment manager for Richard Branson's Virgin Group in South Africa, mature and confident. She attributed her success to loveLife. When she was twelve, her mother died of AIDS: her father followed four years later. "Before I joined loveLife, I had a serious history of self-destruction," she said. "I saw my life ending up in the township, pregnant, not knowing who the father of my child is."

She managed to get through high school. When a friend told her about loveLife, she began going to its programs. "I had been engaging in highly risky behavior, but I pulled back," she said. "LoveLife made me realize there were things I wanted to achieve in my life, and I couldn't afford to have sex without a condom. The reality is that every young person has a dream, but a lot of us look at our situation and think, 'Who are we kidding?' But the minute someone triggers in your brain that [the dream] is possible, so much changes. You start looking at life in a different way."

"Seeing billboards of a dying person didn't tell me about me," said Sibaca. "But when someone says, 'You have such amazing potential that HIV shouldn't be a part of it'—then it wasn't about HIV. It was about me. No one is wagging a finger at me, just young people, peers, telling me the way you've lived your life is not good and we're going to help you. These were people the same age as me. It wasn't a celebrity telling me their story living in a million-dollar house. It was another young person from the same township as me."

She applied to be a groundBREAKER. LoveLife trained her to do motivational speaking and gave her facts and ways to talk about teen pregnancy, peer pressure, HIV, and other issues. She went to work in a high school, teaching a class of twenty people a half hour to an hour a day for twenty-one weeks.

She told me about one girl she had in class, a girl from Sibaca's own township. "She was fifteen and came to me and said, 'My boyfriend is pressuring me to have sex without a condom.' Her fear was that her boyfriend would break up with her if she said no, and she had to hold on to him because he gave her money and clothes that her family could not provide her with. I gave her all the different choices and consequences, and said, 'Are you willing to live with those consequences at age sixteen?

"She came to me the next week and said, 'I'm single.' She had broken up with her boyfriend. I hugged her and started crying—she saw her fears and was willing to go through with it anyway." Sibaca saw the young woman again several years later. "She was not HIV-positive and not pregnant, and she was going to study law the next year."

WHEN LOVELIFE BEGAN IN late 1999, its founders set a goal of cutting in half South Africa's rate of new AIDS infections within three to five years—in other words, by 2004 at the latest. This did not happen. From 2000 to 2004, there was no progress—the HIV prevalence rate among pregnant teenagers (pregnant women are the only people the government tests every year) was 16.1 percent in those years. And while no one in South Africa was happy about this, loveLife had been controversial, arrogant, and large enough that some people who worked on AIDS projects enjoyed seeing it taken down.

Clearly, the claim was one that loveLife's founders never should have made. But the dismaying stubbornness of the AIDS numbers did not mean that the program had failed. The national HIV rates are not a fair measure of any program's success or failure—especially prevalence rates, which do not tally how many people became infected in a specific year. merely how many people *are* infected. Many factors combine to steer an epidemic up or down, from economics (one theory goes that Zimbabwe's economic collapse has driven down AIDS rates, as men there can no longer afford to maintain girlfriends on the side) to the availability of surgery (widespread adoption of circumcision would dramatically curtail the spread of AIDS) to the fact that epidemics run a natural course. LoveLife is far from the only factor affecting the spread of AIDS. It is also not South Africa's only AIDS-prevention program, although it is by far the largest and most comprehensive one, and the only national program aimed at teenagers.

Then there is the issue of size. Although it is a national program, loveLife has always been broke and has never reached more than 40 percent of South African teenagers with face-to-face programs in any given year. David Harrison, loveLife's former executive director, estimated that to really crack the epidemic, the organization needed to reach 60 or 70 percent of teens. So even if it were the only thing affecting HIV rates, it would have to have a huge effect on the people it did touch in order to have much impact on the overall numbers.

Judged by other, more reasonable standards, however, there is evidence that loveLife is working.

In 2003, the Reproductive Health and HIV Research Unit of the University of the Witwatersrand in Johannesburg did a nationwide survey of fifteen- to twenty-four-year-olds. It found that those who had participated in loveLife's programs were only 60 percent as likely to be infected with HIV as those who had not, and the association was stronger for those who had participated in more than one program. In other words, people who participated a little in loveLife had *somewhat* lower infection rates; those who participated a lot had *much* lower infection rates. The survey also found a strong association between loveLife participation and increased condom use, the likelihood of talking about AIDS with friends and family, getting an AIDS test, and a greater sense of optimism about the future. But the survey did not find any statistically significant effect on a reduction in the number of partners.

Another study of loveLife's effects was conducted in 2007 in one area of KwaZulu-Natal, the province with the country's highest rates of AIDS infection. LoveLife was the only AIDS-prevention program operating in the area. The study confirmed most of what was found in 2003 in terms of loveLife's affect on teen behavior, but it did no AIDS testing and so could not confirm whether loveLife's programs were associated with lower rates of infection.

As for South Africa and AIDS, five years after loveLife began, something remarkable happened. Teen AIDS rates in South Africa began to stabilize, and then to drop. By 2007, 12.9 percent of teenage women in prenatal clinics were HIV-positive, down from 16.1 percent in 2004—a 20 percent drop. National household surveys conducted in 2002, 2005, and 2008 also showed that teen AIDS rates were dropping, by enormous margins. The rate of new infections among teenagers went up between

2002 and 2005 and then plummeted. Among eighteen-year-olds, for example, it fell by 55 percent between 2005 and 2008.

At the time the news of the decline in teenage HIV rates broke, there was little celebration. HIV rates were still terrifyingly high, and some 400,000 people a year were dying of the disease. The government was dragging its feet—not just President Mbeki but also his disastrous health minister, Dr. Manto Tshabalala-Msimang, who put obstacle after obstacle in the way of antiretroviral treatment and was derided as "Dr. Beetroot" for her statement that eating local foods was the way to deal with AIDS. She, at least, was rejoicing at the new AIDS figures. "I think it's something we must celebrate as South Africans, and say 'thank you' to the youth of this country, because we think they are beginning to take prevention messages seriously," she told journalists in 2007.

But it turned out that on the issue of whether there was something to celebrate, Dr. Beetroot was right. Some of the reduction may have been due to the maturing of the epidemic—HIV rates are beginning to stabilize in many countries. Indeed, the AIDS infection rate is beginning to drop in South Africa in general, but that is only because the decline among young women has been so stunning. For women aged fifteen to twenty-four, the best estimates show that the new infection rate dropped by 60 percent between the early part of the decade (2000–2010) and the latter part. (New infections, while difficult to measure, are a far more accurate indicator of the epidemic than prevalence, especially in countries like South Africa where prevalence figures are inflated by the new-widespread use of antiretroviral medicines.) This decline is much greater than that seen among young people in other high-prevalence countries, such as Botswana and Namibia.

Something is happening to teenagers in South Africa that is not happening to adults, and is not happening elsewhere.

The bad news is that as teenagers are wont to do, they are still having plenty of sex, and they have it early, and with multiple partners. The good news is that condom use has soared. Nearly 90 percent of males aged fifteen to twenty-four reported using a condom the last time they had sex. That same figure was under 60 percent in 2002. Condom use is much higher among young people than among adults.

Is this loveLife's doing? There is no way to tell, but the evidence indicates that it is likely a key factor in young people's behavior change. The national household survey showed that the loveLife program had by far the highest reach, especially among young people—the 2008 study found that it reached 80 percent of people between fifteen and twenty-four. And we know that loveLife's programs are associated with increased condom usage. Teenagers in South Africa have begun to think about the future. It is likely that one important reason is that loveLife has offered them a way to, as David Harrison said, "be like my friend, whose life has changed."

Even as more teenagers are using condoms, however, there is another challenge for loveLife: safe behavior doesn't last. At age eighteen, there is a sharp increase in infection; prevalence rates for women in their early twenties are more than double the rates for women in their teens. It is the time of greatest exposure to AIDS—about a third of all infections occur in those between the ages of eighteen and twenty-three.

What happens to teenagers around the age of eighteen is that they leave school. "Almost half the lifetime probability of HIV is crammed into just four or five years after leaving school," David Harrison and two colleagues wrote in a research paper. School protects. One 2008 study of teenagers in the province of Limpopo found that teens out of school had ten times the HIV rates of teens in school (although the relationship may not be causal—they may both be symptoms of a risk-taking personality).

It's not what they are learning that is keeping students HIV-free. It's simply being in school. When students leave school, two things happen: They lose their community, their social network, and they lose a sense of progression toward the future. They are in limbo, waiting for something better to happen.

"Without a sense that tomorrow can be any different from today, being HIV-free is not that great when you're looking at ten years of hustling to get by," Harrison said. "The analysis was that two really important factors that contribute to high tolerance of risk are a general sense of lack of choice and opportunity, and lack of social cohesion or solidarity. Aimless, excluded and alienated individuals are at highest risk for HIV infection." Young people just waiting for something to happen live for now. To a girl out of school, with no job, living in a bad neighborhood, taking on a sugar daddy can make sense. Why not have unprotected sex if it brings clothes, spending money, and a new cell phone? There's no hope for a future, therefore no reason to sacrifice.

To respond to this phenomenon, said Harrison in 2008, "our approach has shifted somewhat. The center of our construct is no longer promoting healthy sexuality, but changing perceptions of day-to-day opportunity for young people." LoveLife is trying to create connections for young people after they leave school and to help them negotiate the choices they will face. One TV spot showed a boy sitting by the side of the road, waiting to wash the windows of passing cars, only to be pushed away by a crowd of other window-washers. The slogan is "Make Your Move."

Harrison said that if he could restart loveLife from scratch, "I would have created a system of branded clubs in schools that transcend school-leaving." The clubs would be places to go after school and after leaving school. "We need to support people at their time of greatest vulnerability," he said.

What does this have to do with AIDS? The same thing as the "Get Attitude" billboards did—nothing and everything. "In Africa you don't see behavioral risk factors explaining what you want them to explain," said Audrey Pettifor, a professor of epidemiology at the University of North Carolina who has researched South Africa's AIDS programs extensively and was one of the authors of the 2005 Reproductive Health and HIV Research Unit study. "But you do see things like graduating from high school. We should keep giving correct factual information, but it is right to be saying: let's focus on bigger-picture issues that influence whether kids want to use condoms and get into risky relationships or not." LoveLife is betting that the way to keep teenagers healthy is to make them feel a part of something.

THE SELF-DECEPTION PRACTICED BY South Africa's teenagers is hardly a South African phenomenon. In America, we know we should quit smoking. We know we should have that lump checked out. We know we should give up the french fries. But we don't always do it. South Africa struggles to keep teenagers HIV-free. We struggle to keep teenagers off drugs and cigarettes. In America, as around the world, a good amount of sickness and death is at least in part self-inflicted—the product of behavioral choices we make even when we know we should not. Lack of information isn't the problem—is there anyone who doesn't know that smoking is bad for you? Just like South African teenagers, we understand the risk—in the abstract, or for other people.

We can all too easily invent dozens of reasons to avoid applying this information to ourselves. By the time I'm older, they'll have found a cure for lung cancer. I'm not going to listen to what adults say—they're just trying to tell me what to do. Exercising will be easier after I've lost some weight. One bacon cheeseburger isn't going to kill me. I can keep it to just one drink. I just like to get relaxed. I control my habit—it doesn't control me. My new boyfriend looks so healthy—I'm sure he couldn't have HIV. He loves me—he couldn't have HIV.

Beyond matters of health, people are also expert at finding justifications for bad behavior—from filching office supplies at work (I'm underpaid!) to selling drugs (if they don't buy it from me, they'll just buy it from someone else!). We have many reasons not to do things that are difficult or unpleasant in the short term, even if we know they are in our long-term best interests, such as saving money for retirement.

Particularly striking, however, are bad decisions about health, as the consequences can include death. Such bad decisions are particularly common, for the same reason—it is very difficult to think about death. A dramatic example of the lengths people will go to in order to avoid psychological discomfort can be seen in South Africa's challenges in getting people to do what should not be a challenge: take the medications that keep AIDS patients healthy.

In 2006, antiretroviral drugs that have successfully treated AIDS patients around the world finally were becoming available all over South Africa. President Mbeki, otherwise a sane and reasonable leader, had been inexplicably hostile to antiretrovirals; his government delayed and delayed their rollout, arguing that there were African ways to treat AIDS and that the drugs were part of a plot by multinational pharmaceutical companies to take advantage of South Africa's misery. Eventually, the strength of hundreds of thousands of AIDS activists and the sheer numbers of the dying forced the government to listen. The public-health system went from zero to 175,000 people on anti-retroviral drugs between 2004 and 2006. They were available for free, in neighborhood health clinics. (Mbeki's successor as president, Jacob Zuma, also heeded the call. In 2010, his government finally began to deal with AIDS as if it were fighting World War III. It began promoting circumcision, made HIV tests available in pharmacies, and planned to double the number of people on antiretroviral drugs, which by 2010 was half a million.)

Availability of antiretrovirals did not guarantee that people would take them. They do now in South Africa, because the lifesaving effects of these drugs have become visible to all. But in the beginning, South Africa indeed had to sell AIDS treatment—and it was a hard sell. "People think the health department wants them to be dead," said Sylvia Maguma, a *sangoma* (traditional healer) in the township of Bekkersdal. Many others said this. It might have been a hangover from the apartheid years, when it was literally true. More recently, the government had spent years criticizing as poisonous the same drugs it was giving out now. Some antiretrovirals do have awful side effects, especially at first. Another problem was the widespread stigma attached to AIDS. Everyone who was doing well on antiretrovirals hid the illness; only the dying were visible. Most didn't want to acknowledge that they could have HIV. Many sought help only when death was imminent, when it was way too late.

Instead of taking the drugs, people often turned to magic. In 2006, reports of an AIDS "cure" called the mopane worm appeared on the front pages of the tabloid newspapers. Government health officials' embrace of a long line of charlatans has encouraged a thriving industry in such cures; hundreds of *sangomas* sell them. It seemed that practically every traditional healer had his or her own special treatment. Many *sangomas* also pushed the popular concept that sex with a virgin could cure AIDS.

People embrace such magic because they need to—it brings hope. AIDS sufferers in South Africa are mostly desperate, overwhelmed, and alone. Middle-class Americans have far more resources and education, yet we can be depended upon to pay money for diet books and drinks that promise we will lose twenty pounds in a month without deprivation or exercise. Are these so-called panaceas really that different? One must willfully ignore reality to think they will work, but people do—over and over. People in Johannesburg, South Africa, have herbal potions from witch doctors; people in Harrisburg, Pennsylvania, have Laetrile and pyramids and angels.

What was happening in South Africa was universal. For the sick, psychological comfort was paramount—sometimes even more important than staying alive. They were stricken with a terrifying, stigmatized plague, a disease shrouded in the dark and forbidden—sex, drug use, betrayal, rejection, death, rape, the struggles of intimate relationships. At the Western-medicine clinic, they could have gotten a new, lifesaving AIDS treatment—but at the price of increasing the anxiety and isolation they already felt. Instead, they went to the familiar healer they had known all their lives—the *sangoma*.

Wanting to understand this behavior, I went to one, too. When I met Grace Mhaula in 2006, she was an enormous woman of fifty-four, wearing fuzzy pink slippers and a muumuu in the brilliant colors of the South African flag. She lived in Tembisa, a township outside Johannesburg, its dusty and treeless streets filled with jobless men. The only businesses I saw were hair-straightening salons, phone stations, chicken restaurants, and funeral parlors. Parts of Tembisa were squatter settlements, shacks with tarps for roofs; Mhaula's neighborhood had paved roads and solid houses. Hers was a stucco building with a nice kitchen and living room. In the back, off her patio, was her *indumba* (consulting room).

Mhaula inherited her calling from her parents, *sangomas* both. She had a collection of the bones of seven ancestors, and she would read the bones to provide advice, medical and otherwise, for 50 rand, or about $8.50. She also prescribed herbal medicines. The cement floor of her *indumba* was spread with mats and animal skins; the tables were crammed with candles, traditional clothes and beads, and dozens and dozens of jars of herbs. A single bare lightbulb hung from the tin roof.

Mhaula was an unusual *sangoma*: for twenty-seven years, she had worked as a lab technician for Glaxo Wellcome (now GlaxoSmithKline), and the company had sent her to college. Arthritis had forced her to retire from Glaxo, but she was bored at home. At Tembisa's health clinic, she received training in HIV counseling and caring for the terminally ill. For a sick person—she was vastly overweight and walked with difficulty, and she died of sepsis just three weeks after I met her—she seemed more active than three people half her age. Her own daughter had died of AIDS six years earlier, and Mhaula was raising her daughter's child. She also received government money to run a home-based care business with a staff of fifteen local women who visited, nursed, and fed AIDS patients in the neighborhood. In addition, she conducted workshops for *sangomas* to teach them about AIDS. At the workshop I attended, Mhaula and her family had also cooked lunch for about thirty people.

She moved easily back and forth between African and Western medicine, reflecting a fluidity of cultural forces quite common in Africa. Her clients visited her when they believed themselves bewitched, when their car was stolen and they felt their ancestors were angry, when they had sexually transmitted diseases or cancer or persistent cough, but increasingly they came because of AIDS. "When someone comes in with symptoms of AIDS," she told me, "I always say, 'What do you want me to do? Think about it—we live in a modern age. Don't you think we should go to the clinic? You will be in a safe environment.'

"They say, 'will you go with me?' I say, 'Yes.' Sometimes they just want me to go get their test results and they say, 'Don't tell me the results, just give me *imbiza* [the herbal mixture she prepares]'"

She gestured to the door of the consulting room, where white plastic tubs filled with an herbal mixture were stacked. This was her *imbiza*. The clinic offers free antiretroviral treatment, but Mhaula offered comfort, which many of her patients preferred. "We get more respect than the clinic," she said. "When we talk to them, we have time for them.

We sit down and listen." What Mhaula was particularly good at was combining Western and traditional medicines—her presence took the mystery and coldness out of the clinic.

She was careful not to call her *imbiza* a cure for AIDS—many other *sangomas* in South Africa are not as responsible. Mhaula called her *imbiza* an immune-system booster. "With us, you don't have to take it for the rest of your life." Mhaula said. "And there are no side effects. Patients come in, and they are so afraid, and then I give them the *imbiza* and I give them some porridge to eat. And it's all right."

Her mixture might indeed boost the immune system—it has never been tested, so no one knows—but it seemed unlikely to me that it could compete with the antiretroviral drugs that were saving lives worldwide. Mhaula maintained that her *imbiza* could not be taken with antiretrovirals, so her patients had to choose.

I met one of them, thirty-three-year-old Vusi Ziqubu. "He was gone," said Mhaula of the moment she first saw Ziqubu. "He was frail, smelling of death." Mhaula gave him her *imbiza* to drink four times a day. When I visited him in his house, he was thin but looked strong and was up and around.

Imbiza seemed to be helping Ziqubu—for the moment. But there was another patient taking Mhaula's *imbiza*, a close family friend, a mother of three children. She was doing well, Mhaula told me—please come talk to her. Two days later, I returned to meet the woman. But she had already died.

It is the universal hunger for psychological comfort, people's willingness to sacrifice everything to be respected and reassured right now, that makes it necessary to find strategies that save people from AIDS in a way that also offers emotional consolation today. When you think about it, this is an extremely circuitous route to saving lives. The whole enterprise, in fact, has a touch of the absurd. It should not be necessary to have to employ sophisticated strategies to steer people away from behavior they are aware may lead to a very early, very unpleasant death. Surely it should be enough just to warn people of the extreme consequences.

Yet we know that warnings do not work—not in South Africa, not in America, not anywhere. To understand the value of the social cure, it is first essential to look at why this should be: what we harbor in our psyches, our genes, our economics, and our culture that makes us act so illogically.

Chapter Two

The Empire of Irrationality

THE SOCIAL CURE IS NECESSARY BECAUSE WE HUMAN beings are disturbingly unreasonable creatures, helpless to act in our own interests. No amount of information can budge us when we refuse to be budged. The catalog of justifications for destructive behavior is a tribute to human ingenuity—or it would be if these activities were done consciously. They can be. We often lie to others about our bad behavior, but the more interesting and powerful excuses come when we lie to ourselves. You smoke. Someone comments. You tell him that you're not hooked. You can quit any time! He doesn't believe it. But the funny thing is—you do.

This is the mind playing games. When you smoke, you are doing something startling: twenty or so times a day, you make a choice to perform an act that is likely to cause you serious illness and very possibly a premature death. This fact is intolerable. So the mind does tricks to make it more tolerable.

In his classic work *The Ego and Its Defenses*, Henry P. Laughlin describes twenty-two major and twenty-six minor ego defenses. It is a catalog of the bizarrities of the human personality, of the ways the mind fools itself. One of the most important tricks is rationalization. "In a demonstration to a group of medical students," writes Laughlin, "a volunteer was given the following suggestion while under hypnosis. 'Shortly after you return to a nontrance state I will light a cigarette. This will be a signal for you to remove your shirt, fold it neatly and place it on the podium. . . . You will not remember having received this suggestion.'"

The volunteer was awakened. The hypnotist lit a cigarette. The volunteer took off his shirt, folded it neatly, and placed it on the podium.

"Now, why did you just do that?" the hypnotist asked him. The subject's answer came fluidly and easily: he was very interested in how people react to the unexpected. So he thought it would be interesting to observe how the class reacted to his unusual behavior.

The subject had a justification that was ready, earnest, and completely untrue. Rationalization is a self-deceptive attempt to justify an intolerable behavior by finding motives that are tolerable. Among the other important defenses is displacement: we know we shouldn't hate Dad, so the mind makes us think we instead hate a boss who resembles him. There is regression: we are unable to cope with our current position, so we revert emotionally to a less mature level of development, as a child may suddenly resume bedwetting to greet the arrival of a new baby in the house. There is reaction formation: the development of outward behaviors that are the opposite of consciously disowned behaviors, notably found in the vociferous homophobe whose bullying conceals his own homosexual feelings.

The three defenses on Laughlin's list most relevant to the social cure are the familiar ones of rationalization, repression, and denial. They are closely related. Repression is the banishment of intolerable information from the conscious mind into the unconscious—for example, when a child who accidentally sets the house afire cannot remember the incident in later life. Denial occurs when the unconscious mind deals with the unacceptable information by claiming it does not exist—I don't have a drinking problem; I could quit smoking tomorrow if I wanted to.

The power of denial is so strong that it can even outweigh maternal love. The vast majority of hospitals and clinics in South Africa offer pregnant HIV-positive women a tablet of nevirapine when they begin labor. That pill, plus some nevirapine drops for the newborn, cuts in half the chance that the baby will contract the AIDS virus from her mother during birth. Yet Pauline Molotsi, an obstetrical nurse in the hospital in Alexandra, a township on the outskirts of Johannesburg, said that some women choose to keep the pill in their pocket.

Molotsi said that about twice a week, a woman beginning labor is HIV-positive but refuses to take the nevirapine tablet. Even though the only person who will find out is the nurse—who already knows the woman's HIV status, as it is written on her chart—the woman refuses. "She says, 'Oh no, I don't need that. I'm not positive,'" said Molotsi. "They have not accepted their status. They are still in denial."

Molotsi has figured out a solution. She thrusts a piece of paper and a pen toward the woman. "Would you really like your baby to have the virus?" she asks. "If you don't take the pill, you will have to sign."

"That usually works," she said. "They are scared to commit in writing—so scared that they take the pill."

The need to justify a destructive habit becomes a vicious circle. In extreme form, it can end up enveloping us in a cocoon that protects us from anyone or anything that can challenge our behavior. One way this works is a phenomenon called cognitive dissonance.

In the 1950s, social psychologist Leon Festinger and two colleagues infiltrated a doomsday cult that prophesied that the earth would be flooded on December 21, 1954. The group's leader, Dorothy Martin, had told members that she had received messages from a planet named Clarion that a flying saucer would come to take them away to safety at midnight on the day before the flood. They met in her suburban living room to await their rescuers.

Midnight passed. No spaceship appeared. The world did not end. After nearly five more hours of waiting, the cult's leader had a new revelation: the faith of the group had saved the world.

One would suppose that after Martin was proven wrong, the cult members would desert their leader. After all, many of them had left their jobs, gathered their families, and given away their belongings in anticipation of the spaceship's arrival; considerable irritation at Martin would be justified. But Festinger predicted otherwise: he thought the failure of the prophecy would lead the cult's members to strengthen their commitment.

Festinger was right. Only two members of the cult left. The rest not only stayed but also increased their activities on behalf of Martin and her prophecies. The cult had never proselytized before, but after that date the members went out into the streets and contacted newspapers to try to recruit new adherents. Martin's most enthusiastic follower, a local doctor, said, "I've given up just about everything. I've cut every tie. I've burned every bridge. I've turned my back on the world. I can't afford to doubt. I have to believe."

Festinger called what he saw "cognitive dissonance." It is uncomfortable to hold two contradictory ideas in our head at the same time, so we modify our beliefs to make them compatible. The stronger our commitment to a belief, the more we are invested in proving it right, and we interpret all other information in the light most favorable to our belief. We also seek out information that confirms the rightness of our beliefs.

Social psychologist Elliot Aronson has since proposed that what is really in conflict is not two beliefs, but a belief and a vital self-concept. A person who tells a lie, despite wanting to think of himself as truthful, must find a justification for the lie.

Political conservatives watch the news on Fox, liberals watch MSNBC. Smokers will gleefully seize on studies that show that nicotine stimulates intellectual activity and smoking helps keep you thin. Recent purchasers of houses will suddenly realize that the local schools are much better than they had thought. Cognitive dissonance is one reason prosecutors end up convicting innocent defendants—once they have their suspect, they seek out information that confirms guilt but discard information confirming innocence. The phenomenon can make it much more difficult to overcome self-destructive behaviors, as people can end up cutting off anyone who might question those behaviors. Drug addicts, for example, often choose to socialize only with fellow addicts because this group will never cause them the psychological discomfort of criticizing their behavior or trying to get them to quit.

Cognitive dissonance is so powerful that it negates the effects of something we assume to be helpful—venting our anger. In fact, venting often makes us feel worse. In 1966, Michael Kahn published an article entitled "The Physiology of Catharsis." Kahn, then a Harvard graduate student, designed a study he thought would demonstrate the benefits of catharsis. He brought in thirty-six male Harvard students and told them he was doing a medical study. He took their blood pressure and put them through a lie-detector test. During the test, he acted like a jerk, insulting the students.

Some of the students were given the opportunity to vent their anger—they had the chance to tell Kahn's boss about his misbehavior. Strangely, the polygraph tests showed that these students thought he was a bigger jerk than the students who didn't get a chance to vent. And after twenty minutes, the blood pressure of those who expressed their anger was higher than that of students who had swallowed it. Catharsis didn't work. What was happening, Kahn concluded, was cognitive dissonance—the students who vented had gotten him into trouble, or so they thought. They had to justify it by telling themselves he was indeed a bad guy.

Everyone uses ego defenses; they are strongest in children and teenagers and diminish with emotional maturity. Adolescence is the single biggest risk factor for destructive behavior; bad judgment is built into the teenage years. Adolescents develop their personalities through rebellion, contrasting themselves with the adults and the (relatively) rational world around them. There are physiological reasons as well: the prefrontal cortex, the part of the brain that regulates judgment, self-control, and conscience, is the last part of the brain to mature. The amygdala, which processes emotional reactions, is also controlled better with age. If it is often hard for adults to confront bad news or dedicate themselves to healthy behavior for their long-term good, it is nearly impossible for teenagers to do so.

Humans have ego defenses for the same reason the body has endorphins: they help us avoid pain and make life tolerable. We could not live without them. Taken to extremes, however, they make us mentally ill and facilitate behaviors that can make us physically ill.

Ego defenses are not the only explanation for our failure to act in our long-term self-interest. Research shows that, in part, this fallibility lies in our physical makeup—in our brains and our genes.

Between 30 and 50 percent of those who try cigarettes will get hooked. It's roughly the same in any population, suggesting that nicotine addiction can be partly genetic. One important reason some can drink without becoming alcoholics while others cannot is a genetic predisposition to addiction, which about 10 percent seem to have. From 50 to 70 percent of the variation in susceptibility to addiction is likely genetic. The children of alcoholics are four times more likely than the average person to become alcoholics. The propensity to follow their biological parents into alcoholism holds even if the children of alcoholics are given up for adoption at birth and raised by teetotalers.

Studies of twins show that impulsivity is largely a genetic trait, as is thrill-seeking. Both are linked to low levels of serotonin in the brain. Certain drugs can change the brain's functioning to make humans less disciplined, more susceptible to the lures of risk and loss of control. People with Parkinson's who take dopamine agonists, for example, are more likely to fall into compulsive behaviors like gambling. They are also less able to be future-oriented—to plan and to make decisions based on the consequences those decisions will bring later.

Some criminal behaviors can also result from physical malformations in the brain. At the annual meeting of the American Neurological Association in 2002, two doctors from the University of Virginia presented the case of a forty-year-old man with no history of abnormal sexual behavior who began to molest children after he developed a brain tumor. The egg-size tumor was in the area of the brain responsible for self-control. When the tumor was removed, his aberrant behavior stopped. Later, he began molesting again—and an MRI showed the tumor had returned. Again, after its removal, the man returned to normal.

For a remarkable example of the physiological roots of denial, consider the experiments of Dr. Vilayanur Ramachandran, a psychologist and neurologist at the University of California at San Diego. People with left-brain stroke, which affects the right side of the body, never or rarely deny their stroke, while about 5 percent of people with right-brain stroke deny it. In one experiment, Ramachandran asked a woman with this syndrome, known as anosognosia, to touch his nose with her paralyzed left arm. Her arm, of course, did not stray from her lap. But she insisted that her hand was two inches from the doctor's nose. Then he asked her to clap. She half-clapped, right hand only. But she claimed that she was clapping with both hands.

Ramachandran found that when asked to move their left arm, these patients will not say they cannot. Either they announce that it *is* moving or that they are simply too tired today, or they might even insist that the arm is not theirs. When Dr. Ramachandran filled a syringe with ice water and irrigated a patient's left ear canal (a process that may arouse the right-brain hemisphere), the patient acknowledged, "I can use my right arm but not my left arm. I want to move it, but it doesn't move," and said that she had been paralyzed for several days. But when the water dried again, she not only denied her paralysis but also insisted she had never admitted it. Her brain was perfectly able to process information correctly about the world around her—except for the fact of her own body's devastation.

Why are humans so bent on replacing reality with denial, justification, and defense? "You would have thought," said Robert Trivers, a prominent evolutionary biologist at Rutgers University, "that after natural selection ground away for four billion years and produced these eyeballs capable of such subtlety—color, motion-detection, the details of granularity that we see—you would have perfected the organs for interpretation of reality such that they wouldn't systematically distort the information once it reaches you. That seems like a strange way to design a railroad."

Let's look at it through the lens of evolution, a lens nowadays borrowed to examine almost every aspect of human behavior. The genre of evolutionary psychology arose in the 1970s, in large part thanks to a series of papers written by Trivers. It was popularized in books such as Richard Dawkins's *The Selfish Gene* and E. O. Wilson's *Sociobiology* in the 1970s, and later in Matt Ridley's *The Origins of Virtue* and *The Red Queen*, Robert Wright's *The Moral Animal* and Steven Pinker's *How the Mind Works*.

For many tasks, self-deception wins no genetic prizes. An animal able to recognize where the meat lies is better equipped to propel his genes into the next generation than an animal that constructs a fancy story but can't find the food.

On the other hand, said Trivers, there are many circumstances central to reproductive success in which selective self-deception can help. Explanations of this sort always seem reverse-engineered—we're here, and we're irrational, so it must be evolutionarily useful. Here's Trivers's theory, elaborated in his 2000 paper "The Elements of a Scientific Theory of Self-Deception": "In the past twenty years an important literature has grown up which appears to demonstrate that there are intrinsic benefits to having a higher perceived ability to affect an outcome, a higher self-perception, and a more optimistic view of the future than facts would seem to justify."

Animals better at deception—at rearing up and intimidating a stronger beast into avoiding a fight, for example—win more food and have more sex. But deception is difficult. As any poker player knows, people leave "tells": behaviors such as drumming fingers on the table that we do unconsciously when we are bluffing. There are some, however, who don't leave tells: people who believe their own stories. According to Trivers, this can be a huge advantage. When two animals are evaluating each other before fighting or mating, he writes, evolution has primed them to be intimidated by the other animal's confidence and motivation. Both of these, he said, "can be boosted by selective forgetting, as in humans."

Selective self-deception is also useful in inflating self-esteem, as potential sexual partners find high self-esteem attractive, and a bit of flash will often raise even a mediocre candidate for professional success or sexual partnership to the top of the list. You also try harder and persevere more in any pursuit if you are under the impression, however false, that you are likely to succeed and have chosen the right strategy. You can—and do—deceive yourself into feeling less pain and stress. So even a false impression can be useful. This is why we live, Wobegon-style, in a place where all the children are above average. Trivers even documents it in his own world: fully 94 percent of academics, he reports, believe they are in the top half of their profession.

■   ■   ■   ■

TO THE WEIGHT OF our genes and mind, we need to add another
factor that lures us into self-destructive behavior: the profit motive.
Why do teens smoke? Well, they start smoking because their friends
think it looks cool, and they like to rebel. They continue to smoke
because it's addictive. But none of those is the truest answer. The truest
answer is that they smoke because tobacco companies want them to.
Someone is spending $35 million a day, in very sophisticated fashion,
to persuade them to smoke.

Advertising usually fails when it is trying to get people to quit smoking, follow a diet of brown rice and steamed vegetables, or save for
retirement. This is why other means (the social cure, for example) are
necessary to achieve those goals.

Advertising is very effective, however, when it is pushing immediate
gratification. It is easy to use advertising to get people to start smoking,
order a Big Mac, or simply to spend beyond their means. Ad wizards
have put a lot of time and money into figuring out how to do it well,
and it works—especially with children and teens. Marketing food to
children is at least a $10 billion-per-year industry—and none of that
money goes to selling watermelon. One study carried out by researchers
at the Johns Hopkins Bloomberg School of Public Health found that
preschool children—three- to five-year-olds—found food a lot tastier
when it came in McDonald's packaging than when the same food was
presented in a plain wrapper. And the more televisions in a child's home,
the more likely the child was to prefer the branded food.

As everyone knows, childhood obesity in America has been rising—
the rate of overweight children aged six to eleven tripled from 1980 to
2008, and the same increase went for teenagers. Commercials promoting soda, sugar cereal, candy, and fast food are one big reason. One
large national study of 13,000 children found that for adolescents, the
obesity rate was directly linked to the hours of television they watched.
The reason wasn't that they were sitting; TV tended to replace other
sedentary activities. The reason was the commercials.

That's not to say that junk-food advertising should be banned entirely, but it probably should be banned from children's TV shows. It's worth remembering, however, that a lot of self-destructive behaviors are backed by powerful interests, which need to be figured into any counterplan.

There is no better example than teen smoking. Teens smoke to rebel, but the irony is that they are actually not rebelling at all. They are acting like marionettes, their movements controlled by Big Tobacco. As with loveLife's billboards, incomprehensible to adults, much of cigarette advertising seems to skip right over adults and burrow itself deeply into some crevice of the adolescent brain. The Joe Camel ads that ran from 1988 to 1997 seemed to the adult eye like a complete waste of R. J. Reynolds's money. But they got millions of kids to start smoking, and to start earlier, moving smoking onset down to the level of twelve- to fifteen-year-olds.

Here's how clever the tobacco companies can be. As part of a campaign to counteract their toxic image while major lawsuits were proceeding, cigarette companies in the late 1990s began to run ads that ostensibly discouraged kids from smoking. Beginning in 1998, Philip Morris, which manufactures Marlboros, aired ads with the tagline "Think. Don't Smoke," which was supposed to encourage ten- to fourteen-year-olds not to give in to peer pressure to smoke. An ad aimed at parents: "Talk. They'll Listen," was aimed at promoting conversations with kids about smoking. Another tobacco company, Lorillard, ran ads with the tagline "Tobacco is Whacko if You're a Teen."

R. J. Reynolds, maker of Camel and Winston cigarettes, based its campaign on the idea that parents should tell their children not to smoke. Some of the ads showed parents how to do this even if they were themselves smokers. Parents liked these campaigns, which made them feel that they had influence over their children's choices, and that they could do some good—even if they were modeling smoking to their children twenty times a day.

These ads were diabolically brilliant. They made the companies look good. According to Dr. John Pierce, who led the evaluation of California's programs to prevent teen smoking, research showed they were very popular with parents, and especially with people fifty and older—the same people who would likely make up a jury pool in future lawsuits against the companies.

But none of these campaigns discouraged teen smoking. On the contrary, a study published in the *American Journal of Public Health* in 2006 found that teens who saw the ads had *greater* intention to start smoking and had *lower* recall of real antitobacco advertising. Compared with eight-graders who didn't see them, eight-graders who saw the ads were more likely to think that the harm of smoking had been exaggerated. Tenth- and twelfth-graders who viewed the ads thought tobacco did less harm, had stronger approval of smoking, and, in fact, were more likely to smoke.

Teens smoke to defy authority and be cool with their peers. Faced with ads telling them, "Don't be like your peers," "Smoking is only for adults, not kids," and "Do what your parents say," many teens responded in classic teen fashion—by lighting up.

THERE IS ONE MORE thing that conspires to rob us of rationality when it comes to acting in our long-term interests, something virtually invisible to those living in its grip, and that is culture. Most living beings are groupists. Animals run in packs, and they figure out how to behave by fitting in with the goose flying just ahead in the flock, or the fish swimming around them in the school. For millions of years, we humans have lived in communities, learning to get along with those in our group and to distrust those who are not. Following the group's rules and meeting its expectations was crucial to survival. It was also crucial to the survival of our genes, as groups until very recently were made up mainly of relatives. For obvious evolutionary reasons, a good part of our brains is devoted to functioning as social beings. It is now possible to survive as a hermit, but our brains still behave as if it were not.

Fitting in with the group is still a basic drive. The power of the group was demonstrated in the 1950s in a series of classic experiments carried out by Swarthmore College social psychologist Solomon Asch. A small group of people—one experimental subject and a varying number of secret confederates—were seated in a room and given charts of lines to look at. They were then asked questions about the lengths of the lines. The questions were to be answered out loud, and the confederates always went first. The questions were easy to get right, but after hearing all the confederates answer a question incorrectly, the lone experimental subject usually joined their opinion. The effect was the strongest when there were at least three confederates and they all gave the same wrong answer. In the face of strong public pressure to conform, most people conform. The classic joke from the Marx Brothers movie *Duck Soup*—"Who are you gonna believe, me or your own eyes?"—would seem to have been answered.

One of Asch's students, Stanley Milgram, went on to carry out perhaps the most famous experiments in all of social psychology. While teaching at Yale University, Milgram recruited groups of forty people into what he told them was an experiment testing the effects of punishment on learning. They were assigned to administer electric shocks in escalating doses to a subject sitting in the next room when he gave a wrong answer to a question. In reality, the subject was a confederate and there were no shocks; a tape of a person in pain would play when the "shock" was administered. The results were chilling: twenty-six of forty participants administered "shocks" up to the maximum 450-volt level. Not a single participant demanded that the experiment be stopped.

The experiments tested obedience to authority. Milgram conducted the first of them a few months after the trial of Nazi officer Adolf Eichmann began in Jerusalem in 1961. Milgram unleashed the little war criminal most of us carry inside; it seems that most of us will completely throw aside our moral compass when an authority figure asks us to do so.

During the experiments, one interesting exception to this pattern emerged: we will defy authority when peers signal us to. One of the variations Milgram tried (variation 17) included two other confederates supposedly administering shocks alongside the real subject. When the confederates pretended to have had enough and refused to administer the shocks, only four of the forty participants continued to administer shocks up to the maximum level. Milgram carried out at least nineteen variations on the basic experiment, testing such things as whether people were more likely to defy the authority figure if they were physically closer to the victim, if they were in a less fancy setting, or if they were women. The most defiance was produced by variation 17, the revolt of the peer group. The peer group's creation of a social norm of human kindness was the most effective way to encourage defiance to an immoral order.

Most of us never get the chance to sit in a classroom and answer psychology researchers' questions, but every human being does get to participate, every minute of every day, in the real-world version of essentially the same experiment: we live in a group culture. *Culture*—which for this book's purpose I define as whatever allows a group to express its groupness—is very big and very small. What society expects of its members is informally enforced by a very large group, but people typically measure themselves and set their own rules by looking at the social norms of a handful of peers. Those peers' judgments about our behavior rule our lives. When a prostitute in Mexico City's Zona Rosa considers whether to demand that her customers use condoms, it doesn't matter much to her what the wider world thinks. But she will take very seriously what the other prostitutes in the Zona Rosa think. High school students crave certain fashions not because they saw them on TV but because they saw them on the cool kids in their school.

These communities make us who we are. Our personal identities are in part defined by identification with a group and separation from other groups. "A community," argued Frederic Brunel, who teaches marketing at Boston University, "is conscious of a kind of intrinsic connection between members: we are one symbolic entity, we share values and principles. We are different from non-members. There's an us vs. them. And we share knowing that we belong together."

The community also creates shared rituals and traditions that are a public way of showing the group's values—be they through the ritual of female genital mutilation, backward baseball caps, face paint, smoking cigarettes, or wearing four-inch heels. These things publicly indicate joint membership.

The norms of the community become especially important when we face something new. Robert Cialdini, a prominent psychologist, marketing expert, and author of the book *Influence: Science and Practice*, argues that when people are uncertain about how to behave, they usually look around them to see what their peers are doing. "When things are changing, new or in flux, people won't look inside themselves for answers—all they see is ambiguity," he said. "They look outside, to legitimately constituted experts and to peers. That provides a shortcut way of determining what they should do in that situation without having to get smart on the topic."

The famous theory of the broken window is an illustration of how people respond to what their peers are doing. In the 1960s, Stanford University psychologist Philip Zimbardo and his colleagues left two seemingly abandoned cars—no license plates, hoods up—on roadsides, one in wealthy Palo Alto, California, and one in the Bronx. Looters started by taking the battery out of the Bronx car within ten minutes; twenty-four hours later, it had been completely stripped. (The looters were mostly white and did not appear to be poor.) In Palo Alto, the car was untouched for a week—until Zimbardo smashed a window with a sledgehammer. Then it was looted within a few hours.

It took an extra step in Palo Alto to shift the social norm, but in both places the car eventually sent out a signal that in this neighborhood, no one cares. Other researchers have confirmed this—if there is litter on the ground or graffiti on the wall, people will not only litter and draw graffiti, they will begin to commit crimes. People adjust their behavior to fit the message sent by their physical surroundings about what a neighborhood finds acceptable. It is possible that one contributor to the declining crime rate in New York City in the 1990s was citizens' awareness of a declining crime rate. And the reverse, of course, can also occur—an escalation of crime that builds on itself as the perception of social norms changes. Shifts in social norms can create vicious or virtuous circles, which is the phenomenon Malcolm Gladwell wrote about in *The Tipping Point*, published in 2000.

To those inside it, culture is unconscious. Most of us are the inhabitants of the cave in the Allegory of the Cave in book VII of Plato's *Republic*, destined to see only shadows on a wall and think it is reality. It is normal for a professional woman in Minneapolis, Minnesota, to go to the office dressed in chunky low-heeled pumps, a calf-length skirt, big square glasses, and no makeup, and normal for a professional woman in Caracas, Venezuela, to dress for the office in four-inch spike heels, a low-cut blouse that prominently features the results of her breast implant surgery, and false eyelashes. Neither would consciously say, "This is what my culture decrees," because both would have internalized what they are expected to do—indeed, what they want to do. If they are aware that cultural norms in other places are different, they will certainly believe that those others dress or behave bizarrely.

Culture only becomes visible once you step outside it, or start wanting to. In the Allegory of the Cave, one inhabitant is freed to see what has been casting the shadows. He suddenly understands what it is he has been seeing all his life. But Plato argued that if he goes back into the cave, those who are still prisoner will reject him and call his views "corrupted."

In real life, too, violating the expectations of the community is cause for rejection. In some contexts, it is relatively easy to leave one community and join another—that's one reason people who feel they don't fit in elsewhere flee to New York and other big cities. But if relocation is not an option, defying the group's expectations can bring about social isolation that is acutely dangerous. There are mothers in Africa who realize that practicing female genital mutilation on their daughters is cruel, but they know it would be crueler still to save a daughter from the practice and leave her as a social outcast, unable to marry. I met women in Johannesburg who understand perfectly well that breast-feeding can transmit HIV to their babies. Yet they continue to breast-feed, because bottle-feeding is tantamount to telling the world they are HIV-positive. In much of South Africa, women who make this announcement, although no longer stoned to death like Gugu Dlamini, can be cast from their houses and deserted by their husbands—who likely gave them the disease to begin with. (These husbands are employing the ego defense of reaction formation.)

History is full of cultures that maintain the traditions of a privileged group at the sorrowful expense of another—slavery, for example. But culture can be sustained even by its victims, like a parasite that propagates even while killing its host. Female genital mutilation is one example—always performed by women, and fiercely upheld by mothers so their daughters will fit in. The rule in American inner-city neighborhoods that a man must answer disrespect with violence, a rule upheld by the men themselves, has condemned thousands of young men to early deaths.

The majestic seclusion of American suburbia, where each family drives its SUV straight into the garage and the children play on their own swingset in a fenced-in backyard, is a perfect hothouse for cultivating toxic isolation, alienated lives without community. The growth of the suburbs is one factor that has contributed to a mighty decline in group life in America. And the consequences are great—doing things in groups is associated with better education, safer neighborhoods, more prosperous families, and better health. But because we live inside this culture, we see the isolation of suburban life as normal.

Culture can be small—the norms followed by prostitutes in Mexico City's Zona Rosa in the age of AIDS, the particular shade of blonde highlights adopted by fifty-something women on Manhattan's Upper East Side—or it can be huge, affecting billions of people over hundreds of years. One example is India's caste system.

SHORTLY AFTER THE ARYAN invasion of India, some 3,500 years ago, India's rulers began dividing their subjects into four different castes. Although the word *caste,* from the Portuguese, means "breed" or "race," there is no physical or genetic difference among the members of India's varied castes; the divisions are entirely manmade. A family's caste depends on its *varna*—the body part of the cosmic soul Purusha from which each group was created. Then there is a group with no *varna* at all—Untouchables, or, as they prefer to be called today, Dalits, from the Hindi word for "oppressed." They traditionally do society's unclean work: cleaning up after funerals, dealing with garbage, hunting animals.

Caste was inherited, intermarriage was discouraged, and caste features became intermingled with the Hindu religion, so the caste system continued century after century virtually unchanged. There are parts of India today where caste matters little: among some tribal hill people and in big cities. But in rural, traditional India, the caste system still rules the social structure. And just as persistent in Indian culture is discrimination against women.

The effects of these twin discriminations can be seen in the stories of Babai Sathe and two of her colleagues in the Jamkhed district of India's Maharashtra state. The way these women lived their early lives is virtually indistinguishable from the way their female ancestors lived half a millennium ago.

Americans have always romanticized Indian mysticism, but now Americans are also romanticizing India's growth and modernity. Globalization and an end to inward-looking economic policies in India have created modern industries, such as computer-software companies and call centers, that have given rise to a middle class larger than the population of the United States. In *The World Is Flat, New York Times* columnist Thomas L. Friedman, India's most influential deifier in America, paints the country as the dynamic driver of the forces leveling the globe's playing field.

Jamkhed is not Thomas Friedman's India. Jamkhed is part of the other 75 percent of India—900 million people who live largely as their ancestors did, barely feeding themselves by hoeing small patches of grain. They live in houses they build themselves with walls of mud and cow dung, or even oilcloth lashed to logs, and roofs of thatch. The roads run through small patches of sorghum. There is no local industry, no train service, little water. During severe droughts, conditions here approach famine. Jamkhed is a place to understand the destructive side of culture, to see the relentless persistence over 3,500 years of social norms that have kept literally billions of people in misery.

One of them is Surekha Sadafule—a Dalit, like Babai Sathe. She was twenty-six in 2008, a beautiful woman with a solid figure, a strong jaw, and long dark hair. After a few minutes of conversation, she hiked up her sari to display a flower of scar tissue on her left hip. "My husband cut me with a knife," she said—one of three attempts he made on her life.

Here is her story. As with virtually every village woman in the Jamkhed area, Surekha's marriage was arranged. She was thirteen years old. Like all women in rural India, she went to live with her husband in her mother-in-law's house. Nine months after the wedding, she gave birth to a daughter. Her husband drank and beat her; his parents beat her, too. They wanted a son. One day, however, her husband approached her—for once, sweetly. He suggested that since the day was fine, they should go for a walk. When they passed a well, her husband stopped—and pushed her in. Then he ran. A nearby farmhand had seen the whole thing, and he came running. He got Surekha out of the well and took her to the hospital, where the water was pumped from her lungs. But when hospital officials asked Surekha how she fell in the well, she remained silent. She was too afraid of more violence.

Surekha then went to her parents' house, but they did not welcome her. "Once you marry, you stick it out," her mother told her. "Don't come back to us. Go back to him. Whatever he's given you, you must suffer it. That is Indian culture."

Surekha returned to her husband and soon was pregnant again. Again he took her on a walk, stopping at a particular tree. He proposed making some medicine from the tree's roots to help the cold that was afflicting her—something not uncommon in rural India. He made a liquid, which he had Surekha drink. She fell unconscious, but a neighbor discovered her and took her to the hospital. Again she was saved. Again she did not accuse her husband.

This time, her parents took her in. At their house, she delivered another daughter. When her husband heard about the birth, he came to the house. He picked up the child and threw her on the ground. Then he cursed Surekha and attacked her with a knife. Telling her he was leaving for good, he walked out.

Again she did not go to the police. "You need money for a police case," she explained. "We were very poor. And I was afraid he would do more bad things." Instead, Surekha—terrified, depressed, impoverished—decided to commit suicide. She drank rat poison and insecticide. Her mother took her to the hospital, where she was saved yet again. It was the fourth attempt on her life. She was but sixteen.

Surekha's story was perhaps more dramatic than those of many other women in Jamkhed, but not by much. At least she wasn't married until she was thirteen; I met one woman who was married at the age of two and a half.

The strictures of local culture are taught to children early, often by their mothers. Lalenbai Kadam, now a wrinkled woman in her late sixties, and also a Dalit, told me of two childhood memories. "When I was small, I would go with my mother to the house of high-caste families to work," she recalled. "While she worked, I would clean the cowshed and collect dung and collect firewood. When I finished, my mother would say, 'Don't touch anything—just sit here quietly.' Once the children from that house sat down to eat. I went to them and started to eat with them. Their aunt scolded me and beat me. My mother also beat me. She said, 'Why do you talk with them?' Even as small children, you cannot go near higher-caste children. You cannot ask anything, or touch their hand."

Instead of receiving money, Lalenbai and her mother were paid only in leftover bread and vegetable curry from the family's dinner the night before. The scraps were their only meal of the day.

Another time she went with her mother to the farm of a high-caste family that owned mango trees with ripe fruit. "I asked my mother, 'Can I eat it?' My mother said no, but I took it anyway." A member of the family saw her and beat her. "And they threw away the fruit," Lalenbai said, sadly. Sixty years later, she still remembers the fruit.

Surekha, Lalenbai, and Babai have endured such misery because their culture informs them that this is the way it has always been. Dalits—there are about 160 million of them in India—have been limited to the most menial and ritually impure jobs. They may not touch their higher-caste neighbors or anything they might eat or drink. Higher-caste people will throw away valuable food if it even touches the hem of a Dalit woman's sari. They will even avoid touching a Dalit's shadow. Traditionally, Dalits had to sweep behind them to remove the taint of their footprints.

Dalits lived on the outskirts of their villages. Within the village, they were required to go barefoot, to take off their sandals and carry them. They could not enter the temple to pray. When they laundered clothes in the river, they occupied a spot downstream from higher-caste women. Tradition demanded that they could not even touch the handle of the village water pump. Babai used to spend five or six hours a day waiting at the water pump for a high-caste woman to take pity on her and pump her water.

These forms of discrimination are softening—a bit. Among some members of the middle class, caste is finally becoming irrelevant. It is now illegal in India to practice untouchability, and Dalits benefit from many government affirmative-action programs. Yet caste discrimination, especially against Untouchables, persists. The laws prohibiting the practice of untouchability are rarely enforced. Dalit children are still often denied education; the women frequently are raped. Crimes against Dalits are common because their perpetrators rarely are punished.

India's most admired and powerful modern politician, Indira Gandhi, was a woman. The country's middle class now has tens of millions of educated and professional women. So it becomes easy for many abroad to overlook the other India that persists—a place that might as well be Afghanistan. There is a mystery in India: where are the missing girls? In most countries, women outnumber men. But there are only 933 women for every thousand men in India—tens of millions of women are missing. They were aborted, after their families learned of their child's gender through a sonogram. Or, if they were born to families who did not have access to sonograms, they were killed. Selective abortion is so pervasive that the use of sonograms is now controlled by law—on paper, at least, as enforcement is haphazard. Abortion of girl children is even more common among educated and wealthier families, and it is more common in the rich Indian states in the north and west than in poorer states. Wealthier and more educated parents have the same desire for sons that poor families do, but they have smaller families, so the urgency to have sons is greater, and they enjoy easier access to sonograms. The prejudice against daughters in Indian culture is so strong that the daughter deficit persists even among Indians living in Britain and the United States.

Girls are undesirable because Indian culture makes them costly.

Some sonogram practitioners even advertise: "Spend a little now to save a lot later." To marry her off, a woman's family will have to pay her husband's family a substantial dowry—at times, a dowry amounting to many years' worth of the family's income. (Paying dowries was outlawed in 1961, but it is still done everywhere, even among the urban elite.) The wife will join the husband's family and her mother-in-law's household, essentially becoming her servant. Because the benefits of a girl's labor go to her husband's family, her own parents have very little incentive to invest in her health or education. Parents of a sick girl are less likely to take her to the doctor than parents of a sick boy. The infant mortality rate for girls is 30 percent higher than for boys. Girls also get less schooling. Spending money on girls, the saying goes, is like planting a seed in a neighbor's garden.

In many parts of India, a young bride in her mother-in-law's house is not allowed to take food if her mother-in-law has not offered it. "Even a pregnant woman cannot take food until her mother-in-law gives it to her," said Lalenbai Kadam. "They feed the daughter-in-law like an animal. The other family members get bread from other grains, but the daughter-in-law gets only sorghum flour," which is less tasty and lower in protein. If she fails to bear a son, or becomes injured and unable to carry heavy buckets of water or perform other physical labor, she may be divorced, abandoned, beaten or, in extreme cases, killed. Each year, thousands of Indian brides are burned to death by their husbands and mothers-in-law because their dowry was deemed insufficient or because the woman's family did not meet ever-escalating demands for money— demands that nowadays include kitchen appliances and televisions. The number of reported dowry deaths each year is rising.

The cultural practices of caste and gender discrimination continue to keep much of India backward. Uneducated women make worse mothers—their children are sicker and less likely to be educated themselves. And women who lack education are more likely to put store in harmful superstitions. In many villages, the beliefs are common that breast-feeding should only begin when a baby is five days old, and that someone bitten by a cobra should be rushed to the temple, not to the hospital. The idea is widespread that pregnant women should eat very little. In fact, they often go hungry, as women in general eat last and least. It is a vicious circle: malnourished mothers give birth to malnourished children.

We are herd animals, walking off a cliff if that's what others do, desperate to follow the rules by which our neighbors live, to win their acceptance and respect. Humans have been known to commit suicide because the group is doing so—think of Jonestown in Guyana—or to commit mass murder for the same reason, as did Serbs and Rwandan Hutus in the 1990s. But these events are rare. More commonly, people commit mass suicide or murder slowly, over decades, by beating daughters-in-law or taking a mango from the hand of a hungry Dalit child.

There are many factors conspiring to push us into destructive behavior, but the strongest of these is culture, because it is the very expression of our bonds as a group. It can be the most damaging and the hardest to escape. The power of culture is why Surekha, Lalenbai, and Babai suffered so in their early years.

And yet, their lives have had a second act. The same need to belong offered them a way to transform the destructive parts of their culture. These women have all become community health workers, through the program based in the city of Jamkhed. They are all now respected authorities in their villages, which also have changed. Because of the work of these women, their communities are healthier and more prosperous, Dalits endure less discrimination, and women have come out of isolation. Lalenbai, forbidden as a child to talk to higher-caste children, has become a venerated teacher and public speaker. Surekha, once too timid and vulnerable to accuse a man who thrice tried to kill her, now owns and is lead singer in a fifteen-member brass band. And Babai, who never attended a day of school in her life, was elected mayor of her village. The hold that traditional Indian culture has over women and Dalits is as entrenched and powerful as any culture on the planet. But even where it is at its strongest, there is a way to fight back.

Chapter Three

Righteous Rebels

BEHAVIOR CHANGE HAS A BAD REPUTATION. TIME AFTER time, new campaigns are announced to get people to do the things they know they should. Most often, these campaigns fail. Safe-sex messages are everywhere, yet so many people do not use condoms. Teens have been told over and over that cigarettes kill, yet they take up smoking. People start diets and stay on them for only three weeks. Young men get out of prison—a behavior-change palace in 24/7 Sensurround—and slip right back into selling drugs or burgling apartments. The conventional wisdom, amply supported by the evidence, is bleak: people don't change.

It is indeed very difficult to convince people to postpone gratification for the sake of their long-term good—much more difficult than convincing them to indulge. But too often, organized behavior-change efforts haven't worked because they weren't seriously tried. Looking back at the history of attempts at behavioral improvement, it is notable that, in many cases, the organizers didn't even consider persuasion to be important. People trying to change the behavior of others seemed to think—in some cases still do—that their job ends when they cast their messages out on the wind.

When behavior-change experts have tried to persuade, they have often chosen strategies that were poorly thought out and doomed to fail, usually because they appealed to the strategists but not to their target audience. They failed to take into account those human foibles that can hold us back from acting in our own self-interest. Commercial advertisers know these foibles, and know that what moves people to act must often be more than new information or an appeal to reason. And yet, the selling of such life-or-death matters as safe sex or lawful conduct has rarely employed any of the effective techniques used to sell hair color.

Look hard at behaviors that supposedly can't be changed, and you will often find that the behavior-change efforts have been pathetically amateurish. Take, for example, patient adherence—failure to carry out a doctor's orders. Poor patient adherence is a serious problem; dozens of studies have shown this. Only a fourth of the people on blood-pressure drugs in one study took their medicines correctly. Only 13 percent of diabetes patients taking certain drugs complied with their regimens for a year. Three-quarters of patients in a study did not keep follow-up appointments and 50 percent of patients with chronic illnesses dropped out of treatment within a year. Even people taking medicine they know is saving their life—AIDS patients taking antiretrovirals, or transplant recipients taking pills to prevent rejection—often do not take it properly. Nor do medical students take their medicines. Doctors, too, are notorious for ignoring the advice they receive when they seek medical care. And as for complying with doctors' instructions to lose weight, quit smoking, reduce stress, and make other lifestyle changes, patients do even worse.

Poor adherence is responsible for an increase in bacteria resistant to antibiotics, millions of hospitalizations, hundreds of billions of dollars in wasted health care, and immeasurable patient suffering. The American medical system decries it, but it does not do much about it. If a patient skips pill doses or stops going to the gym or never calls to make the biopsy appointment, we are accustomed to thinking of this as the patient's fault.

It is not. It is the fault of the health system for paying no attention to helping people follow medical advice. If patients are getting sicker and dying because of poor adherence, then finding a way to increase adherence should be an important part of a doctor's job, but it isn't. Doctors normally rely on the assumption that if they point out that certain behaviors are in patients' self-interest, patients will do them. This is puzzling, as anyone who has practiced medicine for more than a few weeks is well aware that this assumption is not true. A big problem is that doctors are uncomfortable wrestling with compliance; it is too fuzzy, too irrational for them. "I'm not a policeman," they say. Some simply refuse to treat noncompliant patients, preferring to maintain that compliance is just not part of their territory. It is the patient's problem.

When a doctor writes a prescription, it is the rare one who will also talk to the patient about what might get in the way of taking the pills. Adherence to lifestyle changes usually gets no more attention. "Oh, and do quit smoking," says the doctor as you walk out the door. "Here's a diet plan you should follow," the doctor says, handing you a sheet of paper. This is malpractice.

The failure to think about persuasion is a global health problem. Look at AIDS services—testing, condoms, antiretroviral treatment. A lot of attention has been paid to making such services available, but very little attention has been focused on getting people to want to use them. It's a lifeline, the logic goes. Surely no one would throw it back. The international agencies that work on fighting AIDS usually set their goals for progress in terms of what percentage of people have "access" to a service, such as counseling, condoms, nevirapine, or antiretroviral treatment.

Nevertheless, people do throw back lifelines, especially when their culture tells them to, and *access* and *accessed* are two very different things. As South Africa shows, there were many reasons people were afraid to take antiretroviral drugs: they preferred the familiar traditional remedies, they were afraid someone would find out they were sick, they had heard rumors that the drugs could kill, even their government had called them worthless. There was a lifeline available, but patients had to be convinced to grab it. It is wonderful news that South Africa can get a nevirapine pill to a woman in labor, but as Pauline Molotsi reminds us, the job is not done until she puts it in her mouth.

Since AIDS was first identified in 1981 by the Centers for Disease Control and Prevention (CDC), we have learned how to keep people from dying of the disease, and we know how to keep people from catching it in the first place. Where we fall short is in getting people to overcome the social, psychological, and cultural barriers to taking advantage of these solutions. Anyone who dies of AIDS in a place where condoms and antiretroviral drugs are available is dying of stigma, denial, and silence. Those are maladies that only persuasion can cure. "The technology is doing okay—it's moving," said Peter Piot, the executive director of the United Nations AIDS agency until 2008, "but we have grossly, grossly neglected the social, cultural and personal stuff that makes it work."

Public health has never been particularly interested in the "stuff that makes it work." As Judi Nwokedi said, the custom is to assemble teenagers and give them a long, boring lecture on proper behavior that sends them running in the other direction. Such a lecture will often contain little that relates the information to the lives of the listeners or gives them reasons to change their behavior or practical help at getting started. Often, the talk comes without services that could help people act on the information if they did want to. Just because teenagers can go to a lecture on condom use does not mean they can find condoms.

When public-health advocates have tried to persuade, even their most basic efforts often have been ineffective. One usual technique is to start a message about behavior change by decrying the dimension of the problem—telling an audience of teenagers how many of them don't use condoms, or telling an audience of Latinas that one in four of them have diabetes. "Alcohol is the drug most widely used by African-American youth," warns Mothers Against Drunk Driving in a message aimed at exactly these young people.

Perhaps it seems like a good way to wake people up and get them to change their behavior, but it isn't. This strategy asks people to buck their own crowd. Robert Cialdini, the psychologist and marketing expert, researched this phenomenon when he was a professor at Arizona State University. Arizona is home to the Petrified Forest National Park, where the biggest problem is that visitors steal its wood—about a ton of petrified wood each month. To try to prevent theft, park officials have put up signs for visitors: "Your heritage is being vandalized every day by theft losses of petrified wood of 14 tons a year, mostly a small piece at a time."

Cialdini said that one of his graduate students was traveling to Arizona from California with his fiancée, whom he described as the world's most honest person. When the couple visited the park, the woman read the sign, punched her boyfriend in the arm, and said, "We'd better get ours now."

"What could turn this honest person into an environmental thief who would loot a national treasure?" Cialdini asked.

Cialdini obtained permission from park officials to do an experiment. He and his colleagues scattered secretly marked pieces of petrified wood on pathways displaying two different signs. One sign said, "Many past visitors have removed petrified wood from the Park, changing the natural state of the Petrified Forest"; it had pictures of three people taking wood. The other sign simply said, "Please don't remove the petrified wood from the Park, in order to preserve the natural state of the Petrified Forest." This sign had a picture of one lone visitor stealing wood, with a red circle-and-bar "don't" symbol over his hand.

For the next five weeks, Cialdini and his team measured how much of the marked wood was stolen. On the path marked with the sign that said many people were thieves, five times as much wood was missing. The signage, Cialdini concluded, was telling people that everyone was stealing. It made stealing wood the social norm. "The key is not to normalize behavior but to marginalize it," he said. You want to show that the lonely thief is committing an act disapproved of by his peers.

It is not always necessary to be explicit in order to have a counterproductive effect. Cialdini cites possibly the single most famous and lauded public-service advertisement of all time, the one showing a Native American in buckskin clothes who paddles his canoe up a polluted river and then watches from the litter-filled side of a highway as yet another bag of garbage is thrown out of a car and splatters open on the ground. He sheds a single tear, and words appear: "People Start Pollution. People Can Stop It."

The spot, known as "Iron Eyes Cody," after the actor playing the Native American, aired countless times in the 1970s and 1980s and won a *TV Guide* award as the sixteenth-best television commercial of all time. Yet there is no evidence it was effective in preventing litter. Cialdini argues that the ad made a big mistake: it showed that the road and the river were already littered, making littering a social norm. Cialdini proposed revising the Iron Eyes Cody spot to show the bag of trash landing in a clean environment, thus demonstrating that the social norm is one of environmental protection and the litterer is isolated in violating it.

"Public service communicators tell us how many teenagers are committing suicide, how many people drink and drive," he said. "This makes contact with the most primitive of our responses: what is the crowd doing?"

At their worst, persuasive messages can be unintentionally hilarious. When behavior-change advocates have decided they needed more than lectures, they often have turned to fear. Theoretically, this is a step up; getting people to feel something is a more powerful motivator than getting them to know certain facts.

Fear is a logical appeal, given that the task is to warn people off behaviors that can bring dire consequences. Hence the "AIDS Kills" billboards, the antismoking ads talking about emphysema or showing rows of gravestones. The problem, however, is that fear doesn't work very well. With teenagers, who are immortal, it doesn't work at all. In 2005, Dolores Albarracin, then at the University of Florida (now a professor of psychology at the University of Illinois), examined the methodologies and results obtained by 354 AIDS-prevention programs. Threats and fear never worked to increase condom usage. What worked for teenagers, not shockingly, was the message that their fellow teens approved of condoms and were using condoms themselves. In other words, peer pressure.

Fear messages have another problem, one emblematic of the deficiencies of most behavior-change efforts: they are particularly susceptible to being perceived as ridiculous by their target audience.

The iconic example of misspending the power of human emotion is the 1936 film *Reefer Madness*. The movie opens with a high school principal talking to parents at a PTA meeting. He tells the story of kids lured into "marihuana" and their rapid descent into crime, suicide, and madness. At the end of the tragic story, the principal points to parents in the audience and says that the next to fall could be *their* children. "Or yours," he warns viewers, pointing directly at the camera. The screen fills with the message "Tell Your Children."

The film was financed by a church group and did not have wide distribution until the early 1970s, when it was revived, much beloved, as kitsch for the drug culture—get high, go watch *Reefer Madness*. Later, the movie received a further tribute—it was made into a musical comedy of the same name. Apparently the plot didn't need much tinkering.

The one thing that can be said for *Reefer Madness* as a piece of public-health propaganda is that at least it didn't settle for simply providing information. It sought to use emotion to keep kids off drugs, a relatively sophisticated notion. But the story was so incredible to young people that it made pot smoking look even hipper.

Reefer Madness conveys a useful lesson for behavior-change proponents: credibility with your audience matters. There is nothing wrong with employing emotion, as long as it is true to the people you are trying to reach. But *Reefer Madness* fails the same way Judi Nwokedi's five-hour lecture fails: it doesn't seek to get into the heads of its target audience. The people who made the film no doubt felt the fear it induced was effective. But then, they were grownups—religious grownups particularly alarmed about drugs. It is unlikely that they enlisted any teenagers in writing the script.

The error of *Reefer Madness* is a very common one: its creators based their persuasive efforts on what would move *them* to take action—which is very different from what moves ordinary people. Experts are already interested; ordinary people need to have their attention captured. Experts have a context for the information they disseminate;

ordinary people don't evaluate it in the same way. Experts prioritize the behaviors they are advocating; ordinary people have other priorities. It is a very basic tenet of advertising that one should look at a problem from the viewpoint of the person whose behavior you are attempting to change. People selling cars and toothpaste know this; people selling healthy lifestyles and lawful behavior and sane political systems have treated this as an afterthought.

NOWHERE HAS THE NEGLECT of persuasion been more widespread or damaging than in campaigns to keep teenagers and cigarettes apart. Efforts to prevent teen smoking used to be considered doomed. Their failure was so consistent that it was common to hear experts acknowledge that they had no idea what to do, and some people advocated simply giving up.

That was in the mid-1990s. Today the battle is a completely different one. An effective new approach has brought astonishing and rapid success nationwide. The problem today is one of political will: how to keep the effort from backsliding in the face of the tobacco industry's political and financial clout.

The major change is that teen antismoking campaigns used to be chosen with very little attention to what interests teens. But in 1998, a new strategy made its debut, one as sophisticated in its message and delivery system (if nowhere near as well financed) as the tobacco ads themselves. Its designers started by asking the obvious question: Why do teens start to smoke? The answer was not the attractiveness of cigarettes. Teens want to feel autonomous, and they want to be admired by their peers for being rebellious. Smoking cigarettes is a symbol of rebellion.

The new approach seeks to provide the rebellious satisfactions teens look for in cigarettes in a healthier way, by offering them a target for their rebellion: the tobacco industry. Many of the states that are now enjoying the most success with their antismoking efforts use the social cure; part of their campaign was to establish clubs for teens. They are not antismoking clubs—indeed, they do not criticize smoking or smokers. Instead, they provide a new peer group of fellow antitobacco revolutionaries, gathering teenagers to tell the tobacco industry that teens are tired of being manipulated. The clubs also intersect with an innovative media campaign in a way that makes both more effective.

The shift in the fortunes of teen antismoking efforts carries many important lessons for using the social cure. The journey from hopeless cause to stunning success shows why behavioral change has been done so clumsily in the past, and how failing strategies can be traded for successful ones. It also reveals the value of borrowing from the world of commerce. The techniques behind many successful examples of the social cure—teen smoking among them—are taken directly from commercial advertising and marketing. Indeed, the anti–teen-smoking campaigners were stealing moves from the tobacco industry. Healthful behavior isn't hair color, and it shouldn't be treated like a commercial object—not completely, anyway. But it is useful to employ strategies designed by people who understand the powers of persuasion—and who lose their livelihoods if they do it wrong. They do things that behavior-change advocates should do, too.

South Carolina is high school football country. On any Friday night in the fall, all over the state, entire towns assemble in the stands behind the local high school. In traditional football powerhouses, the stands are packed, the mood feverish, and the noise thunderous.

Gaffney, South Carolina, is such a place—a few miles from the North Carolina border, a good two hours from the coast. Anyone driving down Interstate 85 can find Gaffney by turning off the highway at the Million-Gallon Peach, a peach-shaped water tower complete with green leaf on top. Gaffney makes its living from peaches, and everything that can be made from a peach, but it is also famous for football. The Gaffney Indians have won the South Carolina state championship sixteen times, a state record.

On a freezing Friday night in November 2007, the Gaffney Indians beat the Lexington Wildcats in a playoff game. Gaffney High School has 2,100 students—it has 124 teachers—and it looked like all of them were at the game. A few hundred people had even come from Lexington, two hours away.

There was more going on than football. Although most people

in the stands were unaware of the fact when the game started, the Gaffney–Lexington playoff game was also a public-health event, one aimed at keeping teenagers off cigarettes. It didn't look like one of Judi Nwokedi's bogeymen—the long, boring lecture in church hall or school auditorium about proper behavior. And it didn't look like more recent attempts at swaying teens—the booklets and posters showing rows of graveyards and cancer statistics. What was happening that Friday night was a new approach, taking the strategies designed to sell cigarettes and using them to keep teens from smoking.

Among the crowd in Gaffney's football stadium that night were about fifteen high school and college students from Rage Against the Haze, South Carolina's teen antismoking movement, in which student volunteers spend their Friday nights going from game to game around the state, putting on a show. That night in Gaffney, they were giving out stickers and gear (such as T-shirts) that said, "I Love My Lungs," and "Smoking Robs Me of My Superhero Powers," videotaping the fans for the Friday Night Rage Web site, throwing NERF footballs into the crowd, leading text-messaging competitions, and working the seats— plunking down in the midst of shivering Gaffney students to tell them how they were being played by Big Tobacco. At most football games, thirty to ninety teens typically sign up to become members of Rage. There were some games where the Rage kids were greeted by rows of students holding up Rage signs, and one memorable game where the signs were held by shirtless students wearing body paint.

Earlier in the day, Matt Geib and Joe Dannelly, who made up Rage's entire paid staff, had visited classroom after classroom at Gaffney High. Matt and Joe were twenty-three but looked younger. "I'm in tenth grade, too," Matt was telling a group of four girls in the Gaffney lunchroom as he handed out stickers. "No, really." The two men seemed to have taken their hair and fashion cues, such as flip-flops in winter, from the Dude in *The Big Lebowski*, though with the addition of religious tattoos on their arms.

They went around the school with Brandon McCluney, Gaffney's student-body president, who knocked on classroom doors, checked with the teacher, and then took Matt and Joe inside.

"We're not like anything you've ever seen," they told each class. "We're not telling anyone how to live their life. We're not against smokers or smoking. We're just here to give you information on how tobacco companies are manipulating you. We'll talk about how tobacco companies target teens and in an underground way hook teens into being customers."

Matt told the students that before the game, Rage would have a tent outside the gates, where they could play *Guitar Hero III* on a plasma screen.

"I'm there!" shouted a student.

"You can come hang out with us and have fun and sign up," Joe said. "We have tons of stuff to give away—we're giving out T-shirts and hoodies. If you see us, you can say you saw us in school. We're a movement 3,000 strong—all people who are passionate about making a difference. Rage is about everybody having their own voice, their own talents. With our movement, you'll have a more powerful way to use your voice."

Joe and Matt gave their talk to class after class: that teens are being manipulated, that they can make a difference, that they can be in control, that no one is judging them, that they can hang out and play a hot video game, that they can get an edge with their friends because they've already met Rage.

Here's what they didn't say: cigarette smoking is addictive, smoking kills, you shouldn't smoke. "They expect the usual," said Joe later. "Then they hear what we're saying and they are open to hearing the rest."

At the Rage tent outside the stadium gate at nightfall, kids were playing *Guitar Hero* and poring over trays of stickers, bracelets, and fuzzy dolls with Rage messages. The Rage kids were hanging out. Among them were Emily Ayers, the perky blonde student-body president of J. L. Mann High School, and Bradley Phillips, a quiet artist. There was Luis Gonzales, a soft-spoken young man who seemed younger than eighteen, planning to start the next year at Furman, the state's most elite university. Some, like Quentin James, were "Ragers" now in college who still liked to come back on Fridays. Quentin had been a skinny ninth-grader with no direction when he first came upon Rage, which he said changed his life. Now a sophomore at Furman, he was taking off the next year during elections to organize college students for Barack Obama. If Obama had not become the country's first black president, almost everyone who knows Quentin was betting he would be. There was Cris Ivan, an engineering major at Clemson, always telling jokes in his strong Romanian accent. There was George Dorrah, a music and communications student at Claflin University who was also a manager at Radio Shack. George wore baggy jeans, braids, a do-rag, and heavy gold chains. "I've never tried cigarettes or drugs, and people look at me and say, 'Wow, he looks like he's having a good time,'" he said.

Many of them were wearing T-shirts and hoodies with "Dum Spiro Spero," the South Carolina motto since 1776, which happens to mean "While I breathe, I hope." The motto is practically the only favor South Carolina has done for its antismoking movement. The state's hostility to antismoking efforts has been truly epic. It has the lowest tax on cigarettes of any state—just 7 cents per pack. (Missouri is next lowest, at 17 cents. New York's tax is $4.35.) South Carolina has the worst laws; only eleven of eighty-six school districts were smoke-free in 2007.

In November 1998, the attorneys general of forty-six states and five territories signed what was known as the Master Settlement Agreement with the five largest tobacco manufacturers, who would pay the states $206 billion in compensation for taxpayer spending on tobacco-related diseases. In return for protection from further lawsuits, the companies pledged to stop targeting teenagers and to open many of their internal documents to the public, among other things. The states received huge settlements and were supposed to use large chunks of the money to combat smoking.

South Carolina took its $900 million in a lump sum and spent one-third of 1 percent of it on smoking prevention. While the CDC recommended that South Carolina spend $62 million a year on antismoking programs, the state spent a grand total of $3.34 million between 2000 and 2008. Rage Against the Haze started in 2002 with a budget of $800,000 a year, and that budget fell by half in 2003. In 2004, Rage's budget from the state was zero. After a furious editorial in *The State* newspaper, a nonprofit group called South Carolina Physicians Care Charity wrote a check for $50,000—and then the state Department of Health and Environmental Control managed to find $45,000 more. Despite the fact that the Master Settlement Agreement money was supposed to be paying for teen smoking prevention, the nickel-and-diming continues. In 2009, Rage's only money was a $25,000 sponsorship from Blue Cross Blue Shield. Both Matt and Joe fell victim to layoffs. In 2010, Rage no longer had a single paid employee.

This was exactly what Geno Church had feared when Rage began. Church works at Brains on Fire, a quirky, hip advertising agency in Greenville, South Carolina, that won the contract from the state to start a teen antismoking program. He knew that the budget was likely to be nibbled to death, so he needed the kind of advertising campaign that could survive anyway. Other states were running television ads, but that was not a possibility in South Carolina. Church needed sustainable and he needed cheap. A face-to-face campaign was the answer.

Church convened a group of teenagers to design the program. They chose the name Rage Against the Haze. "Adults hate it," said Church. "It sounds violent." Rage's delivery system for its messages was person-to-person contact—"viralmentalism," the kids called it, and those who spread the word are "sneezers"—supported by a Web site that told kids, "You're ready to change the world. You just don't know it yet," and any stories they can gin up in local media. Rage holds summer camps to train kids—nearly a thousand of them by the time of my visit in 2007—who then train other kids. Only a small part of the curriculum is about tobacco; the rest is about how to clarify goals and how to reach them. "To be passionate about something in your life, you need to learn how to be yourself. You're easily persuaded by others if you don't know who you are," said Luis Gonzales.

Rage bought a vintage blue-velvet couch, dubbed it Marilyn, and took it on a tour around the state, parking it in front of local landmarks and inviting people to sit down and chat. Its Web site (in 2010 down to a single page—also a victim of budget cuts) asked members to do missions, such as make Rage posters to hold at sporting events, write and perform Rage-related rap lyrics (and send Rage the video), or call radio shows. Rage held events such as Amazing Races and a takeover of the smoking section at a Shoney's restaurant. The latter ended, to the students' delight, when the manager called the police and the students fled into the Walmart next door. The big event, though, was football. Besides going to games, Rage sponsored South Carolina's "Mr. Football" contest to choose the state's best player.

The group's infrastructure was designed to turn on its head the rebellion that draws kids into cigarette smoking. Ragers tell people: "You think you're being independent by smoking? You're actually a puppet." They quote liberally from internal tobacco-industry documents detailing how the industry must recruit young smokers to replace the thousand or so tobacco customers who die every day.

One of Rage's favorite quotes, possibly apocryphal, was attributed to an R. J. Reynolds executive, when asked by the Winston Man model whether he smoked: "Are you kidding? We reserve that for the young, the poor, the black, and the stupid."

In a sense, the antismoking movement is about itself. Matt, Joe, and the Rage kids often found themselves pitching the group's own "groupness." One of the commercials for Rage that had been on Brains on Fire's Web site was a clip of a girl saying, "At the beginning of the year we didn't have any members. Now we have 600. Zero to 600. It's viral, it's spreading, you can't stop it." That's the whole ad. What is Rage? Doesn't say, but it sure is growing.

One of the attractions of Rage for teens is its anarchic, be-your-own-movement philosophy. "What I've seen Rage do is build pockets of Rage groups in different schools," Quentin James said. "People identify with them and student leaders take the movement back home. We'd love to take credit for this, but it's really kids we may see once a year—somebody wearing that T-shirt starting a viral movement."

Teens are like Soviet citizens—they will jump into a queue when they see one and then afterward ask what's for sale. Quentin was such a Soviet shopper. "What drew me in had nothing to do with the issue. That came later," he said. "What attracted me was the fact that I was watching video where young people were doing everything—from interviews to street marketing. We were at Myrtle Beach passing out palm cards. We wore bright clothes and people would stop us to ask, 'Are you famous?'"

Then he heard the quote about smoking being "for the young, poor, black, and stupid." "That caught my attention," he said.

"It's youth reacting to youth," said Greenville's Emily Ayers. "A lot of my friends do smoke. I don't know anyone who doesn't know it's bad for you. Kids will do it because their friends do it. If people see me at a football game, passing out gear, they say, 'Let's go check her out.' They see people who are cool and involved in other things and they say we don't have to do that."

"Having Rage gives them two peer pressures," said Luis Gonzales. "Then they can decide."

"If one of my friends tells me about a new band, I look up the new band," said Bradley Williams. "There's no way to change anyone with stuff like cool design—you have to talk to people. People may already agree and want to take action, but it's a lot easier and more comfortable if you have a lot of people you're doing it with."

RAGE AGAINST THE HAZE is an illustration of a new strategy, one that has been an important part of an astounding drop in teen smoking since the turn of this century—a strategy that will save millions of lives.

In 2000, it was impossible to envision such success. Teen smoking was rising and rising, impervious to governments' best efforts to block it. In *The Tipping Point*, Malcolm Gladwell wrote about teen smoking: "No one really knows how to fight it, or even, for that matter, what it is." His argument was that we should try to reduce the addictiveness of cigarettes, since we have failed utterly at preventing teenagers from taking up smoking them.

While he was writing that first edition of his book, Gladwell was correct that the United States seemed helpless to combat teen smoking. The study "Monitoring the Future," conducted each year by researchers at the University of Michigan, found that in 1997, 36.5 percent of high school seniors were current smokers. That figure was almost exactly the same as in 1975. Despair was widespread. "Officials Seek a Path to

Cut into Haze of Youth Smoking—The Bottom Line: No One Knows What Works," read a headline in the *Washington Post* in 1997.

It was not that the numbers didn't fall. Sometimes they did, but the tobacco companies could always drive them up again. In 1971, when tobacco ads were banned from television in the United States, teen smoking rates fell. Then in 1988 came the debut of Joe Camel, an icon incomprehensible to adults—who often didn't take it seriously—but one with great appeal to teens and even younger kids. By 1991, according to a study published in the *Journal of the American Medical Association*, more than 91 percent of six-year-olds could match Joe Camel to a picture of a cigarette. Among children aged three to six, more knew Joe Camel than they did Mickey Mouse.

Joe Camel was very effective. In 1988, teens spent $6 million on Camel cigarettes. By 1992, the figure was $476 million. In 1991, teen smoking rates began to soar, and the rise continued until 1997, when the Joe Camel ads ceased. As part of a settlement in a lawsuit, R. J. Reynolds agreed to stop them. From that year onward, teen smoking rates dropped.

In the late 1960s, a similar bulge in teen smoking had taken place, entirely among girls. From 1967 to 1973, rates of smoking by twelve-year-old girls rose 110 percent. The reason was an advertising push for three "women's" cigarettes: Silva Thins, Eve, and Virginia Slims. It should not be surprising that young people are particularly susceptible to advertising. The Centers for Disease Control found that 86 percent of teenagers preferred one of three heavily advertised brands: Camel, Marlboro, or Newport. Among smokers over twenty-six, only a third preferred one of those brands.

The problem of fighting cigarettes is different from the problem of fighting AIDS. AIDS fights back in its own way, through widespread societal customs conducive to its spread. But at least AIDS isn't spending millions of dollars every day to market and advertise itself. Think for a moment about a cigarette—an item that will be a significant lifelong expense, is designed to enslave you with its addictive power, and will likely kill you. It doesn't even get you high. Almost no one enjoys that first cigarette—you have to get used to it. It would be difficult to design a less attractive product. Yet 1.3 billion people—one-fifth of all the humans on the planet—smoke. Obviously, Big Tobacco's marketing force knows what it is doing.

The addictive power of nicotine helps. All tobacco companies have to do is get you to try cigarettes for a little while. Of those who do try them, just under half will be hooked. But really, why would anyone try such a product? The answer is that cigarette companies know how to get inside the heads of the people in their target market: young people (if you don't start smoking by your high school graduation, chances are you never will). Teenagers don't try cigarettes because they think they will like cigarettes. They try them for what cigarettes represent; smoking is sophisticated. It is rebellion. It is devil-may-care, live-for-now. It is a rite affirming a teenager's membership in the cool group. It represents autonomy, independence. The very danger of smoking to teens—the fact that it is forbidden and for adults only and may well kill you some day far off in the future when you are decrepit and old and ugly anyway—is its very lure.

After the first *Surgeon General's Report on Smoking and Health* (1964) concluded that smoking was addictive and harmful, antismoking activists began running campaigns to try to keep teenagers from taking up cigarettes. But these campaigns seemed to pay very little attention to the reasons that teens smoke. In the 1990s, Iowa, for example, put up billboards showing fields of gravestones: "430,000 people die a year from smoking," read the billboard. Massachusetts produced ads with Pam Laffin, a woman in her late twenties who had smoked since age ten and was dying of emphysema. She spoke movingly about trying to get children to learn from her life—her face puffed up from medication, wearing an oxygen mask, hooked up to tubes. (She died at the age of thirty-one.)

In New Jersey and elsewhere, a prominent poster campaign showed a duck with a cigarette hanging from its beak. "It Looks Just as Stupid When You Do It," the slogan said. In Illinois, billboards went up showing one smiling, colorful fish swimming with seventeen less-colorful fish, who were smoking. "Dare to be different, please don't smoke!" was the message.

In the mid-1990s, Arizona decided to spend $30 million to attack teen smoking. The state decided that kids wanted edgy, so it would give them edgy. The slogan was: "Tobacco. Tumor causing, teeth staining, smelly puking habit." Beginning in 1996, the slogan surfaced on billboards and such teen gear as T-shirts, baseball caps, and even boxer shorts.

These ads perfectly capture what had gone wrong in fighting teen smoking. The ads with the gravestones and the Pam Laffin spots relied on by far the most common argument of antismoking messages: fear. Smoking kills. But teenagers already know this. In fact, they *over-estimate* the dangers of smoking—they believe cigarettes are even more deadly than they are. Clearly, this is not a deterrent to teens. The problem is that it is abstract to them—they don't apply it to themselves. They do not feel vulnerable. Death is very far away to teenagers, and besides, someone will invent a cure for cancer by then. The message lacks credibility because they have not yet become sick. When I was in junior high school, I remember an eleven-year-old classmate telling me: "I've been smoking since I was seven, and nothing's happened to me."

What's more, teenagers have heard "smoking kills" way too much. They resent it—it symbolizes the heavy hand of grownups. What is salient to teenagers is being free to make their own decisions, and ads they perceive as telling them what to do may make them seek to assert their freedom even more.

As for the duck ad, it is smarter, since looking stupid is worse than death for most teenagers. The problem is that the message isn't credible. Smoking looks stupid when ducks do it precisely because they aren't humans. People happen to look sexy when they smoke. Even though the duck ad had proven its ineffectiveness, the CDC kept it on its list of approved campaigns.

The ad with the eighteen fish was the winner of an Illinois competition for an antismoking ad, a competition held among children aged eight to eleven. The idea, perhaps, was to involve kids in designing antismoking messages, an activity that was seen as giving them a closer identification with being a nonsmoker. It might have been a good idea if Illinois hadn't used the finished product. The message it sent to teenagers was that all your friends smoke, and you are an oddball if you don't.

That's the most powerful message possible—if you want to get kids to smoke. Nor is it smart to run antismoking ads obviously designed by children. Teens smoke to look older and feel older, which is why the tobacco industry's framing of the issue—smoking is for grownups!—is so effective at getting kids to smoke.

Arizona's campaign was edgy, but it still relied on the same principles: tell teens about the negative effects of smoking. It didn't work. The T-shirts became ironic gear, collected by smokers who burned holes in them with their cigarettes and wore them proudly—a double emblem of defiance. Teenagers already know the sensible reasons why they shouldn't smoke, and they are not persuaded by them, no matter what language the message employs.

Little wonder that efforts to keep teenagers off cigarettes weren't succeeding. On one side were the tobacco companies, spending millions of dollars each day to recruit smokers. They had done the research to know what campaigns worked, and they had the budgets to make their advertising seen and heard. On the other side were public-health experts, armed with the truth about smoking but very little money, and no idea about how to persuade teenagers.

Health expertise, it turned out, was a liability. The public-health people knew about the dangers of smoking and cared desperately about them, but their knowledge and intense passion were handicaps when trying to convince others. "They were like evangelists," said Paul Keye, a California advertising executive who would create the ads for the first really effective antismoking campaign. "They are told repeatedly that you don't want to hear what they have to say and that just excites them— they feel if you really knew the good news your life would be changed." The 1964 *Surgeon General's Report* on *Smoking and Health*, they felt, would close the case. "The health community believed that with that declaration, the war was over and they won," said Keye. The truth was now out there—so who would continue to smoke? The experts were shocked and paralyzed when the answer came back: almost everyone.

The most important problem was not that the people running antismoking campaigns were amateurish marketers. The problem was that they were professional health experts. They were so committed and knowledgeable that they could not put themselves inside the heads of those who are not. Antismoking experts were mired in the same muck as most of their colleagues in the public-health and good-guy persuasion world: they were marketing to themselves.

Some public-health experts welcomed the skills of the advertisers, but some felt threatened by the idea of using ad men with no medical background to design campaigns. The admen returned the sentiment. When public-health people set out to create an antismoking campaign, Keye said exasperatedly, "there are so many ways to do this wrong. It's the downside of community work—it's always a reassemblage of amateurs. However earnest or bright they are, you have to go through the whole life cycle of the fruit fly." No matter how much they are told about the need for professional expertise, they don't accept it. "There's always someone in the meeting who says, 'Our situation is different.' Which means: I want my wife to play the piano."

The Centers for Disease Control and Prevention, being health experts, fell into the same traps. The CDC recommended that antismoking campaigns focus on health effects. These guidelines were followed religiously by state health-department officials—harried bureaucrats who, if they were lucky, had just about enough money to hire a bad advertising agency. But even when an ad agency was brought in, government officials often told them that the only acceptable campaign was "Smoking is bad for you." Often the health departments didn't even measure whether or not their programs were working. They would define success as changing attitudes about tobacco, not as fewer kids taking up smoking—two completely different phenomena.

Then something new happened. It began in the late 1980s in California, where the politicians were so captive to Big Tobacco that the legislature had rejected thirty-seven bills to raise tobacco taxes since 1967. A small group of health and environmental activists decided that they had to work around the legislature. And because this was California in the years after the antitax initiative Proposition 13, they decided to have a ballot initiative. It would end up producing an advertising campaign that transformed public health.

Chapter Four

Corporate
Tools

EVEN IN HIS EARLY EIGHTIES, PAUL KEYE RETAINS
a loopy and inquiring brain that has long allowed him to
look at the same problem as everyone else in the room and
come up with a different solution. To promote Harry's
Bar and American Grill, which opened in 1972 in Century
City, California, Keye began the International Imitation
Hemingway Competition in 1978, challenging entrants to
come up with a page of the best bad Hemingway they could
muster. Since Hemingway was an aficionado of Harry's Bar
in Venice, all "Bad Hemingway" entrants had to mention
Harry's. The contest went on for a quarter-century and
drew thousands of entries a year.

Keye is an ad man, and this was a project to promote,
yes, a restaurant, but it is one that became legend. With a
media budget of $30,000, Keye won worldwide fame and
created an indelible brand for his client. It was not his only
success. In 1987, Keye was the creative director for the

iconic fried-egg "This is your brain on drugs" ad (the egg idea was not his, but he refined it) for the Partnership for a Drug-Free America. Two years later, Keye would again make an antidrug ad, this one perhaps the most revolutionary and successful public-health message ever produced.

In 1989, California's voters had just passed Proposition 99 with 58 percent of the vote. The proposition slapped a 25-cent tax hike on every pack of cigarettes, with 5 cents per pack going to antismoking initiatives. For the first time in history, a state had a large and sustained pot of money for antitobacco efforts.

As a result of Proposition 99, California opened a competition for a $28.6 million contract to create an advertising campaign. Keye's firm, Keye/Donna/Pearlstein, won. Keye's proposed ads were nothing revolutionary: variations on the same theme of "Smoking will kill you" that everyone was doing. That's what California had asked for. The health department instructed Keye to go to work on a series of health ads aimed at different audiences—heavy smokers, pregnant women, teens.

Then Keye had an idea. "I had the sense," he recalled, "that we weren't talking about the guy in the raincoat behind the tree." It was just intuition, not research, but it was intuition from an ad man who knew what he was doing. "Paul Keye was the real genius," said Stanton Glantz, professor of medicine at the University of California, San Francisco, and a veteran antismoking campaigner. "His bid was very traditional—you know, smoke and you'll die. Kids shouldn't smoke. But when he got the contract and sat down to do the ads, it suddenly dawned on him that sitting in the shadows out of sight controlling everything were the smoke folk—tobacco companies."

Keye reasoned that while cigarette smoking was an epidemic, it was not a naturally occurring one. It happened because tobacco companies were putting millions of dollars a day into creating that epidemic, and smoking rates rose and fell in direct response to advertising.

To the Californians' credit, Keye, Tobacco Education section chief Dileep Bal, and Ken Kizer, then California's director of health services, managed to convince the politicians that they needed to take on the tobacco industry. Even the Republican governor, George Deukmejian, signed on. "We had to show that smoking isn't coming from cigarettes.

It's coming from cigarette marketing," said Keye. "We re-triangulated the argument. It had always been parents vs. children, teachers vs. students, healthy vs. risky. Suddenly, by putting tobacco companies out in the sunlight, it was tobacco companies vs. the rest of us."

A year and a half after the ballot victory, California brought out two advertising campaigns. One, aimed at trying to get adult smokers to quit, was a fairly traditional campaign about the dangers of secondhand smoke. A typical ad showed a man calmly smoking at a table and blowing smoke in the face of his pregnant wife. The smoke then came out of her mouth. It was creepy, but the message was standard.

The other campaign was something radically different. On April 10, 1990, a thirty-second ad entitled "Industry Spokesman" made its debut. It presented a claustrophobic boardroom of tobacco executives, hazy with smoke. One of the actors says, "Gentlemen, gentlemen, the tobacco industry has a very serious multibillion-dollar problem. We need more cigarette smokers, pure and simple. Every day 2,000 Americans stop smoking. And another 1,100 also quit. Actually, technically, they die. That means this business needs 3,000 fresh, new volunteers every day. So, forget all that 'cancer, heart disease, stroke' stuff. Gentlemen, we're not in this business for our health." The people in the room cackle maniacally.

"Industry Spokesman" was the first in a series of ads that made Big Tobacco a character. In another ad, black rappers attacked the tobacco industry for using menthol cigarettes to get blacks to smoke. The ad ended with the line: "We used to pick it; now they want us to smoke it."

In Keye's later advertisements, the industry was personified by a sophisticated line drawing of a crocodile boasting about the tobacco industry's nefarious strategies. The industry-manipulation campaign goes on. A California TV commercial running in 2009, called "Programmed," shows a split screen. A man smokes a cigarette in one half of the screen. In the other half, a laboratory rat in a cage sucks on a spigot marked "nicotine." Carousel music plays. An announcer says, "The tobacco industry designs cigarettes to be addictive. How long will you let them control you?" Words come up: "Undo the manipulation."

The industry-manipulation campaign was constantly on the air, thanks to the largesse of California's smokers and the taxes they paid with each puff. One of its advantages was that it did double duty. The strategy not only put out a powerful message of its own, it also undermined the tobacco industry. Tobacco companies' own advertisements suddenly had less credibility, commented Glantz. And the companies' political power was dented, which helped politicians to resist tobacco-industry pressure to lower tobacco taxes and gut indoor clean-air laws.

The campaign worked best in adults, and smoking prevalence among adults dropped precipitously. The ads were not aimed at teenagers, and no special campaign for teenagers was used; Keye didn't believe in it. "When you address teenagers as a group, it comes off as a sermon. It's about as effective as yelling at birds," he said. But he hoped the theme would be effective, as it was the opposite of the typical approach. "We did not say ever, 'Boys and girls, smoking is for big people,'" said Keye. The campaign nonetheless did have some effect on teens. While teen smoking still rose slightly during the 1990s in California, peaking in 1995, research found that the increase was less than in the rest of the country—and that this achievement was due to the media campaign, not to the cigarette-tax increase.

But soon Florida would produce something more dramatic. Florida borrowed California's powerful anti-industry message, aimed it directly at teenagers—and added the social cure. The combination ended up creating what Stanton Glantz would call "the most amazing reduction in youth smoking I've ever seen."

THE CALIFORNIA CAMPAIGN HELPED to slow the rate of growth in teen smoking even though it was not aimed at young people. But teenagers were so important—they are virtually the only people who start smoking—that it was worth asking if more could be done.

Florida could ask this question because, like California, it suddenly had money to devote to teen-smoking prevention. The source in this instance was not tobacco taxes but a state lawsuit against the tobacco companies. Smokers had filed many suits against tobacco companies, but they usually lost. The tobacco industry had good lawyers who were able to convince juries that the plaintiffs were aware of the risks of smoking—they could read the warnings on the pack—and chose to smoke anyway. The states had a different and better case. Smoking-related illnesses were forcing the states to spend millions of dollars in Medicaid money to treat them. Mississippi was the first state to sue over these expenses. In 1995, under Governor Lawton Chiles, Florida became the second. Two years later, a settlement restricted tobacco advertising and sales in Florida and awarded the state $11.3 billion. The first $200 million of that money was to be used to finance a campaign to reduce teen smoking. No state had ever before enjoyed sustained financing for teen-smoking prevention.

The state asked for bids on an advertising strategy. The contract was won by Crispin Porter + Bogusky, an agency that had never worked on a government account but had done marketing to teens. It was probably the first time that people in any ad agency had sat down to think seriously about what could keep teenagers from smoking. Tom Adams, who became the creative director for the campaign, said that Florida's assured stream of money gave those designing the campaign the luxury of thinking about it in a more serious way than their predecessors. "Before this, a lot of people had thought, 'Oh, we have some money, let's tell teens something about smoking.' But no one was approaching it as a brand, an ongoing battle, a conversation with teens," he said.

"We did a lot of research during the course of the pitch on social marketing to youth related to tobacco," said Jeff Hicks, president and CEO of the ad agency. When the agency's directors sat down and read the marketing strategies that had been approved by the CDC, they became more and more frustrated.

"We couldn't make them work," Hicks recalled. "One was on romantic rejection—you should tell kids that tobacco makes them less romantic. Well, that was the same year the movie *Titanic* was released, with Leonardo DiCaprio smoking on the bow. We're supposed to tell you that tobacco makes you less sexy? It was so false and lacked any credibility. With the other strategies, too, we kept running into dead ends. Talk to youth about health effects and they're like, 'I'm never going to die.' Or, 'I'll quit.' They believe you can quit—cessation advertising has done a lot to continue a myth that it's easy to quit smoking. We couldn't make any of their strategies work."

The clue to what worked lay in another potent weapon Florida had acquired. Both California and Florida had money, but Florida had something else: a trove of internal documents from the tobacco industry—the industry's internal marketing strategies, memos, and studies.

Florida had the documents because the Mississippi and Florida tobacco lawsuits had paved the way for a national lawsuit, which ended in the 1998 Master Settlement Agreement, the largest civil settlement in American history.

As part of the settlement, companies and their marketing arms had to release internal documents. These showed that the cigarette executives knew exactly how damaging tobacco was, and that they had lied to Congress when they said they did not know. Although in their public statements tobacco executives consistently denied marketing cigarettes to teenagers, again the documents showed otherwise. A memo from R. J. Reynolds in 1975, for example, said, "To ensure increased and longer-term growth for the Camel Filter, the brand must increase its share penetration among the 14–24 age group which have a new set of more liberal values and which represent tomorrow's cigarette business." From the same company's 1976 forecasting report: "Evidence is now available to indicate that the 14–18 year old group is an increasing segment of the smoking population. RJR-T [R. J. Reynolds Tobacco] must soon establish a successful new brand in this market if our position in the industry is to be maintained in the long term."

Governor Chiles chose Chuck Wolfe, one of his top aides, to be the director of Florida's teen antismoking program. One of the first things Wolfe did was go to California, along with Peter Mitchell, the marketing director for the Florida Department of Health. California's Department of Health Services had been doing focus groups on whether an anti-industry strategy would work with teenagers. The answer was a resounding *yes,* and the bolder the better. The officials dumped the research in the laps of Wolfe and Mitchell.

They knew that a campaign aimed at teenagers had to be much more radical and audacious than even Keye's boardroom ad had been. The problem was that such advertising was a hot potato for Florida's health department. Even in California, the anti-industry camp had not had an easy time getting the governor to approve its campaign. Florida was a much more conservative state.

Wolfe solved the problem by drawing on his past. When he was in college, Wolfe had been the National Explorer president of the Boy Scouts, and he had served on the Boy Scouts national leadership board. The Scouts themselves had revised the Scouting program. Wolfe knew that if Florida's teens were given the chance to design the campaign, it would help in several ways. The campaign would be more believable to teens, it would get teen leaders from across the state involved in antitobacco work, it would produce a more radical message, and— perhaps most important to Wolfe at the time—it would give some cover to legislators nervous about the state's suddenly taking on the tobacco industry. Florida could blame it on the kids.

So the state held the first Teen Tobacco Summit in March 1998, assembling 600 teenagers from all over Florida. There the kids watched commercial after commercial and studied other states' campaigns. Almost all of them received a thumbs-down. "The 'Smoking will kill you,' 'Smoking will turn your teeth yellow' didn't work," said Jared Perez, then a tenth-grader from the Tampa Bay area. "The ads were health stuff, and the one, you know, with animals smoking cigarettes and 'It looks just as stupid when you do it.' My reaction, which was typical, was that these were messages you've heard before."

By contrast, the tobacco-industry documents enraged the teenag- ers. "These documents were something I'd *never* heard before," Perez said. "It was more compelling than 'Smoking is bad for you.' It was a truth issue." Then and there, at the Teen Tobacco Summit, the kids decided to make two commercials. Crispin Porter served as midwife and adviser, but the decisions belonged to the teens, some of whom stayed up all night to write the scripts. One ad starts with the camera on one young woman's face, then pans out to reveal hundreds of kids. In unison, they tell the tobacco companies something to the effect of: "We're smarter than you and faster than you and younger than you, and we thought we should introduce ourselves." Then they say they are tired of being manipulated and lied to by the tobacco industry. The other commercial was shot in stop-action video, with the kids wearing ski masks and acting like bank robbers holding a roomful of hostages. A girl whose voice is electronically altered demands that the industry stop targeting teenagers. "We know you've been targeting us," she says, "getting us to replace the 1,000 smokers who quit every day–you know, because they died."

The advertisements hit Florida's airwaves and billboards just a month later, in April 1998. At the teenagers' insistence, the campaign was dubbed "truth." (Among the many things the "truth" brand shares with loveLife is a preference for quirky and cool typography that includes an aversion to initial capital letters.) It became a brand for a collection of TV ads focusing on industry manipulation. Every ad was approved by a panel of teenagers, and some of the ads featured those same teens. The campaign borrowed from California's "industry manipulation" theme, but it added outrageous quotes from the tobacco-company documents and adapted the campaign to a teenage audience by making the ads mischievous. Florida's ads not only would target Big Tobacco; they also would show teenagers having fun at Big Tobacco's expense.

In one TV spot, Florida teenagers drove to Philip Morris headquarters in Richmond, Virginia, and asked to speak to the Marlboro Man, only to be told by an apparently clueless security guard at the front gate that he was dead. (The principal actor who played the Marlboro Man had, in fact, just died of lung cancer.)

Another ad showed a girl calling Lucky Strike's advertising account coordinator. "What is the 'lucky' part about Lucky Strike cigarettes?" she asks. "I really have no idea," the executive answers testily. The girl: "I mean, is it because . . . I might live?" After the ad executive hangs up on her, you can hear a group of girls laughing.

In another commercial, Perez and another teen call an ad agency that advertises cigarettes. They offer the hapless person on the line an award for killing more teens than anyone else. Ad after ad showed teenagers getting people from the tobacco-industrial complex on the phone—and then torturing them. It is likely that never before in the history of public health had anyone done a media campaign based on prank phone calls.

"California came up with the idea that the industry is manipulating you," said Peter Mitchell, who oversaw the "truth" campaign. "No one likes to be manipulated. But Crispin Porter took it to the next step. What do teenagers want? They are shopping for a way to rebel against their parents. Well, these people are even less cool than your parents."

FLORIDA THEN TOOK ITS campaign for the teenage mind a step farther: it reinforced the message of rebellion by using the social cure. The state set up SWAT—Students Working Against Tobacco—groups of teenagers in every county who were the forerunners of Rage Against the Haze and similar antitobacco groups in other states. SWAT recruited thousands of youngsters and trained them in leadership skills and organizing. The SWAT kids created some of the "truth" ads themselves, and they had final approval over all of them. SWAT had a "truth train" that went from city to city, at each stop picking up local kids and giving them onboard workshops before they got off at the next stop. There was a concert each time the train stopped; at the end of its run, in Miami, the train was welcomed with a concert by the group 'N Sync. There was plenty of gear—T-shirts, baseball caps, and more.

Like Rage, SWAT stayed away from the predictable messages to teens. "We never said, 'Don't smoke,'" recounted Jared Perez, who was later hired to run SWAT. "We got a bunch of kids together to make a statement to the tobacco industry—to rebel against them." SWAT used the same messages as "truth," but in the form of guerrilla warfare.

Each of Florida's sixty-seven SWAT chapters—one for each county—selected a different foreign country and researched how the tobacco industry marketed cigarettes in that country. The chapters tried to collect examples of cigarette marketing and tried to contact youth antismoking groups there. Some of the SWAT groups even persuaded their counterparts overseas to make videos about tobacco marketing, and SWAT showed the videos at Florida's Teen Tobacco Summit, which became an annual event. One Orlando-area chapter, for example, began corresponding with a high school in Novosibirsk, Siberia, and a Siberian tobacco researcher came to the Teen Tobacco Summit to bring back strategies and information to teens there. SWAT also published ten guidelines for the international tobacco industry. The list began: "The youth of the world must no longer be lied to or manipulated by the tobacco industry."

SWAT and "truth" reinforced each other; "'truth'" is the message, SWAT is the messenger," the program announced. Some people referred to the relationship as air war and ground troops. "The thinking on SWAT was that the media campaign provided the glue, the overarching message, but you really needed to drill down into the community and have the peer-to-peer activities going on to build a grassroots movement," said Ursula Bauer, a former leader of Florida's antismoking program.

"Because the 'truth' product is information, we try to find ways to make the brand tangible," said Tom Adams, the Crispin Porter ad executive. "Groups like SWAT make it tangible." Whenever a new "truth" TV spot came out, a network of kids was already in place, responding to it and amplifying it—creating a buzz about it. (A lot of teenagers in Florida were able to recite those "truth" ads by heart.) And the reach of TV made SWAT's antismoking peer pressure more powerful. The "truth" ads made it seem as though teen rebellion against the tobacco companies was everywhere.

Some of the "truth" ads themselves overtly reinforced the "your peers are doing it" message. Ads like the one filmed at the Teen Tobacco Summit, with hundreds of kids yelling at Big Tobacco in unison, try to show that antitobacco rebellion is widespread. But all the "truth" ads benefited from the peer effect.

Peter Mitchell said that right away SWAT turned the television "truth" ads into a form of peer pressure. "Not that many kids were in SWAT," he said, "but other kids *knew* it existed, and it made what was happening on TV real—not just an ad campaign."

SWAT's existence, Mitchell said, also erased the grownups from the "truth" ads for many teens, which made the messages much more credible. He ran focus groups to ask teenagers who was behind "truth." Nobody got the right answer: the Florida Department of Health. Most kids thought other teenagers were funding it. ("Their grasp of finance was not that great," said Mitchell.) "Truth" became a media version of a friend, a statement on a massive scale of what other teens were thinking and doing. The combination of the two was more than the sum of its parts. Without SWAT, "truth" was a very good media campaign. With SWAT, "truth" began to transcend television and become adopted by teenagers as the voice of their peers. A series of TV ads had become, in effect, part of a social cure.

WHEN GOVERNOR LAWTON CHILES died of a sudden heart attack in 1998, his lieutenant governor took office for a few weeks and then was succeeded by Jeb Bush, brother of the future president. Under a Republican governor and legislature, Florida became far more responsive to the lobbying of tobacco companies. The most outspoken student leaders, including Jared Perez, were fired. (The justification was budgetary, but Perez was being paid only $6 an hour.) Governor Bush nominally defended the program, but behind the scenes he was doing little to protect it from those who wanted to see it go away.

Without the shelter offered by Governor Chiles, the program was left at the mercy of its powerful enemies. Florida's legislature had never been comfortable with the "truth" campaign; it was too anti-authority. Many legislators felt that encouraging teenage rebellion went against Florida's values. Peter Mitchell, who had been a Republican staff member of Florida's legislature, was called in by the people for whom he used to work. They accused him of teaching teenagers to make prank phone calls. "Oh, that's been going on forever," he replied. "We're just improving the quality." A campaign based on disrespecting your elders apparently had its risks. Mitchell was fired.

Fortunately, Florida was completing its evaluation of the year-old campaign. The 1999 report was released the same day Mitchell lost his job. Newspaper headlines across the state read "Program Successful, Director Fired." More than 90 percent of Florida's teens were aware of the program. The evaluation showed not only attitude change among teenagers but measurable behavior change—fewer middle school and high school students were taking up smoking. In one year, current cigarette use among middle school students dropped from 18.5 percent to 15 percent, and among high school students from 27.4 to 25.2 percent—the biggest single-year drop seen in any state in the last two decades.

"It shows that Florida has perhaps the most effective antitobacco program in the world," said Ed Trapido, the University of Miami epidemiologist who carried out the evaluation. Stanton Glantz, the California antitobacco campaigner, agreed. But Glantz also put his finger on a powerful political truth: "With most state programs, the better they work, the more they get to keep going," he told the *Tuscaloosa News.* "With tobacco, the better they work, the less they get."

SWAT kids descended on the Florida legislature to argue for keeping the program, and it was saved, although its budget was cut by half. The next year's evaluation in 2000 showed continued success—the number of high school smokers had dropped to 22.6 percent—a fall of 17.5 percent in two years.

Florida's teen smoking rate continued to drop, and by 2007, the high school smoking rate was down to 14.5 percent—cut in half in less than a decade. But the decline greatly slowed beginning in 2002, the same year that "truth" and SWAT began to fall victim to budget cuts. That year, the state stopped increasing cigarette prices, and Governor Bush cut the financing for "truth" and SWAT to $1 million a year. While teen smoking dropped by 35 percent between 1998 and 2002, it only dropped by 19 percent in the seven years measured since then, and smoking for younger teens was again rising by 2009.

Interestingly, progress has stalled despite the fact that Florida is once again spending heavily on fighting teen smoking. In 2006, the state's voters approved a constitutional amendment mandating that 15 percent of the roughly $360 million Florida gets every year in Master Settlement money must go to antismoking campaigns, particularly those directed at young people. The antismoking budget in 2008 was back up to $60 million.

But Florida's Department of Health lost interest in themes of industry manipulation. In 2008, one theme of the ads, produced by a new ad agency, was "I Care," based on the idea that refraining from smoking shows you care about your health and the health of those around you.

One TV spot shows a video game. After destroying numerous enemies, the player lights a cigarette. "Each year smoking kills over 400,000 people," the announcer intones. "Don't be your own worst enemy." Another commercial shows a boy playing catch by himself. He throws a baseball and then starts walking to retrieve it. "Each year, smoking leaves 31,000 children fatherless," the announcer says. They are evocative and well-made ads—but for teenagers, probably useless.

Researchers at the North Carolina nonprofit institute RTI International did Florida the favor of asking Florida teens about their beliefs and seeing which of those beliefs correlated with smoking rates. They found that only two beliefs related to a lower likelihood of smoking: cigarette companies lie, and cigarette companies try to get young people to start smoking. Teenagers who agreed with those statements, in other words, were much less likely to smoke than teens who didn't. The other beliefs failed to resonate: smoking makes people look cool, nonsmokers don't like to date someone who smokes, smoking shows you like to take risks, smoking keeps your weight down, one out of three smokers will die, it's safe to smoke for a year or two as long as you quit. The implication of the survey is that the theme of industry manipulation works, while other themes are ineffective in ads aimed at teenagers. Yet Florida no longer uses industry manipulation, nor do many other states. "The better they work, the less [funding] they get," said Stanton Glantz about antismoking campaigns. This turned out to be prophetic.

IT WOULD SEEM LOGICAL that once Florida had proven what worked to fight teen smoking, its program would quickly be adopted everywhere. Since there are new teenagers every year, teen smoking prevention by nature needs to be a permanent campaign. It requires constant attention, steady financing, and an ongoing commitment to spending that money on the most effective strategies. We know what those strategies are, so financing them adequately and using them should simply become the way things are done. Yet this is not what happened. Not only did Florida move away from what works, but the same ups and downs occurred on a national level.

Just as Florida started with dramatic success, so did the United States as a whole. Part of the money from the national Master Settlement Agreement went to create the American Legacy Foundation, whose job was to run national antitobacco advertising and help states carry out the other parts of the campaign. Legacy went with what had worked. It adopted Florida's advertising and messages, hired its chief, and took its ad agency. Florida's Chuck Wolfe became executive vice president and chief operating officer, and Legacy began a national "truth" campaign in 2000, with ads created by Florida's Crispin Porter + Bogusky.

While Florida saw a 47 percent drop in teen smoking between 1998 and 2007, the nationwide "truth" ads helped many other states to do almost as well. States have also benefited from an increase in the federal cigarette tax, state cigarette-tax increases, and a general toughening of public opinion and laws on smoking. There are more smoke-free areas now, and enforcement is tougher on selling to minors. Social norms on smoking have changed. The rise of cell phones may be another reason why teen smoking has dropped—it has never been studied, but some researchers have hypothesized that phones may give teenagers something to do with their hands and a way to be cool that doesn't involve cigarettes (which may actually provide teens with a new rationale for high texting charges). In the decade from 1997 to 2007, the drop in teen smoking nationwide was 45 percent. Almost all of that drop occurred between 2001 and 2003—exactly the years that the Florida-style campaign went national.

States with the will to keep spending money on effective programs now are finding that they can keep reducing teen smoking. New York, for example, has a particularly aggressive and well-funded antismoking program (although it is not directed at teens), and public officials such as New York City mayor Michael Bloomberg, who is an antismoking crusader. Cigarette taxes are particularly high. In 2010, a pack of cigarettes cost more than $11 in New York City and more than half the price—$5.85—went for taxes. (In South Carolina at the same time, a pack of Marlboros cost $4.49, with $1.08 of that going for federal and state taxes.) Psychologist Robert Cialdini would approve of New York City's strict smoke-free laws—no one must feel more lonely, more in

violation of his group's social norms, than the guy who has to leave
a party and stand outside to smoke his cigarette. New York also has
a social-cure group called Reality Check, the state's version of Rage
Against the Haze. Reality Check has adopted the mission of writing
letters to movie actors and studio executives to get cigarettes out of
movies that kids see. New York City saw a staggering 63 percent drop
in teen smoking between 1997 and 2007.

But very few states resemble New York. As in Florida, most states have
seen a serious erosion of their political commitment to the antismoking
fight, and they are doing less and less of the right stuff. Florida's new
ballot initiative makes it one of the few states to actually use its settlement funds for antismoking campaigns. Nationwide, less than 5 percent
of the Master Settlement Agreement money has been used to prevent
smoking. The rest goes to—well, whatever politicians want it to go to.
Nearly half the states securitized their payments, taking a lump sum of
some 30 cents on the dollar and giving up future payments—politicians'
way of making sure that they, and not future administrations, would get
to do all the spending. In 2008, ten years after the Master Settlement
Agreement, states had spent only 3.2 percent of their revenues from
the agreement on smoking prevention or stop-smoking programs. It is
simply too tempting to raid the fund to finance other priorities.

Despite abundant evidence that they work, teen antismoking campaigns have been gutted in most states, in some cases to pay for campaigns to fight childhood obesity. And when states do spend money on
antismoking campaigns, many choose strategies that have been proven
ineffective. Like Florida, many have gone back to the bad-old-days campaigns based on health concerns. On the surface, this is inexplicable. If
it costs the same to make effective ads, why not make them?

The reason, of course, is that the tobacco companies don't want them
to. Not only does cigarette marketing and advertising provide constant
pressure on teens to smoke, the companies spend billions in lobbying
and political donations in hopes of persuading politicians to make their
antismoking campaigns as puny and ineffective as possible. Michael
Thun, chief epidemiologist for the American Cancer Society, said the
tobacco industry spent $100 million in 2006 just to defeat various state

efforts at passing stronger antismoking laws. In 2007, Oregon voters
had to decide on a measure that would have raised the state's cigarette
tax by 84 cents a pack to finance health care for uninsured children.
The tobacco industry spent nearly $12 million to defeat the proposal,
which failed—59 percent to 41 percent. The industry's strategy was to
create and finance "front groups" with names that sounded like ordinary citizens were behind them, such as Oregonians Against the Blank
Check, which was financed by R. J. Reynolds. These groups painted
the ballot measure as yet another tax hike. It worked.

Antismoking spending matters. A paper in the *American Journal of
Public Health* found that if states had spent the minimum amount on
teen tobacco control recommended by the CDC, teen smoking would
be between 3.3 percent and 13.5 percent lower than what it has been.

How the money is spent also matters. The subtlety of Big Tobacco
is a marvel. If it becomes evident that states are going to run antismoking campaigns, the industry is brilliant at getting them to choose ineffective themes. Even the Master Settlement Agreement fell into this
trap—states could use their settlement money only on ads "regarding
the addictiveness, health effects and social costs related to the use of
tobacco products and shall not be used for any personal attack on, or
vilification of, any person (whether by name or business affiliation),
company, or governmental agency, whether individually or collectively."
The tobacco industry gave its approval to themes of addictiveness,
health effects, and social costs because they were the proven failures.
The states probably agreed to them at the time because they didn't
know better.

Big Tobacco pushes states to focus their antismoking campaigns on
pregnant women and young children, or on telling teenagers they'll get
sick and their teeth will turn yellow. Even many politicians who know
this approach is ineffective are content to use it, as it makes the tobacco
industry happy and the public can't tell the difference. To the public,
these messages seem as though they would work.

What alarms the tobacco industry is the social-cure theme of rebellion, messages that make teenagers feel cool by turning against the cigarette companies. The industry hates the "truth" ads. Lorillard, maker

of Newport cigarettes, sued the American Legacy Foundation, trying to stop its ads on the grounds that they amounted to vilification. The ad in question was called "Dog Walker." In the ad, a man identifying himself as a dog walker called Lorillard to propose a business idea— that he collect dog pee and sell it to the company. "Dog pee is full of urea and that's one of the chemicals in cigarettes," says the dog walker. Lorillard eventually admitted that there was urea in cigarettes, but it took the position that the truth didn't matter—it was still vilification. A Delaware court did not agree. The foundation won, but not until it had spent millions of dollars defending itself. The tobacco industry is highly litigious, and it can channel its wealth into legal harassment with great success. Politicians contemplating aggressive advertising remember this—which is just what the tobacco industry wants them to do.

Given the failure to spend the necessary money, and to spend it on what works, it is hardly surprising that teen smoking is no longer declining in many states. The year 2003 saw a big decline in the states' antitobacco funding and a flattening of cigarette prices through industry discounts to compensate for state tax increases. That was the year the dramatic drop in teen smoking ended, and by the end of the decade in many states it was rising again.

ONE WOULD EXPECT THAT if the tobacco industry was successfully fighting back nationwide, it would be doing even better in South Carolina. There, the industry has been extremely powerful. It has kept South Carolina's cigarette tax the lowest in the country and cigarettes there are the cheapest in the nation. Its antismoking laws are among the weakest, its spending on smoking prevention among the lowest. In 2009, the state legislature passed a bill raising the state cigarette tax from 7 cents a pack to 57 cents, with the money going to health care and antismoking programs—Rage Against the Haze was to get $3 to $5 million a year. But the governor, Republican Mark Sanford, vetoed it. The state has continued its near-perfect record of doing nothing.

Yet teen smoking in South Carolina dropped nearly 54 percent between 1997 and 2007—one of the biggest declines anywhere, and not terribly far behind the crusaders in New York City. Antismoking experts couldn't explain it. "That's a big drop," said April Schweitzer, associate director for youth advocacy at the Campaign for Tobacco-Free Kids. "We usually only see drops like that when there's a lot of prevention funding being spent and a statewide youth advocacy empowerment program." Said Meg Riordan, the director of policy research at the Campaign for Tobacco-Free Kids: "South Carolina could be pointed to as *the* outlier."

Could the reason be Rage Against the Haze? We know that face-to-face programs can work if done right. Smoking experts call them very powerful. Stanton Glantz has studied South Carolina's antismoking program and believes that Rage is the main reason teen smoking has dropped: "These programs when they are well done are wonderful. They increase the social unacceptability of smoking."

Glantz's California colleague John Pierce, a professor at the University of California at San Diego Medical Center, was hired to evaluate California's antismoking programs. He likes to tell a story about a video he had kids make in a Monterey high school where he had spent three months. It was only a ten-minute video, but "the kids poured their hearts out. Smokers talked about how difficult it was to quit, about trying every day."

The videotaped students were what Pierce called the "power group" in the school—leaders, opinion makers, cool kids. All were smokers. He showed the video to two classes. "The whole school had turned against us within half an hour," he said. Students came up and withdrew permission to use them in the video. They accused Pierce of fabricating the tape, of manipulating them.

About six months later, Pierce visited the school again. A student who had been in the video told him that nearly all of those in the film had stopped smoking. It turned out that the kids in the video felt like they had been under attack. "What it showed was this very cool group in school couldn't control their own behavior," he said. "The power group in the school was getting devalued. They wouldn't talk to me for three months. But the experience was so strong that they all eventually quit.

"We got permission to use the video in other schools. But it had no impact. It wasn't *their* power group. It had the effect of other videos—which is to say, not much."

Pierce believes that antismoking peer pressure can have a huge impact if the power group in a school takes an active stand. "We made our video because kids weren't talking about smoking. For the power group to do that was our goal. That's a huge change. You would not have gotten the power group in any school to do what is happening in South Carolina—taking on smoking issues."

But there remains a mystery. Let's assume for a moment that Rage Against the Haze is tremendously effective at changing the behavior of the students it reaches through peer contact. Still, the number of students it reaches directly was never large. Yet there was nothing else visible that could explain South Carolina's bigger-than-average decline in teen smoking. Rage has been the only game going.

Perhaps, as with SWAT in Florida, this social cure has a reach beyond the students who get personally involved. Perhaps simply hearing about the group, just seeing the logo on the Mr. Football contest, for example, makes a large group of teenagers think that Rage is larger than it is—that thousands of their peers are rebelling against the tobacco industry.

No one would argue that South Carolina chose the right strategy in doing virtually nothing, or that groups like Rage alone are enough. The variety of states that had success with persuading teenagers not to smoke between 1998 and 2003 show that the more you do, the better: tax increases on cigarettes, more enforcement of prohibitions on selling to minors, smoke-free laws, "truth" ads on TV and radio, face-to-face youth peer programs. Florida showed that for teenagers, the combination of industry-manipulation–themed TV ads and face-to-face teen peer groups is particularly potent. But TV ads have a problem: they cost money—lots of it—and states aren't spending.

The example of South Carolina indicates that when times are lean and states are not willing to spend money, what little they spend might go to the social cure. Many states now have Rage-like groups: REBEL (Reaching Everyone By Exposing Lies) in New Jersey, Reality Check in New York, Just Eliminate Lies in Iowa, TRU (Tobacco Reality Unfiltered) in North Carolina, reACT! Against Corporate Tobacco in Montana, and REAL in Hawaii, among others. These groups give durability to a teen antismoking campaign. Because of the (volunteer) passion of its teenagers, Rage Against the Haze showed a remarkable ability to bloom in a desert. Stanton Glantz cautioned that while these rebel-youth clubs need care and feeding—which means money—they are hardier species than other kinds of antismoking programs: "If kids are doing what kids do and they have information, they go off and do it." He also felt that youth-empowerment programs such as Rage are harder for politicians to attack: "Media campaigns are a lot easier for politicians to control—they're produced centrally. Youth-empowerment programs are harder to stomp out," he said.

"We have kids educated and trained, and they can replicate it in their home towns for very little money," Geno Church, the Brains on Fire executive who runs the Rage account, said in 2007. "Today it has 8,000 members, and some of them still do events and talk to their friends. I'm glad we built it the way we did, or it would have died."

At that time, Rage was still functioning only because it was powered by teenage rebellion. But in the end, there are no perpetual-motion machines. By 2010, Rage was too poor even to have a Web site, and once again teen smoking rates in South Carolina were on the rise.

Social change does not happen in a vacuum. Any decision on strategy must take into account the difficulty of building and maintaining political support, especially when the opponent is formidable. The money is theoretically there for antitobacco campaigns—from the Master Settlement Agreement. The expertise is there—we know what works. Yet only one state—North Dakota—is spending the money that the CDC recommends be spent on tobacco control. Only nine other states spend half the recommended amount. And many states that are spending money on programs have chosen ineffective ones.

With the money and documents unleashed by the Master Settlement Agreement, the turn of the twenty-first century very likely saw the most auspicious convergence of events we will ever see for smoking prevention. Yet through ignorance, indifference, or outright corruption, politicians have squandered this good fortune.

THIS STORY IS A TESTAMENT to the value of the ad man. Yet the cultures of social activism and commercial advertising have never trusted one another. They have long viewed each other as do-gooders vs. corporate tools, hopeless naifs vs. frivolous sellouts. This tension has been destructive. The history of antismoking campaigns shows that behavior-change advocates desperately need help from the world of hair color and soft drinks. They need the advertisers for the perspective they bring: the public-health experts tended to assume that people would respond to information alone, but advertisers knew that they would not. Advertisers understand the need to sell. They could look at smoking through the eyes of the target audience—something health experts could not do.

Behavior change also needs the techniques that the commercial advertisers use, such strategies as branding, word-of-mouth and experiential marketing—all borrowed by the Florida campaign against teen smoking. The idea of having to convince someone of the utility of these strategies is laughable in the commercial world, where branding was already in wide use in the late 1800s. But public-health and other behavior-change campaigners confronted with branding are almost like grandma looking warily at e-mail.

The array of weapons employed to sell hair color not only is useful by itself for those trying to help their fellow humans to straighten up and fly right. It also is necessary for the success of the most powerful of these techniques: the social cure.

Although the social cure's mechanism for change is peer pressure, people don't find their new peers by themselves—they have to get to a meeting or join a group. Luring them there is not always easy—by definition, the issues that the social cure addresses are a hard sell. With some types of behavior, getting people to show up is most of the battle. Young people in South Africa who attend just a single loveLife

program are less likely than their peers to get HIV. And if the organization can provide people with groups that are particularly useful or
particularly fun, they will come back again and again. If 90 percent of
life is showing up, it can be 95 percent of behavior change.

So there's the major challenge: getting people to show up. More specifically, it is how to get those who are *not* enthusiastic natural allies
to show up. There is always a small group of the faithful—committed
antismokers, kids who would never think of having unprotected sex.
They will be first in line for your meeting, but they are not the ones
at risk. For the social cure to be successful, it must reach beyond this
core audience.

In the world of fast food, the first thing an advertiser would do is
create a brand. Nothing is more standard in the commercial world, yet
branding is widely ignored by social activists. If campaigners have a hope
of persuading people to change their behaviors, they must embrace the
idea of brands. A brand creates loyalty, affinity, and consistent expectations for the experience people will have with a product. Brands create
emotional associations—when you hear the name, you feel something.
All these are invaluable for behavior change. Florida's Crispin Porter +
Bogusky knew that it needed to make "truth" a brand, to break teens'
strong loyalty to the Marlboro, Camel, and Newport brands.

The founders of loveLife went even further: their goal was to brand a
lifestyle. The end of apartheid had done several things at once to elevate
the importance of brands to South African youth. It had brought electricity, and hence television, to people who had never had it. It plugged
a once-isolated country into global fashion, music and youth culture.
And it ushered in an era of consumerism for newly empowered blacks.
Add them up, and you get an environment of very high awareness of and
loyalty to advertised commercial brands—Coca-Cola, KFC, Vodacom,
and South African brands such as Castle Lager beer. LoveLife's founders knew that teens would embrace a brand, that identifying loveLife as
a brand standing for a positive, upbeat approach to life in the company
of other cool kids would be alluring to teens. So they branded loveLife
with recognizable logos, typographical flourishes, and stylish signature
design, and they tried to impart a consistent upbeat and fun flavor to

the loveLife experience. LoveLife's Web site, for example, effectively announces that this is no ordinary AIDS-prevention campaign. The home page changes regularly but often doesn't even mention AIDS. In one typical week, it featured profiles of TV stars and MTV video jockeys, and there was a teaser for green careers. Pictures of great-looking young people adorned the page. Absolutely nothing on the portal indicated that it was anything other than an online fashion, gossip, and lifestyle magazine for teenagers—which is just what loveLife wants.

The branding stuck—loveLife is one of the most recognized brands in South Africa. It was named the tenth-favorite brand outside major cities, and its TV ads are the fourth best liked.

Beyond branding are more sophisticated techniques valuable for the social cure. One is identity marketing—selling not the Porsche but the self-image a buyer would enjoy as a Porsche driver. Identity marketing is ubiquitous in the world of luxury goods and personal products. Many commercials for auto dealerships or cars show beautiful women standing next to the products. They are there not because they know about cars but to appeal to male shoppers' fantasies of what life would be like driving these cars. Think of those Ralph Lauren Polo ads—the gorgeous photos of rich, WASPy-looking, patrician, beautiful people. It's hard to remember the cut of the clothes they wear but easy to remember the association with wealth and good taste the ads inspire. Liquor ads feature slinky models in party clothes. L'Oreal hair-color models say, "It costs a little more, but I'm worth it." Cigarette ads show people who look really cool and are clearly having fun.

At first glance, it would seem that identity marketing wouldn't work very well in the service of the social cure. Identity marketing is good for selling fun: expensive clothes and cosmetics, drinking, sports cars, cigarettes. But the challenge of selling behavioral change is to get people to give up their fun in exchange for their long-term well-being. No more free sex, drinking, crime, environmentally destructive gas-guzzling cars, big spending—all that stuff identity marketing is so good at making you want. People want to think of themselves as Porsche drivers. How many people fantasize about life as the driver of the car I own—a Ford Taurus station wagon?

But in fact, because people's desired identity is multilayered, identity marketing does work for behavioral change. Commercial identity marketing assumes people want to be rich and beautiful. And they do. But the social cure goes deeper. Behind the desire for wealth and beauty is (in part) the need for connection, recognition, respect, and the admiration of one's peers.

There are other ways to satisfy those needs than by wearing Polo clothes and using expensive hair color, as Florida's experience shows. Cigarettes are perhaps the world's most successful example of identity marketing. Their selling point is pure self-image (the product itself is repulsive). The big "aha moment" for Crispin Porter + Bogusky came with the realization that they could give teenagers a different route to the same desired identity—a healthier way to be rebellious and autonomous, to stand up to adults.

Marketers now have become more interested in word-of-mouth: the idea that the most credible spokespeople for a brand are peers—special, socially influential peers, but peers people know and trust. Word-of-mouth itself is very, very old—cave-dwellers no doubt used it to barter their animal skins for more berries, or marry off their daughters to a wealthier class of son-in-law. But in the last few years, the advertising and marketing industries have looked to word-of-mouth—which today also effectively means word-of-e-mail and word-of-Facebook—as a response to media overload. It's a way to break through the clutter of the thousands of media messages and hundreds of media vehicles the average consumer encounters every day. It is also a response to the fact that the audience for media has splintered. Any mass media must by nature be homogeneous—and therefore irrelevant to many of its consumers.

Word-of-mouth-marketing experts say that it isn't simply good products that inspire customers to text or call or e-mail their friends. It's about the way that product affects the customer's identity. "I would share because it makes me look good to be part of the hip group," said Andy Sernovitz, a word-of-mouth guru in Chicago. "It's the Ritz problem. You go stay at the Ritz. It's wonderful—the food is great, the room is perfect. But you never call a friend to tell them about it. But say you go stay at the Doubletree for $79 a night, and when you check in, they have cookies. Now you call someone—they have cookies!

"With traditional politics, you talk about the party and no one cares. But when I join Obama's page on Facebook, I'm cool. I'm part of the group. It's not about the topic. It's about the emotions. It's 'How am I going to look good?'"

According to Sernovitz, another key component is that people will talk about a product when they can claim some stake in it: "If it's something new and different and I'm there at the beginning, I can belong to this and feel special. I change the ownership. When I tell my friend about something new, it conveys status to me."

This is especially important among young people. "They abhor overt positioning and the feeling they are being marketed to," said Jennifer Stephen, vice president of GIO Global Intelligence, an international marketing company based in Chicago. "When the recommendation comes from a trusted friend or influence," she said, "they feel they have circumvented a manufactured desire for something."

This phenomenon allows consumers to claim a piece of the product as theirs. Taking this farther are consumer-generated media, which allow people to help create a product or its campaigns. The desire for ownership, to add value, is something consumers respond to in the oddest forms. Take ketchup. A few years ago, Heinz ran a competition— grand prize: $57,000 and national airtime—asking people to create a thirty-second TV commercial for its ketchup and upload it to YouTube. In its second year, the ad agency that worked with Heinz said that it received 8,000 commercials, which had 2.3 million hits on YouTube. People spent more than 80,000 hours of their valuable time watching— one supposes voluntarily—amateur ketchup commercials on YouTube. Consumers chose the winner, Matt Cozza of Chicago, whose commercial featured people in a restaurant swiping ketchup from the next table and pouring it on their french fries and burgers. A man and a woman sit down at their ketchup-free table and look dismayed until a waitress drops a new bottle in front of them. Words come up next to the bottle: "Now We Can Eat."

It was a pretty good commercial, by any measure, but even if it hadn't been good, it still might have been effective. Sernovitz believes that consumer-generated media are more credible than standard commercials, which consumers think of as "corporate and branded and well executed and not yours."

Word-of-mouth and consumer-generated media can and should be used as stand-alone strategies in the realm of behavior change. But they have even more relevance if activists are trying to use the social cure. There is no better way to get someone to attend an event or join a group than to have a trusted peer recommend that group or event. The social cure, like word-of-mouth, relies on peers to create credibility and weight. The social cure also works much the same way as product campaigns that let the consumer add value. People are more committed to a cause if they invest some of themselves in it. In part, this is cognitive dissonance at work—since they have put money or time into a cause, they'd best believe in it. But the investment also keeps them in contact with other people at various stages of the same journey. LoveLife's groundBREAKERS say that their work persuading others helps them maintain their own commitment to a healthy lifestyle. Alcoholics Anonymous is another group where members' commitment to sobriety is strengthened by supporting others in the same struggle and helping them to stay sober. AA's program in which more experienced members sponsor new ones is a proven success—for the sponsor. Being a sponsor helps keep you sober, but being sponsored, research shows, does not. Behavior change, of course, is bigger even than choosing a hotel or buying ketchup, so for the social cure the interaction with peers generally must be more intense than a simple e-mail, Facebook post, or conversation.

The most useful concept that social-cure founders can borrow from corporate life is experiential marketing, an idea that combines several other strategies. Judi Nwokedi used it when she modeled loveLife on a Sprite relaunch in South Africa. Experiential marketing tries to involve people in an experience, not just a purchase, even if the purpose is getting them to buy. Tobacco manufacturers are masters of it: after cigarette advertising was banned from television, tobacco companies turned their dollars to sponsoring events, especially sports and concerts that young people like. Experiential marketing tries to build a community, one that transmits its new norms to its members. It gives them activities to go to and do, people to meet, a group that revolves around the product. The social cure is essentially a supercharged, ongoing, face-to-face version of experiential marketing—one focused on something huge and life-altering.

Social activists interested in experiential marketing can learn from the single most successful example of experiential marketing in American business history—the closest a for-profit business has ever come to a social cure. The campaign was, in fact, designed to address the perception of a social ill—in this case, the midlife crisis—but its main purpose was to sell a product. The campaign created a new group of peers that large numbers of people chose to join and see face-to-face on a regular basis, changing their identities and something fundamental about their lives in the process. The product is a motorcycle.

In the early 1980s, Harley-Davidson was in deep trouble. Its reputation was suffering from the plethora of biker-gang movies portraying motorcycle riders as outlaws. In 1969, the company had been bought by AMF, which cut labor costs and lowered the quality of its motorcycles. After that, Harley sales had dropped, pushed out by better-made Japanese bikes.

When AMF sold the company in 1981, quality began to improve. Harley began to shed its outlaw image by persuading police officers to use its bikes. The results were dramatic. In 1983, Harley started the Harley Owners Group—playing on the fact that big bikes have long been known as Hogs. Today, HOG has more than a million members, and they are far from who you think they are. By 2005, the average Harley owner was forty-seven, with a median income of $83,000. Bike owners play a large role in directing the organization, but Harley manages the process. The company organizes rides for everything from going out to dinner to cross-country tours and charity events. It promotes the HOG this way: "Who says you can't choose your family? Become a part of HOG and meet the thousands of brothers and sisters you've always wanted."

Harley-Davidson is considered the iconic cult brand—so cultlike, in fact, that Harley has had to tone it down. In the late 1990s, the marketing department realized that the mystique of the Harley rider was starting to scare away new customers. The group-ness of HOG made potential customers feel too much like outsiders to buy a Harley, and they started to turn to other brands. Harley responded by offering courses at its dealerships to teach motorcycle novices to ride, even offering courses in group riding. The idea was to soften some of the intimidation outsiders felt when facing the passion of the Harley owner.

Experiential marketing has been very good for Harley-Davidson. Until the economy weakened in 2007, the company enjoyed year after year of record-breaking sales. According to the company, $100 invested at the end of 1986 would have been worth $9,000 at the end of 2009— and only $782 if it had been invested in the S&P 500 Index. The brand is so valuable that 7 percent of the company's revenue comes from licensing products. There are not many companies whose customers tattoo its name on their arms.

What all these marketing strategies (beyond branding) have in common is that they sell the idea that buying the product will make the customer more respected and embraced by his or her peer group. "If you want people to rally to the cause, it has to be about *them*, not the cause," said Andy Sernovitz. "But there aren't a lot of marketers and organizers who start with the premise of 'What's in it for our helpers?'" There are even fewer among behavior-change advocates.

ANYONE HAVING EVEN A CASUAL acquaintance with the world of marketing or social change will find a glaring omission in this inventory of marketing techniques useful for behavioral change and the social cure: there has been very little mention of the Internet, even though the conventional wisdom is that the Internet is *the* tool for social change. Facebook members can join hundreds of different groups focusing on Darfur. The world got to see the cruelty of Iran's regime when video of the shooting of protester Neda Soltan was uploaded onto YouTube. Web chat groups and communities link people around the world interested in subjects such as crime statistics or climate change. Web sites such as kiva.org hook up farmers in Cambodia who need $162 to raise pigs with people in Chicago who have $162 to invest. It would seem that the Internet would make the social cure easy, if not irrelevant.

But is this the case? As we think about what techniques from the business world social activists can adopt, it is useful to look at how the Internet intersects with the social cure. The Internet, of course, is not a strategy. It is a platform—like television, radio, newspapers, skywriting, or traveling minstrels, a vehicle for disseminating a message. Its impact on social change in general is a fascinating and complex subject, but it has been widely debated and that conversation need not be repeated here. The questions most relevant to the social cure are two: Can the Internet help facilitate a join-the-club solution? And can it *be* one, replacing the face-to-face version?

The answer to whether the Internet can be useful in a social cure is a resounding *yes*. Like other platforms, it can introduce people to your social cure and bring them to your meetings. It can help link up like-minded people and raise money. Used in the way loveLife does, it can reinforce your brand.

The big limitation of the Internet, of course, is that it has been very difficult to use it to reach people who aren't already looking for you— and these people make up your most important audience. A "truth" commercial on *Gossip Girl* would be seen by everyone watching the show, whether they had ever given a thought to tobacco-industry malfeasance or not, but only those who looked for it would find the loveLife Web site. Alas, there are no "truth" commercials on *Gossip Girl*, because they would be too expensive. The loveLife Web site, by contrast, does exist. This is perhaps the most important advantage of the Internet over other platforms: it is almost free.

It is increasingly possible to use the Internet to talk to people who didn't realize they could be interested in what you have to say. Social-networking sites accomplish this—your information reaches new people if their friends post a link on their Facebook page or suggest they become a fan. The message has added impact because it comes from a trusted source.

"The things we did ten years ago are valuable—having events, bringing people in and talking to them," said Jared Perez of Florida's SWAT, reflecting a decade later. "But only so many people are going to come to your booth. Technology offers the opportunity to overcome the preaching-to-the-choir effect. There's a huge potential for person-to-person communication of youth-directed messages. You can put a 'truth' commercial on your page. So many things with pop-cult status come from YouTube or some kid somewhere and spread." (The music video *Chocolate Rain* and the Chicken Noodle Soup dance are two examples.) And while TV viewers are passive recipients of a message, Internet users can be interactive. People in your target group can add their own content, sign up for membership, upload videos, buy gear—steps that can bring them closer to personal commitment.

Every organization knows that a Web site is important. But as the "truth" campaign TV commercials did for Florida's antismoking efforts, a Web site can have extra value for a social-cure group. It can work as a booster, giving a movement weight and scope. It can make a small peer group seem like a large peer group. Teenagers, especially, want to do what everyone else is doing (and call it rebellion!). A South Carolina teenager who meets five people from Rage Against the Haze at a football game may be intrigued, but she may not decide to join until she goes to the Facebook page and sees postings from other teenagers all over the state. In this way, the Internet works no differently than television or other platforms. It can guide people into a social cure, facilitating an introduction to real groups with other real, live humans. And it can provide proof that a social norm is widespread.

It is an open question, though, whether the Internet can substitute for human contact in *being* a social cure. Information on the Internet cannot, nor can information from anywhere else. Information alone is a very poor propellant of behavior change. The Internet, however, offers something that other platforms do not—the virtual community of a chat room.

We know that Internet chat rooms can contribute to *negative* behavior change. There is evidence from several cases. One is Internet-assisted group suicide in Japan, where people interested in killing themselves use the Internet to find each other. Several dozen people a year die this way, many of them in their twenties, and the number is rising. Some go to the sites just to talk to others, but some are determined to find a suicide group. They arrange to meet and decide who will bring the materials—the preferred suicide method involves a sealed car and burning charcoal. Often three people will kill themselves together.

From other societies, we know that suicide can be socially contagious, especially among young people. In the United States, a small proportion of teen suicides—100 or 200 a year—seem to be due to clusters: teens who kill themselves following the suicide of someone in their school or church, or after widespread media reports of the suicide of a well-known person. The mechanism, supposedly, is that each death makes suicide seem more like normal, accepted behavior. (Some of the evidence, however, goes the other way—a Houston study published in the *American Journal of Epidemiology*, for example, found that people exposed to the suicide of a friend or acquaintance are *less* likely to try to kill themselves.)

Internet suicide chat groups do help someone join up in person with a transformative peer group—the usual role the Internet can play—but they also in their own way transform. Even doing Internet chatting with others thinking about suicide probably intensifies people's desire to do the same. Since everyone on the site is interested in suicide, a pro-suicide social norm is created that counters the stigmatization of suicide by society in general.

The Internet also has a demonstrated effect on another form of suicide: it can assist in the creation of radical Islamic terrorists. Until a few years ago, young men with radical views might meet at an extremist mosque and hang out in a local *halal* restaurant or in someone's apartment. Now, according to Marc Sageman, as the locations where budding suicide bombers meet have increasingly come under police surveillance, some have turned to the Internet.

Sageman is a forensic psychiatrist and former CIA officer; from 1987 to 1989, he was in Islamabad, Pakistan, working with the Afghan mujahideen. He has combined his two careers in a third, as a writer and consultant on terrorism. In *Leaderless Jihad,* Sageman writes that the most effective engine of radicalization on the Internet is not the

extremist documents excoriating America or Jews or the videos showing massacres of Muslims in Bosnia or Israeli soldiers shooting into
crowds of Palestinian children. It is the chat rooms. In these virtual
venues, radicalized young Muslims who are attracted to violence can
find endless discussions of what they see as outrages committed against
Muslims and justifications for the use of violence—almost always with
very little basis in Islam. Those who become disillusioned with this way
of thinking usually drop out of chat rooms. They do not stay to offer
opposing views. So the only people remaining in the conversation are
pro-violence. The discourse ratchets up, getting angrier and angrier as
people push each other into more extremist positions. For people who
isolate themselves from personal contact and immerse themselves in
the world of the chat room, the online conversation creates a powerful
pro-violence social norm. (A way to counter that norm, using a join-
the-club strategy, will be discussed in chapter 10.)

The Japanese suicide groups and the terrorist chat rooms, of course,
are examples of negative peer pressure. But they do offer evidence that
individuals can strengthen and intensify an incipient new identity
through social relationships on the Internet alone. There is less con-
clusive evidence, however, about whether the Internet could, by itself,
start you on the way to that new identity—or, more to the point for
the purposes of social change, about whether Internet relationships can
bring about *positive* personal transformation.

There is some evidence that, in the area of health, having an Internet
"buddy" helps. Kate Lorig, professor emerita of medicine at Stanford
University, has conducted or worked on several studies that provide people with Internet or e-mail buddy groups to help with the management
of heart or lung disease, diabetes, arthritis, or back pain. The online
buddy offers advice, asks whether you have taken your daily walk, and
just listens to your complaints. The groups helped—one study of an
online group found that results were similar to those of face-to-face
peer groups. "Anonymity takes away a lot of inhibitions, and people
are more frank on the Internet," Lorig explained. "Besides, since you
cannot see the person, race, ethnicity, age, etc., are not important factors for most stuff."

In other cases, however, an Internet peer group has not been as effective. A study of an Internet-based social-support group for patients with depression, for example, found some improvement, but none in the crucial-for-depression area of social support—an outcome that might be expected with an Internet peer group.

As with a face-to-face group, good design can make the difference between success and failure. An effective Internet social-cure group needs not only community but also accountability. People who join the four-person weight-loss groups at www.peertrainer.com, for example, say that what matters most to them when reaching for a cookie is the thought that they will have to report having eaten that cookie to their three online companions. You have to keep a log of everything you eat—and your companions will read it. It's nice to have support, but it's probably more useful to picture your peers' disapproval and disappointment when you are contemplating a second dessert.

Even if the Internet cannot offer a social cure as effective as personal contact, there is still a good argument for using it: because of its convenience and anonymity, it is the only social cure some people will actually carry out. No matter how effective a weekly in-person support group might be for someone who has diabetes or is trying to lose sixty pounds, it will do her no good if she can't make the time or is too embarrassed to go.

We cannot say for sure that an online group like peertrainer.com falls short of the in-person meetings of Weight Watchers, as this has never been measured. (Weight Watchers has its own online program but has not measured its effectiveness.) It seems intuitive, however, that for people with a choice, face-to-face is going to be best. People we see and know and care about have a more compelling pull. The relationships we create in person are simply stronger. (In fact, when face-to-face groups fail, it is often because the human connection is too strong—people empathize too much and the necessary "tough love" gets lost.)

What matters to us most is our relationships with fellow humans—the most commanding force for change. Relationships not only are powerful, they also are versatile. The ability of the social groups around us to affect our behavior is not limited to whether we poison ourselves or live healthily, become criminals or good citizens, become civic-minded or sit at home and bury ourselves in TV. Done right, the social cure has solved even problems seemingly completely divorced from questions of behavior. Surely the most curious example is the story of the calculus club.

Chapter Five

The Calculus Club

AT FIRST GLANCE—AND PROBABLY ALSO SECOND and third—the question of how to raise black and Latino achievement in college calculus would seem to have little in common with the challenge of keeping teenagers from taking up cigarettes. Teen smoking is clearly about behavioral choices. Succeeding in math, it would appear, is not.

That even well-prepared minority students with high test scores often do poorly in calculus has been a phenomenon in American universities since the 1960s, when university education opened up to nonwhite students on a large scale. Even minority students who did well in calculus in high school often didn't pass it in college. Theories about the reasons for this were myriad and often ugly: the students' high schools weren't good enough, their parents didn't support them, they were unmotivated, they shouldn't really be at a university. One even heard that blacks just aren't cut out for math.

Then came an idea put forth in the 1970s by Uri

Treisman, a doctoral student in math at the University of California at Berkeley. Trying to understand why some groups did better in calculus than others, he spent eighteen months living with and filming two groups of math students, one successful and one unsuccessful. What he found gave rise to an idea—using the social cure—that has now been implemented in dozens, if not hundreds, of universities across America, with stunning success. Using Treisman's concept, university after university has helped its minority students to excel in calculus, to the point where they outperform white and Asian students.

One way to find the calculus club is to listen for the noise. In the math department at the University of Texas at Austin in the spring of 2008, three days a week from 1 to 3 p.m., about twenty students in freshman-level calculus met with their teaching assistant for their discussion section. This happens at every university in the country. Freshman calculus here has some 450 students. Usually, the students are divided into sections, and they meet several times a week with a graduate student, who stands at the blackboard answering questions from students and going over homework assigned by the professor. Except for the teaching assistant's explanations and the scratching of chalk, discussion sections usually are quiet.

This one was not. There was nothing on the blackboard, and no one mentioned homework. Todd Geldon, the graduate student teaching the section, didn't even answer questions. That was the students' job.

Todd walked in, deposited some boxes of giant cookies on a table, and asked the students to number off. They did that, split into their groups, and pulled their desks into a circle. Then the students spread out sheets of paper with problems that Todd had written.

He didn't care whether they got the right answers, or any answers—he didn't even have an answer key. Nor was he planning to go to the blackboard, or, indeed, tell them anything at all. Nor would Raul Sánchez or Tatiana Peixoto, Todd's student assistants—sophomores who had taken this class the year before. Geldon and the student assistants hovered over the groups, asking leading questions. But the students taught each other.

One group of students argued about whether a partial answer to one of Todd's problems was $2xy$ or $2xy^2$. "How do you convert the data into a vector?" asked a tall man with a disorganized beard. In another group, a woman was sketching a graph at which another woman was squinting. "Is that always 90 degrees?" asked the squinter. The first woman shook her head.

In another group, four men were working. "I see how you did that," said one. "I calculated the gradient incorrectly—I switched the x and y values." They realized that they were solving for the wrong thing. "Can we flip this?" asked another man. "Or make it negative?" He thought for a minute. "No, that won't work."

Todd walked over to a man and a woman struggling with a problem and glanced at their work. "It's a little bit different this time and you're going to tell me why in a second," he said to the man.

"Do I have to do it twice?" asked Kishan Patel.

"Do you have to do it twice?" Todd responded.

"Do you?"

"I'm asking *you*," Todd said, determinedly uninformative.

He went over to the group of four men. "Did you have a question?" he said to Daniel Mendoza.

"He already answered it," said Daniel, gesturing at another student. Todd smiled—that was the response he was looking for.

The students worked in their groups for two hours. They didn't care about finishing the problems—no one ever finished them. The questions were too hard—much harder than the class homework the professor gave out—because Todd wrote them to teach the concepts of calculus. Understand the concepts and the homework will be easy.

This class was itself designed as the answer to a problem, a really hard problem—the struggles of minority students to do well in college calculus, an issue consistently seen in universities across the country. It affects not only individual students but the future of America's ability to compete in the world. The student body in the United States is becoming blacker and browner. Doing well in calculus is the gateway to a career in math, engineering, or the hard sciences. If minorities do not succeed in calculus, an increasingly large percentage of Americans will be excluded from these crucial professions.

This story is a lesson in how to study calculus—how to study many things, really. It is a tale about the fragility of cherished assumptions, such as assumptions about why certain groups of people do well and others may have trouble in school.

It is also a lesson about when to reach for the social cure. Many problems don't seem solvable with behavior change of the social-cure variety. Flunking calculus is one—what is behavioral, after all, about learning math? But a close look at Treisman's calculus clubs hints at the wide variety of problems that can, in fact, be solved this way. A good number of problems that don't *seem* behavioral do have a hidden behavioral component, one that can be altered through the creative application of peer pressure. But finding it usually requires inventive thinking, and indirect attack—such as the ingenious one Uri Treisman conceived.

TREISMAN'S SOCIAL CURE WAS born at a time of great opportunity in American universities. In the late 1960s and early 1970s, American universities were expanding. The baby-boom generation was going to college. Universities were beginning to pay attention to diversity, to the importance of getting black and Latino students into professional careers.

The sciences were where minority students encountered a roadblock. At the University of California at Berkeley, 60 percent of black or Latino students who completed first-term freshman calculus scored a D or an F. From 1973 to 1975, the *average* grade for black students in calculus was D+. As for blacks in higher-level math, there were very, very few, because many didn't pass calculus.

These were students who should have done much better. They had scored well on the math SAT, a test that supposedly predicts success in college math. Many of them had done well in a Berkeley program that offered college-level calculus classes in high schools in the minority area of East Oakland in the tenth and eleventh grades. In high school, they were excelling in calculus. "But when they got to Berkeley, they did very poorly in these courses," said Treisman. "It was sort of a shock—students who clearly understood the math not being able to use what they knew."

Treisman, the child of leftist Jews from Brooklyn, was determined to find out why this was happening. In the mid-1970s, he and his faculty mentor, Leon Henkin, sent a letter with the pass-rate data to 400 Berkeley faculty members, asking them to comment. The responses they received fell under roughly four different hypotheses. One was that there was a motivation gap—Asian and Jewish kids were super-motivated, and kids who had only average motivation couldn't compete. The second hypothesis was that these kids came from low-income families, and income is often a reliable predictor of success in college. Third, they had uneducated parents who couldn't provide guidance. Or fourth, they had attended weak high schools, so even if they had received good grades, they really hadn't learned very much.

None of these assumptions turned out to be true. Motivation? Treisman examined the students' backgrounds. He found that many had been their high school valedictorians and leaders of church youth groups. Their dedication to schooling had kept them apart from their communities—sustaining it had required amazing motivation, much more than that required of nonminorities. They could not turn back.

He interviewed their families and found that many parents had decided even before they had had children that those kids would go to college. Many of the parents were college graduates themselves, often working as teachers in the public school system.

As for the other two factors, they correlated negatively. It turned out that the better the student's math SAT score, the *worse* he or she did in calculus. "The supposedly best-prepared students failed the most and the few successes came from kids near the bottom," Treisman said. (This was also true in other classes. From 1973 to 1976, only five black students passed premed organic chemistry or sophomore-level differential equations—the third class in the calculus sequence—with an A or a B. Of those five, four were from poor families, had graduated from largely minority high schools, and were the first in their families to attend college. Two of the four were affirmative-action students, admitted to Berkeley despite not meeting the standard criteria.)

Higher family income, Treisman found, also correlated with worse performance—possibly because some of the lower-income black parents were teachers.

"The only interesting response to our survey," Treisman said in a lecture, came from a professor who was vocal about his belief in the genetic inferiority of blacks. "He said that according to his calculations—he was big into pseudostatistics—'population characteristics' (by which he meant 'race') could only account for about four percent of the failure. But the observed failure was so great that only the institution's behavior could account for it. What an irony—he was the only one to assert that something might actually be wrong with the institution."

This was intriguing. If there was something Berkeley was doing wrong, perhaps Berkeley could fix the problem.

Treisman asked math teaching assistants for the names of their best and worst students. The best students were disproportionately Chinese American and the weakest students were disproportionately black. Treisman chose twenty of each who were enrolled in first-semester calculus for scientists and engineers. Then he got a movie camera and moved into their dorms. He spent eighteen months talking to them about math and how they studied, and observing them studying and working in their dorms, libraries, and homes.

When he had finished, here's the most important thing Treisman had found: The Chinese students studied alone part of the time, but in the evenings they gathered to study with classmates; The black students only studied alone, keeping their academic life completely separate from their social life.

The two approaches may have diverged because the Chinese students came from a culture that values the group. Or the reason may have been that black students were accustomed to studying alone. One way or another, many black students at Berkeley had been alone in high school. Either they were the rare black kid in a white high school, or the rare academically minded kid in a largely minority high school where studying was seen as "acting white." They had learned to compartmentalize. They had earned their way into Berkeley through individual effort and were suspicious of people who needed outside help.

This seemingly mundane difference in study habits turned out to be of momentous consequence.

Their study groups helped the Chinese students to learn math better. They gave each other ideas on techniques for solving problems. Working in groups gave the students the opportunity to ask questions. Black students had no one to ask—unless they were willing to stand up before forty people in their discussion sections and ask the teaching assistant something that might or might not make them sound like an idiot, an option very few people ever chose.

Working in groups had many other advantages besides helping with math knowledge. It gave the Chinese students a sense of how they were doing. Faced with a problem that they could not solve, black students would give up, concluding that their math skills were hopeless. Chinese students would go to the teacher and say, "This is not a fair problem, sir." And how did they know? Because no one in their group could solve it. Confident that the problem was hard for everyone, the Chinese students felt far more liberated to ask questions about it in the forty-student discussion section, or even in the 450-student class. They always knew where they stood. The black students were sometimes taken completely by surprise when they flunked a test.

The groups also shared advice that allowed students to navigate the course and school better: whether it was okay to write in pencil, how to get more financial aid, how to approach the professor. Someone's cousin would show up who had had the same professor before. This behavior goes by another name—networking. People from a dominant culture take networking for granted. They do it unconsciously. Neither the black nor the Chinese students had access to the standard Berkeley white network. The Chinese kids created a network for themselves; the black kids didn't.

Studying in a group—often with food on the table—also encouraged the students to study more. The Chinese kids quickly learned that they needed to spend more than the conventionally prescribed two hours of study for every hour of class. The black students were dutifully putting in eight hours of study a week for their four-hour class, but the Chinese students were putting in fourteen hours.

Perhaps most important, the study groups gave Chinese students academically oriented friends, a social group interested in math that encouraged its members to succeed in math. These students had peers who told them it was OK to be a math nerd. Black students did not have this. Black students had friends and they had academic colleagues, but those two groups usually did not overlap.

BY 1978, URI TREISMAN was ready to try an experiment to see if he could solve the problems that studying alone seemed to be creating for black math students. Treisman chose a group of black and Latino freshmen who were enrolled in calculus. They attended the same lecture as all the other students, but he created a new kind of discussion section for them to attend.

Treisman's discussion section met more often than the usual one—six hours a week instead of the more typical four. These students did not do what is typically done in discussion sections: homework problems. The teaching assistants in Treisman's program—which has come to be called Emerging Scholars—were trained to create extremely challenging problems that helped students understand the concepts of calculus. Those problems—much harder than homework—were what the students worked on in their discussion sections. Then they were expected to apply their understanding to the homework outside of class.

Students were invited into the special class with letters welcoming them to a challenging math honors program where they would be expected to graduate with a degree in math or the sciences and be encouraged, even expected, to go on to graduate school. "Who wants to put all their energy into passing rather than excelling?" Treisman said. "It's easier to aim for an A than a C. Aim for an A, and when they fail they get a B."

The other difference was that Emerging Scholars sections were collaborative efforts. Students worked in groups of three or four, asking each other questions and learning from one another—the only way these difficult problems could be solved. If students were stumped and asked the teaching assistant for help, they would get only a series of leading questions—like Todd Geldon's "Do you have to do it twice?"—to help them come up with the answer themselves.

Emerging Scholars produced stunning results. In the four years at Berkeley before the program began, 131 black students enrolled in first-semester calculus. Of those students, twenty-nine of them got As or Bs: only 22 percent. Then, in 1978, Emerging Scholars began. Over the next four years, 188 black students took Emerging Scholars calculus, and 102 of them got As or Bs: 54 percent.

Of course, Treisman was cherry-picking, admitting only the most promising students (sometimes not the students with the best SAT scores or grades). So the fairer comparison would include all black calculus students, even those in traditional calculus sections. The numbers continue to impress. From 1978 to 1982, a total of 331 black students enrolled in calculus, both Emerging Scholars and traditional sections, and 125 of these students, or 38 percent, got As or Bs. So overall, the percentage of black students doing well in calculus moved from 22 percent to 38 percent. And many more black students were studying math. Berkeley went from having twenty-nine black students successful in calculus in a four-year period to having 125.

Black students in Emerging Scholars calculus did so well that those with math SAT scores in the low 600s were performing comparably to white and Asian students whose math SAT scores were much higher, in the mid-700s.

In every SAT level students did much better in Emerging Scholars. Among black calculus students who had scored in the top third on the SAT, only 28 percent got As or Bs if they were not in Emerging Scholars. But put them in Emerging Scholars and 71 percent of these students got As or Bs.

FOR THE CALCULUS CLUBS to be a replicable model for solving other problems, it is important to understand how they work, to identify the mechanism through which they improve student achievement. One advantage of Emerging Scholars has nothing whatsoever to do with the social cure: it simply forces students to do more math. There are three discussion sections a week instead of the usual two. And in a normal, non-Emerging Scholar discussion section, students watch the teaching assistant do problems. In an Emerging Scholar section, the students do problems themselves. "Math is not a spectator sport," said Stephen MacAdam, the professor who taught the Texas calculus class I visited in 2008. Math people agree: you don't learn math by watching someone else solve a problem.

The collaborative aspects of all this were terribly important, however. You can learn more by asking others for their strategies and methods, but you also deepen your understanding when others ask you. "You have to be able to articulate it," said Raul Sánchez, one of Todd Geldon's student assistants. "It definitely helps you understand it to try to explain it to your peers." Sánchez, an army kid from San Antonio, was a self-assured double major in math and philosophy; no one else in the calculus room was carrying around books by Nietzsche.

Being part of a group also encourages you to get help when you don't understand. Rose Asera, a senior scholar at the Carnegie Foundation for the Advancement of Teaching who has studied Emerging Scholars programs in dozens of colleges, believes that the group setting changes the nature of asking questions. "Questions are viewed as positive interactions with the material, not as indications of ignorance," she wrote.

"Everyone does better in Emerging Scholars programs, but in particular minority students do much better," said Concha Gómez. She was a student of Treisman's who earned a PhD in math and later landed at the University of Wisconsin, where she taught math and ran the Emerging Scholars programs until 2009. "Minorities tend to isolate themselves when they come to university. They are less likely to form study groups. They are more likely to have done very well in high school by studying alone, and that's what they're used to, or they feel unwelcome in a white environment to form a study group. They are less inclined to visit the professor during office hours or the TA [teaching assistant] during office hours. I experienced this. If I had to ask someone for help, well, I must be stupid or they must think I'm stupid. Because I'm a minority, I'm more likely to be viewed as stupid—I didn't want people even to get a hint of what was going on. But in Emerging Scholars programs, everyone is encouraged to ask questions, and they are more likely to visit the TA and professors. They are told they're smart, and if they don't understand it, it must be very hard."

"Here you have no reservation about being wrong," said Raul Sánchez. "You also have no reservation about speaking out and being *right* about things."

This was the other advantage of the group. The students didn't just solve problems. Todd Geldon's students talked about their cars, or a run-in with a guy hawking Scientology. They gossiped about other students and teachers. In other words, they made friends, math friends, a peer group that permitted them to be interested in math.

"I'm from a part of San Antonio where, well, let's just say twenty people from my high school went to college. Math was not cool to any of them," Jaron Crawford, one of Geldon's students, told me after class. "Even my family. Once when I was home I wanted to tell someone something cool—something to do with calculus and computer graphics. They weren't interested in it and didn't get it. I'm the first in my family to go straight to college out of high school. I'm the first to take more than college algebra. The most in-depth question I get from my family is 'How's it going?'"

Crawford was a serious black man with glasses and a goatee, wearing jeans and a Texas Longhorns T-shirt. He had enrolled in the University of Texas as a physics major and received a letter about the Emerging Scholars program. He had switched his major to electrical engineering but was still glad to have the extra help with calculus. He was engaged to be married, and he worried about getting the education that would allow him to meet the responsibilities that awaited him. "I'm going to have to end up taking care of my mom and my girlfriend's parents," he said. It was now his second term in the section. "I would not have passed calculus without Emerging Scholars," he said. "I would not still be here. The group just makes things a whole lot better. You don't just have one perspective. Going to a predominantly black high school, most African American students fall into stereotype because they think it's cool. This class counters the stereotype. It's OK to like math."

One analysis of Emerging Scholars found that the key was the development of academic friends. Susan Elaine Moreno, a sociologist who earned her PhD at Texas, wrote her dissertation about why the Emerging Scholars program works. She analyzed friendship patterns and concluded that good grades depended on making friends to study with—and fewer friends to go to movies or a bar with. The more academic activities students said they did with their friends, the better their grades, and the more social activities they did with their friends, the worse their grades. The more friends students had in Emerging Scholars, the higher their grades in calculus. This was even truer for women and minorities.

The Emerging Scholars students at Texas included several who had wholeheartedly embraced this idea. "We tell silly calculus jokes," said Hannah Laster, a sophomore who had taken the course the year before. Calculus jokes? What's a calculus joke? "I wish I were your derivative so I could lie tangent to your curve," she said, rolling her eyes. Two other women, Ana Berrizbeitia and Lucia Simonelli, were juniors and roommates who had met in the Emerging Scholars program. Simonelli said her experience in the class and the friends she made persuaded her to switch her major from biology to math. Ana is president and Lucia vice president of Texas's math club. The two of them lifted their arms to show me the tattoos on the insides of their wrists—matching Möbius strips.

THE SUCCESS OF MINORITY STUDENTS who joined the calculus clubs is an intriguing part of a larger debate about why students succeed or fail in college, and what universities can do to tip the balance. The development of Emerging Scholars added a weapon to the very limited armamentarium universities had relied on to help their struggling students succeed. That armamentarium had consisted almost entirely of one strategy: remediation, which meant taking students off the track temporarily and giving them classes to strengthen basic skills and allow them to catch up. About a third of first-year college students nationwide are placed in remedial math or English courses.

It is very hard to know whether remediation works in general.

Students in remedial classes are much less likely than those in regular classes to go on to academic success, but since this group of students is by definition ill-prepared for college, this is not necessarily an indictment of remediation. The real question is how do students in remediation compare with equally struggling students who are *not* in remedial classes.

Here the research is sparse. One study, published as a working paper in 2005 by the National Bureau of Economic Research, took advantage of the fact that standards for remediation are not uniform—for example, at some schools a student with an SAT score of 500 in English would be put into remediation, while at other schools the student would be in regular classes. Authors Eric P. Bettinger and Bridget Terry Long compared Ohio students of similar abilities who differed only in whether or not their schools had put them into remedial classes. They found that remediation was helpful. Students taking remedial math classes were 15 percent more likely to graduate in four years than similar students in regular math classes. With English, the difference was somewhat smaller, but students in remediation still did better. This study, however, has its limits. It looked only at students teetering between needing and not needing remediation—a group better prepared than remedial students as a whole. And the students were all in four-year colleges, whereas the vast bulk of remediation occurs in community colleges.

Other researchers are more skeptical about the value of remediation. Patricia Gándara, professor of education at the University of California at Los Angeles, said that there was an informal natural experiment in that some students who need remediation at community colleges, mainly Asian, stubbornly avoid remedial classes. "They will struggle like crazy and not get great grades and their English is weak, but at least they get the credits. This group is often more successful by avoiding the remedial track.

"In community colleges many students require remediation in English or math," she said. "In the period of time they are in remedial courses, they are not getting credits toward graduation. They can spend a year or year and a half in remedial courses and at the end they are no closer to getting their degree. That uses up your financial aid and discourages people. We believe it's related to the very high dropout rate in community colleges."

Berkeley, an elite university, of course is different. But here, too, remediation was failing in the early 1970s, at least in math. The math department created a course called pre-calculus. It wasn't formally remediation, but it was designed for students who weren't ready for calculus in the first term of their freshman year. "One year 422 students enrolled in the course, only one of whom, Danny Lescano, went on to receive a grade of B- or higher in second semester calculus," Uri Treisman said. "It makes you want to name the course after him. The evidence is overwhelming that few students who take remedial courses ever complete science degrees."

It is not obvious why this happens. It should matter a little if a student mastered the basics during high school and not college, but it shouldn't be so utterly determinative. There is no clear reason why remedial classes teaching what a student didn't get in high school would be unable to prepare that student for college—after all, these were students bright and well prepared enough to get into an elite university. A student who got an A or B in pre-calculus at Berkeley should be able to do just as well—or better—in calculus as someone who didn't need pre-calculus.

Remedial classes are overwhelmingly filled with blacks and Latinos. Perhaps there is something else going on, something that particularly affects minorities? According to psychologists Joshua Aronson and Claude Steele, there is. They call it "stereotype threat," describing a phenomenon in which the objects of a stereotype can find their performance greatly affected by it simply by being reminded that it exists.

Their most important paper on the subject was published in 1995 in the *Journal of Personality and Social Psychology*. (Aronson is now a professor at New York University; Steele is the provost of Columbia University and author of the 2010 book *Whistling Vivaldi*.) Steele and Aronson administered a difficult word test to two groups of students, one black and one white. When the students were told the test was a problem-solving exercise that didn't measure underlying ability, the two groups did equally well. When they were told instead that the test *was* a measure of their intellectual abilities, the black students did worse than the whites. The researchers also found that black students who were told that a test was a measure of their intellectual abilities were more aware of their race and had less confidence than those who were told the test didn't measure their abilities. And among those told the test was not diagnostic, black student performance dropped if the students were asked first about their race.

This experiment is dismaying, in a sense—it seems absurdly easy to activate a stereotype threat in people's minds. But the flip side is that it can be easily fought.

A second group of researchers administered a math test to a group of Asian female students, members of two groups at once: Asians, who are stereotyped as doing well in math, and women, who are stereotyped as doing poorly. The test was administered after the women filled out one of three kinds of questionnaires. One questionnaire asked about their gender, one about their ethnic identity, and one about neither. No questionnaire said anything about stereotypes or math performance. But the students' heads apparently did: those who were reminded they were Asian did the best on the math test, and those reminded they were women did the worst. Those who had received the neutral questionnaire scored in the middle.

In another study, two groups of math students were given a rigorous calculus test. These were top students, going on to math and science careers. In one group, men and women performed equally. In the second, women did better, outperforming all the others. The difference was that, before taking the test, the second group read a statement claiming that the test had been given to many students, and men and women did equally well—there were no gender differences. Even these top-performing women, it seemed, had been hampered by stereotype threat and liberated when it was neutralized.

The most intriguing experiment came later. In 2008, on four different occasions, researchers gave a short test, consisting of twenty questions drawn from the Graduate Record Exam, to groups of American adults. On two of those occasions, whites scored much better than blacks. But on the other two dates, the two groups' scores were statistically equal.

What made the difference? Barack Obama. Black scores improved when they took the test on two occasions when Obama was dominating the headlines: right after his speech accepting the Democratic nomination—but only among people who watched the speech—and just after his election. The study, published in the *Journal of Experimental Social Psychology* in 2009, concluded that when Obama was especially salient to black test-takers, his example helped them overcome stereotype threat. It raises the tantalizing possibility that the example of a black president could raise black academic achievement. One of this study's authors, Ray Friedman, a professor at Vanderbilt University's Owen School of Management, suggested that black families concerned about their children's grades might want to keep Obama visible and present in the household.

Stereotype threat affects many aspects of academic performance. It makes students study less and reduces their interest in pursuing a subject in which they are not "supposed to" succeed. It can drive them into different majors—in the case of women, blacks, and Latinos, out of the sciences.

This research suggests that if students assigned to remedial classes do worse, a major reason might be *simply because they are there*. Remediation is a constant reminder that the students in it are expected to fail. They may have less confidence, study less, take less interest in their subjects. (Bettinger and Long found that remediation does discourage students from majoring in that subject.) In other words, simply labeling a student "remedial" might undermine his or her performance.

If remediation does not work, then something else must take its place. Students lacking the skills and preparation to succeed in mainstream classes cannot simply be tossed into them. They will drown. The solution, however, may be something more creative than remediation. Researcher after researcher has shown that in college, smarts and preparation are far from the sole determinants of success. Many other things factor in—whether you have good study habits and time management skills, a strong social circle that makes you feel part of the university, a network that can provide tips on navigating courses, and some degree of happiness. A black student accustomed to studying alone, who feels isolated in school, who sees the professors as mysterious and distant, and who doesn't have a plugged-in peer network to give him advice may be plenty smart and well prepared but may still flunk out of college. He may not need remediation. He may need, instead, the social cure.

EMERGING SCHOLARS–STYLE PROGRAMS continue at Berkeley and in dozens of other American universities. The idea has been successful virtually everywhere it has been measured—Cal Poly, Rutgers, the City University of New York, Wisconsin, just to cite a smattering of schools that use it.

Before Emerging Scholars began at Texas, Treisman described the math department as "looking like Taiwan and Connecticut had merged. I mean you could not tell you were in the state of Texas." In 1988, the University of Texas at Austin had ten minority math majors. But things changed rapidly with Emerging Scholars. By 1992, UT Austin had 113 black or Latino math majors. Blacks and Latinos in Emerging Scholars were averaging a B+; whites and Asians, who were in traditional sections, were averaging a C-.

A 2006 Berkeley study took students in Emerging Scholars and matched them statistically with students who were identical, or nearly so, on important measures—same professor, same class, same race, math SAT, high school grades, gender, income, parents' education, and rates of being first-generation collegians in their family. The only difference was that they studied calculus in traditional sections. Blacks and Latinos in the Emerging Scholars sections averaged two-thirds of a grade point higher than their traditional-calculus counterparts.

Emerging Scholars is no longer only for minorities. Challenges to affirmative action have led most universities to open Emerging Scholars to other students. But it doesn't have as strong an effect on these students, perhaps because they are not under the sway of stereotype threat. At Berkeley, although whites and Asians in Emerging Scholars also do better than their matched pairs in traditional calculus, the difference is smaller than with blacks and Latinos. They average just over half a grade point higher than their matched pairs. Something about Emerging Scholars is more helpful to minorities.

Even though the usefulness of Emerging Scholars is undisputed, curiously, not many schools are using it now. In the mid-1990s, about 150 different schools had Emerging Scholars programs. The number is much lower today. And in some of those programs, the Emerging Scholars classrooms are whiter than they used to be. Only one black student and one Latino were in the Texas program in the spring of 2008, for example. (Both student assistants were Latinos.) There were a lot of women and people from small towns—two other groups Texas considers eligible for Emerging Scholars.

As with the fortunes of Florida's teen smoking-prevention program— a proven success that surprisingly few states decided to emulate and that Florida itself has moved away from—the explanation has to do with politics and money. Although there is no equivalent of the tobacco industry fighting back against Emerging Scholars, the programs must compete for scarce university resources.

Running an Emerging Scholars calculus section is more expensive than the normal section. The classes are smaller and meet more often. Student assistants must be paid, and the graduate teaching assistants must be given higher salaries or smaller course loads. A professor has to run the program, and someone has to do the recruiting and arrange the logistics. If there is room for luxuries, it's nice to be able to use an empty classroom, perhaps equipped with a used sofa or two and petty cash for pizza, to encourage students to hang out and study together.

The money and time involved are trivial when compared with the expected return. But in academia, even the pittance needed for a student assistant can matter enough to stop a program cold. "You're paying us to do something and we're not really teaching," said Sue Hahn, a math professor at Kean University in New Jersey. There are no graduate students at Kean, which puts an extra burden on the professor. Hahn used to run an Emerging Scholars program at Kean and thought it worked well. "It was a really good idea," she said, "but we don't have anyone who is willing to do it now."

The biggest obstacle is frustratingly basic: finding someone committed

to Emerging Scholars who will fight for it and run it. Graduate students
are busy writing their dissertations. Professors looking for tenure concentrate on publishing the research that will win it. Professors with
tenure often consider themselves too senior to be putting extra time
into a freshman course. At Michigan State University, the Emerging
Scholars program has been run since 1992 by Richard Hill, a professor
who was approaching seventy in 2009. He had found another professor to continue running the program, but he warned that there was
never any certainty. "It takes a lot of commitment and energy to start a
program," he said, "and once you've done that, you are involved. New
people don't have that level of commitment."

The dearth of Emerging Scholars programs seems to make little
sense. If there is a minority graduate student or young professor in a
math department at an American university, it is very possible that he
or she came out of Emerging Scholars. Nonminorities, too, are likely
to be aware of its value and may themselves be alumni. There must be
dozens of young math professors who know the program well, appreciate its value, and could start one in their schools.

But they don't. Natasha Speer, an assistant professor of mathematics
education at the University of Maine, recalled going to a math-education
workshop and listening to a graduate student give an enthusiastic talk
about Emerging Scholars. You've been at your university for five years,
someone asked him. "Have you started a program?" He had not. He'd
been busy with other things, he said. Speer was standing there with
three other graduate students, and they realized that none of them knew
anyone who had started a program. "What a waste," she said.

Speer surveyed graduate students about why they hadn't started
Emerging Scholars programs. She found that it simply hadn't occurred
to them that, as new faculty, they could. They also didn't know how
to get the resources—not just the money, but something as basic as
copies of good calculus problem sets. And they worried that the time
involved would get in the way of preparing for tenure. Inertia, lack of
a champion, and the absence of a system for getting started can kill a
successful program as surely as tobacco-industry lobbying.

But these things are easier to overcome than the opposition of Big

Tobacco. Speer now runs workshops at math-education conferences to encourage former Emerging Scholars participants to start programs themselves, to help them get the resources, and to arm them with arguments for making the case to their universities. Perhaps her most important contribution is to help those interested in Emerging Scholars by providing a template: the steps needed to start a program, all written out. This hand-holding seems silly, but it is the way to overcome an important barrier to getting started. Speer has made a difference. She now knows four graduate students who have started new programs and two or three who have serious plans to do so.

Perhaps the more difficult obstacle for Emerging Scholars programs to overcome has been political—the competition among students for scarce places at good universities. The form this takes is a battle between advocates of affirmative action and its challengers. To understand the importance of political will to the success of—well, anything, but in this case, the calculus clubs, it is instructive to compare what has happened to Emerging Scholars programs at the University of Texas and at Berkeley.

In Texas, the calculus clubs have become a program serving more women and white rural students than blacks and Latinos. The change began with a court decision about affirmative action. The repercussions were felt nationwide, but the case happened to come from Texas. In 1992, Cheryl J. Hopwood, a white student, was denied entrance to the University of Texas School of Law in Austin while minority students with lower test scores were admitted. She and three other white plaintiffs sued the school and won. In 1996, a federal court ruled that Texas could no longer use race as an admission criterion. The next year, Texas's attorney general, Dan Morales, issued an opinion that broadened the decision: race could no longer be a criterion in financial aid, scholarships, fellowships, and other university decisions.

Also in 1997, however, Texas took a step to mitigate the effects of those decisions. The legislature created a new formula for university admission, one that admits the top 10 percent of every high school graduating class in the state to the Texas public university of their choice. The thinking was that since Texas's high schools tend to be segregated, assuring university entrance to some students from each school would ensure diversity. And since success in high school generally is a good predictor of success in college, these students should do well.

The formula has succeeded on both grounds. The student body at the University of Texas at Austin—as the top public school in the state, the one most affected—is more diverse, and students admitted under the 10 percent rule have done better than any other group at UT, with fewer dropouts and higher graduation rates. The law has encouraged applications from students who would not otherwise have thought UT Austin a possibility, and they have generally done well.

After the Hopwood case, American courts swung back toward affirmative action. In a 2003 decision (*Grutter v. Bollinger*), the United States Supreme Court ruled that colleges may use race as a consideration in admissions, as long as it is done on an individual basis and is part of a diversity agenda that encompasses more than race.

Given that it had the 10 percent rule and the flexibility to seek a diverse group of math and science majors, the University of Texas should not be seeing Emerging Scholars classes with only one black and one Latino student. Yet it is. Lisa Wyatt, a sociologist as well as a biologist, is the University of Texas official in charge of helping minorities succeed in the natural sciences. She said the scarcity of minorities in the Emerging Scholars program was due to faculty problems—there were no professors available for spring term, which changes the mix of students.

Uri Treisman did not agree with that assessment. He is now in Austin, running a University of Texas–affiliated center dedicated to researching and disseminating new ideas about education. Ironically, the university has not embraced his ideas about the importance of producing minority science scholars. Treisman's explanation for the whiteness of Emerging Scholars is that many influential people at Texas preferred the classes that way—a conspiracy theory borne out by the university's strenuous opposition to the 10 percent rule. "It wasn't that long ago that this was a segregated campus," he said. "A lot of people at the university were happy to see affirmative action go bye-bye. Some people on the Board of Regents were literally dancing with joy."

Treisman argued that Texas used the Hopwood decision as an excuse
for whitening the campus. He said the university went well beyond the
requirements of Hopwood, even barring the Emerging Scholars program from identifying students by their ethnicity. "We could be doing
an enormous amount more of directed outreach to recruit minority
students," he said.

The founders of UT's Emerging Scholars program also believe that
the university's restrictions have gone farther than what the law requires.
Efraim Armendariz, a UT math professor, established the Emerging
Scholars program there and was its first teacher. He argued that Latinos
were well represented in math at Texas; it was just an anomaly that they
weren't in that particular Emerging Scholars calculus section. (Everyone
agrees that black students are not well represented.) He agreed with
Treisman, however, that Texas isn't doing enough. "Hopwood has been
a problem and the university has not made big efforts," he said. "Before
the decision, we could write to students who were potentially debating
coming here and promise them entry into Emerging Scholars and work
to get them registered. We could recruit students who had applied and
make Emerging Scholars one attractive feature.

"Now we can't make admission into any academic program be based
on race, including programs like Emerging Scholars. We're restricted
from going after a student who is debating between going here and
someplace else. Our recruitment for [Emerging Scholars] students has
to wait until after they are accepted."

It is likely that the University of Texas at Austin, and its Emerging
Scholars programs, will become even less diverse over the next few
years. In June 2009, the Texas legislature amended the 10 percent rule,
a change that will mainly affect the Austin campus. The school had
lobbied hard to relax the rule, arguing that because it was the best
public university in Texas, it was overwhelmed with the 10 percent
students and so had little room to recruit top athletes or fill certain
majors. Perhaps the more important opposition, however, came from
legislators in largely white suburbs, who were seeing many of their "11
percent" students, who would have gotten in before, now turned away
in favor of inner-city black and Latino and rural white students from

less competitive high schools. The rule was relaxed. Now UT must admit only 75 percent of its student body under the 10 percent rule, and it can do as it pleases with the rest.

The Emerging Scholars program at the University of Texas did not have to end up with very few blacks or Hispanics. This did not happen in California, a state operating under many of the same constraints as Texas. California was (and still is) working under a ban on affirmative action. The 1996 ballot initiative Proposition 209 made it illegal for the state to give preferential treatment to or discriminate against any racial or ethnic group. But the ban has had very little impact on the makeup of Emerging Scholars: at Berkeley, Emerging Scholars sections are still between two-thirds and three-quarters black and Latino.

"After Proposition 209 was passed, we didn't revise what we were doing immediately," said Steven Chin, the Berkeley math professor who runs Emerging Scholars there. "The letters and e-mails we'd send were considered informational outreach, and we had a policy statement from the office of the president of the University of California that this was an allowed activity. But about five years after Prop 209 they sent out another recommendation—we needed to contact more students and give them the opportunity to hear about the program. So we did expand our informational program by e-mail. Before 209 we would send out letters to maybe a couple thousand students. We currently send out e-mail to 11,000. And we continue to send out letters."

Berkeley and Texas had similar rules. They couldn't invite students to apply for Emerging Scholars based on race. Most of Berkeley's thousands of letters went to white and Asian students, yet Berkeley still had Emerging Scholars sections made up largely of the racial groups that had been having disproportionate trouble—the people it was designed to help.

One reason was that the e-mails went to everyone who was admitted to Berkeley and accepted a place; the letters went to minorities. "Maybe e-mails don't work as well," Chin said innocently. In addition, the e-mails and the letters never mentioned race. They just invited the student to examine a "prestigious program" that would "accelerate you towards your intended career goals." But they arrived on letterhead from something called the Coalition for Excellence and Diversity in Mathematics, Science and Engineering. Is it possible that white students looked at something with "diversity" in the title and deleted the e-mail or threw the letter in the trash?

"Maybe people self-select," said Chin. And with very little effort, apparently, on Berkeley's part. Treisman was right; Texas just wasn't trying. The admissions rules were similar, yet Berkeley's program was still helping minorities excel in college calculus and Texas's program was largely not. What mattered was political will.

There is a larger irony here about affirmative action. The ban on affirmative action is based on the fiction that the numbers do tell who is "qualified" for college—that a student's standing and test scores really do predict who will succeed. In general, test scores and grades do predict this—which is why schools employ them for admission decisions—but they are far from perfect predictors. Treisman had found that before Emerging Scholars, the handful of successful black students in math or science came disproportionately from those who had scored low on the SAT. (No one knows why.) If introducing a new teaching method, such as Emerging Scholars, can produce such a dramatic change in student achievement, then obviously nothing is immutable about the relationship between past test scores and present grades. Without Emerging Scholars, blacks' test scores overpredicted black students' success in math—they did worse than their test scores indicated they would. But with Emerging Scholars, test scores now underpredict: black students do better at calculus than their test scores say they should. If the correlation between test scores and college success is so elastic, then how much should we be relying on the test scores?

The University of Texas has created a vicious circle. One of the most commonly heard arguments against affirmative action is that college is wasted on "unqualified" students with test scores below the normal cutoff—they just don't make it. The success of the calculus club confirms, however, that doing well in school depends on many things besides high test scores—especially for minority students, who are disproportionately helped by this social cure. If a university such as Texas decides not to go out of its way to attract minority students to Emerging

Scholars, it is keeping black and Latino students out of the very pro-grams that allow them to succeed—the very programs that allow them to challenge the traditional measuring posts of university success.

THE STORY OF URI TREISMAN'S calculus club is rich with lessons about where to use a join-the-club strategy. We already know the general description of when the social cure can be useful: (1) people are in trouble because of behavioral choices they make that offer comfort, pleasure, or acceptance in the short term but lead to harm in the long term; (2) that behavior can be changed through identification with a new peer group.

It's easy to see how some behaviors fit into the first category, such as having risky sex, smoking, overspending, overeating, substance abuse—pretty much anything that you could picture looking like the classic AA group, anything you might put "anonymous" after. What is not obvious is how calculus fits in, yet it's a very successful example of the social cure working when other solutions fail. The challenge, then, is to pinpoint just how the behavioral component works with calculus, and how Uri Treisman found it. That will provide clues to identifying other problems that are like math failure—problems that don't fit neatly into the AA-style support-group model and don't seem to be susceptible to the social cure but really are.

The oddest aspect of the calculus club as social cure is that the problem seemed to be missing the most important condition: bad behavioral choices. No one looking at the problem of minority achievement in math at Berkeley would have suspected that students' choice of conduct was the explanation for math failure. There were plenty of *other* explanations. Treisman investigated four of them: lack of motivation to succeed, lack of parental support, low income, and weak preparation. What they all had in common (in addition to being wrong) was that none involved the students' choices about whether to do X or Y.

Nonetheless, a behavioral problem existed. It was hidden because—unlike the decision, say, to refrain from drinking—it didn't even seem like a behavioral choice. The black students didn't think about studying in groups and discard the idea—they just didn't consider it. And for the Chinese students, gathering to work on math problems was just how it was done. Culture is invisible from the inside.

Studying alone also didn't seem to be a toxic choice—the same way a drug user decides to buy just one more bag or a chronic overspender chooses to take out a credit card. There was no I-shouldn't-but-I-can't-resist internal struggle. That concept is absurd—calculus is not a guilty pleasure.

Nor is it any kind of pleasure at all. Studying alone didn't offer any kind of short-term high. No one would confuse it with doing coke or buying a pair of Manolo Blahnik shoes. Instead, what it offered students was the comfort of doing things the normal way, the comfort of doing what fit their culture. Any other study method would have produced discomfort. For those who aren't used to it, approaching another student to do calculus together might seem rather weird.

Treisman, of course, did not set out to try to apply the power of peer pressure. He was simply looking for the reason minorities tend to do poorly in math. Instead of accepting the usual assumptions, he tested them—and threw them out. Then he did a long investigation, finding a difference between successful and unsuccessful students that few would notice.

Treisman not only noticed it, he realized it was crucial. The habit of solitary study was not merely hard to find. Before Treisman, even people who had seen it did not grasp its importance. Studying in groups is not obviously related to doing well in calculus. Study habits also make up only a piece of what determines math failure or success—alongside talent, drive, discipline, good preparation, and other factors.

A join-the-club strategy in its classic form attacks a problem in its entirety. AA meetings, for example, use the social cure to enforce sobriety, the solution to alcoholism. It is a total solution. In fact, it's a tautology—the solution is to refrain from the behavior causing the problem, and the new peer group can help. It's easy to see how the social cure works in those cases.

The social cure can't always go after the whole problem—how does anyone, for example, refrain from flunking calculus? It has no meaning.

But a join-the-club approach can still work by attacking only part of a problem—if it is a key part, a bottleneck. For calculus, obviously, one of those bottlenecks was study habits.

This is important. What Treisman did shows that the social cure can be useful for many more problems than the obvious AA-style behavioral issues. Treisman reduced a complex problem to small pieces to find the bottleneck. His success allows us to do the same—but we have the advantage of knowing what we are looking for. We can creatively dissect a big issue to see whether a part of the problem depends on people's choices, choices that can be influenced by peer pressure.

As it turns out, the scope of problems vulnerable to the imaginative application of a social cure proves to be stunning. Few major societal ills, in fact, are immune. Since so much of our behavior is shaped by our peers, so much of it can be changed with peer pressure. This includes the pieces of what we do that then affect those around us. Peer pressure changes you, and in turn you change a community, a bureaucracy, a culture, a government—a world.

Chapter Six

Angels of Change

IF YOU ASKED POVERTY EXPERTS TO NAME THE single most significant new concept in the field in the last few decades, chances are they would say, "Microcredit." Microcredit is the lending of heartbreakingly tiny sums to heartbreakingly poor people so they can buy a sewing machine or piglets to raise. It reaches nearly 100 million clients in more than 100 countries.

For many reasons, microcredit is a unique way to fight poverty. It does not need to be administered by governments, so it can work even in countries where corruption and political favoritism have gutted other social programs. Once the infrastructure is in place, it does not require large donations. It is sustainable, as sums repaid at rather high rates of interest are then lent to the next person. It can be easily targeted to the people who need it most. And what makes it work? The social cure.

Like poor performance in college calculus, world poverty

does not initially appear to be a problem susceptible to the social cure. But both are—a fact of signal importance. It shows that a join-the-club strategy can be used to help a wide spectrum of people and to solve a wide variety of problems.

The challenge is to find them. One way to do this is to analyze some of the various approaches the social cure can take, to see the different aspects of a problem that are susceptible to a join-the-club attack. Then it becomes easier to identify problems with similar vulnerabilities. We must start by taking a close look at several social-cure success stories.

Poverty is infinitely intricate. There are many different reasons why people are poor. In very poor countries, most of the reasons are structural—there are few good jobs, minimal government services (such as decent schools and clean water), and sometimes no infrastructure (like passable roads). Cultural issues compound the situation, as with the discrimination suffered by Dalits. There are also political reasons— poor people have little political clout to change things. And then there are the behaviors through which poverty perpetuates itself: poor people need their children's labor, so they take them out of school; they can't spend two extra hours to gather firewood to boil water, so their children get diarrhea; or they can afford only rice, so they suffer from malnutrition. And that list doesn't even touch the myriad reasons why countries themselves are poor.

When people talk about fighting poverty, they talk about making agriculture more productive, educating girls, passing laws to prohibit discrimination, building roads, fighting traditional superstitions about health, changing widespread negative attitudes about women and girls, equalizing the balance of trade between countries—there are endless solutions, because poverty is endlessly complicated.

Microcredit, however, attacks an aspect of poverty that did not often show up on the list of usual suspects: the poor could have better lives if they could borrow money.

The guru of microcredit is Bangladeshi economist Muhammad Yunus. In 1974, during a terrible famine in Bangladesh, Yunus was a young professor of economics. He came upon a woman named Sufia Khatun, who made stools out of bamboo. She told him that since she did not have 22 cents to buy her materials every day, she used those lent to her by a moneylender, who demanded she sell the finished product to him at the end of the day for the price he set. She made 2 cents profit on the day. Yunus realized that a loan of less than a quarter could allow her to buy her materials in advance and therefore sell her crafts at the market price. Yunus asked one of his students to find other people in the same situation, and the student found forty-two. Yunus then lent them a total of $27—an average of 64 cents per person. The loan meant that Khatun could make a profit of $1.25 a day instead of 2 cents. Her 22-cent loan bought more than bamboo. It bought her freedom.

Yunus's idea had already occurred to others. The first documented microloan, in fact, took place in 1973, in Recife, Brazil, lent by Acción International, a group that has now lent more than $10 billion. But it was Yunus who developed a model now in use globally. His ideas made lending to the poor possible on a gigantic scale.

Grameen Bank, the organization Yunus founded in 1983, has lent $9 billion in small sums of money to nearly eight million people in Bangladesh, almost all of them women—many of them women who had never before touched money. Grameen has turned microcredit into microfinance, offering savings plans, insurance, home mortgages, pension funds, and scholarships. It also provides credit for families to buy fertilizer, build latrines, or dig wells, and it has a program of no-interest loans for beggars, so they can offer candy or chiles for sale as they go house to house. Grameen is not a charity and does not accept donations. As other banks do, it runs on the interest it charges borrowers. The difference is that its repayment rates are far higher than those of traditional banks. The typical bank in Bangladesh sees less than half its loans paid back, and it stays afloat only by grace of government subsidies and bailouts. Grameen, by contrast, has had a repayment rate of 98.5 percent and makes millions of dollars in profit most years.

Like Uri Treisman, Yunus did not set out to find a social cure. He simply saw a specific problem—the enslavement of artisans because they had no access to credit—and sought to solve it. If he had been looking to apply a join-the-club approach to the huge problem of poverty, his first step would have been to carry out a painstaking search, looking far beyond the list of usual suspects—just as Treisman did with calculus.

Both of them found the answer in a bottleneck—a small but crucial part of the issue. And in both cases, the bottleneck was hidden from view. For microcredit, the solution was even further hidden. The behavioral bottleneck that microcredit attacks is not the behavior of the poor. The key behavior Yunus sought to change was that of the organizations that refused to lend to the very poor—the banks.

The moderately poor—people with assets that could be used as collateral—had always borrowed money from village loan sharks at exorbitant rates of interest, often losing their farms or businesses in the process. But even loan sharks wouldn't lend to the really poor, who had nothing they would consider as collateral. Banks didn't go to villages or rural areas at all; the very poor didn't fit into bankers' normal view of clients. Very few of the rural poor even know what a bank is, and many of them can't even sign their names. The very poorest in Bangladesh are women, who have absolutely nothing that could be repossessed. They have no credit record, little education, no formal employment history. The costs of checking these borrowers' creditworthiness and servicing their loans would be an astronomical percentage of the tiny amounts they would borrow.

Yunus decided that there was another way to look at banking. The poor don't have collateral in the traditional way banks see capital and collateral, but he realized that the poor do have one kind of collateral: their standing among their peers. The brilliance of Grameen was to use this to build a model that made it viable for a bank to offer very large numbers of very small loans at fair rates of interest. Grameen formed its borrowers into groups of five women each. The group had to approve each new loan, and members could only get new loans if their fellow borrowers were current on their repayments, a rule known as joint liability. Effectively, the whole group would be held hostage to one delinquent repayer.

Peer pressure made this run. In a small village, the opinion of one's neighbors takes on supreme importance. The women know intimate details of each other's lives. Grameen used peer pressure to lift the expensive burdens of determining creditworthiness and monitoring repayment from the bank's shoulders and put them on the shoulders of the borrower's neighbors. They wouldn't let a woman into their group if she were a default risk, and they met weekly to check on loan-repayment progress. This system produced unheard-of repayment levels.

Grameen's officials initially believed that the joint-liability rule was key to this success rate, but that turned out not to be important. It was not the threat to the group that made the women repay their loans on time—it was the simple desire to protect their reputations. Grameen began to realize that the joint-liability requirement was unnecessary and seldom enforced, and in 2001 Grameen dropped it entirely. A borrower's desire for the respect of her peers was enough.

The social cure here is buried three layers deep. Poverty has multiple bottlenecks, and microcredit addresses a hidden bottleneck—indirectly. By using peer pressure on borrowers to make them more assured repayers, microcredit changes the behavior of lenders. Microcredit uses the social cure to turn poor people into catalysts for *someone else's* change—a change that eventually benefits the poor.

This is labyrinthine indeed, but the multitude of steps between problem and solution is useful. It is evidence that societal ills may have many different points of attack, and perhaps more than one where a join-the-club attack can help.

The utility of an indirect solution—the use of the social cure in one group to procure change in *another* group's behavior—is important. It opens wide the universe of susceptible problems. The social cure can be directly applied if people want to change their behavior or can be convinced to want to by a new peer group. Unfortunately, however, not everyone who *should* change *wants* to change. Bangladesh's commercial banks did not convince each other to look for ways to lend money so destitute women could buy chickens. Stepping down as president of Yugoslavia was not Slobodan Milošević's idea, and the notion that a group of his fellow-dictator peers would try to convince him is the stuff of a magic-realist García Márquez novel. American carmakers are not volunteering to subscribe to higher emissions standards. Every person and institution on the planet, however, can be swayed by something.

Bankers and automakers follow the scent of profit; dictators react when their citizens become disobedient; government officials respond to activism, votes, and contributions. These forms of persuasion are not the social cure. But the social cure can amass people to exert these forms of persuasion—by creating catalysts.

FEW PEOPLE TRYING TO create a more just and prosperous India would have thought that the social cure offered any possible solution, but it does—through the use of catalysts. The catalysts are Surekha, Babai, Lalenbai, and hundreds of other village women in a remote part of India. Their story shows how the social cure can work to fight against the destructive aspects of a 3,000-year-old culture.

Surekha Sadafule, Babai Sathe, and Lalenbai Kadam seem unlikely agents of change. As we saw earlier, they knew only victimization and suffering, having experienced the full oppression their culture metes out to women and Dalits. But their lives had second acts, triumphant ones. They were recruited to join a village health program that relies heavily on the social cure. Once changed, they went back and transformed their villages.

Cultures do evolve—especially in tandem with economic developments that dramatically alter how people live—but they evolve slowly, over generations. In India, for example, women who work in the call centers in urban areas—the new India—suffer far less discrimination than their old-India villager sisters. The hardships faced by Surekha, Babai, and Lalenbai as women and as Dalits no longer occur among the urban middle class. But people like Surekha still make up the vast majority of Indians, and it will be many, many decades before real economic transformation touches women like them, if it ever comes at all. And some discriminatory aspects of Indian culture—such as the payment of dowry and the abortion of daughters—remain and even have increased among the elite. Waiting for economic change to alter a culture is a task for the very patient.

And for the impatient?

Jamkhed is the name of a city and the district of villages scattered around it in the eastern part of Maharashtra state. If you go to Jamkhed today, you will find that life in many villages is far different than it was a few years ago. Not substantially richer, no—there is still drought, no industry, only rain-fed agriculture—but better. Women are out of the house and working on village-improvement projects such as sanitation systems and vegetable gardens. They start small businesses. People eat more nutritious foods, use toilets instead of the woods, and wash their hands and bodies with the clean water now piped into their backyard pumps. They know how to prevent the diseases that typically kill poor people. Dalits suffer far less discrimination than before, as do women and girls.

The transformation of Jamkhed began in 1970 with an extraordinary pair of doctors, Raj and Mabelle Arole. Raj graduated second in his class at one of the most prestigious medical schools in India; Mabelle, who died in 1997, was the only student who bested him. She came from a wealthy, scholarly, southern Indian family. Raj, whom she married after medical school, came from a poor family of schoolteachers and grew up not far from Jamkhed. The couple shared not only medical talent but also a dissatisfaction with the kind of medicine they were being taught—curative medicine, the kind in use in wealthy countries. "Medical graduates found it easier to work in hospitals in America than in a rural hospital in India," Raj Arole told me. So, in order to become doctors in rural India, they decided to go to America to learn about public health. They first studied curative medicine in Cleveland, then spent a summer on a Navajo reservation, and finally studied public health at Johns Hopkins University in Baltimore, Maryland.

Then they moved back to Jamkhed, a location they chose largely for its desolation. People stayed alive by raising small patches of sorghum. "We wanted to choose the poorest area where nobody wanted to go, the most needy villages—an area where no change was likely to take place," Raj said.

The way to help those villages was not with doctors—the vast majority of doctors simply wouldn't go to them. Even doctors assigned by the government to rural posts in India often visit only once a week, spending the rest of the time in the city treating patients who can pay. There are even doctors who take the bus from the city to their assigned job at a clinic in the countryside, punch their time cards while the bus driver is on his tea break, and get back on the same bus.

More important, the Aroles concluded that rural villages don't need doctors: they just don't help much. Doctors do not help people prevent illness. Doctors do not spend time teaching people about handwashing, nutrition, breast-feeding, hygiene, boiling water, and making simple home remedies such as oral-rehydration salts. They don't help villages acquire clean water and sanitation systems and improve their farming practices—ways to eliminate the root causes of disease. They don't work to dispel popular myths that keep people sick. They don't combat the discrimination against women and, in India, lower castes, which is toxic to good health.

Uri Treisman found that students learn best when they learn from and teach each other. The formal math professors and teaching assistants were too distant from the students, and the setting too intimidating. This imposed passivity on the students. The Aroles reacted similarly. Doctors in rural India held themselves very much apart from their patients. They didn't explain things, didn't try to involve patients in their own health. Going to a doctor to get a pill or injection furthered the sense that people were passive and ignorant, unable to do anything to make themselves or their children healthier.

Doctors, in fact, tended to put obstacles in the way of health for the poor. They are a closed and conservative group. If a new malaria drug comes out, doctors often will resist it. They are hard to train—in part because poor countries do not require them to update their skills, and there is no organized way to assemble them to transmit new information. They also present a powerful institutional lobby that can block the real solution for places like Jamkhed: training village health workers like Lalenbai, Babai, and Surekha. "Doctors promote medical care, because that's where the money is," said Raj Arole. "We promote health."

At first, the Aroles tried to put auxiliary nurses—women with eight years of schooling and two years of training in nursing and midwifery—in the villages. Few wanted to go, some who went wouldn't stay, and those who stayed didn't succeed. Their education and urbanity made them foreign to villagers. And they brought top-down concepts of medicine. They were comfortable administering mysterious medicine to sick people, not forming relationships with villagers to teach them about preventive measures such as nutrition, vaccination, and hygiene. Some were openly disdainful of the uneducated villagers.

The Aroles then thought of training village residents in nursing—people who presumably wouldn't up and move to the big city. "But we needed high school graduates," said Arole—a requirement for entry to nursing school, "and there was not a single one."

One day in 1971, Raj Arole was visiting the village of Sakat, where the Jamkhed program had placed an auxiliary nurse. The nurse was very good at curing illnesses, but she had not been able to convince villagers to change their ways in order to prevent disease. The mayor told Arole that the nurse was too foreign and too young—she had no children of her own, so she had little credibility with village mothers. Then the mayor mentioned a woman from a nearby village named Mrs. Joshibai, who was employed by the government as a promoter of family planning. When he watched her work, the mayor said, he marveled at her ability to connect with and explain things to village women. Part of the reason, he said, is that she was one of them.

Mrs. Joshibai had gone to school for only four years. It suddenly occurred to the Aroles that instead of being a handicap, her lack of education might be an *advantage*. She understood how to reach the people who most needed reaching: illiterate, poor village women. She knew how they thought and lived, because she was one of them.

So the Aroles made a very curious decision: they would go completely in the opposite direction from doctors and nurses. They would train villagers to care for their neighbors' health, and they would ask villages to choose as their health workers capable and intelligent women who were among the most downtrodden. These women often would be Dalits and usually victims of early marriage. Every single village health worker I met had been married by the age of thirteen, and quite a few earlier than that. Many had been abandoned by their husbands when they gave birth to girls or had physical injuries that prevented them from doing heavy work. In the beginning, virtually all the women chosen were completely illiterate.

For the Aroles, no one was too much of an outcast. When Sakubai Gite was chosen as a village health worker, she had been long cured of the leprosy that had afflicted her as a teenager, nearly twenty years earlier, but her hands were still gnarled and deformed, with parts of her fingers missing. Leprosy was common at the time, and lepers often were thrown out of their villages. "We wanted to remove the stigma," she said. "We wanted to show that a cured leprosy patient can be a village health worker."

The health workers were chosen by their own villages, using criteria established by the Aroles. To revolutionize villages, the Aroles set out to find the least influential people imaginable.

The Aroles concluded that empathy, knowledge of how the poor live, and willingness to work with the poor were more important than prestige and skills—including the ability to read. "We do not equate illiteracy with lack of wisdom and intellect," Arole said. "Literacy is a good tool, but not so great that you can't do without it. We wanted to work for the most downtrodden. An educated woman likely comes from a high caste—she may not work for the poorest of the poor."

Mabelle Arole reasoned that the illiterate had learned to cook, clean, care for children, raise animals and plants, and do everything else in their daily lives without reading. They learned by listening, asking questions, and doing. Surely they could learn basic health care the same way. When they were cooking, they could distinguish among the different bags of spices they owned and measure the correct amounts without reading. They could prescribe, identify, and dispense medicines in the same way.

The Aroles were confident that illiterate women could be successful because the vast majority of rural problems did not require complicated diagnosis and treatment. "Rural problems are simple," Raj Arole said. "Most health problems prominent in rural areas are related to nutrition and the environment—sanitation, for example. Good health is diet, water supply, environment, and attitudes. Infant mortality is three things: chronic starvation, diarrhea, and respiratory infections. For all three conditions, we do not need experts. An array of women like village health workers is enough, properly trained and supported."

The Aroles believed that transforming village thinking and practices was far more important than giving out pills or injections. "It's giving education to the people," they had said, "and the educational processes can best be given by the people who share the culture of the people, who share the life of the people, and that means the local village people." In other words, peers—even the most scorned—were more effective at changing their villages than prestigious outsiders like doctors or nurses.

The other advantage of having health information come from your neighbor is that it demystifies health, just as learning from a fellow student demystifies calculus. Rural people were used to thinking about health and disease as something that came from the gods as a punishment or reward for their conduct. They did not think of health as something that was in their hands, within their abilities.

The initial problem with recruiting the planet's most downtrodden people as village health workers was not that they couldn't read and write—it was their complete absence of confidence. Their entire lives had been a lesson in keeping their heads down. They had been told since birth that they had no worth or intelligence, possessed no skill. It is hard for anyone in a Western culture to imagine exactly how oppressed these women were, how limited their lives. Now suddenly they had been plucked from their familiar surroundings and sent to a building in an overwhelming city, to be talked to by doctors—people with education and status.

For some of the women, it was too much—they simply refused. Others arrived in the city, but were cowering in fear. Lalenbai Kadam, for example, had been selected by the mayor of her village in 1972. He knew her because she was his servant. She took care of his animals, cleaned the cowshed, and formed cow dung into cakes for fuel. But this was the world she knew. She didn't want to go to the Aroles' training center in the city of Jamkhed, but she had to obey.

At the Jamkhed center, she was terrified to sit with the others, as Dalits are not supposed to share the same carpet as higher-caste people. "I wouldn't look at anyone," Lalenbai said. "I would sit like this"—she folded herself up and put her sari over her face. "I thought they would tell us to sweep the room. I had only a torn and dirty sari and blouse."

Then Mabelle Arole went over and asked Lalenbai what problems she saw in her village. "I couldn't talk—my tongue got stuck," Lalenbai recalled. Mabelle reassuringly brought her a glass of water.

The Aroles' daughter, Shobha, a doctor who now directs the day-to-day operations of the Jamkhed program, helped her mother with a lot of the training, beginning in the 1980s. "I would ask, 'What's your name?' and they would say the village they came from and their caste. They had no self-identity. They would be totally veiled. They wouldn't look into your eyes or talk to you. They didn't even feel that a woman has intelligence. My mother asked them: 'Who's more intelligent, a woman or a rat?' They'd say, 'The rat.'"

Mabelle would have the women practice saying their names in front of a mirror. She would ask a question: "Who is the one person who will never leave you?" Then they would go behind a curtain and see the mirror. "Everyone can give technical knowledge," said Shobha. "What makes it successful is time spent building up their confidence."

"Only half the training was devoted to teaching the women about health," Raj Arole said. "The other 50 percent went to helping the women learn money-making skills, and to teach self-confidence and women's rights. They had to realize who they were and how they could have their dignity. These women were so poor—they had a little scythe to cut grass. We talked about income generation before talking about health. It's important in a village—the successful people are the ones who get power."

From the very beginning (in the early 1970s), the Aroles and their staff taught the women business skills and helped them get bank loans. Women borrowed $20 and bought dried fish to sell in their villages, bangles to sell, a goat to raise. The Aroles told them it was important to get their names on their land and houses, not just their husband's names. "That way," Raj told them, "your husband cannot just kick you out because you didn't produce a son or were not good-looking."

When they did talk about health, it was health in a very broad sense: Why is it important to work together? How do you start a self-help group? Why am I as a woman treated differently? Bettering their villages' health meant dealing with agriculture, nutrition, certain societal problems like early marriage, alcoholism, dowry, violence against women. The Jamkhed program focused on the value of doing things together.

The women learned a lot from the Jamkhed staff. The reason those lessons were so effective is that, as with the calculus clubs, they were pulling each other up from the ground. At first conscious of caste, the village health workers soon realized that Dalits and higher-caste women could sit together and eat together and sleep under the same blanket and nothing terrible would happen. New village health workers went in groups of three or four to stay with a more experienced peer in her village for a week. They watched their mentor as she greeted her neighbors with confidence, went down to the well to be able to speak with young women out of earshot of their mothers-in-law, worked with local all-male farmers' clubs, saw patients, and taught mothers about breastfeeding and purifying water. When the women saw that she kept her sandals on even though she was a Dalit, it was as important a lesson as if they had watched her weigh a baby.

In watching the more experienced woman work, the novices could see their own future. They saw someone transformed from passive to bold, and they could imagine how they might be able to make the same journey.

Lalenbai said that after she had been a health worker a short time, in the early 1970s, Mabelle Arole took her to a meeting in a hill village, far from Jamkhed; it was time for Lalenbai to give a speech. She was tongue-tied. She started to talk, but after two sentences her tongue got stuck again. Mabelle got up and said, "Please bring a glass with water for Lalenbai." Lalenbai drank the water and then spoke for twenty minutes about prenatal care and child immunizations. Everyone clapped. Today, she is an experienced teacher who spends most of her time at the Jamkhed campus training other health workers. She still marvels at that memory.

After the women complete their initial training, they can return to the Jamkhed campus every week, arriving Tuesday afternoon, staying till Wednesday morning. There are always new women joining the program, so there are always novices mixed in alongside women with decades of experience. They sleep together under one big blanket they sewed together from smaller ones. Every week they talk about a new health topic, one that usually arises from the women's reports of what they see in their villages—from women's rights to heart disease. Often the discussions are led by more experienced village health workers.

Mainly the women come to Jamkhed for the fellowship—"to tell each other our problems," said Surekha. For many, it became the first time in their lives they could complain. In their normal lives, they could not even tell their troubles to their own mothers and expect sympathy. "It's your fate in life," they would invariably be told. But at Jamkhed they could talk to women who would say instead: "I was there, and here's what I did."

WHEN THE JAMKHED WOMEN finish their initial training and go back to their villages, they see village problems with different eyes. What once appeared normal no longer does. Ideas and conditions that their village has accepted for centuries now appear more like bankrupt superstition. A typical example was Sarubai Salve, the senior health worker in Babai Sathe's village of Jawalke. She had joined the Jamkhed program in 1984.

"When I started, the children all had scabies and there was filth everywhere," she said. "Small kids used to die. Pregnant women died during and after delivery. Mothers did not space their children." Standing water—the perfect mosquito-breeding ground—was everywhere, which meant malaria was, too. Tuberculosis and leprosy were common, and sufferers were ostracized, sometimes driven out of the village. Many mothers and babies died of tetanus because a dirty knife had been used to cut the umbilical cord.

As in South Africa, where some people preferred the *sangoma*'s potions to the clinic's antiretrovirals, many people died of superstition. "If a mother died of tetanus, no one would take care of the child," said Sarubai. "People said the mother would become a ghost and come and take the child away." There were superstitions about pregnancy—pregnant women were not supposed to eat very much, so many had low-birthweight babies. The babies themselves often did not thrive, as mothers would not start breast-feeding until the baby was three or five days old, and in some places infants were not given anything but breast milk until they were a year old. Cobra bites were common, and even though an antivenin was available at hospitals, the victims would be rushed to the temple for the gods to cure. The gods usually failed.

In her first few weeks after returning to Jawalke, Sarubai could not imagine that she would be able to make a difference. She was an impoverished Dalit who had only finished fourth grade. After her initial training at Jamkhed, Sarubai's attitudes had been transformed, but how would she transform her village? Her head was full of useful knowledge and she had become assertive—she would never again remove her sandals to walk in the village. But that might even make people less willing to hear what she knew. How could she persuade people to listen?

There was no magic in it. The answer turned out to be the expected factors: time, demonstrable success, and support. At first, in fact, no one did listen. People didn't want her advice, didn't send for her when someone was sick, didn't ask her to deliver their babies. There were months, for some women years of frustration, tempered by the soothing words of fellow village health workers, who had gone through the same thing. But eventually, mothers of sick children called Sarubai out of desperation, when going to the temple didn't work. "I was called by the mother of a two-year-old boy with a high fever," Sarubai said. "I went there and brought cold water and put it on his head. The child got better. People were very surprised, and they began to have faith in me."

All of the health workers said they had started out being ignored, but then came a moment of change. It would come when a family, usually of a high caste, called them as a last resort. Their success in curing a child's diarrhea or delivering a baby after a difficult labor would be the turning point. After that, people started listening when they also talked about clean water, breast-feeding, and nutrition.

"For me, the hardest fight was to break castism," Sarubai said. "I am from Jawalke and I know everyone. I would go to the houses of high-caste friends and call them 'aunt' and 'big sister.' They would give me tea. But at first it was in a separate cup"—the broken cup and saucer reserved for Dalits. "But I helped them with safe delivery of their babies. I used to visit them in pregnancy and explain things to them. I gave them love and affection—that makes a difference. When I came for delivery, I would cook for them. Then they started to eat my food. They started to give me tea from a normal cup. Then they would ask me to eat with them. And slowly castism goes away. They observe that I cooked for them, and they realize that if I eat with them, nothing will happen. Slowly they changed their attitude. And it changed for all Dalits, not just for me."

The women's breakthroughs were helped by the fact that they were not completely on their own in their villages. Every week, each village would have a visit from one of the Jamkhed program's mobile teams, which usually consisted of social workers and nurses, and sometimes doctors. The mobile teams carried out health surveys and saw tough cases, but their most important job was to reinforce the credibility of the village health worker. Surekha said that once, early in her tenure, the mobile team went with her on a visit to a high-caste woman. The woman made tea for the others but not for Surekha, because she was a Dalit. "The social worker put her cup in my hand," Surekha said. She had prescribed some medicine, but the high-caste woman didn't trust her, so she asked the mobile team the same question. The Jamkhed nurse asked Surekha to bring her bag. She took out the same medicine that Surekha had offered the woman and gave it to the patient.

THE GREAT MYSTERY OF JAMKHED is the way it encourages poor, sometimes destitute, women with overwhelming burdens to spend hours each day on work that offers them no money—only the occasional gift of a papaya from a grateful patient. But something clearly is working. Most health workers are lifers; very few leave. The reason turns out to be a key lesson in what motivates people—a lesson that reveals the power of the social cure.

Raj Arole contended that it was better that the health workers were unpaid. Paying the women, he said, would alter the balance between the Jamkhed program and the health workers—turning them from partners into servants. This always seemed like a justification: he had to make the best out of the fact that Jamkhed has never had the money to pay them.

Instead of paying a salary, Jamkhed compensates the women by teaching them how to run small businesses and helping them get loans. "When I worked in the fields, I earned 3 rupees a day," said Leelabai Amte, a health worker in the village of Halgaon. "Now I know how to make money. I earn 150 rupees a day selling bangles"—the glass bracelets every woman wears by the armful. "When there is a marriage ceremony in Halgaon and everyone needs new bangles, I can make 2500 rupees in a day." That's almost $60—a fortune by local standards.

This is a good strategy for Jamkhed—the wealthier the health worker, the more weight her ideas will carry in the village. But it doesn't explain why Leelabai still spends hours every day checking blood pressures when she could be selling bangles.

The real benefits, the women say, cannot be measured in rupees—a lesson for anyone who believes that the poor are motivated simply by material needs and not the desire for respect, community, and recognition. A big part of the health workers' desire to stay with the program is the fellowship they share with their sister health workers. But they also have acquired a new identity in their own villages. "When I am useful to any family, when they apply my knowledge successfully, they will give me respect," Leelabai told me. "If you want respect, do something for the poor."

THE TRANSFORMATIONS OF THE Jamkhed-program women and of their villages work in tandem. The women acquire their new self-image in part through their new role in the village, the satisfaction of helping their neighbors, and the respect they have earned from the villagers. As a result of the knowledge and skills of the Jamkhed women, the villages change.

The Jamkhed villages with a long-standing, assertive health-care worker now look very different from the villages around them that have not yet joined the program. At one of the Tuesday meetings at Jamkhed in 2008, the health workers talked about the biggest health problems in their villages. One after another, they mentioned diabetes, hypertension, and arthritis. These are rich-country diseases; only the luckiest die of such illnesses in rural India. In Jamkhed villages, there is no more malaria, no more active leprosy and tuberculosis, very little diarrhea. Women no longer die in childbirth, and birth weights have risen, because pregnant women now know what to eat and there is no more nonsense about starving them.

Jamkhed villages have clean water, and many have pipes carrying that water to a pump in every backyard. Most houses have soak pits, a simple and cheap drainage system dug outside every house that eliminates standing wastewater; they are moving on to toilets. In an area nearly barren of trees, Jamkhed villages have planted millions. Jamkhed villagers have kitchen gardens, so they eat spinach and papaya along with their sorghum bread. Dalits are less oppressed and upper-caste women are freer to leave the confines of their houses. Women are more educated and more interested in educating their girls.

India's health statistics show that the program has had a dramatic effect. Jamkhed-program villages have an infant-mortality rate of twenty-two per 1,000 births, less than half the average for rural Maharashtra. Almost half of all Indian children under five are malnourished, while there were not enough cases to register in Jamkhed villages. Jamkhed villages have far higher rates of vaccination and far lower rates of diseases such as tuberculosis and leprosy than India as a whole. A rigorous study led by the London School of Hygiene and Tropical Medicine published in 2010 found that death rates for children ages one through five were 30 percent lower in Jamkhed villages than in villages not in the program.

ONE WAY TO APPRECIATE the power of the Jamkhed village-health program is to accompany an experienced Jamkhed health worker on her rounds. Twice a day, at nine in the morning and six at night,

Leelabai Amte sets off through the streets of Halgaon, her village of 6,000 people. Amte is sixty, a very thin woman with thick glasses and no front teeth. She is a higher-caste Maratha, not a Dalit, but she was totally illiterate when she became a village health worker—she has since learned to read and write. She was married at ten and had her first son at thirteen.

In the streets of Halgaon, Leelabai carried a blood-pressure cuff and a baby scale in her black shoulder bag, along with a logbook. She visited old people, pregnant women, and the newborns she had delivered. Her first stop one morning in January was the home of Savita Baba Pacharne, whose son was three days old. Leelabai watched the baby suckle and then tied him in a light cloth sling and hooked it to her scale. He weighed three and a half kilos—a remarkable gain over his three-kilo birthweight. She murmured approvingly. "Don't put anything on the umbilical cord," she advised the mother. "And keep the child in the sunlight in the morning."

"Twenty years ago," Leelabai told me, "mothers waited three days to breast-feed their babies"—a superstition that deprived babies of valuable colostrum and reduced the mothers' supply of milk. Today, Leelabai has banished this and dozens of other superstitions from Halgaon. When she started working in the village in 1977, families had six or seven children. The children often had scabies and other skin diseases; they were unvaccinated and often sick; night blindness due to Vitamin A deficiency was everywhere; tuberculosis and leprosy were common, and their sufferers were ostracized. People attributed illness to curses from the gods.

Today, preventable disease is rare. Mothers eat better—the average birthweight of a baby has increased from two kilos to three.

Leelabai's next stop was the home of Tukaram Kumbhar, an old man in white clothes with a white beard, who has been cured of leprosy. There are no active cases of leprosy in Halgaon, but Leelabai always checks the arms, legs, and eyes of former patients for signs of recurrence.

Tukaram sat with his wife, Keshar, on a mat in the courtyard of their house. "You are feeling well?" Leelabai asked him. She inspected his hands, feet, and heels. "Take care of your feet," she said, advising him to wear sandals that are glued together, not nailed. "Massage your feet at night."

She removed his glasses gently. "Let me see your eyes. Have you consulted with an eye specialist?" He had. "I cannot see anything from my left eye," he said. "The eye surgeon says I have glaucoma."

Leprosy is actually a disease like any other. It is contagious only through contact with open wounds and is easily curable with medicines. There is no reason the patient cannot live at home and work normally. But when Leelabai began working, the stigma attached to lepers was overwhelming. "Previously, if you had leprosy you'd be kicked out of the village," she said. "When I started as a health worker, people used to say to me: 'Don't come to my house—you visited a leprosy patient and touched him.' I had one leprosy patient who had made his living carrying water. When he got sick, people refused to take it. Another man ran a grocery shop, but no one would buy from him after he got leprosy." Having a leper in the family usually ruined the children's marriage prospects.

The most difficult prejudice to attack, she said, was her own. "I had to clean so many wounds. It was a very difficult job, cleaning infected legs and noses. I was thinking: why should I have to clean it out? There are doctors in the hospital. Slowly I changed my mind. I decided I'm a human being and this patient is, too. And Dr. Arole said to me: 'If you get leprosy, I am there.'" Today, one of Leelabai's sons is married to the sister of a leprosy patient.

Part of Leelabai's job, it seemed, was to bust taboos, one after the other. One morning, at a busy corner in the village center, Leelabai was in the middle of a crowd of about twenty men, talking about installing toilets in Halgaon's houses. Village women in India do not speak out to men, but Leelabai does. (She also became the talk of the village when she turned down a dowry for her son, part of her efforts to reduce the practice of demanding dowry.) In the street, she spotted the husband of one of her pregnant patients—a woman overdue for her prenatal visit to the Jamkhed program's hospital. "Why is your wife not coming to the hospital?" she scolded him. "We'll check everything, give her blood tests." The man had the grace to look sheepish. "I've been busy with farming," he told Leelabai. "Next month I'll bring her."

One of Leelabai's biggest achievements, she said, was that she has taught others about health. She has trained three village women to deliver babies. New mothers learn from her how to feed and care for a baby, the importance of immunization, how to treat diarrhea and fever. At one house, she quizzed a high school girl. "If a child has a fever, what do you do?" Leelabai asked.

"Cold compresses," said the girl promptly.

"And diarrhea?"

"You give oral-rehydration mixture," came the answer.

"Do they teach you about health in school?" asked Leelabai, eyes twinkling. "Do they tell you about safe drinking water and keeping yourself clean?"

"No," the girl replied, "you are the one who talks about that."

All the Jamkhed health workers agree that the most important thing they do is teach others. Each of them organizes a women's group in her village, gathering eight to ten women. At first they meet to discuss what women most want to know about: making money. The health worker teaches the women the business skills Jamkhed taught her, and she shares advice on getting loans. In a scheme called *bhishi*, each woman puts a few rupees in the pot, to be lent to one member. When she repays the loan, it goes to someone else. As other women see the advantages of joining a group, the health worker organizes more of them.

The women's groups also become a venue for teaching people the health lessons learned during their weekly gatherings at the Jamkhed campus. Often what is learned on a Tuesday night is all over the village a few days later. These groups also provide a way to organize village-improvement projects. In Jawalke, for example, the groups decided that the village needed a high school for girls—the local school only went up to seventh grade and families were unwilling to send their girls six kilometers to the nearest high school. The groups endorsed the collection of a rupee from every household to pay a teacher's salary. School could be held in the village community hall. The women's groups have also organized the planting of hundreds of thousands of fruit trees—combating malnutrition and deforestation at the same time.

In 2008, the Jawalke women's groups were working on their latest campaign: toilets for all. About 85 of 240 families already had one. It required pouring water in to make it work, and the waste went into a soak pit dug next to the house (there were no sewers), but it was still hugely more sanitary and convenient than the usual places that served as toilets: the woods and the street.

Babai Sathe—Sarubai Salve's colleague and Jawalke's mayor—spread two mats on the patio of a house and nine women sat down. Babai and a government representative told the women that the government would pay part of the money to build the toilets, but villagers had to provide some materials and the labor.

"All of the people in the village must be involved," Babai told the group. "Of 100 houses, we must have 100, not 99. We can do this: you work with me for two days and I'll work with you for two days." She reminded them of an earlier campaign to build soak pits. "Some people weren't willing to do it, so we made them for those people. Then they were ashamed and started doing it themselves."

"We're not going to do that now," said a confident woman in a red sari, Nandabai Kantilal Borate. ("She owns cattle," someone whispered to me as Borate began to talk.) "You're not a master and I'm not a servant. If you want a toilet, come and work." They talked for a while about how to get everyone's participation.

It was clear that these women had undertaken such campaigns before, successfully. Organizing had been hard at first, because of castism and the constraints on women's behavior. Higher-caste women have privileges Dalits don't have, but they are also kept secluded in their houses. At first the only women in the organized groups were Dalits, but then the higher-caste women noticed that the women's-group members were starting businesses and making money. At one early meeting of a women's group in Sarubai's house, a high-caste woman was present. Her husband broke into the meeting with a stick, furious that his wife was inside a Dalit house. Sarubai and Babai pulled the stick from his hand, telling him, "You'll have to beat us first." Then they invited him to sit down and listen.

Times have changed. "I have a small poultry business, and goats and a cow," said Alka Gokul Kamble, a group member in an orange sari. "Previously, if I wanted a sari, my husband would buy it for me but now I will go with him. I help make decisions about our bullock. I am registered on our property—I am one of the owners now. Selling milk and eggs, I make 50 rupees a day."

She was very proud of those 50 rupees a day. It was the equivalent of about $1.50. She was poor enough that this sum was a victory. But because of the work of Babai and Sarubai, she did not live like a poor person. It was not just the impending toilets, the vaccinated children, backyard water pumps, vegetable gardens, or other visible changes that mattered most. It was that now she knew what constituted a better life. And she demanded it.

TO APPRECIATE THE SCOPE of the social cure, it is useful to understand some of the ways it can attack a problem—by targeting a bottleneck, by affecting hidden factors, or by using peer pressure to create catalysts for change. It is also important to examine whether certain kinds of people and situations lend themselves to a join-the-club approach more easily than others do.

One group that is a natural fit for the social cure is the poor. The benefits of peer pressure are one kind of valuable social capital; they are a resource. People often talk about resources as if there were only money and skills—financial capital and human capital. But everyone has something else that's often overlooked—bonds with other people.

Social capital is the only resource that the poor have in abundance. The wretched of the earth have the problems most urgently in need of answers, but they do not have money. Many don't have the education or health necessary to develop and use advanced skills. Nevertheless, they do have social capital—the value generated by social networks in reciprocal favors, information, and collective action.

Social capital exists because people are better off living and working together than alone. The value two farmers accrue when they together harvest each man's corn as it ripens, in philosopher David

Hume's famous example, is social capital. So is the money saved by three suburban families who share a snowblower. Consider, too, the savings in burglaries averted by the inner-city block that organizes a neighborhood watch committee; the improvements in their children's education reaped by parents who are involved in the kids' elementary school; and the better health enjoyed by the elderly women who meet at McDonald's two mornings a week for coffee and conversation. All represent social capital.

For the poor of the world, the benefits of social capital are crucial. In the Mexican village of Paso de Coyutla, Veracruz, for example, I watched a ritual repeated in countless places: a villager had returned from working in Louisiana with enough money for cement and other building materials for a new house, but he didn't have enough to pay workmen, and he couldn't build the house alone. So the unemployed men in the village—there were a lot of them—gathered every day to help him build it. He would, in turn, help to build theirs. This is the only way houses get built in 75 percent of the world.

The formation of a group of reciprocal house-builders is not a social cure. There are many ways to create and use social capital, and not every community activity is a social cure. Building each other's houses, for example, involves no identity change. There is a peer group—fellow house-builders—but it isn't trying to change *you*. It's just trying to build a house. When people harvest each other's corn or share ownership of a snowblower, that's not the social cure. Nor need it be. You don't need a social cure to bring a village together to build a house or to organize slum-dwellers to convince the government to pave a road. An appeal to enlightened self-interest often suffices.

Sometimes, though, the power of peer pressure to change people is needed. The social cure is social capital in its mightiest form. Not only does it make us more effective together, it also influences each of us to be better alone than we were before. In places that lack financial and human capital, it is a strategy that is likely to work well. It is cheap—substituting social capital for financial capital—low tech, and sustainable. And people understand it instinctively—peer pressure has been both the blessing and the curse of village life for centuries. In a village, especially one with few other forms of entertainment, people amuse themselves by knowing each other's business. The Bangladeshi village woman instantly grasps the idea that she must monitor her neighbor's progress in repaying a loan. (She may even seize on this task gleefully.) It is not a mysterious, far-off solution.

A join-the-club approach can work in the developing world even where more expensive and high-tech solutions have not. For a powerful example, look at tuberculosis, a disease that kills nearly two million people a year. The paradox of tuberculosis is that it is curable with a course of four antibiotics costing as little as $11. Yet even many people who start taking those antibiotics are not cured, because a course of treatment must run six to nine months. In China in 1990, for example, less than half the people who started treatment were cured. The former Soviet Union tried to force compliance by hospitalizing TB patients for months at a time. It was expensive, horrible enough to the patient that it drove many cases of TB underground, and, worst of all, ineffective. The cure rate was still very low.

Was there a better solution, using a social cure? There are many parts of TB in which behavior matters. Choices in living quarters are important. You are more apt to get sick if you live in cramped quarters, close to others who are sick. One way to prevent TB, then, is to help people find less-crowded housing. A person is also fifty times more likely to develop TB if he or she has the AIDS virus—TB is resurgent today, in fact, because of AIDS. So it pays to help people stay HIV-negative.

Decent housing and freedom from HIV are, of course, worthy causes, but they are even harder problems to solve than curing TB. And even if they could be solved, it would do nothing for those who already have tuberculosis. There is, however, another relevant behavior that we *can* change, and fairly easily: the way people take, or don't take, their pills.

Once a patient starts taking antibiotics, the most important reason treatment fails is that the patient stops taking them. As we know, it is hard even for people with great advantages in life to take just a short course of medicine properly. It is even harder for TB patients, who tend to be extremely poor and lead chaotic lives. It is very difficult for them to be faithful to a treatment regime lasting for six to nine months—even after they stop coughing, even though the medicines cause nasty side effects.

If a patient starts but does not finish his course of medicines, he will stay sick, and chances are that his TB will now be resistant to the basic drugs. He will now need a two-year course of new medicines—costing $10,000 instead of $11. Cases of tuberculosis resistant to the basic drugs are soaring; some parts of the former Soviet Union are finding multiple drug resistance in 22 percent of new TB cases. Because of poor patient adherence, resistance has reached the point where some forms of TB are approaching incurability—the first-line drugs and some of the second-line ones are useless. These cases, called XDR-TB (extreme drug resistance), now make up 5 percent of multiple-drug-resistant cases. South Africa is battling an outbreak of XDR-TB and fifty-seven other countries have documented at least one case. No doubt many other places have it as well—they just don't know it yet.

Because of the long duration of treatment needed to cure tuberculosis, and the deadly implications of stopping early, patient adherence has become the Armageddon of tuberculosis. Health systems were at a loss for how to address the problem other than to simply exhort people to finish their medicines or keep them virtual prisoners in hospital beds. Slowly, however, a new strategy emerged, one that did not rely on hospitalization. First used in the 1950s in India, it has now become the world standard for treating TB. To ensure that patients finish their treatments, it uses the social cure. The strategy is called DOTS—for directly observed treatment, short-course. DOTS has several components—among them, good supply management and diagnosis—but the major paradigm shift it brings is what it is named for: someone observes the patient swallowing her medicines. This can be a community health worker or a nurse, but it also can be a neighbor or a family member. People who will not take their medicine regularly on their own, it seems, will take it when they must be accountable to a peer.

DOTS is not as widespread as it should be—ideally, every single person with tuberculosis should have DOTS—but it does cover about 60 percent of the world's diagnosed TB cases; where it is used, it greatly improves the chance of cure. When DOTS arrived in Ukraine, the cure

rate rose from 57 percent to 81 percent. In 1991, China began pilot programs using DOTS and the cure rate rose in DOTS areas from under
50 percent to 94 percent. Prevalence of the disease fell by 40 percent
over the next ten years in areas where DOTS was used, and rates of
the development of drug-resistant TB also fell. Today, DOTS programs
cover 700 million Chinese and have prevented 30,000 deaths from TB
a year. The global cure rate with DOTS averages 82 percent.

DOTS is one of the world's most cost-effective health programs;
each cure costs a total of $100 and brings a return of $60 for every
dollar spent. DOTS has proven that patient adherence can be vastly
improved—sustainably and cheaply. The model is also being used with
great success in administering antiretroviral drugs to AIDS patients.
The Boston-based organization Partners In Health uses *accompagnateurs* in its programs in Haiti, Rwanda, Peru, and elsewhere—villagers
who are paid stipends to visit their neighbors each day and watch them
take their AIDS medicines. Compliance rates are nearly 100 percent.
Developing-world public-health specialists want to adapt DOTS to the
management of all sorts of different diseases.

The need for DOTS is not limited to the developing world, and neither is its effectiveness. Organizations that are starting to use DOTS in
poor neighborhoods in America are having the same success that DOTS
enjoys in the rest of the world. Partners In Health, for example, works
with AIDS patients in inner-city Boston neighborhoods in what is called
the PACT program (Prevention and Access to Care and Treatment).
The patients receive visits from PACT health promoters, who also do
such things as prepare them for doctors' visits, go with them to appointments, and encourage friends and family to provide better support.
Those who need it also receive a visit either daily or every weekday by
a DOTS specialist, who sits with them while they take their medicines.
The DOTS specialist tries to recruit a friend or family member to watch
the patient take medicines the rest of the time, if necessary.

The health promoters and DOTS specialists are chosen for their
compassion and their ability to establish trust and put themselves in the
patients' shoes—some DOTS workers have not finished high school.
They are people from the same or similar neighborhoods, and many

have also gone through what the patients are suffering. "They are not just going in and saying you need to take your pills," said Dr. Heidi Behforouz, who runs the PACT program. "They can say, 'I was in your situation and really sick and dying, and I just made a decision that I have to love myself and take my pills and here I am.' This is incredibly powerful, and it can't come from people who look different from you and wear a white coat in a clinic."

Partners In Health selected these patients for the PACT program because they have multiple serious problems—among them, AIDS, diabetes, drug abuse, alcoholism, and histories of abuse and domestic violence. Many of the patients receiving visits from the DOTS specialists are, not surprisingly, also suffering from significant depression. Many stopped (or didn't start) taking their medicines because they felt there was no point. "If you ask the DOTS specialists what they do every day, they will say, 'I teach people how to learn to love themselves,'" said Behforouz. "A beeper to remind them to take their pills doesn't do that. Someone is going in and having a cup of coffee with them and reminding them *why* they are taking their pills." The program has been successful, and the staff has trained representatives from hospitals in New York and Miami.

DOTS is an excellent example of how the social cure can use the comparative advantage of the poor—their connections to other people—to solve problems. But the poor of the world, whether in India or China or Boston, are not the only ones with qualities that make a join-the-club solution effective. Identifying other groups of people with such characteristics can help find other ways to use the social cure.

Teenagers are a group with even stronger social bonds. Adolescence—a time when peer approval is as important as oxygen and water—offers the most obvious natural habitat for the social cure. People who live in groups of peers, such as college students or soldiers, also have exceptionally strong social connections.

Beyond groups of people who place high value on peer approval, there are other categories of people well situated for success with a join-the-club strategy. One type is those with addictions—to food, drugs, alcohol, overspending, what have you. Because of Alcoholics

Anonymous, we have grown comfortable with the idea of overcoming addiction with the help of a support group.

Also receptive are those with very serious problems, ones so overwhelming that they have come to the realization that they must break with their daily routine to solve them. The social cure may not require a lot of money, but it does require time. A fifty-five-year-old with poor eating and exercise habits may not make time in his life to join a group to help him live more healthily, but he is likely to do so after suffering his first heart attack.

Then there are people who will devote nearly all their time to a new peer group, such as recently released prisoners or people trying to get out of gang life. They are shedding their old lives and starting anew, and they have to completely redesign how they live. In doing so, they may be vague about the road to a productive life, so it would help them tremendously to surround themselves with like-minded peers, with guidance from people who have already been through the same process.

Examining what these groups have in common is a way of answering the question of what makes the social cure seem like a natural fit. The people in these categories meet one or both of two conditions. First, they live in close proximity to peers, and their main relationships are with peers. They may live in groups, like college students, or simply spend all their time running in packs, as teenagers do even while they live with their families. These people are desperately interested in the opinions and practices of their peers and are highly susceptible to anything those peers suggest.

The second condition is that they have very big problems. The social cure is a strange remedy, one whose effectiveness increases with the severity of the issue to be attacked. The social cure works by offering people a new identity, anchored by a new peer group that helps them think of themselves in a different way. But changing your identity is not something you do every day, over small issues. Even if going to join-the-club meetings is attractive because of the relationships you've made there, meetings take up a lot of time. And altering something as deeply rooted as your self-concept is not done to fix something minor.

Passing calculus may not be a salient issue to most people in the world, but for the students enrolled in it—whose plans for their lives as engineers or scientists must begin with a B or better in Calc 101—it is damned important. Bangladeshi village women do not have abundant free time, but they will spend it in group meetings if it allows them to borrow the money to raise chickens or improve their status in the village—which can make the difference between feeding their family or not. A former prisoner seeking to build a law-abiding life, or a gang member desperate to escape the streets, will uproot himself completely and start over in order to break free. The regulars at AA meetings go because they feel the group is quite literally saving their lives.

There are a great many people on the planet, however, whose circumstances are not so dire. Many of us do not need to attend meetings to keep from drowning. Nor do we have time to hang out with a new peer group. We are already too busy with family and work and barely have time for the people already in our lives, so we are resistant to the idea of solutions to our problems that involve more people and more demands on our time. Middle-class people in Western countries may think, in short, that the social cure is irrelevant to our lives.

It is not. There are various ways a join-the-club strategy can be helpful—indeed, indispensable—in a settled and comfortable life. One example concerns the issue of patient adherence—not just a problem for tuberculosis sufferers in rural China. We know that Americans are also terrible at taking medicines on time, much less following doctors' orders to diet, exercise, or give up smoking. This failure causes immeasurable sickness, death, and hospitalization and costs billions of dollars every year. "There is no impending pharmaceutical discovery, surgical innovation, or governmental policy change with greater potential for improving the health of patients and the efficacy of the healthcare system than simply increasing the percentage of treatment plans that patients carry out as prescribed," writes Allan Showalter, a Chicago-area psychiatrist who founded and runs a Web site on patient adherence.

Showalter's argument is that we should throw out our traditional notion of adherence, in which the doctor dictates what he or she considers the ideal treatment plan and instructs the patient to carry it out. Instead, he argues for "alignment"—patient and doctor together should design a treatment plan that might be less effective but *would* be carried out. In other words, an imperfect treatment plan that the patient follows is better than a perfect one that the patient ignores.

It's hard to argue with this idea, but his justification is revealing. The reason to settle for second best, said Showalter, is that increasing adherence has proven to be nearly impossible. He has seen dozens of programs come and go—counseling, patient information brochures, electronic beeping pillboxes, automated-reminder phone calls. None of them, he said, can get people to take their pills more than half the time. "Almost every program helps with someone," he said. But it's usually the same people—those who are disciplined enough to take their medicine anyway.

What about DOTS? Showalter acknowledged that DOTS is successful—elsewhere. He didn't think Americans would accept a prescription that included getting a family member to watch the patient take his pills. "With kids—okay," he said, "but with older people—lots of people won't let anyone else monitor them. They feel stigmatized. It's tricky to tell a 45-year-old adult, independent in every way, that you've got to let your wife watch you take your pill."

It didn't seem that tricky to me. Some middle-class, middle-aged Americans might balk at having their spouses watch them take their medicine, but others would not. If a doctor learned to explain that it was a proven way to improve treatment success, why should "take with wife" or "take with child" (a kid would love this job) be that different from "take with food"?

In fact, medical programs in various parts of the United States are experimenting with using peer groups to help people stick to their treatment plans, and it is working. Michele Heisler, associate professor of internal medicine at the University of Michigan, has produced a booklet describing various models that use peers to help people take care of their health—to help others launch similar programs. Some of these programs involve doctors. The Cleveland Veterans Affairs Medical Center, for example, holds group sessions—about fifteen patients with diabetes meet, with doctors and nurses rotating in and out. Patients do get one-on-one time with a doctor, but perhaps more useful is the

opportunity to hear how other patients have dealt with similar struggles. Other programs depend completely on the patients themselves.
The National Kidney Foundation, for example, recruits dialysis patients
who are successfully managing their disease and trains them to talk
to other patients receiving dialysis at the same time. Others, such as
California's Latino Health Access, recruit, train, and pay local people to
work in their own communities (and language). There are also patient-
to-patient support groups—in person, by phone, and on the Internet.

Dr. Heisler said that while programs using community health
workers are fairly widespread in the United States, enlisting patients
to help each other is not. But having the patients support each other,
whether through meetings or phone calls, may have advantages over a
community-health-worker model. For a start, patients work for free,
the main cost being their initial training. They also receive a double
benefit: they get help and they help others. Heisler believes that helping others may be even more important. Other researchers have borne
out this finding—in programs such as AA or ones that provide newly
released prisoners with mentors, the mentors and sponsors benefit more
than the protégés.

The apparent success of some Web-based versions of medical peer-
group programs, such as the Internet "buddy" groups discussed in chapter 4, shows that some people can use an Internet social cure to help
them manage chronic disease. Even busy people seem to find endless
time to spend on the Internet. As Dr. Showalter would say, an imperfect
social cure that people will carry out is better than a perfect one they
won't.

While programs using peers to help manage health conditions are
currently sparse and small, there is plenty of incentive to broaden them:
in addition to curing people, they save money. The Partners In Health
program in Massachusetts is a particularly dramatic example, because
it works with the very patients who tend to cost the health system the
most. A study of forty patients in the Partners In Health PACT program showed they went to the hospital much less often and their stays
were shorter. Their medical costs dropped by half. At the same time,
another study, which also showed huge cost savings, found that the

patients were increasing their use of appropriate medicines—their use of antiretroviral drugs rose by 30 percent. Three-quarters of the patients saw clinical improvement in their AIDS, and half of them managed to drop the viral load in their blood to undetectable levels. In any modern health system, 20 percent of the patients account for 80 percent of the costs, and these patients were in the 20-percent category—people who constantly ended up in the emergency room. In the United States, where soaring medical costs are an overwhelming problem for individuals and for the government, there should be considerable enthusiasm about a program that can bring down health costs while improving patient care.

THERE IS A CULTURAL DIVIDE here, and it is about something much bigger than the social cure. Americans and people in other wealthy countries have a blind spot about the tremendous value of community and social capital. We believe we don't have time for people; we already have enough friends; we want to keep our private lives private.

But a join-the-club strategy can work in a comfortable society when the foundation is properly laid. The scope of problems susceptible to the social cure is very wide, including issues with which people grapple in a middle-class life. We care about problems affecting our neighborhoods: the quality of the schools and the level of crime around us. We care about problems in our country and the rest of the world. Americans do spend time trying to get Washington to stop genocide in Darfur, or trying to persuade fellow citizens to take action against climate change. We use all kinds of strategies to try to accomplish these larger societal goals, though the social cure is rarely used. Later in this narrative, however, we will see how the social cure can work where other social-change strategies have failed.

There is another way the social cure can be useful in a conventionally settled life, although it will always be a harder sell. There is a growing realization, at least in America, that so much of people's dissatisfaction with modern life results from its isolation. In a country that has strayed from its community origins, the evidence today says that Americans, especially young people, are once again looking for community, connection, authenticity. Perhaps it is time, then, that the social cure, complete with burdensome meetings and loss of privacy, might come to be accepted by the overwhelmed and underconnected middle class as a way to solve important personal problems, a way to bring meaning to our personal lives. In fact, this is being done—in places where it might be least expected.

Chapter Seven

A Problem
That Has
No Name

THE CHURCH IN AMERICA IS A NATURAL PLACE TO
look at the transformative power of peers. For hundreds
of years, a person's church was his community. Families
went to neighborhood parishes and churches, worshipping
alongside a hundred or so others. Their parents had worshipped together and they anticipated that their children
would do so as well. People walked to church, and after
services they broke bread with fellow parishioners. From
the time America was first settled in the early 1600s, church
was where families marked their joys and tragedies, and
those who shared their pews were a family's support. If a
family was in trouble, it turned to the church and to fellow
worshippers.

But church has changed; a congregant from a century

ago stepping into a modern American church might not even know what kind of building he had entered. Ten percent of American worshippers attend a megachurch—a Protestant church with at least 2,000 people at weekly services—and megachurches are the fastest-growing churches in America. Indeed, the most influential church in America is a megachurch: Willow Creek Community Church. Its main campus, a brick-and-black-glass complex resembling a junior college, is in South Barrington, Illinois, a far suburb of Chicago. More than 18,000 people attend weekend services here, and every one of them arrives in a car. The parking lot is a vast ocean of minivans and family sedans, and woe to those who forget whether they parked at D3 or E1. Four other Willow Creek campuses, in Chicago and other suburbs, see 6,000 more worshippers each weekend.

Willow Creek is a nondenominational evangelical church. Not only is it unaffiliated with any traditional denomination, it has in effect started its own. Through the Willow Creek Association, a grouping of about 11,000 churches in thirty-five countries, Willow Creek's ideas reach millions of people. Several people I talked to referred to Bill Hybels, Willow Creek's founding pastor, as the "Protestant Pope."

Despite the "community" in its name, there was little community in Willow Creek for the first few decades of its existence. The very idea of the church, its founding mission, was to provide anonymity: to allow those beginning a relationship with God to come pursue it at their own pace and in their own way. The seeker—Willow Creek calls him "Unchurched Harry"—could come to Willow Creek and would not be asked to say anything, sign anything, or sing anything. No one would push him or even approach him. He was free to sit in the back row and talk to God—or not—unmolested by humans. Then he could slip out again.

Willow Creek, then, might seem an odd place to set a story of the social cure. But Willow Creek has changed: it has taken very seriously the idea of community and the way to create it. One area where it has done so is in the structure of the church's small groups. Today, almost every medium-size or large church in America encourages its members to join a small group—usually eight to twelve people who have something in common, such as a recent divorce, a job on the night shift, or an ailing parent. But Willow Creek took it further than other churches. It created conventional small groups, and it did this better than most other churches and bigger than virtually all of them. But then Willow Creek surveyed the congregation about those groups and found that many members said the groups didn't help them grow spiritually.

So Willow Creek scrapped that model and started something more radical. The path to God, Willow Creek announced, winds through your neighbor's dining-room table. It encouraged its members to deepen their relationship with God by forming the closest thing to communes that suburban life permits—a particularly shocking notion in the wealthy and staid exurbs of Chicago. Members were instructed to form groups with eight or ten neighbors, preferably those within walking distance, and make community with those neighbors part of every-day life: meet to talk about God, the Bible, and their own problems, but also eat together, go camping together, jog together, serve those in need together, console each other, and hold each other accountable. It was attempting to reestablish one of the traditional ways churches in America had served their members.

The idea did not succeed for many Willow Creek congregants; it simply asked too much of very busy people steeped in today's suburban culture of autonomy, people for whom interconnectedness is foreign. Willow Creek was attempting to use the social cure to transform the behavior of its membership, which is made up largely of middle-class and some upper-class suburbanites—South Barrington is one of the hundred wealthiest communities in the United States. Their lifestyles and beliefs tend not to fit naturally with the social cure.

Nonetheless, it did reach some. For the groups of Willow Creek wor-shippers who chose to invest the time and take the risks involved, the experiment did succeed. They were rewarded with deeper relationships with Christ and more closely knit communities.

Willow Creek, a huge organization, imposed the social cure from the top. In doing so, it did certain things right—for example, this is a church that measures and evaluates.

Willow Creek also did some things wrong. In switching from

traditional small groups to neighborhood-based groups, with the expectation of a more communal style of living, the church's leadership failed to prepare its membership adequately for the change. It was expecting a revolutionary new behavior but didn't fully explain the hows and whys.

The experiment with neighborhood groups shows the challenges of making a social cure relevant to suburban life. It also shows how the social cure can work, even in the American suburbs, to solve problems beyond addictions (for which the social cure, in the form of AA-style groups, is now the standard treatment). A close look at Willow Creek's experience reveals the mechanics of a social cure run by a large organization: the struggle to lay the foundation, build the new model, refine it, and keep it running.

Willow Creek was also grappling with larger questions: What is it about small groups that brings people closer to God? How does community work to encourage people to meet their goals? How is that community created and sustained? How can it be produced in mass quantities?

MEGACHURCHES ARE NOT JUST an American phenomenon. The Yoido Full Gospel Church in Seoul, South Korea, for example, has more than 800,000 members. Nor are megachurches new. Aimee Semple McPherson, the charismatic forerunner of the televangelists, achieved fame in the 1920s with her Pentecostal radio sermons from the Angelus Temple in Los Angeles. The temple filled its 5,300-seat auditorium three times a day for services that, like Willow Creek's, were theater. At the Angelus Temple, services sometimes featured live camels and motorcycles. Thousands of people lined up to get in.

After World War II, the megachurch movement really grew as part of the American suburban expansion. The massive scale of the suburbs made it possible for a church to have big buildings and big parking lots—ergo, the megachurches. They were made possible by highways and urban sprawl and in turn promote more of both. In 1980, there were fifty Protestant megachurches in America; in 2005, there were 1,200.

Bill Hybels was a college student in 1972, when a minister asked him to lead a Bible-study class for high school students. Hybels was talented and the group became a success. One day, Hybels asked the students if they wanted to invite friends whom they would like to see become Christians. The students told him they'd be embarrassed to bring their friends—the group met in a dingy basement, sang sappy songs, and listened every week to Hybels preach for more than an hour. The students assured Hybels that, as believers, they liked these services, but they told him that their non-Christian friends would not.

Hybels quickly grasped an important lesson—believers and not-yet-believers needed two different things. Deciding that his mission would be to establish a church for people known as seekers—people who didn't go to church—he designed a service specifically for those seekers, with short, punchy sermons on relevant topics, delivered in an attractive setting. A year later, he was preaching to more than a thousand kids, and hundreds of them became Christians. Then Hybels asked them to invite their parents.

Before he designed the "seeker service" for adults, Hybels conducted what would become a Willow Creek hallmark, a market survey. He had his high school students go door to door and ask people if they went to church, and if they didn't, then why not?

People gave several reasons for not going to church: services are boring and predictable, the church is always asking for money, the messages aren't relevant and you walk away feeling guilty and ignorant. Hybels then set out to design his church to remove the barriers to reaching Unchurched Harry. He wanted to make comfortable a person who had had little experience of church or who was left cold by a scripture-and-hymnal church or who felt bullied by a hellfire-and-damnation church. (His focus was Harry, not Mary; Hybels had determined that if he could get the men into church, the women would follow.)

"The idea," said Bill Donahue, a longtime Willow Creek leader, "was that people wanted to be investigative but not accosted. The 'Let me shake your hand, here's a name tag' was too much right away. People felt pressured to give. They didn't like that the church wanted them to start singing. I visited churches and felt unwelcome. It was like being at a family dinner where they tell insider jokes. You feel, 'This isn't for me right now.' If someone had the courage to show up at services with people they didn't know, we weren't going to attack them. Let's meet them where they're at."

Hybels preached his first sermon for adults in 1975, when he was twenty-three, and 125 people attended. Two years later, he had a church of 2,000. In the beginning, Willow Creek's music was secular, with no mention of Jesus; the pastors wore jeans. There were no scripture readings or prayers for the seeker to mumble; his participation consisted of singing a few lines of a chorus and greeting his neighbors. The sanctuary looked like a theater, with no crosses or religious icons of any kind. An acting troupe often performed sketches to introduce the message of the day; the sermon was usually as dramatic as a gripping play. At first, the sanctuary literally *was* a theater—the Willow Creek name comes from Hybels's first location, the Willow Creek movie theater in the Chicago suburb of Palatine.

The same attention to the needs of his target audience helped Hybels build Willow Creek into the pastoral empire it is today. He is always asking: What environment would make the unchurched feel comfortable? What form of message would they feel at ease receiving? What experience do they want? What will help them begin a relationship with God? Hybels hung a poster outside his office with a quotation from management guru Peter Drucker: "What is our business? Who is our customer? What does the customer consider value?"

In the early 1990s, Willow Creek began surveying its congregants periodically to measure what aspects of church they liked and disliked, and their responses were fed back into the design of church programs. When congregants requested the ability to relisten to sermons in their cars, Hybels began taping them and making copies instantly available at the door as people left. Congregants complained that sermons always told them to change their lives but lacked specifics, so Hybels began to conclude his sermons with specifics. Committed Christians complained that the seeker-oriented weekend service was not meaty enough for them, so Willow Creek added a midweek service for "mature believers." Drucker even cited Willow Creek's clear sense of mission and focus on results in his classic 1989 article in the *Harvard Business Review*,

"What Business Can Learn from Nonprofits." Hybels used marketing techniques familiar to the business world but seldom used for the job of gathering souls to Christianity.

At the same time as Willow Creek was becoming famous for its embrace of anonymity, other churches were discovering they needed just the opposite. Organized religion in America was adopting the small group.

The traditional neighborhood church in America had little need of a small group, because it more or less was one. Community was built in. It was small enough that everyone knew each other. As churches grew, however, they needed a way to keep the fellowship and intimacy. The desire for fellowship is the reason many people join a church, even many who are not believers. They want to be with members of their own religious faith or ethnic group, or they just want the sense of rooted-ness that comes from a community built around something as central as religion. For many churchgoers, it's the people who draw them in; God comes afterward.

Fellowship is also important in church because it helps make a person's relationship with God deeper and more meaningful. As has been documented repeatedly by researchers such as Robert Wuthnow, the Princeton University sociologist and scholar of American religion, small groups can serve as a powerful vehicle to help people intensify their faith or change their lives. Nothing makes people holier than being sur-rounded by others also struggling to be holy. Religious small groups, in other words, are a classic social cure.

Religions have always known the value of small-group fellowship. Jesus and his disciples were a small group. Religious Jews need a minyan—a gathering of ten adults—for public prayer. The Talmud says that when ten Jews gather to pray or study the law, the spirit of the Lord dwells among them.

American churches began using small groups in the late 1960s, drawing on that decade's fascination with encounter groups, but the practice became widespread in churches in the 1980s, about the same time that the megachurch movement exploded. Megachurches were in obvious need of human scale and intimacy, but both the megachurch movement and the small-group movement were a product of the same phenomenon: we have left our traditional neighborhoods to move to the suburbs, toward anonymity and the breakdown of traditional support structures of family and clan.

IN THE 1980S, as churches across America began to establish small groups, Willow Creek did so as well. But from the beginning, the church has struggled with them, changing the model every few years. It was not that Willow Creek did worse at small groups than other churches—indeed, by all traditional measures, Willow Creek's small groups have been relatively successful. What set Willow Creek apart is that, unlike other churches, it surveyed its members to see whether they believe church programs are working. And it found that achieving real spiritual growth in a small group is not as easy as people had believed.

"In the beginning here, everyone knew everyone," said Bill Donahue, who until 2010 led small-group programs at the Willow Creek Association, the arm of Willow Creek that serves its member churches. "Then we went from a few hundred people to a few thousand. When we got larger, we realized we also needed to get smaller."

Willow Creek's first foray into small groups used a curriculum the church developed called "Walking with God." Three times a week, members were expected to pray alone, with their Bible and a prayer journal. Then they would meet three or four times a month with the others in their group to talk about what they had read, written, and prayed.

It was a one-size-fits-all model, geared to already-believing Christians who were willing to make a long-term commitment, but many didn't want or need that—some were still seeking, and even many committed Christians were not ready to sign up for a long course of study. Lots of people started the curriculum, but almost as many stopped. "The issue we were wrestling with was the size of Willow, and how do you get connected," said Russ Robinson, who worked on small groups at Willow Creek and has left Willow Creek periodically to pastor his own church. "The front door was working well. But the back door was also working well—too well."

In 1992, Willow Creek's management began to completely restructure the church program around the concept of small groups. It went from being a church *with* small groups to a church *of* small groups. "We believe that life-change happens best in small groups," says the church's *Participating Membership Manual* of 1995. By 1997, every area of the ministry was built around a small-group structure. There were small groups for singles or alcoholics but also for motorcycle riders, O'Hare-based airline pilots with erratic schedules, people who wanted to do carpentry work, even second-graders. People who managed traffic in Willow Creek's parking lot during weekend services had their own small group, gathering twenty minutes before work began to share prayer requests. A small group of vacuum-cleaner repairmen met to talk, study the Bible, and pray together before getting to work fixing Willow Creek's dozens of vacuum cleaners. A small group of hairdressers would have their meetings before cutting and styling the hair of homeless women.

The main point of connection was affinity: profession, hobby, marital status, struggle with a particular issue, or desire to help with a certain type of service project. "A number of guys like to bang a hammer," said Donahue. "They're not going to show up to talk about feelings, but if you say you're going to build stuff for Habitat, they're there in a moment. When you pause for breaks, you build in a component of communal life. People will stay around for a half hour afterward to have coffee and read a devotional. If you give people a taste of genuine community they want more."

At one point, said Russ Robinson, there were more people in Willow's small groups than the 21,000 who at that time attended services on the weekend—not everyone goes to services every weekend. So many people wanted to get into a small group that there was a waiting list of two months—Willow Creek didn't have enough trained leaders.

It certainly appeared that small groups were a big success at Willow Creek. Then, in 2004, the church did something that churches rarely do but that is absolutely crucial to the effectiveness of the social cure: it asked for the congregation's view. Even though it had been doing basic congregational surveys for twelve years, now it carried out a more in-depth survey to determine how different parts of Willow Creek affected members' spiritual development.

The results, Bill Hybels wrote, were "almost unbearable."

The survey was not just about small groups, but since Willow had put so much effort into its small-group programs, the congregation's response on this issue was particularly disheartening. The church also conducted a separate survey of more than 200 leaders of small groups. While many people were satisfied with the church and its small groups, about a third of the parishioners described themselves as spiritually "stalled" or "dissatisfied" with the role of the church in their spiritual growth; the higher the level of their engagement with the church, the less satisfied they were with it. The people least happy with the church were the ones at the most mature stage of the spiritual journey—the church's most active and valuable members. Many said that the church lacked depth and was not helping them grow spiritually. A large percentage of small-group leaders reported that their groups had never seen a significant conflict among members—a sign that the groups weren't getting below the surface. A third of the leaders said that they did not ask other group members to pray for them about significant personal issues and didn't encourage their members to, either—another sign of superficial relationships. Willow Creek concluded: "It is clear the current state of affairs is a long way from the ideal that we seek. . . . We have to admit that we have sometimes become overly concerned with just getting people into groups of any kind while paying not enough attention to how those groups were supporting the spiritual growth of their members."

Some organizational leaders might have put the surveys in a drawer and locked it. Hybels, characteristically, did not. He called the results "the wake-up call of my adult life . . . one of the hardest things I've ever had to digest as a leader." But being Bill Hybels, he figured out a way to turn the bad news to good employ. He publicized the survey results and used them to overhaul Willow Creek's programs. After that, Willow Creek branded the study, calling it "Reveal," and proceeded to conduct the same survey in other Willow Creek Association churches: first six, then twenty-three, then 200, then 1,000. Since then, it has also aggressively marketed Reveal-related videos, conferences, and books (such as *Focus: The Top Ten Things People Want and Need from You and Your Church*). The products are sold to leaders of other churches as tools to move their churches "from good to great." Few organizations have ever put dismaying information to better use.

DOUG YONAMINE DID NOT need a survey to tell him that Willow Creek's small groups were not satisfying the spiritual needs of the church's mature believers. He knew that from his own experience. On the scale of commitment to Christianity, Doug was near the top. He grew up worshipping with his family at a Baptist church and then at a small ethnic-Japanese church in Chicago. When he was eleven, Doug said, "I discovered who Christ was, and asked him to be Lord of my life."

After college, he was living in Evanston. When he was twenty-three, in 1987, he attended a weekend service at Willow Creek. "I hated it," he said. "I grew up in a church of 125, and church just wasn't supposed to be that large. The service wasn't very participatory. There wasn't a lot of singing or scripture reading. Their understanding of the seeker was that the seeker didn't connect with scripture. I felt it wasn't much of a worship service."

He tried the midweek service for committed believers and found it a better fit, so Doug settled in to Willow Creek. He found the services engaging and challenging, but he lacked meaningful friendships at Willow Creek. So in 1992, he decided to give priority to building relationships around the church. He struggled with what this would mean for his friends who didn't attend the church. "I thought, 'What am I going to do when old friends call me up?'" How was he going to tell them gently that he didn't have as much time to spend with them?

It turned out not to be an issue—not one of his friends called him. "I was single and not dating; I had no close friends. I realized that I was the planner and organizer," he said.

Willow Creek then had a small-group program for singles called Prime Time, so Doug signed up. His group consisted of five men from various parts of the Chicago area. It met every other week; Doug drove forty-five minutes to get there. The group used a formal small-group study guide for curriculum or studied a particular book of the Bible. When that group ended after a few months, he joined another one like it.

"People talked about their lives, but I don't recall there being much depth in terms of taking risks and sharing things we were struggling with," he said. "I'm just as guilty. I'd put on my game face. I felt like the session was to learn more about the Bible, which wasn't a bad thing. But we weren't really connecting." Doug did not feel pushed or challenged by his group; he felt it didn't address the real spiritual issues with which each man struggled.

After the groups ended, so did his relationship with the men in it. "I don't remember successfully getting into the rhythm of meeting outside our formal meetings, so once it ended, no one made the effort," he said. "Once I ran into the leader of my small group. I told him I thought he had gone to California. He said, 'No, I'm here.'"

Doug ran up against the inherent limitations of the standard small group. "If you meet every two weeks, you spend time catching up," said Ryan Boldt, the Willow Creek area pastor for the region that includes Algonquin, where Doug lives now. "You can spend the whole time on that, or if one person has a problem, you can work on that the whole time. Then next time you catch up again. The church had groups for whatever you like to do. But a lot of the groups tended not to last. The relationships didn't last. You have to drive to Schaumburg. If you have kids, you have to get a babysitter. No one gets to know you at a super-deep level. Many of these groups never got to the level of 'let's be honest, we all have problems.'"

Small groups had become Willow Creek's main mechanism for moving people on their spiritual journey, but the congregational survey of 2004 uncovered what Doug Yonamine already knew—they didn't go deep enough to produce transformation. It was hard to find transformation in a small group made up of strangers you would see twice a month—and that was if you could persuade yourself to get into the car to go to the meeting.

"Some small groups merely provide occasions for individuals to focus on themselves in the presence of others," wrote Princeton's Robert Wuthnow in *Sharing the Journey*, a 1994 study of support groups and community in America. "The social contract binding members together asserts only the weakest of obligations. Come if you have time. Talk if you feel like it. Respect everyone's opinion. Never criticize. Leave quietly if you become dissatisfied. Families would never survive by following these operating norms. Close-knit communities in the past did not, either."

Buried in Willow Creek's 2004 bad-news congregational survey lay clues to a possible solution. Willow Creek had asked people to provide specifics about what they felt was useful about their groups and what had failed. Three of the main things that produced satisfaction were genuine friendships, shared experiences of helping others, and personal accountability. Respondents consistently said their groups were too structured. The church's analysis of the answers noted that people needed to go through often painful self-examination and deep grieving, and needed a supportive and non-shaming environment to accomplish this. They needed less curriculum and more community—a community that would really listen, accept them, and walk with them through their troubles. But this analysis circled back to the same question: How do you build that depth of community in six hours a month?

WILLOW CREEK FOUND AN ANSWER, one that completely upended its small-group structure and replaced it with something radically new. The answer was: You don't. It came from Randy Frazee, a pastor at Pantego Bible Church, perched on the highway in Arlington, Texas, between Dallas and Fort Worth. Frazee is a slightly built man with hip glasses and thinning blond hair. He had some ideas on this question—ideas he has described in two books, *The Connecting Church* and *Making Room for Life*. Bill Donahue had gone to seminary with Frazee in the 1980s, but Frazee's introduction to the rest of the Willow Creek staff came at a Willow Creek Association conference on small-group leadership in 2004. A pastor who was supposed to speak at the conference had had a heart attack and couldn't make it. Donahue recommended asking

Frazee, who was already coming, to speak in his place. His presentation drew thunderous applause, and shortly afterward Willow Creek invited him to move to Illinois.

Frazee's idea, the subject of his talk, was that proximity is community. If your small group is made up of the people next door, you can plan meetings with them that don't require long drives, or any drives. You don't need to get a babysitter, because you can bring your children to those meetings—all the kids are probably already friends. Your neighbors see you in various different settings. They know your family. You run into them at school and Brownies and the grocery store and the gym. That's a small group that produces community, which in turn produces transformation.

The idea is several thousand years old, but it has fallen out of favor in the fractured, high-tech, multitasked modern world. Frazee preached it with creativity and determination. He called it "doing life together." When he spoke about it at conferences, he was often viewed as a curiosity. "The amazing two-headed pastor!" he joked. But his ideas intrigued Willow Creek. The church's analysis of its small-group problems said this: "People who live closer in proximity with a transformational community are far more likely to be influenced by it. Geography matters because it affords participants many more opportunities to be in relationship with one another."

The problem, said Gene Appel, the lead pastor at Willow Creek's main church, was that Willow Creek had so many church activities that people didn't have time to carry out the most basic of Jesus's instructions: Love thy neighbor.

Bill Hybels, who has the money and clout to do these things, hired Frazee away from Pantego in 2005. Initially Frazee said no—"After all, I've talked so violently against mobility." But how could he pass up the chance to carry out his ideas about doing life together at the most influential church in America? So Willow Creek, formerly a temple of anonymity, was suddenly pushing its membership into a kind of community seldom seen in the American suburbs.

Randy Frazee's unlikely mutiny against the isolation of suburban life began at Pantego. Like all pastors of big churches, when he arrived at

Pantego in 1990, he knew the church needed small groups. Frazee made small-group membership a requirement for Pantego's staff—everyone had to be in one. He and his wife, Rozanne, formed their small group, as Frazee described it, "on the same concept as a sandlot team. You pick captains based on strength. Boys line up from the strongest to the mutt. And you pick the strongest guys for your team. You choose going from strongest to weakest—strongest being people like us, people you want to be around. It was the model for most American church small groups.

"I was the senior minister, the alpha dog, so I had my pick of the litter. We had three couples, all genetically well put-together physically and financially. I called it the mother of all small groups. The wealth, beauty, and business success was the best we could put together." The group met every other Friday night.

Members chose a book, read a few chapters and discussed them, and talked about a few things going on in their lives. Occasionally the members skipped discussing the book and went out to dinner instead.

"It was a miserable experience," Frazee said. "Not because of the people—it was because we were doing meetings together and not doing life. But our lives weren't structured to make more of it. Life can't be reduced to every other Friday. With your family, you do life together— it's constant. But a church-sponsored small group competes with many activities—the lake home, season tickets to sporting events. The more money you have, the more fragmentation you can purchase."

He said that the others in the group were more satisfied with it than he was. "They'd never been in another group, and it was a feather in their cap to be with the senior minister. It helped them. It was better than nothing." Soon, however, he decided there was something much better.

While the small groups were beginning, a new neighbor moved in two doors away from the Frazees. His name was Tom, and he was a retired policeman from Minnesota starting a new career in sales. He and his wife, Bonnie, an antiques dealer, had two children a little older than the Frazees' kids. "He worked out of his home and was very gregarious," Frazee said. "They introduced us to the couple across the street, the Rosettis—we were so busy at the church that we didn't know our neighbors. Tom didn't go to church. He wasn't against Christ, but Christ didn't make the short list. Because he worked out of his house, he was not overwhelmed with commuting and meetings in his office. I'd come home from work and he'd be hanging out two doors down. We began to share tools and had millions of little encounters. It snuck up on us—we found ourselves enjoying this relationship by accident."

One night during football season, a couple in the Frazees' small group canceled the Friday-night meeting because they had football tickets. "That's fantastic," Frazee said to Rozanne. "I'm exhausted. Let's call Tom and Bonnie and see if they can come over." They arrived in sweatpants.

Then, one Saturday morning after mowing the lawn, Frazee went into his house for a glass of water, only to find Tom sitting in the family room reading the newspaper—uninvited. Frazee's first thought was, "Uh, oh, I'm not going to get my chores done." It must have been visible to Tom, who suggested that Frazee go back outside and keep mowing the lawn. Frazee asked if Tom wanted something to drink. "I've already made a pot of coffee in your kitchen," Tom replied. "Well, that's invasive," Frazee thought, as he was walking out of the garage. At the same time, he realized he didn't really mind that Tom was sitting and reading his newspaper.

The "aha!" moment came on a summer Friday night. In the Frazees' neighborhood, people were grilling in their front yards; elderly people were sitting on the lawns watching the kids play kickball. But it was Friday night, time to go to small group. Frazee drove to get the babysitter and went to the bank for some cash. He and Rozanne pulled out of their driveway, waving to the neighbors.

"I don't want to go," Rozanne said.

"I know," said Frazee, "but we can't not go. The whole staff is going. I made them sign this covenant."

Then Rozanne said, "You're the senior pastor. You can change the rules. Why don't you change what it means to be in a small group? What if you allowed the neighborhood to count?"

She was right, thought Frazee. "These were the kinds of relationships I was looking for," he said.

Soon after, Pantego had a retreat day for the church's staff, held at the vacation house of one of the members of Frazee's small group. From one side of the pool table, a staff member confessed she didn't like her small group. "But we can't quit," she said. "Randy's very serious."

"Once that was airborne, it took over like the black plague," said Frazee. Other staff members said that they, too, were not satisfied. After listening to his staff, Frazee also confessed that he, too, was just going through the motions.

The small group he was in, Frazee said, was not community. It was just offering a place for people to talk about their own spiritual journeys in the presence of other people, as Wuthnow had said. There was no social contract. In *The Connecting Church*, Frazee explores five characteristics that make up a real community: A community has the authority to hold members accountable; it has a shared understanding of beliefs and practices; it has traditions, standards, and a common mission. Frazee felt that his small group lacked most of those characteristics.

So at the end of the 1990s, Pantego redrew its small groups, creating them along neighborhood lines, attempting to create real community. Frazee's relationship with Tom and Bonnie and the Rosettis was the starting point, but that relationship was missing something rather important for a church: God. "Barbecue is not enough," Frazee said. "I don't think my relationship with Tom and Bonnie and the Rosettis was church. The church expresses itself where two or more people are gathered together 'in my name.' But instead of sticking them in the basement of the church, you put them out in the middle where they are needed. Instead of Tom coming to the church, we took the church to Tom."

Pantego still organizes almost all its small groups around neighborhoods and is still enthusiastic about proximity-based groups. Small groups there are made up of five to seven families who live within a quarter-mile or a half-mile of each other. Their formal meeting is once a week for dinner, but they also see each other at the grocery store, soccer matches, and school activities. There is no set curriculum: groups read books together but also gather to serve food to the poor or see a play featuring the child of one of the group's families.

David Daniels, who took over as senior pastor when Frazee went to

Willow Creek, came to the idea of neighborhood groups as an outsider but was quickly persuaded. "It just makes logical sense that proximity to one another facilitates spiritual growth," he said. "There is genuine connection. I can say anecdotally people are better off and they would say that they're better people for it."

One factor that has been key, he said, was time. Every year has brought progress in understanding and refining how the small groups work. "We're almost ten years in and we're starting to sand down some of the corners and figure out how this works in reality. But I don't know if we'll ever arrive."

Frazee argues that neighborhood-based groups not only are effective, they are true to the Bible. "The idea that I'm going to get on my camel and go to Bethany out of Jerusalem, which is not that far, to be in a small group, was just a foreign idea," he has said. "That's why the scripture doesn't talk about place-based community. Because it's really only been within the last 100 years that anybody's experienced anything but place-based communities. Our goals mirror the first 300 years of the church."

Randy Frazee is mild-mannered, conservative in habits. Ohio-born and transplanted to Texas, he is an unlikely person to be confused with Jane Jacobs, the defender of the raucous urban jumble. He voted for John McCain in 2008, but he acknowledges that his interest in community has brought him into territory largely populated by liberals. In his books and speeches, his critique of the individualism of American suburban life is radical indeed. "A modern-day prison," he labeled the suburbs in one of his books. "The suburbs are segregated so I don't have to see poverty," he said. "The isolation of American culture is showing, and the outcome is pandemic dysfunction. Adolescents have never been better off financially, but never been worse off emotionally. The solution is not medicine, but authoritative community."

Frazee cites the affection and nostalgia many people have for the deep community they experienced in their college years. Researchers at the Massachusetts Institute of Technology, he said, did a study about how friendships form. "The hypothesis was that friendships are based on affinity, but it ended up that proximity was more important—your next door neighbor is your best friend. But people don't know that proximity is meaningful."

He thinks the megachurch is unsustainable. "Build a large church on the freeway and they will come—this era seems to be coming to an end," he said. "People are affected by rising gas prices. Town centers are being built. We have to change to a way of life that values wasting time on the front porch, rather than putting your kids in yet another adult-driven activity across town. We're down to a level where the average person has only one person to share things with."

As a pastor, Frazee comes to his critique of American suburban life through the path of Christianity and the difficulty of attempting spiritual growth without community. Yet in attacking suburban anomie he has diagnosed a syndrome that afflicts many Americans, religious or not, and before returning to the subject of Willow Creek, it is useful to understand it. The syndrome has been present for several decades, but only now is the realization dawning on dissatisfied suburbanites that their life of majestic isolation—so much a part of American cultural aspiration—is the very reason for their unhappiness.

IN 1963, BETTY FRIEDAN published *The Feminine Mystique*, describing the gnawing despair many stay-at-home women felt—and didn't know why they felt, and felt guilty for feeling. Focusing mainly on educated white women in the suburbs, the book threw a grenade at the pervasive post–World War II belief that women could find fulfillment solely by taking care of husband and children. It ignited the American feminist movement.

Randy Frazee's Suburban Mystique is aimed at another part of the 1950s American dream: the big house in the suburbs with the two-car garage and enclosed backyard where the kids can play. This idea has outlasted the feminine mystique and remains the way many Americans aspire to live. We are too rich, too busy, too private, and we live too far apart, to have community in our lives. We think we are so evolved that we don't need people anymore.

From its founding, America was a society built on associations and civic groups, which is why Alexis de Tocqueville had very high hopes for the American political system. But we have grown very poor at embracing community. Two landmark books marshal the arguments. The general critique is the 1985 study *Habits of the Heart: Individualism and Commitment in American Life*, written by a group of sociologists led by Berkeley professor Robert N. Bellah. The researchers asked Americans about their work and private lives, where they found meaning in their lives, and why they lived the way they did. It examined how they described their lives and how they related to their communities, religions, cultures, and traditions. The book laments that modern life has pushed Americans (or at least the group of white, middle-class Americans the sociologists studied) out of the community and moral structure of the past and into individualism, and it proposes a new model of American life based on community.

The second book is *Bowling Alone: The Collapse and Revival of American Community*, published in 2000 by Robert Putnam, professor of public policy at Harvard. *Bowling Alone* is a more direct and evidence-based inquiry into American habits of associating with others. Putnam has mined dozens of surveys and studies of every imaginable kind of civic association to find that, from playing cards to visiting neighbors to donating blood to attending town meetings to voting, Americans since roughly the mid-1970s have joined with others less than they used to.

Putnam blames the decline of community on four different factors. One is new time pressures, especially those on two-career families. It is no longer possible for most American families to survive on the income from one job, and many people now work hours much longer than nine-to-five. A second factor is suburbanization, which brings isolation in itself, and long commutes that reduce the time people can devote even to those they *want* to see. Then there is the rise of television, a form of entertainment that does not require human contact and swallows more than four hours a day of the average American's time. The fourth factor is generational change, which Putnam believes is especially important. The generation marked by World War II was uniquely community-minded—probably because of the collective sacrifice demanded by the war. As these Americans die off or retire from community life, they are being replaced by generations that are much less inclined to join groups. As for the Internet, Putnam says it is too early to predict its effects—but he is convinced that it is not responsible for the turn inward that he reports. "Voting, giving, trusting, meeting, visiting and so on had all begun to decline while Bill Gates was still in grade school," he writes.

To confirm Americans' reluctance to join groups, I don't need to look farther than my own life. I have three young girls and a job. I love the *idea* of joining groups (obviously). I have structured my life so there are a lot of people in it—my husband and I chose our neighborhood, on Manhattan's Lower East Side, because close friends live here. We see them frequently and I love the small-town feel of the neighborhood, love walking everywhere and seeing familiar faces at the kids' playgrounds and on the street. My apartment is often crammed with my daughters' friends.

Nonetheless, I belong to very few groups. Off and on, I sing in a Yiddish chorus that rehearses weekly; it's always a struggle to find the time to go. I volunteer at my girls' public elementary school, but probably not as much as a parent with three kids there should volunteer. When I am invited to join a group, my first thought is to say, "Yes." My second thought is to ask, "When do we meet? Between 5 and 6 in the morning?" When I get mad about something, I don't volunteer; I give money so a professional can change the world on my behalf. I live in a city and work at home, so I don't spend time commuting. Except for sometimes catching the last inning of the day's Mets game after the girls are in bed, I don't watch TV. If anyone should belong to a lot of groups, I should. Yet I don't.

Like most people I know, I don't have time. When we have problems, we look for solutions that require the least commitment of time. To help us remember to take our medicines, we turn to the beeping pillbox—*accompagnateurs* are for rural Haiti. When we decide to lose weight, we buy a treadmill or a new diet book—we tend not to join groups or commit to going to meetings. If we want to work for social change, we are not out there protesting in person. Even when we "join" an environmental or human-rights or other group, that joining consists mainly of writing a check. In America, our political campaigns center on raising money and buying advertising, not knocking on doors and having face-to-face conversations, although the Obama presidential campaign did mark a return to an earlier era of volunteering.

Lester Salamon, director of the Center for Civil Society Studies at Johns Hopkins University and an expert on the nonprofit sector, said that even if the form has changed, Americans are just as involved in public life as before. Yes, he agreed, the traditional organizations such as labor unions, the Girl Scouts, and Rotary Clubs are declining in membership, but that doesn't mean that Americans aren't interested in solving community problems. "We've been through an amazing revolution of citizen engagement," he said. "The women's movement, consumer movement, environmental movement, antiwar movement—they were popular movements, and many of them have grown into significant, enduring institutions. They aren't now bringing people out onto the street, but people are engaged through e-mail, letter-writing to congress."

He argued that the Internet has fostered community, "even if people don't get together to go bowling every other week. I'm in five or ten different networks—I've got a network of colleagues in forty different countries."

The generation that has grown up with the Internet also has grown up with a democratized view of civic life. On the Internet, everyone can be an expert—the blogger in her kitchen can give her opinion, and for some readers it will carry weight equal to that of Thomas Friedman. The Internet is the most bottom-up, open, transparent, and participatory form of communication ever designed. It turns the user from object into subject. People who have grown up with the Internet become accustomed to the idea that they are talkers and writers, not just listeners and readers.

One consequence of this shift in self-image is that these empowered people are striking out to create their own groups. Americans may not be eager to join associations, but one subgroup of Americans has grown—those who start them. The number of independent-sector groups has more than doubled since the mid-1980s, and the nonprofit sector is growing at a faster rate than the business sector.

The problem remains that while writing a check or being part of an Internet group may be effective ways to produce social change, they do not satisfy the basic human hunger for community that we have so widely repressed since the mid-twentieth century. Compared to a genuine organization with real humans, they are not enough.

What makes people happy? Researchers have studied the issue, polling people worldwide on the question of how happy they are—from villagers in Bangladesh to burghers in Scarsdale. The answers are surprising. Most people on the planet report that they are reasonably happy—even the very poor. As long as people have enough to eat and basic physical security, their income level does not directly correlate with happiness. From 1947 to 1970, per-capita income in the United States tripled but levels of happiness stayed about the same. Lottery winners are no happier than people who are confined to wheelchairs after an accident, and the lottery winners take less pleasure than the accident victims in the events of their daily lives. A lot of what we aspire to because we think it will increase our happiness has no such effect.

What does increase people's happiness, readers of this book will not be surprised to learn, is joining a club. Literally: joining a group that meets once a month will increase your happiness as much as doubling your income. Marriage is helpful—a good marriage is much, much more important to happiness than professional success. In terms of daily life, a British study concluded that people find the greatest happiness in socializing after work, having dinner, and especially having sex. If you want to decrease your happiness, arrange your life so you have a long commute. A study in Germany found that the longer the commute, the lower people's satisfaction with life. The short answer to the question of what makes people happy is this: other people.

There is considerable evidence that the trend toward isolation is slowing. The polling organization Harris Interactive has been doing periodic surveys of new college graduates, research commissioned by the insurance company Northwestern Mutual. The study supervisor, Harlan Wahrman, said the results show it is a "We Generation, not a Me Generation." People in their early twenties are entrepreneurial; they don't want to work for big corporations. They consider face-to-face time with family and friends sacrosanct, and many say they get together with friends or family every day. They list their most important job requirements as finding work that helps others, allows them to impact their world, surrounds them with idealistic and committed coworkers, and requires creativity. And nearly three-fourths say that how they spend their time is more important than how much money they make.

Even older people may be starting to structure their lives to give more emphasis to community. In the 1950s, the era of the great American suburban explosion, the middle class's desire to escape city life was enabled by government policy—the building of highways, the tax deduction for mortgage interest that encourages home ownership, tax policies that shield drivers from the real economic and environmental costs of their commute, government spending on schools and sewers, tolerance of redlining that excluded people who looked different, and suburban zoning that limited population density, separated housing from commercial areas and, in some places, effectively ensured there was no room for the poor. Although most of those policies are still in place, today there is a backlash against the isolation of modern life, especially suburban life. People are less likely to choose to conduct their lives from car to garage to fenced-in backyard, more likely to look for authenticity and connection.

One new trend, prominent since the early 1990s but only taking off now, is the construction or retrofitting of suburbs to make them more like small towns, with walkable neighborhoods, parks, a mix of apartments and houses, stores near dwellings and access to mass transit. These are suburbs where you can take the train into the city to work and on the weekends can walk to stores, restaurants, and parks: suburbs where you may not even need a car. "It's the opposite of the default setting for development from 1950 on," said Rob Steuteville, the editor and publisher of a magazine called *New Urban News*. This kind of design—what architects call New Urbanism and policy planners call Smart Growth—has become the focus of an Obama administration project to promote environmental-friendly and livable communities.

Smart Growth is much more than just a government push—these communities increasingly are where people *want* to live. Home prices have been dropping fastest in the sprawling exurbs, with their long commutes, and have dropped least in urban areas and in Smart Growth suburbs with town centers. A 2010 study by the U.S. Environmental Protection Agency showed that new housing is increasingly being built in cities, not in suburbs. Living downtown used to be for poor people; now it is more expensive than the suburbs. And the suburbs are changing—the places that are drawing premiums are suburbs that feel like small cities. People will pay from 40 percent to 200 percent more per square foot to live in a walkable place than one accessible only by car.

Part of the reason for the antisprawl revolution is the high price of oil—people want to get to work by train or have shorter commutes, and they can't afford to heat big houses. Another reason is changing family patterns. Americans are marrying later and having fewer children. In 2010, 75 percent of American households did not have school-age children; the percentage has been rising. Having no kids in school removes the main reason people leave cities.

These trends have now meshed with the growing awareness that we are happier when we see other people. The aversion to the traditional sprawling suburb is especially pronounced among young people today, but home buyers in general are looking for an alternative to isolation. "The market is rewarding walkable, compact, mixed-use suburbs vs. driving suburbs," said Ed McMahon, senior resident fellow in sustainable development and environmental policy at the Urban Land Institute in Washington, a membership organization of builders and developers. "These are the suburbs that offer community."

One such New Urban town is Orenco Station, a walkable town-style suburb of Portland, Oregon. Sociologists from Portland's Lewis and Clark College surveyed the town's residents, along with residents of two downtown Portland neighborhoods and a traditional suburb. They asked such questions as whether their neighbors were friendly and whether they belonged to any groups. The researchers found that Orenco Station residents walk to errands more and use mass transit more than the others. Residents there also think their neighbors are friendlier and are twice as likely to belong to a group as residents of the other three places. And while the groups that residents join elsewhere are Neighborhood Watch or homeowners associations—groups concerned with safety or property issues—in Orenco Station people belong to book clubs and dinner groups and go to block parties. If the evidence from the real estate market is to be believed, this kind of community— one with people in it—is increasingly the new American dream.

WILLOW CREEK COMMUNITY CHURCH had been constructed for the seeker who preferred to begin a relationship with Christ unmolested and in privacy—community was considered an intrusion, something that could drive the seeker away. Yet, by the middle of the first decade of the twenty-first century, the national trend was headed firmly in the other direction, toward community. Randy Frazee's arrival in 2005 was a sign that Willow Creek not only had joined that movement, it was preparing to lead it.

People knew something was changing at Willow Creek when the church canceled its Christmas services in 2005. In their place, Willow Creek gave its members DVDs and instructed them to have Christmas at home, invite the neighbors, and watch the DVD together. It was in part a way to give the church's staff and volunteers a break. But it was also the beginning of an idea that would soon come to govern Willow Creek's small groups: instead of bringing your neighbors to Christ, bring Christ to your neighbors.

The affinity-based small groups were not dissolved, but in 2006 Willow Creek stopped providing the administrative structure for them. Instead, Frazee redirected the church's army of small-group staff and group leaders toward building neighborhood-based groups. People were invited to host a Table group—so named because it was usually structured around a potluck dinner—with other members of Willow Creek, ideally those who lived within a two-block radius.

Willow Creek was big enough to have Table groups in virtually every neighborhood of Chicago's northwest suburbs. At the regional meetings of Willow Creek worshippers interested in Table groups, people were shocked to learn that someone to their left whom they had never met lived two doors away. Others recognized their neighbors but had never realized that they attended the same church.

For most of Willow Creek's leadership, the change from affinity-based to place-based small groups was a way to create closer community. Moving to neighborhood-based groups was aimed in part at overcoming two major reasons for missed meetings and superficial interaction: the long drive and the need for a babysitter. At Table meetings, children were welcome as part of the community. A teenager could be assigned to run compatible programs in a downstairs den.

The change would also facilitate the church's key mission, which was evangelization of Unchurched Harry. It was designed to allow worshippers to introduce church to their neighbors without dragging them to a Willow Creek campus. Peter J. Mundey, a Notre Dame sociology student who wrote his master's thesis about Willow Creek's small groups, notes that for Hybels, " 'Christ-centered' people living in neighborhoods are better ambassadors for Christianity than a centralized worship service. . . . [Willow Creek was] dispensing thousands of evangelistic agents throughout the neighborhoods of Chicagoland." Peter Drucker might have considered it the equivalent of a business hiring a force of salespeople to expand into new markets.

To Randy Frazee, this was a change with radical implications. He envisioned that Table groups would mark a dramatic shift in the role of the church in its members' lives. "The idea at Willow Creek has always been to put on a spectacular show for everyone gathered here, on campus," Frazee said. What he wanted was different. "Instead of coming to the church, you are invited to *be* the church," he said. "You'll come here on Sunday and get equipped and inspired to be the church in your neighborhood. You'll come here with stories about how you helped the widow with Alzheimer's, joining up with a couple of other Christ-followers.

"What we're looking for is the starfish, not the spider," said Frazee. "With a spider, you kill it by cutting off its head. But the starfish has no central brain. Each finger contains the whole idea." People in each Table group would determine the purpose and activities of their group. There would be no set curriculum, no required reading. The groups

themselves could decide whether to do service projects in their neighborhood, study a particular book or Bible chapter, or simply get together
to eat and talk about their lives and their relationship with God.

Doug and Jen Yonamine were part of Table groups even before they
were called Table groups. After his second men's small group ended,
Doug didn't go back to formal small groups at Willow Creek. He liked
playing volleyball, however, so he began to play in Willow Creek's gym.
He felt a chemistry with two other men there, and he asked them to
form a group for Bible study and going to church together. They went to
the midweek services, joined by a group of women, and afterward they
would stay around, talking. "We used to close down the auditorium,"
he said. "We'd be the group sitting there while they were flicking the
lights." They also got together twice a month—once for a study session
and once just to socialize.

One of the women in the group became his wife. Jen Tweedie grew
up Presbyterian in upstate New York, attended college in Illinois, and
came to Willow Creek with a high school friend. She was struck by
what she called "a kindness" about the place. "What drew me in was
how they treated each other," she said. Doug and Jen married in 1995.
Doug continued to lead the group for three more years before deciding
that he was spending too much time and energy on it and needed time
off. They left the group right before Jen became pregnant with their
first child. By 2003, they had three children. Doug was working at the
Willow Creek Association and Jen was an at-home mother. They lived
in Algonquin, a twenty-minute drive farther out from Chicago than
Willow Creek.

Jen shared Doug's desire for connection. Although they had three
children under six, they felt the need for more community. Both of them
instinctively felt that a group of neighbors would be a more meaningful relationship than a traditional small group. In February 2004, they
invited ten Algonquin families who had kids in kindergarten to their
house for dessert. No one showed up. Then they tried again, inviting
neighbors to a cookout. Still, nobody came. "It would be hard on anybody," Doug said. "It was especially hard on my wife."

Nevertheless, they kept trying. They hosted a dinner for a few other

Willow Creek families who lived in Algonquin and the neighboring suburb of Crystal Lake. This time, their house was full. "We should have called it dinner for the kids," said Doug. "It was ten adults and fifteen kids under five." But even the fifteen-minute drive between the two towns was too much for some families. "We realized we needed much closer proximity," said Doug, "but that wasn't the way Willow Creek was organized."

In the spring of 2004, the Yonamines read in the church bulletin that Willow Creek was going to try neighborhood groups. A mailing went out to Algonquin families, and twenty-five people showed up at a meeting at the Algonquin Public Library. A good start, but it didn't go anywhere. "The idea was to cast a vision for connecting with neighbors and help people meet each other, and see what happens from there," said Doug. Attendees were supposed to take that idea and go out and invite their neighbors into small groups, but few did. "We could get people to come once, but we couldn't get people to come back," Doug said. "It seemed like there was a yearning there. But it didn't happen. People didn't have a clear path of where this would lead to. There has to be some semblance of a framework—people just didn't know how to live that way, and we didn't do enough to get momentum going."

It was an early warning of problems ahead.

The next year, Frazee arrived at Willow Creek, and the Table groups debuted in June 2006. Thousands of people went to Table groups in their neighborhoods—in part because of Willow Creek's decision to cancel the midweek service and hold the pilot on that night. The church made it easy for people to take the first step—a key social-cure tactic. In October 2006, the groups began in earnest. Willow Creek had hoped 5,000 people would sign up, but the numbers exceeded the leadership's expectations. By December, 8,000 people were attending Table groups. Senior pastor Greg Hawkins told an interviewer that year that Willow Creek was changing the seventh core value in its mission statement. The value had read, "We believe that life-change happens best in small groups." Willow Creek was now replacing "small groups" with "community."

As the Yonamines found, however, the idea was hard to sustain. Even though thousands of Willow Creek members joined Table groups, a lot of them dropped out, disillusioned. The church started out with 700 Table groups—two years later, there were only 200. "I've been doing groups for thirty years," said a man who wished to be identified only by where he lives—Northbrook, a suburb about twenty miles east of Willow Creek—"and this is the first group that didn't work for me. There were so few people who wanted to come that we ended up merging three groups into one—and we still had only eight people at most."

Table groups did not function for many Willow Creek members for various reasons. They are important to understand, as they illustrate some of the challenges in making the social cure work, and the necessity of meticulous attention to training and supporting leaders and preparing participants.

Perhaps most important, Willow Creek had not provided enough groundwork for the switch to Table groups. The church had not fully explained to people why the shift was occurring, why it was biblically justifiable, how it would help them. Some people in the traditional affinity groups, especially the leaders, felt that they had been undercut very suddenly. Small-group members that felt they were simply told that if they were team players, they would enfold their affinity-based groups into new, proximity-based ones. "We felt a little bit that it was imposed on us," said Mr. Northbrook. "It was communicated in a little bit of a dictatorial way." Even if group members were dissatisfied with the shallowness of their traditional small groups—and many were—they were comfortable with that style and had an investment in it.

Nor had the church paid enough attention to training people in the considerable skills necessary for Table-group success. "It was a bunch of branches without a tree," said Bill Donahue. Leading a Table group— a free-form group dedicated to the mysterious concept of "being" the church—was a lot harder and more confusing than conducting a traditional small group. "There is something attractive for a Christian about the concept of 'being the church'—being the light wherever you go," Mr. Northbrook said, "but it requires a leader in each small group to cast a vision. You are sort of starting a bunch of mini-churches, and I don't think the average person has that kind of gift set. You've got to get your neighbors to say, 'Yeah, we'd rather come to your house than do something with our friends.' " In addition, he said, "The couples leading the new groups felt they were not being supported. Willow Creek tried to provide curriculum, but it wasn't that good. So mostly we just shared our lives. And leading that kind of group takes more skill than doing formal things. There was a wide disparity in quality. The small groups were about as good as their leaders. The challenge was reproducibility—could you train a person with average gifts to grow a small group?"

Part of the problem was that any big change at Willow Creek is a major undertaking; the church is so huge that it is like an ocean liner, requiring miles to make a turn. Frazee acknowledged that the congregation never fully grasped the benefits of Table groups, but he argued that, as one of five rotating pastors who gave sermons on Sunday, he never had the opportunity to tell them. "They had just finished building a new auditorium and regional campuses"—changes that were taking up everyone's time—"I was here six months before I even got a chance to meet with the Elders."

Frazee's forte, it turned out, is vision, not management. He is a dreamer, not as skilled at giving people the steps to reach the dream. "There was not enough structure and purpose," said Russ Robinson, a Willow Creek leader. "You need a clear idea about why to go to a meeting, and there never was one."

The difficulties of Table groups, however, were more profound than simply inadequate training and management. Ryan Boldt, the Willow Creek area pastor, saw the biggest obstacle to making Table groups work as a very American lack of time. "Neighborhood small groups give you a better chance at deeper intimacy, a better chance to get more people involved. But they still have to be intentional," he said. "We thought it was going to be a little more magical—we thought it would take off more organically than it did. But it's harder than we thought." He sighed. "But then everything in life is a lot more work than you thought it was. Every project in life takes me two more trips to Home Depot than I had thought.

"Busyness is a cultural tidal wave. It's hard to fight against," said

Boldt. "People say they're going to do things and don't do it—I want to come, but shoot, I forgot about the dance recital." During my visit, he talked about an event he was working on. Willow Creek families were gathering at Eastview Elementary School in Algonquin to package meals to send to orphanages in Zimbabwe. "This event—we signed up 122 people. I asked people to *please* let us know if you can't make it. On Sunday, thirty of the 122 didn't show up. They didn't notify us. I don't think thirty people had emergency appendectomies. It's just that they are too busy to even let you know."

Being busy, however, may not be the real root of the problem. Several Willow Creek leaders mentioned that busyness itself is the product of cultural pressures to work harder and possess more. It is perhaps peculiar to hear a critique of modern consumer culture in a place like South Barrington, Illinois—the epitome of it—but you can hear one from people at Willow Creek who believe that there is something unbiblical about the modern American emphasis on earning and acquisition. "The Bible is written in collective culture," said Scott Vaudrey, who was briefly the director of small groups at Willow Creek and now is the head of the pastoral-care department. "Even if you forget the God stuff, communal life is counterculture to this world. The greatest enemy of missional living is consumerism and individualism, which is at the root of being too busy. Particularly in the suburbs, where we think we don't need anyone's help. We live with the illusion that we have enough on our own. We don't know we're hungry."

Willow Creek was asking people to make time for a small group and to prioritize relations with neighbors over other activities. More than that, it was asking them to think seriously about what they needed to get out of a group and how to structure the group to meet those needs. This was overwhelming. A lot of people will participate in something if they can simply fit into a predesigned structure—something they can do without too much thought. Some people welcome the responsibility of designing it themselves, but they are the minority.

One Willow Creek parishioner said that he and his wife didn't join their neighborhood Table group because the members put his wife on edge. "People were saying—you're telling me I have to invite the guy across the street who doesn't take a bath and I can smell him across the street? It's a risk," he said. True community, several staff members at Willow Creek pointed out, is the place where you'll find the person you least want to spend time with. For most people, this is an acquired taste.

The neighborhood groups' great advantage for personal growth was the closer community it can create with people who track the course of your life as it runs, but the idea of "doing life together," as Frazee put it, is foreign to American suburban life. "Maybe in the South, where Frazee made this work, it's different," said Mr. Northbrook. (David Daniels, the pastor at Pantego, also thought there might be something about Southern hospitality and openness that makes people more receptive to this concept.) "But in the Midwest, you're lucky if people even know their neighbors. 'Doing life together' is not realistic. The only people it works for are people with kids in school or sports. We had young couples, old people in their eighties. Where are we supposed to run into them—at the doctor's office?"

Some people might have been uncomfortable with Table groups because they could work too well. The frequency and proximity of the Table group is designed to allow your neighbors to get to know the real you—that is how they produce behavior change—but such vulnerability can be intimidating and even terrifying. "There's a tremendous fear of community as well as longing for it," said Bill Donahue. "Guys know they need other guys to do life with, but they are afraid to appear vulnerable and weird. Most people don't think we'll be loved if we're really known. We fear rejection. The irony is: we love the self-made man. And at the same time we crave connection and community, and desire to give away something to someone else."

The culture of the self-made man is a powerful reason that the social cure does not come naturally to many middle-class Americans; we are wary of projects designed to solve problems in community. Donahue argued that this, not busyness, is the main obstacle. "People make time for what they value," he said. "Busy people don't have a problem getting to their AA group. But most people don't think they need community." In a previous life, Donahue lived in New York and worked for Procter and Gamble. "If you needed help, you were weak," he said of that culture. "The challenge isn't 'Are you busy?' It's fighting to show people's true brokenness."

The culture of individualism and time pressures that kept people away from the Table groups are the barriers to any join-the-club solution in Western middle-class societies—but they have been especially strong in America. For many Americans, solving problems in close community with others seems as removed from the lives we lead as the rotary-dial telephone. But for those who did embrace the social cure that Willow Creek offered, the rewards have been great.

DOUG AND JEN YONAMINE were among the Willow Creek worshippers who found the rewards. After their discouraging experience with trying to organize neighborhood groups, they were relieved when Tim and Michele Auch, who live half a mile away, volunteered to host an experimental Table in June 2006. The Yonamines joined the Auchs' group, as did four other Algonquin families. Their experience with trying to "do life together" tells a lot about how the social cure works. When Doug invited me (at Randy Frazee's suggestion) to visit the group, he said it had been a struggle for people to make the time. But the members had also experienced gradual small victories: more self-awareness, a more spiritual life, and, for some, a closer relationship with God.

I met three of the six couples on a Saturday night in the spring of 2008 at Willow Creek. Part of what the group does together every week is attend services at 5:30 p.m. (Willow Creek repeats the same service twice on Sunday.) Then the group eats together in the giant food court downstairs. The Auchs, the Yonamines, and Tim and Beth Moss sat down with their trays at a table in the noisy hall; their children sat at a table of their own nearby.

Michele and Tim Auch had met at a church in Ann Arbor, Michigan. Michele had been a student at Eastern Michigan University; Tim was working at an Ann Arbor research firm and was a part-time graduate student at the University of Michigan. In that church, they were part of a small group. "Everyone lived in the same neighborhood," said Tim, a balding man with a goatee and an acerbic intelligence. "It was intense." Only one of the families had children, so the group met at that couple's house. The meetings were so compelling to the members that some lasted more than three hours and people would still linger. The group also pooled resources and shared such things as lawnmowers and freezers.

Tim and Michele left college determined to move to the developing world and work with the poor, but Michele became pregnant right away, so the plan was postponed, indefinitely. Now Michele, a direct and serious woman who looks like the singer Sheryl Crow, worked part-time as an occupational therapist, and Tim was a systems architect at Motorola. They had two children.

The Auchs shared a backyard fence with Tim and Beth Moss. The two families knew each other well and had been taking care of each other's children for ten years before the Table group was born. The Mosses, who had three children, called themselves the skeptics of the Table group, and Tim Moss was always the one with the most questions. They were both tall, big, and gregarious. Beth was a social worker at a shelter for homeless families and Tim was a paramedic.

Formally, the Table group met twice a month, for a potluck at the Auchs' house, with Michele assigning food—Italian one meeting, Middle Eastern or Mexican the next. A typical meeting would start with a discussion of the events of the week and how they affected each person's spiritual life. This often took up much of the meeting—"the last few times, we've been going longer on the highs and lows," said Jen. Then they would discuss a Bible chapter. Often Tim Moss would throw out a question, and it would be the basis of discussion for the rest of the night.

At a meeting shortly before my visit, the group was discussing Bible verses in which God instructs Moses and the Israelites to take revenge on their enemies with wholesale slaughter. "Did God really authorize genocide?" Tim Moss asked. "Everyone tells me that God is always good and doesn't want you to do anything bad. So why tell Moses to go kill women and children?"

"Tim asks the questions that other people wrestle with but don't say out loud," said Doug.

The men in the Table group were starting a group of their own, on Mondays from 8:15 to 10 p.m. They could put their youngest children to bed, duck out the door, go to the meeting, and be back home by 10:05. "The general feeling was that most of us are not looking for anything else to read," said Doug, "so we thought to ask the question: how's your soul?"

Their regular meetings were close by—the Mosses only had to walk into the next yard. And the couples' children were also part of the group. The older kids led a Christian-themed play group of sorts for the younger children while their parents were in their own meeting. These advantages meant that members were much more likely to be able to show up than with traditional small groups. "Beth, you just got home from work," said Jen. "It would be a deal-breaker for you if you had to get in the car again."

"We want to nurture our kids in our home," said Michele. "We don't want to run around and be so busy we're not available to sit and hear stories."

The meetings were not that different from those conducted in affinity -based small groups. By themselves, they would not have offered a dramatic advance in intimacy and accountability. But the advantage of Table groups was what happens in between the scheduled meetings. "We thought—what are people already doing?" Doug said. "Well, a lot of people eat at Willow Creek after services on Saturday." He gestured around him. "Let's start with that."

The men also decided to exercise together—hence the runs at 6 a.m. Sundays, and sometimes Tuesdays and Thursdays.

The Mosses and the Auchs found the Table to be an extension of the relationship the two families had been conducting for years. Long before, they had knocked down a piece of the fence between their yards, as the kids had kept climbing over it. Their kids began to switch houses to do homework and fall asleep in each other's rooms.

This was the advantage of the Table groups—the life between meetings. Randy Frazee likes to say that the test of whether a group is experiencing deep community is that there is no clear answer to the question of when they meet. "I appreciate the time between the gatherings," said

Doug. "I'm a big fan of growth opportunities in the moments. In terms of sustainability, longevity, and depth, that works for us."

"It's like family," said Ryan Boldt. "If you have to schedule meetings with your wife and kids to fit them in your life, then something is seriously wrong." If you are doing Table groups right, he said, "you don't have to schedule meetings at all."

IT IS EASY TO SEE how the Table groups create community, and why they do this better than traditional small groups. But the members of Willow Creek's Table groups did not join with the end goal of achieving community. They joined to become more like Christ. They sought to change themselves, and community was the mechanism. The question is: How does community work to create individual transformation; just what does being close to others trigger to help people change themselves? The success of the social cure—every social cure—depends on this alchemy.

The Yonamines, Auchs, and Mosses have learned how it works for them. One mechanism is openness: with a real community, you can't fake it. In his earlier small groups, Doug had been able to wear his "game face," as he put it. Now he couldn't. People had gotten to know each other too well. "Just being in a place where we see each other more often, it's more difficult to hide something," he said.

If it works well, having a close group around you can also provide the safety necessary to face your problems. People who see you all the time judge you on the totality of your conduct. It becomes less risky to admit to a problem when the problem is just one small piece of what others know of you.

Close community also helps hold you accountable. "Going to services may inspire you to make promises to God, but no one holds up a tape measure the next week to see if you kept them," said Beth. A real community will; you are surrounded by people you do not want to disappoint.

Holding people accountable is perhaps the most difficult step to take, and the Algonquin group had not yet reached that point. Doug said that when one couple was experiencing a problem, he hadn't had the courage to say, "I don't think you're making the right choice." Members of the group had spoken directly to the couple, but perhaps not directly enough. People were tentative; they didn't know whether they had the right to speak—whether they had, as Doug put it, "relational equity."

"If I'm in that situation," Doug told the group, "I would expect each of you to be lovingly intrusive in my life. Now, I'm not going to *like* it. And I will push back. But I want to tell you all that you have enough relational equity with me."

The depth that produces transformation requires work and time. At first, the Table group did not go much below the surface, and Doug spent months worrying about it.

"Nobody has any problems," Tim Auch grumbled at one early meeting, after each member spoke about his or her week. The members shied away from confronting each other; nobody wanted conflict. "But 'no conflict' is a bad thing," Doug said flatly. "My experience with other groups is there haven't been conflicts. When you get to a place where you're comfortable with conflict, that's where growth happens."

"I can't wait for our first fight as a group," Tim Auch said. "That will tell us we're family."

By the time of my visit—nearly two years after the group formed—there had still been no big fights. "Right now we're just talking about Tim behind his back," cracked Doug. But the problems in their lives were increasingly on display. "One of my key learnings is that this takes time," said Doug. People were starting to take risks.

The breakthrough had begun at a seemingly ordinary meeting in the spring of 2008. Tim Auch had started the meeting by asking about the highs and lows of the week. It was the usual question, and members gave the usual answers: Work's busy. I'm stressed. But then one woman in the group spoke up: "Am I going to be authentic or not?" She then began to talk about problems in her marriage.

Then Tim Moss started talking about his relationship with his son. He would yell at the boy, he said, and then hate himself for yelling.

Next it was Doug's turn. He decided that since others had taken risks in speaking out, he could, too. He told the group about an entry he had made in his journal, about a Bible verse in which Solomon asks God for a discerning heart. "But in the car I had turned off the radio and God told me: you picked the wrong verse. You should have journaled about a verse from Proverbs, which says, 'Do not be wise in your own eyes.' "

Doug went on for ten or fifteen minutes. "I babbled about how I tend to feel superior and how I am judgmental," he said later. "A lot was disjointed—I just felt the need to share it." Afterward, a few people told him they had been encouraged by what he said. Tim Moss told Doug that he had never heard him be that open.

That night, Doug told Jen that the Table had reached a depth it had never reached before. He was relieved. "This thing just takes time," he told his wife.

Two years later, in 2010, Doug still saw that meeting as a turning point. He said that the Auchs had always been open and had always put themselves on the line. "But this was the first time I recall anyone else in the group taking a risk. I can't say that every meeting thereafter we all took risks and were extremely vulnerable, but I can say that it happened more regularly."

The discussions of the Table group, he said later, had brought about changes in other parts of his life. He felt that he was more open with Jen. Having the circle of the Table group also allowed him to be more confident with other people. He had a tendency to be too needy for connection, he said. "Now that I have this, I don't feel as needy in that way."

Perhaps the deepest spiritual transformation in the Table group was that of Michele Auch. She came to the Table group in crisis. Since college, she and Tim had almost always been in small groups and had led or co-led several of them, including one at Willow Creek, but before the Table group began, they had dropped out. "During that period, I had a strong disagreement with God and decided I didn't want to talk to Him. I'd say to Tim, OK, I'm ready to try again. I should pray. But I never did. And I never did. And I never did.

"The crisis stemmed from a lot of built-up expectations in college and early in marriage about what my life course would be," she said. "Tim and I had talked about it, and it revolved around serving the poor. But I got pregnant right away, and Tim was uncomfortable about going to a third world country with a baby in tow. We had pictured it, planned for it, and abandoning it brought a lot of stresses."

They moved instead to the Chicago suburbs. When their son was seven, he was diagnosed with Asperger's syndrome. Tim and Michele mainly handled the situation alone. They had no family in the area and few close friends. For several years, the boy did well in a Montessori school, but when he had to move to a public school, he didn't fit in. "I plunged into an ongoing struggle with him and the educational process," Michele said. "Kids would pick on him. He got into fights. Teachers didn't understand him. He would spend two to three hours fighting me over homework. It was very, very hard. I would walk home after walking to school yelling at God, saying you don't have to answer my prayers, but answer his—he's a kid!"

"Does he fit in now?" I asked. She tilted her hand from side to side— more or less. One thing that had changed, she said, is that he was now very responsible. "He's obsessive about homework. He was offered a job mowing the Mosses' lawn for $15, and he said, 'Well, I have homework.'"

Their son's troubles weighed heavily on Michele and Tim. "We had a marriage crisis and didn't know if we were going to stay together," she said. "We went to a marriage counselor and healed a lot of things, but the spiritual side of this didn't really recover." Instinctively, they decided that what they needed was to be close to others. "We got disconnected," Tim said, "then we decided we wanted to be connected to other people. We wanted to hang out, to build community. We started having summer barbecues. It wasn't a spiritual thing."

"Yes, it was," said Michele.

At one point, their son began to get into fights again. Tim saw him hit another child. He grabbed the boy and his anger was palpable; he wanted to "shake him to pieces," Tim said. Fortunately, the Table group stepped in. One family took the boy for a weekend and another family took the Auchs' daughter. "They all agreed to pray for us," Michele said.

For Michele, being part of the group, being involved in other people's problems and involving them in hers, was the start of the renewal of her faith. "What I needed to help me through that crisis was friendship, somebody to demonstrate they cared about me and cared about my kids," she said. "Even having a girlfriend who could stand to sit and listen to me bleed on her—somebody who's willing to listen to me say, 'I have doubts,' without any condemnation or even words of advice. Or someone sending me an e-mail saying, 'Something you did or said touched me.' It made me feel I have value in other people's lives. I've got to think about how this worked, but it did work. It worked because in essence people are the hands and feet of Jesus. I wouldn't have climbed out of this crisis if I hadn't seen the face of Jesus on the people in my community."

In 2010, two years after my visit, Michele and Tim's son was thriving. So was the Algonquin Table group, now three and a half years old. The members still met formally for dinner twice a month, the men met by themselves twice a month, and the women had their own session, staying late after the Table meeting while the men took the children home. The group also still went to church Saturday night and ate together afterward. Some of the men still ran together, as did Michele and Jen.

People's lives were no less busy, and it was still hard for the members to find the informal, impromptu times to be together. "People would like to have a little more interaction during the week, a little more support," said Michele, "but we don't know how to get that."

In April 2010, Willow Creek was holding its annual food challenge in which the church asks its members to try to understand more about the lives of the very poor by eating like the very poor. Participants were allowed 600 calories a day—a cup of oatmeal for breakfast, rice and vegetables for lunch, a cup of rice and beans for dinner. "The most spiritual thing I have done in years," Michele had called it on a Willow Creek blog. Spiritual, yes, but it also left people exhausted and fuzzy-brained. "We talked about what a great idea it was to eat dinners together this week, to support each other and make sure we don't cheat," said Michele, "but we haven't been able to pull it together."

With time, however, the group's discussions had grown more honest and specific. "A few years ago, the women might have alluded to stresses in their marriages, or joked about lack of time in the bedroom," said

Michele. "Today if we open up that subject, it's specific information—he spent four hours on the computer and no time with me. It's more real content than shared experience of frustration. You can't know things about people's lives over time without having more depth."

THE MEMBERS OF THE Algonquin Table group are not the only ones who have reaped spiritual benefits from the increased community provided by neighborhood-based small groups. Dozens of Table groups—although they no longer were called that—continued to meet four years after their birth.

But for too many of Willow Creek's members, the Table groups demanded too much, and the experiment ended in 2008. After less than three years, Randy Frazee left Willow Creek. He moved back to Texas, where his children are in college, to become senior pastor of Oak Hills Church in San Antonio. He had learned about the need for preparation. Instead of bursting in with a new focus on neighborhood life, Frazee built in a two-year plan for teaching the congregation about the biblical mandates for community and the ideas behind the change. In the spring of 2010, nearly two years after arriving at Oak Hills, he was reorganizing the church's staff around neighborhood lines. He was planning to give church members a book to get them started during the summer: *Block Parties and Poker Nights*, containing ideas about how to connect to neighbors. "Not what you normally associate with church," he said, "but it's a way to invite our people to take another step in the wonderful life of staying home, being more green, and letting your heart rate go down." The debut of Table groups was planned for the fall of 2010.

At Willow Creek, small groups went through yet another incarnation after Frazee left. The church would no longer promote Table groups. The new model was a bit of a hybrid. It emphasized affinity groups but also took geography into account. Members could join an affinity group, but it would probably be made up of people only in their area. People who were happy in their existing affinity or Table groups could stay in them.

In theory, this was the ideal solution, allowing all members to find the group that made them comfortable. In practice, though, the system was bound to move Willow Creek eventually back toward exclusively affinity groups. Small groups require attention. The leaders must be trained and be able to rely on a structure of church staff that can help them with problems. The members need to hear from church leadership, often, about why they are doing what they are doing. Staff energy will gravitate toward the more familiar affinity groups, leaving the newer, more foreign, and more challenging Table groups to wither.

Even though Willow Creek largely abandoned the Table groups, many of the neighborhood-focused changes that accompanied them remained. The Table groups were one manifestation of a tectonic shift at Willow Creek: the era of anonymity was over. Willow Creek had changed. In many different ways, it had turned away from its founding idea of allowing Unchurched Harry to stumble, alone, along the path toward God.

Just before Frazee came to Willow Creek, the church established a geographical system of what it called community pastors—now known as area pastors—who are the principal providers of pastoral care. This change seems destined to stick. "The pastors used to complain that when they officiated at funerals, they often didn't know the person they were burying. Now they know them," said Scott Vaudrey, who briefly was in charge of small groups after Frazee left and then became director of pastoral care. "People wave when they drive by. What a difference proximity makes: You can bring food to a woman who is getting divorced. You can have a glass of wine on the porch with your neighbor whose wife has cancer—and you can do it again tomorrow."

Ryan Boldt knew the kind of community he wanted to pastor: his touchstone was Baldwin, Wisconsin, the small town where he grew up. His father had a heating business and his uncle was the insurance guy. His uncle's best friend ran the newspaper store. The men had a coffee club at 9 o'clock every morning, rolling dice to see who paid. When Boldt walked home from school every day, he'd pass his uncle's office. "You'd walk up and down the streets, and you knew everyone," he said.

Boldt's mission, he said, was to have the neighborhood focus at

Willow Creek re-create that small-town feeling in a place to which people flocked in part so they wouldn't have to know anyone, and nobody walks at all. The gathering place nearest to Boldt's house is a small strip mall with a Starbucks, a Quiznos chain restaurant, and a UPS store.

He argued that it didn't matter whether it was a sixty-years-in-the-same-location diner on Main Street or a Starbucks in a strip mall. What did matter, he said, were the relationships among people. At one point, he went to meet one congregation member at Starbucks. "We are standing in line getting coffee," he said. "I realize Kaleen is working at Starbucks now. Then I see Kate, daughter of someone in church. Then three people from church walk through the door for coffee. There are ten people in here and I know eight of them. This feels a lot like my hometown."

The transformation in Willow Creek was also evident in the services. A weekend service at Willow Creek has always been a theatrical production, and this had not changed by 2008. It started with contemporary Christian songs played by a ten-piece rock band, with lyrics for singing along displayed on two enormous TV screens overhead. The sound system and stage, which dropped to disappear into the floor, were top quality. The congregants were mostly dressed in jeans or chinos, and so were the pastors. There were very few children—families were encouraged to drop off their kids in the basement, where there were special children's programs.

The sermon, in the spring of 2008, was a dramatic talk called "Rescued," by Jim Mellado, president of the Willow Creek Association. Mellado recounted an experience that nearly killed him and his son. Vacationing in Baja California, Mexico, the two were swept out to sea. Mellado described the incredible struggle to get back to land, and then he told of his deliverance from kidney failure, which hit him later as a result of muscle breakdown from the exertion and trauma. At the end, a healthy son joined his healthy father on stage.

This was, in classic Willow Creek mode, a "seeker-oriented" service. There was no scripture, no organ music, no visible cross or other religious object. The sermon, while Christian, was a sophisticated presentation of a generic message, designed to inspire someone with very little relationship with Christ to develop one.

What was new here was that the other old hallmark of a Willow Creek weekend service—anonymity—was gone. Mellado asked "people who need hope" to stand, and many did. Then he asked others to put their hands on the standers' shoulders, "so they know they are not alone." Again, many did. Later, he asked people to stand if they had personally witnessed God turning something terrible in their lives into something good. About an eighth of the congregation stood.

The church's new focus on community was evident in a new outward orientation, a desire to engage with the world. Willow Creek was trying to push members not just into the closer relationship with God that everyone was seeking but also into a closer relationship with fellow humans—near or far, known or unfamiliar. In 2007, Bill Hybels told a *New York Times* reporter: "For churches to reach their full redemptive potential, they have to do more than hold services—they have to try to transform their communities."

In 1995, for Willow Creek's twentieth anniversary, the church had rented out Chicago's United Center, where the Chicago Bulls basketball team plays, and held services for 20,000 people. In 2005, Willow Creek celebrated its thirtieth anniversary rather differently—by sponsoring hundreds of service projects all over the community. McHenry County volunteers, for example, received $12,000 to rebuild a house that was being destroyed by mold. The projects were chosen by each neighborhood group. Willow Creek didn't even seek to count or keep track of them.

Since 2003, Hybels has aggressively sought to turn his once virtually all-white church into a more diverse one, and today about a fifth of the members are not white. Willow Creek teamed up with Salem Baptist Church, an enormous black church in Chicago, to organize a bus pilgrimage to historic sites of the civil rights movement in the South. The two churches have traded choirs and youth groups, and senior pastors Hybels and James Meeks have switched pulpits. Willow Creek and Salem Baptist work together on issues such as equalizing financing for public schools across rich and poor school districts. "The playing field simply is not level when it comes to education, employment, housing, and overall opportunities for black Americans," Willow Creek pastor Nancy Beach wrote in a church blog.

The church is asking its members to understand "communities" in the largest sense. Willow Creek has an officer with the title of Advocate for Global Engagement. It is not just anyone—it's Hybels's wife, Lynne. (Pastor Rick Warren's wife, Kay, plays a similar role at Saddleback Church, which often is compared to Willow Creek.) At Lynne Hybels's urging, Willow Creek works in partnerships with pastors in Latin America and Africa. The church also raises awareness of and money for causes such as AIDS in Africa, world poverty, violence against women, and war in the Congo and other places.

Bill Hybels is a Democrat. He was a spiritual adviser to Bill Clinton, meeting monthly with the president, and one of the preachers considered to speak at the 2004 Democratic Convention. Hybels was nixed because he was considered too conservative on some social issues: he opposes abortion rights and gay marriage, for example. But on other issues, he is on the left. Against the backdrop of the Iraq War, Hybels gave a series of sermons articulating the classic approaches to war, talking about interventionism, a "just war" approach, and pacifism. Hybels told his congregants to study and pray and come up with their own conclusions, but he made it clear that he was a pacifist. He is also a leftist on social justice. Hybels has become bluntly critical of the leadership of the evangelical Christian movement, telling the *New York Times* that their rank and file was rebelling. "The Indians are saying to the chiefs, 'We are interested in more than your two or three issues.' We are interested in the poor, in racial reconciliation, in global poverty and AIDS, in the plight of women in the developing world. . . . If there is racial injustice in your community, you have to speak to that. If there is educational injustice, you have to do something there. If the poor are being neglected by the government or being oppressed in some way, then you have to stand up for the poor."

It is likely that in South Barrington, Illinois, one of the wealthiest and whitest communities in the United States, his views are in the minority. There is general agreement at Willow Creek that Hybels and some of his church leadership are considerably to the left of the church's members. Even though his congregants may not agree with Hybels's politics, however, many have strongly embraced his advocacy of engagement with the poor. Ryan Boldt's blog of the Willow Creek news from his region is largely about local service projects—announcements about donating a car to a single mom, packing vegetable seeds to send to Zimbabwe, helping paint a local shelter for abused children, raising funds for a local girl with leukemia, or supporting Willow Creek members running the Chicago Marathon to raise money for the charity World Vision.

During my 2008 visit, Ryan Boldt told his companions on the Sunday 6 a.m. jog, that he hadn't been to church the day before, and he wouldn't be going that day. But in a different way, he had gone to church. Boldt had spent the past weekend, and was spending this one, at the local elementary school supervising the ambitious Willow Creek–led volunteer effort to pack food for orphans in Zimbabwe. The project was organized through the Minnesota-based Christian group Feed My Starving Children. Willow Creek had purchased enormous sacks of bulk food—rice, soybean meal, dehydrated vegetables, and a concentrate of vitamins and minerals. The volunteers scooped the proper proportions of each food into small plastic bags, sealed them, and packed them. When reconstituted with water, the contents of each bag would be a meal for six children.

The Algonquin Table group took an early afternoon shift, along with dozens of other Willow Creek members. Once gathered in the school's basement, the group watched a small skit about the inequality of hunger in the world. It was a graphic, easy-to-grasp depiction of the huge gaps between what Americans eat and what Zimbabweans eat. After hairnets and puffs of hand sanitizer were distributed, everyone took up stations at tables loaded with bins of the foodstuffs, bags, and sealing machines. About half the workers were kids, and even toddlers were scooping cups of rice or soybean meal and pouring them into funnels. Tables competed to finish bags the fastest, while songs such as "Macarena" and "Devil in a Blue Dress" blared from the sound system.

At the end of the shift, the group had packed enough meals to feed ninety-one children for a year. By the end of the weekend, the Willow

Creek volunteers at Eastview Elementary had packed 207,000 meals—a year's worth of food for 567 children. A very tired Boldt thanked the crowd at the end of the shift. "We are better together," he said.

The complement to the meal packing for Willow Creek congregants was the 600-calorie-a-day eating challenge. At the Saturday service, Nancy Beach spoke about the food challenge and the value of limiting consumption—eating more simply, living more simply—and giving the money saved to Feed My Starving Children and other church projects for the poor. (Willow Creek raised $700,000 in 2008. The next year, while charitable giving everywhere was dropping during the recession, the church raised $2 million for that cause. In 2009, the church raised $2.3 million.) Pastor Beach also plugged the World Market taking place in Willow Creek's lobby, featuring coffee, chocolate, soccer balls, and other products made by fair-trade cooperatives in poor countries. Women were walking around with trays of chocolate to sample, and the church's bookstore has a section featuring fair-trade goods.

Just as Willow Creek as a whole was turning outward, so were some of its small groups. At the urging of Matt Lossau, the Algonquin Table began a project to raise money for and provide long-distance solidarity (mostly via Skype video) to the village of Gambella, Kenya. The goal was to raise $5,000 a year for projects that were aimed at making the village self-sustaining, such as digging wells and establishing a health clinic.

The most enthusiastic driver of this change at the ground level in Willow Creek was Sue Dunn, who in 2008 was an area pastor. She is a gray-haired sprite in her sixties who bubbles over with enthusiasm for Jesus and for what she considers His work. Unlike Hybels, Dunn is politically conservative. Like him, she is interested in transforming her community—consumed by it, in fact. Dunn does nothing by halves. When she had a prison ministry, she took one of the released prisoners into her house to live.

The center of Dunn's ministry was Willow Creek's satellite church in McHenry County, close to the Wisconsin border. Fifty miles from Chicago, McHenry is a place of farmland and small town whose residents are police and firefighters, construction workers and small-business owners. When you drive from the megachurch in South Barrington to the McHenry County campus, the towns spread out and the wealth dries up as you go.

Dunn had worked for Willow Creek for eleven years before Randy Frazee arrived, but in his ideas she finally found the ministry she wanted. "When we got the neighborhood piece of it, it made sense to me. I saw years ago that the closer you can get people together, the better," she said. Out of the Table groups in her area she established Cary-Grove Neighborhood Life, an association of Willow Creek and four other churches in the neighboring towns of Cary and Fox River Grove. Dunn has organized hundreds of volunteers for neighborhood service projects: kids set up lemonade stands to finance the local homeless shelters; teams of temporarily unemployed construction workers rebuild roofs and bathrooms in decaying houses.

Soon after Frazee left Willow Creek in 2008, Dunn also left. Neighborhood work was what interested her, and now Willow Creek was telling her that she had to go back to working on traditional small groups. "They never said you can't do neighborhood things," she said, "but they said, 'That's part of your job, Sue, but a small part of your job now.' They don't think they've turned away from neighborhoods. There are still some area pastors dabbling in the neighborhood movement, some little pockets where it's happening. But it's such a powerful, unique new concept that if you don't concentrate on it, it's not going to materialize," she said. She went to work, for no pay, as president of Cary-Grove Neighborhood Life.

One evening when Dunn was still an area pastor at Willow Creek, she met with her Table-group leaders at the McHenry County church. A half-dozen people sat around a conference table and talked about what their Tables were doing. A few of the people present were not only helpers but also had been helped—one woman, Debra Nelson, had lived in an old house that was falling down. Her Table group gathered twenty people who stripped the bathroom to the studs and rebuilt it. "I am thankful to them every time I go into the bathroom," she said, laughing.

They talked about how the Table groups were affecting their relationship with God. "My small group came into my life at a very difficult time," Nelson said. "At the time, I really needed other women who understood what my situation was like. We had one woman who lived nearby and recently lost her husband. Another would talk about her teenage son who had a lot of trouble. You are willing to risk being real."

She was answering a question I had asked of nearly everyone I met at Willow Creek: "How has the Table group affected your religious journey?" Then Mike Singleton began to talk, and I stopped asking the question. I had been thinking of community as a means to an end, and that end was spiritual growth. But when Singleton told his story, I realized that, for some people, it was the other way around.

Singleton was in his sixties, retired from Motorola. During one of Willow Creek's neighborhood service projects, he knocked on a door eight houses away from his own, on the same side of the street. An elderly woman with a round face and short gray hair answered the door. Singleton explained that a group of local people were planning to help out some neighbors, and he asked if she had any chores that needed doing.

"That sounds good," said Betty Geis. She told him she needed her windows washed, gutters cleaned, and flower bed weeded. "I can't do that anymore," she said. Singleton asked if she lived alone. "My husband died two weeks ago," she replied.

"In that nanosecond, I was convicted," Singleton said. "I was so embarrassed not to have known that eight doors down from me, a woman's husband died two weeks ago. I had even driven by the house on the day he died and saw an ambulance out front. She told me that her husband had Parkinson's and was sick for two years. I didn't know that, either." The woman was completely alone, it turned out. She had two daughters from whom she was estranged.

Betty made a list of what she needed done, and soon a group of volunteers arrived at her house to do her tasks. But the next time Singleton knocked on her door, there was no answer. A neighbor told him that Betty was in the hospital with pneumonia. Singleton went to visit her, praying with her at her bedside.

When Betty returned home from the hospital, the Singleton family adopted her and she became their surrogate grandmother. The kids took out her trash and took her to get a nondriver ID card. Mike Singleton became executor of her will and helped her sell her house when she moved into a nursing home. Once, when he asked her if there was something else she needed, she said that her husband used to get her a *Chicago Tribune* and a cup of Starbucks coffee every Sunday. So he did that. And when he couldn't, Sue Dunn did it for him. When Betty Geis died, Mike Singleton was at her bedside.

The group donated Betty's hospital bed to someone else who needed it, a neighbor named Judy. Cheryl McDermott, another Table-group leader at Dunn's meeting that day, met Judy when Cheryl was driving through a winter storm and saw a woman walking on the road, struggling through snowdrifts and 40 mph wind. She said she was on her way to Walgreens to pick up some prescriptions. Cheryl gave Judy a ride and also offered to help her with rides to the grocery store.

"I don't have money to go to the grocery store," said Judy. She had no food at the house, was sleeping on a decrepit couch, and was way behind in her rent.

Cheryl e-mailed her Table group with a prayer request for Judy, but the members did more than pray—they took her to the doctor. They got her a cell phone. One person each week bought groceries for her. The Table group met with Judy's landlord and agreed to settle her back rent by painting the apartment building where she lived. It took five weekends to finish the job, but there it was—blue with white trim. And Judy got Betty Geis's hospital bed.

When I had prodded Randy Frazee on the mechanism that makes a small group work—exactly how community fosters personal change—he had smiled. "You have it backward," he said. "What matters is not what community does for *me*—it's what I do for the community. I'm becoming fully devoted, gentle, and generous, for *your* sake. Individual transformation is the means. Community is the end. The end objective is relationship." For Frazee, community was not a means but a value in itself, the highest value.

When Mike Singleton spoke at the meeting I attended, I suddenly understood what Frazee had meant. The fellowship of these Table members, which they undertook in order to transform themselves—the social cure—had indeed deepened their relationships with God. But in Frazee's view, and Dunn's, and Singleton's, their transformation as individuals was only an indirect route. There was another step. Their individual change turned them outward and produced community, perhaps the small town Ryan Boldt sought. That was what had created a more spiritual life. For them, what brings people closer to God is not any leap in self-understanding, mastery of scripture, or increase in virtue. It is the conveyance of a Sunday newspaper and coffee to an old woman, the offer of a ride to Walgreens to someone struggling through a snowdrift, the dipping of a brush in blue paint and its careful application to the corner of a house.

Chapter Eight

The
Party

WILLOW CREEK IS ONE OF THE WORLD'S MOST
powerful religious institutions. It has money. It wields
enormous influence over the lives of its members and the
behavior of other churches. It enjoys unlimited room to
experiment and maneuver. When it admired a strategy
another church was using for bringing its members closer
to Christ, it adopted that strategy and hired the man who
designed it. But not every person or institution interested
in social change can function as Willow Creek does. Many
people who would like to change the world around them
do not enjoy abundant resources, influence or autonomy.
They have goals but no clear idea how to reach them, and
they cannot simply adapt an already-tested solution from
somewhere else.

Consider a group of people who were as disadvantaged
as Willow Creek is blessed. They were students. They had
no money. They had very little autonomy—they lived under

a dictatorship and were followed, harassed, beaten, and arrested; some were marked for death. Their plans were devised on the fly, through trial and error. Their goal was much broader than to affect the lives of the people who had chosen to join them, as Willow Creek tried to do. They set out to do something audacious: overthrow Slobodan Milošević, who had attained power in 1989 in Yugoslavia and had contrived to preserve that power through a poisonous nationalism. The "Butcher of the Balkans," as he was called, had outmaneuvered countless enemies—a list that eventually would include the combined European and American forces of NATO—and killed tens of thousands of people. These students were amateurs. Getting rid of Milošević did not appear to be a job for amateurs.

"Everyone told us we were completely insane," said Ivan Andrić, one of the eleven founders of Otpor, which means "Resistance" in Serbian. Yet in 2000, two years after they gathered for the first time, the eleven had grown to at least 70,000, and Milošević fell.

By no means was this exclusively an Otpor victory; it belonged to many groups. But it could not have happened without Otpor, which provided the democracy movement's ground troops. They liberated the most important and difficult terrain in overthrowing a dictator—the insides of people's heads. The men and women opposed to Milošević had many obstacles to overcome, but the most daunting was the attitude of their countrymen: fatalistic, cowed, pessimistic, and afraid. Even though most Serbs wanted Milošević to go, the vast majority believed his ouster was simply impossible, and that it was too dangerous to try. Otpor's signal contribution was to change this thinking. It created an energetic, courageous, and confident nonviolent army of young activists, who in turn eroded the fatalism and fear of the Serbian people. Largely improvising, Otpor designed and executed a plan that bulldozed through a fundamental barrier—perhaps *the* fundamental barrier—to political change. And it did so using the social cure.

The story of Milošević's fall is not just a feel-good tale from a country that has not specialized in such things. It carries important lessons for the social cure. Watching Otpor build a movement step-by-step, under some of the most adverse circumstances conceivable, is useful for all who know where they want a join-the-club strategy to take them but don't know how to get there. Otpor's experience also demonstrates that the social cure can be used to address a whole spectrum of important public issues that have no obvious personal component. We know from the success of DOTS and microcredit that the social cure can attack major ills such as tuberculosis and poverty. In those instances, however, the social cure works by facilitating certain changes in behavior among those personally afflicted. Otpor's success shows something larger still: the social cure can be used to amass citizen power.

I LIVED IN TWO DICTATORSHIPS—Chile under Augusto Pinochet and Sandinista Nicaragua—and have visited perhaps a dozen others. I have watched numerous homegrown democracy movements in action and have seen an army of international democracy-promotion experts come and go. I have been an election monitor. I thought I had seen all the meat-and-potatoes of turning dictatorship into democracy. But I had never seen anything like Otpor.

When I lived in Chile in the late 1980s, there was a group of politicians and intellectuals who actively opposed the Pinochet dictatorship. Toppling Pinochet and restoring democracy to Chile was the focus of their lives. These men and women were among the most sophisticated and well-educated democracy activists anywhere in the world. They denounced the regime in journals published overseas and in the few permitted opposition magazines in Chile. (The fact that Pinochet permitted them to be published indicated he didn't consider them much of a threat.) These politicians and intellectuals documented the poverty, income inequality, violence, and human rights abuses that Pinochet had brought to Chile.

I suspect that they didn't think much about whether these articles would actually lead to change—writing them was simply what they felt like doing, an expression of their frustration and anger. If they had thought about how change would come about, they probably theorized that people who understood the evils of the regime would then take to the streets and overthrow the dictator.

Unfortunately, that is not how politics works. Chileans were quite aware of their own poverty—they did not need an intellectual with a PhD from Princeton to point it out to them. Early on, the regime killed and tortured in secret, but by the time I arrived in Chile in 1986, its abuses were widely known—the government even publicized them, in order to scare people back into their houses. What toppling Pinochet required was not an increase in anger at the regime but a way to turn that anger into effective action.

That catalyst should have come from the leaders of Chile's many civic groups. Chile had always been a highly politicized society with a very active civic culture. By 1983, ten years after Pinochet's coup, associations of all kind—mining unions, the medical association, soccer clubs, small businessmen's groups—were united in their opposition to him. Unlike the intellectuals, they decided to organize. They held *cacerolazos*—sessions of simultaneous pot-banging. They held protests and strikes, including a national strike. Santiago was under occupation, with, at times, 18,000 soldiers in the street. In one strike in August 1983, twenty-six people died.

Looking at a dictatorship from the outside, we are always thinking: it could be today; he will fall today. My first reaction upon arriving in Santiago was surprise: Where are the soldiers? The images that had reached the outside world were of protests—students with their fists in the air, burning barricades, policemen scattering demonstrators with water cannons and tear gas. My Chilean friends in exile would listen to the news of the protests and begin mentally packing for their return. "You hear the news of protests, strikes, death, but not of daily things," said a Chilean who was exiled in Holland. "I came back with the image that Chile was all protests, that more people were participating and that the regime was more fragile. Instead, you see people in the center of the city sitting and reading the paper, eating ice cream, getting their shoes shined." From the outside, we have an idea that people crushed by dictatorship struggle heroically, that people who live in repressive countries are obsessed with their repression and single-minded about fighting for democracy. This is a romantic myth. The vast majority of people do not protest, do not fight back. They do not need to be crushed; instead, they can be bought, or simply cowed. The dictator manages to convince the citizens that it is useless to fight, that the price is too high, that there is no alternative that would make life better.

Chile historically was the Latin American country with the strongest tradition of democracy and the most ingrained respect for rights. A Pinochet was never thought possible, and the idea that Chile would not fight him was unbearable. Yet because Chile was in an economic boom, he faced virtually no opposition for the first ten years of his rule—just a small handful of dedicated human-rights lawyers and activists, sheltered to a certain extent by the Catholic Church. There was murder, torture, and mass arrest. But there were no protests. Chile was silent. It was convenient to look the other way.

The protests began in 1983, when the economy crashed—as most protests do. For stretches of a few months in the mid-1980s, life imitated journalistic cliché. Masses of Chileans took to the street, fists in the air, braving tear gas and bullets to raise their voices against the dictator. Political arrests rose to 40,000 in 1984. At one point in 1987, I was teargassed twice a day for a week. Protesting was like being on a roller coaster, climbing and climbing, and you could see the top.

The roller coaster came close, but it never reached the top of the hill, never had a chance to begin the wild, thrilling descent. The protests never led to anything. The moderate parties withdrew from the demonstrations in order to negotiate with the government, and the protests became increasingly dominated by the Left. Thousands of people still were in the street demanding Pinochet's resignation, but he just laughed. Shouting, "Down with Pinochet!" was exhilarating, but it grew hollow after the twentieth time. They were only words, and they were not bringing him down. He was too strong. He still enjoyed support—from the Reagan administration in Washington, his own military and police, and many Chileans who bought Pinochet's argument that he represented order and the opposition represented chaos. The democratic opposition was splintered and its leaders had settled into a predictable and comfortable routine. In the summer, political activity stopped so everyone could go to the beach. The protests, which began in 1983, had no formula for turning their energy into matter; Pinochet lasted another seven years.

"Grievances by themselves don't lead to revolution," said Ivan Marović, a mechanical engineering student who was perhaps the most creative and daring of the Otpor founders. "There has to be an alternative political movement with a plan and a strategy. Revolutions are often seen as spontaneous—it looks like people just went into the street, but it's the result of months or years of preparation. It is very boring until you reach a certain point, where you can organize mass demonstrations or strikes. If it is carefully planned, by the time they start, everything is over in a matter of weeks."

SERBIA, TOO, HAD HAD PROTESTS before Otpor. It is worth understanding them—and why they failed—because they set the stage for what came later. In March 1991, less than two years after Milošević came to power, 100,000 people massed in Belgrade to protest his repression. The government responded with violence, putting tanks in the streets, injuring 200 protesters, and arresting 100. The next day, thousands of students at Belgrade University joined the protest, now adding the resignation of the interior minister to their demands. A week later, Milošević gave in and sacked the interior minister—the first example of what would become his specialty of winning by losing, making small concessions but retaining power. The protests stopped, and soon Milošević had begun the wars in Slovenia, Croatia, and Bosnia that would lead to the disintegration of Yugoslavia.

The next year, the students began again, this time alone, without the support of the opposition parties. In June 1992, they occupied Belgrade University for twenty-six days, demanding Milošević's resignation. This protest failed utterly. As in Chile, it petered out over the summer vacation; when school resumed, Milošević stripped the universities of the autonomy they had enjoyed up to that point.

For four years, there was silence. Then in 1996, the opposition to Milošević—miraculously united in a coalition called *Zajedno* ("Together")—won municipal elections in thirty-two cities and towns, including Belgrade. Zajedno had three leaders. One was Vesna Pešić, an urban intellectual who had few real followers. But the other two were Serbia's most important opposition politicians. Vuk Drašković (pronounced DRASH-koh-vitch—a Serbian š is sh, a ć is tch) was the epitome of old-style politics. His speaking style was florid and poetic and his rhetoric firmly grounded in old Serb tradition. He received the nickname "King of the Squares" for his ability to stir up the crowds in the plaza. Although his political views underwent abrupt shifts, his dominant ideology was nationalist, in support of Greater Serbia—the poisonous idea that wherever Serbs have lived is Serb forever. A man with an unkempt beard and a wild look in his eye, Drašković once challenged Milošević to a duel. Drašković was moody and erratic, and he eventually lost all credibility when he joined the Milošević government.

If Drašković lived in the nineteenth century, Zoran Djindjić (pronounced JIN-jitch) lived in the twenty-first. He earned his PhD in Germany under the renowned philosopher and public intellectual Jürgen Habermas. Djindjić was a politician of extraordinary talents: ferocious intelligence, energy, discipline, charm, movie-star charisma, boundless self-confidence, and physical courage that eventually also became political courage. Alone among Serb politicians, he understood the importance of step-by-step organizing. (His supporters called him "The Manager." On trips to Washington, he would buy armloads of books on organizational and business administration. He bought books in English because he was planning to learn it—which he did, on his own, at the age of forty-six.) He built the Democratic Party into Serbia's only modern political party, training activists to knock on doors and help their neighborhoods solve local problems.

When Djindjić was assassinated in 2003, hundreds of thousands of mourners walked in silence behind his casket through the streets of Belgrade. After his death, he was often called Serbia's Kennedy. But while alive, he was not beloved in Serbia. In part this was the result of the regime's daily campaign against him in the media—he was called a traitor, a spy, a criminal. Djindjić liked to say he was unpopular because of his pro-Western views, which were never echoed by his fellow citizens. But there were other reasons: his role in the opposition's constant infighting, and his ambition, opportunism, and need for control.

Djindjić was a superb organizer and strategist, a Machiavellian always playing chess. Like Drašković, he made deals with the devil, including financing his political activities through relationships with wealthy patrons, some of whom were undoubtedly gangsters. This is how everyone who contested power got the money to do so in Serbia, where it was virtually impossible to acquire wealth legally. "A man must have friends in heaven and hell," Djindjić liked to say; there is no room in Serbian politics for naifs. In the early 1990s, he pretended—not convincingly—to be a nationalist, telling his colleagues it was the only way for the Democratic Party to become more than a party of urban elites. At his lowest point, he shared roast ox with Radovan Karadžić, the über-war criminal who was head of the Bosnian Serbs.

A tactical nationalist is not necessarily better than the real thing— that's what Milošević was, too. But Milošević wielded the cudgel of nationalism to keep the power he held, and it killed 140,000 people. Djindjić, powerless in a small opposition party, supported it in hopes of eventually turning Serbia in the opposite direction. Similarly, he flirted with the hard men, but he was confident that he was using them—not the other way around—and that, in the end, he could outmaneuver them. Djindjić was "easily the most complex politician with whom I had ever had contact," wrote William Montgomery, who became U.S. ambassador to Serbia in 2001. "I am convinced that his fundamental goal was to bring Serbia into the European Union as a 'normal, demo-cratic country' as rapidly as possible. But he also knew better than anyone else that this could not be done in a straight line."

The government annulled the results of the local elections in November 1996. In protest, Serbia went out into the streets. The pro-tests began in the southern city of Niš and spread across the country. Zajedno held marches every evening, beginning on November 17, 1996. In about forty cities across Serbia—including many cities where the elections were not contested—people walked every day. In Belgrade, opposition protesters met at Zajedno headquarters each day at three, already twilight, to march through the snow in a wide circle around the city, past government buildings.

Students held their own protests. University life in Serbia was fertile ground for political activity. Many students approached study rather leisurely, staying at university until well into their mid- or even late twenties. There was no reason to hurry. School was free and being a student conferred important government benefits. In a country lurching from war to war, students received draft deferments until they hit twenty-seven. There were few jobs awaiting them upon graduation, and those that were available paid a pittance—$40 or $50 a month. Not having jobs and families to support, students had little to lose and plenty of time. In Belgrade, students walked downtown from the philosophy faculty every day at noon, demanding recognition of the opposition's victories and the firing of the university rector.

The student protests were immensely creative. A Belgrade art student made a large puppet of Milošević in prison stripes that was carried through the streets. (He was arrested and badly beaten.) Students did street theater with bodies outlined in chalk on the ground, as at a crime scene. They poured detergent on the ground to clean up the streets after a pro-Milošević rally, and they wrote graffiti on government buildings with cockroach powder. When state media called the protests destructive, students built a brick wall in front of the Parliament building to argue that they were, in fact, constructive. Ivan Marović took reporters with him on a trip to Belgrade's zoo to look for the university rector. Students stood in front of the police lines and read the police passages of Plato and Aristotle—for hours.

The protests achieved their narrowest goals: Belgrade University's rector was sacked, and Milošević was forced to recognize the opposition's electoral victories. Djindjić became mayor of Belgrade, and opposition politicians took over municipalities all across Serbia.

The victories, however, proved hollow. Djindjić and Drašković hated each other as much as they hated Milošević, and Zajedno split apart, dooming any possibility that the protests could shake Milošević loose. Djindjić refused to support Drašković's presidential bid against Milošević. Drašković, furious, pulled his support from Djindjić, thus ending his mayoralty after only four months. Drašković then let himself be bought by the regime, becoming Milošević's deputy prime minister.

The opposition controlled most city governments, but Milošević's hold on Serbia was stronger than ever. Even after eighty consecutive days of marches in Belgrade, even with a million people in the streets, the protests, as with those in Chile, had not turned energy into matter.

Once again, the opposition fell back into silence. After Zajedno's demise, the goal of a free Serbia seemed farther away than ever. Milošević passed new laws cracking down on the independent media and tightly controlling the universities, turning academic posts into political ones and firing professors who would not sign contracts pledging loyalty to the regime. The economy was in collapse. In 1998, Milošević started his fourth war of the decade—in Kosovo, a province of Serbia that was majority Albanian but of great historical importance to Serbs. He was in firm control; the opposition political parties had earned the fury and disgust of the nation. "They had no common goal and no common sense," said Milja Jovanović, the only woman among Otpor's eleven founders. "They used their media time to slam each other." After nine years of Milošević, the opposition had nothing to show.

The question of why it had nothing goes to the heart of the way he maintained his rule, and the major challenges that Otpor had to overcome. While to the outside world Milošević was the worst of the worst, he was not particularly brutal to his fellow Serbs. Dissidents were not being tossed from helicopters or burned alive. Inside Serbia, Milošević did not rely on terror to control his people. He did not need to. Until 2000, he did not even need to steal national elections to stay in power. He had ground his citizens into passivity. Life was crumbling, but that simply seemed to increase Serbs' paralysis. He stilled them by convincing them that the world was against them, that he was their protector, that there was no alternative that could make things better. And the opposition played into his hands.

Many of the leaders of the student protests left Serbia—for Hungary, Germany, Canada, the United States. Another group fell into depression, alcoholism, or drug addiction. But a third group decided to organize. During a series of meetings over coffee and cigarettes in October and November 1998, they formed Otpor.

The initial idea came from Srdja Popović (pronounced SERGE-a POH-poh-vitch) He was twenty-five, tall, thin, and sharp-featured. His parents had made careers as part of the Yugoslav intelligentsia. His father, a star reporter at Radio Television Serbia, retired in 1991 when RTS began to push Milošević's nationalism. His mother, who had been editor in chief of the TV news, was gradually demoted because of her son's activities. But Srdja was a protégé of Djindjić and a city council member from the Democratic Party. He was also a marine biology student at the university—when he studied.

Srdja had been active in the protests of 1996 and 1997. Now he wanted to try again, to organize students against the university law—but this time, also against Milošević. He and five other former student activists met at Greenet, a Starbucks-style coffee bar in downtown Belgrade. "It was a meeting of desperate friends," he said. "We were at the bottom of a depression." A few days later, on November 11, five more former student protesters joined the group, meeting in someone's apartment. One of the men, Vukašin Petrović, editor of the student newspaper at the university, offered its headquarters for further meetings. The office, in a building under a bridge, had a few tables, chairs, computers, and posters of Serbian rock bands on the walls. Milja, who had been organizing protests against the dean of her world literature department—a particularly odious bureaucrat—also started attending the meeting.

The eleven founders were far from typical Serbs. All were students— in law, literature, mechanical engineering, biology, economics. They were between twenty-three and twenty-seven. All had been in the previous student protests and one of them, Slobodan Homen, was the chairman of the student parliament. They were all from comfortable homes—Homen's family was wealthy. They had cell phones, their parents could support them, and they had enough spending money to be able to devote full time to politics.

With the exception of Milja, they were men. Otpor would remain that way, no more able to take women seriously than the rest of the country was. There were thousands and thousands of female activists, but of the thirty or so main decision-makers, only two were women—Milja and Jelena Urošević, who led Otpor in the university city of Kragujevac.

The Otpor leaders started out by talking about why the protests had failed—the largest reason being that the political parties in the opposition bickered like children. Only the student movement had remained united, only the students had been able to rise above personal ambition to keep their focus. But the Otpor founders agreed with Srdja that a student movement aimed only at the university was not enough. Even if they won reforms, the same thing would happen as in the past— Milošević could quiet the students by changing the university law, but after the students dispersed, the bad old law would be back again. They had to go after Milošević himself. To do that, they had to recruit more than students—they would have to get a wide swath of Serbian society actively involved in toppling him. That meant they had to overcome people's passivity and fear.

This decision to focus on motivating their fellow citizens, to think about it seriously and creatively—the way no one else in Serbia ever had—was an absolutely key choice. It was central to Otpor's success. "We looked at the history of Serbia to find what had been effective and motivating," said Slobodan Djinović, a mechanical engineering student. Most of what they found had to do with heroic young people—a recurring theme in Serbian history and national myths. Particularly admired were the Yugoslav Partisans, who had fought the Axis powers in World War II. Could a group of comfortable university students become modern-day Partisans?

Well, not with guns. Advocating violence was not a way to win widespread support. Besides, that was a conflict Milošević was sure to win. "If we did that, we'd be killed," said Djinović. "We couldn't fight him— the police are too strong. But we said: let's transfer that idea to nonviolent methods. We could use guerrilla actions and black propaganda—no one would know who was originating it. People would be reminded of 1941 to 1945. Older people would think of us like they were."

Serbia's political parties had typical political-party names, ones that could have come from a Chinese menu: Democratic, National, Radical, Socialist, Serbian, Renewal, Liberal, etc.—just pick any two or three. They had meaning only to their faithful. The students, instead, chose a name that evoked both the Partisans and their current mission— Resistance! Then they appropriated the clenched fist, symbol of the Partisans and of Communist movements everywhere. The fist started as a secret signal, as if this were a kids' clubhouse, but it quickly became the Otpor emblem. Nenad Petrović—known to all by his nickname "Duda"—a graphic designer who had been Srdja's best friend since fifth grade, created Otpor's clenched-fist logo. It was stylized and stark, simple enough to lend itself to a stencil, so it could be hurriedly spray-painted on a wall. "We wanted it to look powerful," he said.

Otpor's fist was a way to mock the government. "We wanted to use their own weapons, their own symbolic imagery and heaviness against them," said Milja. "We thought the irony was obvious. We didn't know it would be taken so seriously." Black humor was key. "I always thought about my immediate friends," she said. "They were very blasé. They felt political activity was beneath you, a waste of time. It sometimes seemed to us that our friends accepted their situation because it gives you an alibi—you can be a slacker all your life. I can't get a job, Milošević is everywhere. People don't want to take personal responsibility for the way they live their lives. That kind of apathy was our biggest enemy—more than the police, more than Milošević.

"We really wanted those people. We needed to penetrate the defense mechanisms of our peers that politics makes you dirty—to get the opinion-makers in their own small circle. For that, the coolness factor was very important. We wanted the coolness of Otpor to be strongly seen by our peers as a way to profile themselves. We wanted to be a brand that signifies something when you put it on yourself."

As they do now, high school students in Serbia at that time grew up with the temptations of Mafia culture. Today in Serbia, organized crime is, in some ways, arguably as powerful as the state. Back in 1998, it *was* the state. Crime and war were the perfect mix. The top Mafia leaders were also warlords and chieftains of paramilitary units. Milošević relied on these men to carry out the mass killings and rapes that were hallmarks of his wars, especially in Kosovo, and they were untouchable. Serbia's nightclubs were full of beefy men with heavy gold chains and miniskirted women from Belgrade's "Silicone Valley"—so named not for computer chips but for breast implants. The future for Serbian students was a choice between a legitimate job paying a pittance each month—if they could get a job at all—or a career as a smuggler of contraband, drugs, cigarettes, weapons, or women.

The lure of the Mafia was powerful. Even many students repulsed by its values ended up drawn in by the money. Otpor tried to provide an alternative route for kids to earn respect and admiration and be part of a desirable group. One day at the university I met a graduate student named Jelena, who had been active in Otpor when she was in high school. One reason she liked it, she said, was that Otpor competed with the prevalent culture. "Otpor offered a place where it was not important to have a gold necklace, to be blonde and thin," she said.

Milja went on to work in advertising, but all the Otpor founders were keenly tuned to the importance of branding, messages, and marketing. Ivan Marović used to say that along with Gandhi and Martin Luther King, Jr., Otpor had another role model: Coca-Cola, with its simple, powerful message and strong brand. Otpor's organizers routinely talked about being in a brand war, with Milošević as the brand to beat.

Otpor reinforced its image with a soundtrack of rock music: Serbian bands, American groups such as Rage Against the Machine, and music from the rest of Europe. One interesting influence was the sly, subversive, intensely political Slovenian band Laibach, famous for using Nazi-style uniforms and props associated with totalitarian Communism or appropriating nationalist political speeches as lyrics. It wasn't the music that attracted Otpor—"Have you heard it?" groaned Srdja—but the group's theatricality. "They created a brand out of nothing," he said.

In truth, all Otpor's music was political—rock in Serbia at the time was a pro-Europe, antinationalist statement. It was also a very clear statement against the Mafiosi, whose anthems came from a particularly Serbian blend called turbo-folk, with lyrics celebrating Serb nationalism and militarism. Its goddess was the singer Ceca, a bombshell who married Arkan, Serbia's most notorious criminal and paramilitary leader.

DESPITE ITS OUTSIZE AMBITIONS, in many ways Otpor was in the position in which many movements find themselves when seeking social change. It had an inspired name, logo and brand. Its founders had a very clear goal: a Serbia without Milošević. For Otpor, as for most organizations, all that was the easy part. The hard part is what to do to reach that goal. Otpor knew that the earlier protests had made mistakes it should not repeat: Miloševći wasn't going to resign just because it held a big march, and it could not simply aim at fellow students if it wanted to defeat a dictator. Otpor knew what it shouldn't do. The question it faced, that every group faces, is what it *should* do—what must be done tomorrow morning after breakfast, and the next morning, and every morning after, to get the roller coaster to the crest of the hill? What concrete, small step should we take next? When the founders of most groups sit down to think about this question, they draw a blank—if they think about it at all. Otpor was determined to find the answer.

Otpor's founders made a list of the movement's assets. It was very short. At the top of the list was the media. The anti-Milošević media were harassed and fined, but they existed. Serbia had many radio stations in what were called "independent"—in fact, opposition—hands, the most important by far being the Belgrade-based B92. There were opposition newspapers, including *Blic*, the country's largest-circulation tabloid. And because the opposition controlled most municipalities, there was opposition TV in almost all cities. In Belgrade, that was Studio B, controlled by Vuk Drašković.

"Our relationship with the independent media was very important," said Jovan Ratković, who joined Otpor immediately after the inner circle widened. "There were twenty of us—we couldn't close a single street in downtown Belgrade. But we needed to create massive support. The strategy became one of surprise, shock, and secrecy—presenting ourselves as a widespread underground movement." Otpor was small, but if it could do things the independent media would cover, it could look big. It could have Serbs asking: Who are these people?

Otpor's first action came on the night of November 2, 1998. Two women and two men spray-painted "Otpor" and the fist on the wall of the Natural Sciences and Mathematics Building at Belgrade University. They were arrested. Two days later, at an afternoon rock concert in a central Belgrade square organized by the Association of Independent Electronic Media, a group of students distributed a leaflet printed with the fist and a short, rather juvenile message: "Resistance is the answer!

There is no other way. It will be too late when someone you know starves to death. When they start killing in the streets, when they put out all the lights and poison the last well, it will be too late. This is not a system, it is a disease. Bite the system. Get a grip. Live the Resistance!"

"Teen angst," Milja called the message. Someone on stage took a leaflet and read it out loud to the crowd.

As Otpor intended, the message was magnified by the independent media. Slavko Ćuruvija, once an ally of Milošević's wife and now publisher of an opposition paper, put the leaflet and the fist on the front page of his *Dnevni Telegraf.* (It was an expensive decision. He was fined $100,000 for it and eventually had to move the paper's production out of the country.)

The graffiti-sprayers were sentenced to ten days in jail. When twenty-six-year-old Teodora Tabacki was released on November 14, she gave an interview to the opposition newspaper *Danas*, where she described in detail their time in jail—which was uncomfortable but not terrible. "Will you withdraw from political activism after this?" *Danas* asked her. "You're kidding, right?" she answered. "I'll just make sure they don't catch me next time."

Tabacki's courage and directness got people talking. The next month, there was an official ceremony at the university that included a group of politicians. Students unfurled a banner bearing the word "Otpor" in front of the visiting VIPs, then ran. On December 15, on his way to a student march, Srdja Popović was pulled from his car, arrested, and beaten up by police. One officer, he said, put a gun in his mouth and told him he wished they were in Iraq, where he could do whatever he wanted with prisoners. Police claimed, falsely, that they had found cocaine in the car.

For the next few months, the fist and the Otpor name appeared on walls regularly, although mostly inside the university. Otpor's organizers also contacted other students who had led protests in 1996–97 in Belgrade and in the other major university cities of Novi Sad, Niš, and Kragujevac. The movement grew, but very slowly. There were perhaps 300 members by late March 1999. Then Otpor announced it was suspending operations because Serbia was about to be bombed.

Before he came to power, Slobodan Milošević had shown no sign of being a Serbian nationalist. Yet over the decade of the 1990s, he began four nationalistic wars. When he could not solve his people's problems, he attempted to unify and divert them by stirring up hatred and paranoia against outsiders. He led largely Serb armies and paramilitary groups to invade the other Yugoslav republics of Slovenia, Croatia, and Bosnia and carry out brutal repression in Kosovo. In each case, he used nationalist propaganda to stir up Serbs' historic grievances against their neighbors, telling the Serbs that if they did not kill the Slovenes, Croats, Bosnian Muslims, and Kosovo Albanians, they themselves would become victims. Mass slaughter and genocide were not new to Europe, but it was Milošević—not Hitler or Stalin—who introduced to the annals of war the term *ethnic cleansing* and persuaded the world to prosecute rape as a war crime. At least 140,000 people were killed in his four wars. He lost them all.

It took the outside world an unconscionable decade to stop treating Milošević as its partner, but by 1999 the West had finally had enough. When negotiations about a Serb withdrawal from Kosovo broke down, NATO began to employ other methods of persuasion. For seventy-eight days, bombs rained down on targets in Serbia and, to a lesser extent, Montenegro, the tiny state (one-fifteenth Serbia's size) that, together with Serbia, then made up Yugoslavia. NATO bombed military installations, oil refineries, bridges, power plants. Warplanes hit at least eleven targets with shells using depleted uranium—a superdense material that can penetrate armor but also leaves lasting radiation. The bombing of the headquarters of Radio Television Serbia (RTS), which broadcast Milošević's nationalist poison, killed at least sixteen people. During the bombing, the government forbade employees to leave the building.

After the bombing, Human Rights Watch documented about 500 civilian deaths. The United Nations Environment Programme was still finding and cleaning up radioactive shells years later. The economy, already in ruins, was further devastated. The bombing rallied most Serbs around Milošević; any dissent would have seemed unpatriotic. Besides, it was perilous. Ćuruvija, the publisher of *Dnevni Telegraf*, warned

Otpor's leaders that the government had prepared a hit list and they were likely on it. Srdja Popović, Ivan Andrić, and Andreja Stamenković, who handled money for Otpor, left Serbia for Montenegro. Then, on April 11, 1999, Ćuruvija was assassinated. A few weeks later, Zoran Djindjić, who had been told by police contacts that he, too, would be murdered, also went to Montenegro. Vuk Drašković (who had by then left the government), Radio B92's Veran Matić, and other civic activists also left Serbia for their own safety for the duration of the war.

On June 10, Milošević capitulated to NATO, agreeing to pull Serbian troops out of Kosovo and turn the region over to the international community. RTS, of course, recast the situation as a historic triumph. But it was not hard for Serbs to understand the implications of Kosovo as a United Nations protectorate: Milošević had lost their Jerusalem.

For the first time, the bombing had brought Milošević's wars home to civilian Serbs. The vast majority of them had never given much thought to what Milošević had done to the rest of the region. (Nor, to this day, do Otpor leaders seem to have done so. It may seem contradictory that people with enough talent for democracy to overthrow Milošević so creatively could live inside a nationalist bubble, but Serbia's political culture was, and continues to be, one of insularity and victimhood.) The NATO bombing served to reinforce Serbs' own sense of victimization. Serbs noted that the bombs now killing civilians were ordered by world leaders who had spent years shaking Milošević's hand. Since Serbs had not been told about Serb abuses of Albanians in Kosovo—and probably would not have believed the stories anyway—NATO's bombing indeed looked like the "fascism" Milošević had labeled it.

After the war, however, the apparent unity it had produced began to melt away. For the first time, Serbs felt in the flesh the effect of Milošević's wars, and they started to blame him for it. They still considered themselves victims, but they began to realize that their leader had brought the suffering upon them.

Otpor began organizing in earnest. Now it would leave the confines of the universities and become a nationwide organization.

■   ■   ■   ■

OTPOR'S MAJOR CHALLENGE WAS to persuade its potential activists to overcome their apathy and distaste for politics. The solution it improvised took the form of the social cure. It would make joining the movement cool, hip, and fun. Otpor set out to make its activists the envy of their friends: wearing the organization's black T-shirt would mean you were an insider at the revolution.

To accomplish this goal, Otpor had to take everything Serbia's political parties did and turn it on its head. Serbia's politicians, for example, loved to hear themselves talk. Except for Djindjić, who actually organized, Serbian politicians tended to believe that speeches were their entire job. So Otpor decreed that it would have no speeches. The students decided that their task was not to persuade people of the evils of Milošević; everyone already knew about them. Otpor didn't have to give anyone any information. What it had to do was motivate people to act: get them out of their houses and into political life. Speeches by men in ties had just the opposite effect on young people: they put kids to sleep and reminded them that politics was something foreign, something creepy, uncool.

History, as is often noted, carries profound weight in the Balkans, where people sometimes speak about events that took place in the fourteenth century as if they had occurred a week ago. Milošević used the Serb identification with historical figures and the relevance of past events to play on his countrymen's sense of victimization and draw them into war after war. The political parties also reached back into history; most claimed to reflect a certain part of Serb tradition and treated certain historical figures as patron saints.

Otpor, too, had a patron saint: Monty Python. Nearly every Otpor founder I talked to recalled growing up watching the British comedy troupe's TV shows. They knew what lumberjacks have for tea and what happens when you try to return an ex-parrot. Appropriating the Pythons' absurdity and irreverence was not entirely a conscious decision—Otpor was, after all, an organization of college students. "For us it was a great party all the time," said Slobodan Homen, and he was perhaps the soberest of the bunch. "We were friends together drinking beer and talking about serious issues. The humor comes up naturally." Many Serbs—in and out of Otpor—also talked about sardonic humor as a prominent feature of Serb culture. Ridicule had been a part of the student protests, but now it became Otpor's central strategy.

The traditional politicians also relied heavily on marches, protests, and rallies—often studded with political speeches. The daily march had also been the bread and butter of the student movement. Not for Otpor. Part of the problem was that mass marches required, well, masses, and these Otpor didn't have. "We couldn't compete on numbers," said Milja. "If the numbers drop, then people see it as a failure. What we wanted was to apply constant pressure, like a bee annoying a big bull. The bull can't do anything—he's not fast enough."

The students decided that the stuff of Otpor, its daily work, would be street actions—pranks, really, pieces of attention-getting public theater. Although wit was perhaps not always achieved, it was always the aim. One of the most famous actions featured an oil barrel painted with the face of Milošević by Otpor's house artist, Duda. Otpor activists took the barrel to Knez Mihailova street, Belgrade's most fashionable pedestrian shopping district, and began to roll it down the middle. People could insert one dinar into a slot in the barrel for the privilege of whacking Milošević with a bat.

Another celebrated action took place right after the police raided the office Otpor had established on Knez Mihailova (in an apartment owned by Homen's mother). Police arrested the staff and carted away boxes of materials, files, and computers. Otpor then announced publicly that it would be bringing in new material in two days.

At noon two days later, hundreds of spectators and dozens of reporters and photographers—all called by Otpor—gathered to watch. Strapping young men began to carry boxes, bending under their weight, from trucks parked two blocks away to the building where Otpor was housed. There was even a pulley rigged up—this was an Ivan Marović production, and he neglected no theatrical detail. Before the men began bringing in the boxes, Marović solemnly told the assembled reporters that "big Joe"—the name of a famous crane in Yugoslavia's old shipbuilding yards—was back in business. (The pulley was actually useless, but no one could see that from outside.) The police pounced, opening the boxes. They were empty.

"Our people knew they would be arrested," said Srdja. "That was no problem. The problem was to keep them from laughing."

It was a classic example of Otpor's favorite kind of prank, a dilemma action. Both the barrel and the boxes left the regime damned either way. Let boxes through and the regime looks weak—and the next day, Otpor would have brought in the real boxes of materials. Something that had been prohibited would now be permitted. But when the police arrested what was essentially a troupe of actors doing a pantomime, the nation sniggered. The same with the oil barrel—if police had let the barrel go, they would be telling Serbia that it was now permitted to ridicule Milošević. So they "arrested" the barrel. Photos of the police loading a barrel into the police van appeared all over the opposition media. The police looked ridiculous.

Otpor made Milošević a giant cake on his birthday, carving it into pieces just as Milošević had carved up Yugoslavia. To celebrate a lunar eclipse, Otpor built a five-meter cardboard telescope. Viewers could look in and see Milošević as a falling star. In Novi Sad, Serbia's second-largest city, a ninety-minute drive northwest of Belgrade, NATO's bombs had destroyed the city's bridges. Milošević had been making a big show out of building new ones, so Otpor dedicated its own new bridge—a Styrofoam toy bridge it placed over a pond in a downtown park. Otpor's Novi Sad branch also took over a small square in town and put out a few stools in front of a cardboard box with two antennae and "RTS" painted on it. Otpor people would sit in front of the box and watch nothing happen on their cardboard TV.

A few of Otpor's actions were on a larger scale. In February 2000, Milošević's Socialist Party of Serbia held its annual party congress, as Socialist parties do. Otpor mocked it by holding a congress of its own, and members came from all over the country. They actually did important business—they changed Otpor officially from a student movement to a people's movement—but what mattered more was the show it put on. Ivan Marović, wearing a long, gray World War II military coat, was surrounded on stage by a crowd of Otpor activists in their black

T-shirts with the white fist. The names of their cities were called, and one by one they went to the front, where Ivan announced that Otpor existed in seventy cities. It was Otpor's show of force.

By all accounts, Otpor's most-talked-about action occurred on New Year's Eve, as the year 2000 began. (Because Serbia uses a different calendar, New Year's Eve falls on January 13.) Otpor had organized a rock concert in front of the National Museum in downtown Belgrade. New Year's Eve in Belgrade always draws people from all over the country; the celebration of the new millennium brought out about 30,000 people who listened to Serbian rock bands in the early evening. "Save Serbia—Slobo, kill yourself!" the crowd chanted. A rumor had circulated that, after midnight, the rock band Red Hot Chili Peppers would appear. Otpor was sly, not confirming or denying it.

Precisely at midnight, the stage went dark. Instead of Red Hot Chili Peppers, a brief film began to play about the disastrous year, with photographs of Serbs and Albanians supposedly killed in Kosovo—the photos were fake—as a deep, resonant voice from offstage intoned names of the dead, which were real. (The voice belonged to Boris Tadić, who was then a Democratic Party member of Parliament and therefore enjoyed legal immunity. Srdja, in hiding at the time, was staying in Tadić's apartment. In 2004, Tadić was elected president of Serbia.) Then the voice said: "You have no reason to celebrate the new millennium . . . go home."

The crowd stood in stunned darkness, waiting. But the event was truly over, and soon everyone shuffled home. It was the first serious Otpor action; Serbs discussed it for months afterward. For many young people, it was the moment they realized Otpor was something worth getting involved in.

Actions had many advantages over marches. People talked about them. Marches often ended in some dreaded speech; actions were cooler. The humor was key to smashing through the wall of fear. Seeing a group of devil-may-care young people ridiculing Milošević made onlookers smile—and encouraged them to think about the regime, and their own role, in a different light. Through actions, Otpor showed that energetic and fearless opposition to the regime was possible.

The Otpor actions also helped keep volunteers busy—very important to growing a movement. "If people aren't busy, they leave," said Srdja. Not everyone wanted to do actions. Many new recruits were happy plastering walls with stickers and posters, or giving out leaflets. But there were always people who came to Otpor with ideas for actions, people who loved to plan them and make the props, people who loved to be out in public doing guerrilla theater.

Actions also helped to grow Otpor. Onlookers would often stay to ask the actors about the mysterious movement, and some filled in the membership forms Otpor passed out. They asked whether there would be another action soon, and to that one, they would bring friends. Otpor called it a "recruit, train, act" triangle: get some people, train them, and do an action, which in turn attracts more people. Then you train the new people and send them out to do more actions.

Even when Otpor was still small, actions made it look big. In Novi Sad, Otpor never had many activists—it was the same people all the time at the actions. But that was hidden from the average resident, who could see the graffiti on the wall—and, when Otpor got money, the stickers and posters—and see the headlines on the newsstands about Otpor's mischief. That was the power of the independent media.

Otpor wasn't aiming for the people who bought newspapers; few Serbs had that kind of disposable income. The valuable real estate for Otpor proved to be the front pages, which, displayed at newsstands, were visible to everyone who walked down the street. "We told the press department [of Otpor] that there will be no press conferences or press releases," said Ivan Marović. "If you want to say something, you do something on the street, and when journalists show up, you can talk to them." Otpor needed the picture an action would generate, and good pictures often made the front page. "A hundred people in the street is not news, but a hundred people on the street doing something crazy is a picture," he said.

For the cost of a barrel and some paint, Otpor could buy itself a front-page picture. During the month of February 2000, Otpor scored twenty-one front-page stories or pictures in the popular tabloid *Blic*.

Arrival of the police usually guaranteed the front page, but Otpor was happy with all publicity. Even small towns—if they were run by the opposition—had tiny TV stations that were happy to broadcast Otpor's actions, the taping sometimes done with the same camcorder that had videotaped the director's daughter's wedding. Jovan Ratković marveled at an interview he did at a TV station in the town of Prokuplje: it was run by one old guy whose studio was his living room; the office was his kitchen. He reached an entire city of 50,000 people with a staff he paid in pizza.

The other strategy that Otpor used to appear massive was to imprint the logo everywhere. When Otpor started to attract money, the spray-painted graffiti and stickers were supplemented by posters and stickers. Stickers were preferred because posters took three men to put up, and it was slow work, which gave the police the opportunity to arrest the group and seize a very expensive stack of dozens of posters. Stickers could be applied by anyone, instantly and nearly secretly, and they were made of paper, nearly impossible to remove. The messages evolved constantly—Otpor wanted Serbs to wake up in the morning to see their neighborhoods covered with new slogans as often as possible. But all Otpor's materials used the stark, modern, aggressive-looking visuals that Duda had begun with the fist logo. The aim was to appear big, powerful, and secret.

To acquire its underground image, Otpor had help from a very above-ground source: corporate marketing experts. Ivan Andrić, in charge of Otpor's marketing, relied on advice from friends at Serbia's large advertising agencies. He had polling done—mostly for free, or nearly free—by two experienced market-research firms. When Otpor wanted to introduce a new message, Andrić organized a focus group. "In the beginning, it was more intuitive, but by 2000, we were more professional," he said. "I read more than 9,000 pages of surveys and public-opinion polls."

The slogans aimed at brevity and impact. "People always want to make slogans it takes days to remember," Duda complained. Not Otpor. Duda was happy; Otpor wanted a very big graphic and very little text. One poster, double the standard size, was of a huge fist bursting out of the bounds of the frame with a small "It's Spreading" at the bottom. There was no need to say what "it" was—like Rage Against the Haze's Web spots, the movement was in a sense about itself. To counter the government's accusations that Otpor's members were CIA agents, or terrorists, Otpor printed a few hundred thousand posters with the fist and "Resistance (Otpor), because I love Serbia" at the bottom, on a black background. "That was a bull's-eye," Duda said. "You look at many of them hung up together, and it looks very powerful." In 2000, Otpor printed more materials than all the political parties in Serbia had printed over the previous ten years. Even in the most remote, tiniest villages in Serbia, the lampposts and walls were plastered with the fist.

Otpor wanted its posters, stickers, flags, and buttons to be everywhere. By contrast, when it came to T-shirts, the movement stumbled upon the advantage of exclusivity, a new way to make Otpor the club everyone wanted to join. The basic T-shirt was black, with a white Otpor fist in a circle and "Otpor!" above. Later some slogans were added: "Resistance until victory," "Live the Resistance," or "Resistance, because I love Serbia." The T-shirts were a hot item from the beginning, but their cachet soared when the only T-shirt printer willing to take the risk of working for Otpor ran low on black shirts. To conserve, new ones were reserved only for important activists. Naturally this drove up their value. People *wanted* one of those T-shirts. Even Milja's blasé friends wanted one. "Having a T-shirt became something that proved something to the people around you," she said. People lined up for them outside the office, but they emerged instead with stickers to put up.

"A black T-shirt made you different from other people," said Jelena, the graduate student who had been a high-school Otpor activist. "Some of the T-shirts were white, and low quality. Everyone had those. But to get a black T-shirt; there was a hierarchy. The fact that there was a limited number of people with black T-shirts was very important."

Otpor had printed a few red shirts, a few with the fist outlined, even a polo-collared shirt. "The T-shirts were like a military ranking. My T-shirt had no letters at all—just a fist," said Srdja. "I was proud of that."

Otpor never wavered from its public explanation—given to the press during interviews and to police during interrogations—that it got the money for these T-shirts, the computers, the fax machines, the tons of posters, the millions of stickers, the hundreds of cell phones, the cars, and the gasoline from discontented Serbs at home and abroad. It was true the first year: Otpor's members were Serbs, and they certainly were discontented. A few fundraising events among Serb communities abroad raised a small amount. But until about mid-1999, Otpor lived on the labor and contributions of its own members and their parents, and on the resources, such as office space, that belonged to the student organizations and a few other congenial groups. The first T-shirts were printed by the radio station B92. Offices were donated and people drove their own cars and paid for their own gas. There were not many activists, and few materials aside from leaflets, stencils, paint, and T-shirts.

After the NATO bombing campaign, Washington began to realize that Otpor was a group that was going to do something. The first person inside the U.S. government to take notice of Otpor was Albert Cevallos, a program officer for the Agency for International Development's Office of Transition Initiatives (OTI), which worked in countries in crisis trying to emerge from repressive regimes. When Srdja met Cevallos through mutual friends, they hit it off. Otpor asked Cevallos for a few hundred dollars to run a small campaign inside Belgrade University to get rid of a particularly hardline dean who had been installed by the government.

OTI supported Otpor with a small grant. "They did a good job, for less than the price of a used car," said Cevallos. "We reported that around Washington, and then we gave them a little more support. They were more successful each time. I had to go to the State Department and convince them that these were good guys to pay attention to, and go to Congress to show them proof of success."

With Cevallos's help, Otpor leaders began to meet people in Washington—democracy activists, reporters, and officials. Soon Slobodan Homen and Nenad Konstantinović went to Washington to meet with Secretary of State Madeleine Albright and others. "How can I help?" was the first question asked of Homen by Albright, who had made the overthrow of Milošević a personal goal. (She had lived in Belgrade as a child, when her father was the Czechoslovak ambassador to Yugoslavia.)

In November 1999, the U.S. government was beginning to work with Serbia's political opposition as well. In the winter of that year, Washington joined a European program to buy heating oil for cities controlled by the political opposition. The program was successful: the oil kept many Serbs from freezing, boosted the popularity of opposition mayors, and showed that foreign governments could distinguish between Milošević and the Serbian people.

That program received millions of dollars; Otpor's efforts required numbers with far fewer zeros. "The beauty of Otpor was that it was not expensive," Albert Cevallos said. "T-shirts, posters, and stickers were not heating oil. There were huge nongovernmental organizations—groups Washington had worked with for years—and they were getting a lot of money and not doing things. But with Otpor, for a couple hundred bucks, you'd get a big return."

Otpor's idealism, which was key to its appeal to Serbs, also helped convince Washington. The largely volunteer nature of the workforce gave Washington more assurance that its money would be used well. (Not everyone was a volunteer. Office managers were paid, as were a few other professionals, such as a security expert. And there were stipends for some Otpor activists, said Peter Wiebler, who was working for Freedom House at the time: "It was small bits of money—we never had the sense they were running some sort of scheme.")

"They were young, abrasive, and foulmouthed, but they were really committed and got stuff done," said Daniel Calingaert, at the time a program officer working on Serbia for the International Republican Institute (IRI), an arm of the Republican Party. "They accounted for their spending a lot better than the others."

The dynamism of Otpor contrasted with the lethargy of the Serbian political parties. Calingaert said that when IRI staff members would meet with political-party leaders and ask what was happening, the Serbs would talk about what Otpor was doing. "We'd say, 'We know. What are *you* doing?'" Calingaert said. "Even going into the summer of 2000, it was hard to picture these guys winning an election. In comparison, Otpor delivered. They were always on the go, doing stuff. They were politically smart—much better focused than the others at promoting unity. They instinctively knew infighting was one of their biggest enemies."

Calingaert was not the only American unenthusiastic about the political parties. His was the prevailing view. "In 1998, the general U.S. attitude was that the political opposition in Serbia wasn't a particularly influential force and wasn't related to the two main issues of Bosnia and Kosovo," said James O'Brien, a senior adviser to Madeleine Albright who was involved in Washington's policy in the Balkans on a day-to-day basis.

Otpor, however, intrigued the Americans. "The signal thing they did that should never be lost is that they made it okay for Serbs to say publicly that the regime was not invincible, that many Serbs shared a sense that change could come," said O'Brien. "They created a space in which Serbs could speak publicly, and they were clever enough and connected enough that the regime couldn't ignore the messages or suppress the messengers."

It is hard to calculate how much financial help Otpor received from Washington, but one U.S. government official estimated that it was probably around $2 million in the year before the election. (Some in Otpor think this estimate is too high.) Until Milošević fell, that story was hidden. About the rest of Otpor's activities, the movement was completely open—about the money, not at all. Otpor concealed the source of its money because the truth would have killed the movement; especially after the NATO bombing, anything from Washington was anathema to Serbs. The government all along had tried to tar Otpor by calling it an agent of imperialism.

This is still a sensitive subject for many in Otpor. What is certainly true is that money from abroad covered only a small part of Otpor's total expenses, given that Serbs contributed their labor, donated offices, and mostly covered other fixed operating costs—expenses that make up the vast bulk of any organization's budget. The cash from outside paid the cell-phone bills and was spent on Otpor's actions, such as the printing of posters and stickers.

More important, the strategies were homegrown. Part of Slobodan Homen's answer to Albright's question about helping was to ask her—diplomatically—to stay as far away as possible. And that routine photo with the secretary of state that gets mailed to the visitor's home? Don't send that. Washington granted Otpor got both of its wishes: money and distance. O'Brien had confidence in Otpor and admired its creativity. He understood that direction from Washington was neither necessary nor helpful. Washington likes to micromanage. This time, it refrained.

FROM ITS INCEPTION, Otpor's mission was very different from that of a political party. It was designed not to inform Serbs of the merits of any particular ideas or people, or even to persuade them to support a certain group, but rather to call them to action in what was an overwhelmingly popular goal—to defeat the dictator. To motivate them to participate, Otpor chose messages that were in large part about the group itself: actions designed to make a tiny group look big, and slogans like "It's Spreading." Otpor had discovered a key principle of a successful social cure: Information rarely motivates people; identification is much more effective.

It was a bit paradoxical—Otpor was the only movement in Serbia that tried to make political activity light, hip, and fun, yet it was completely negative. Like humor, this had a particular appeal to Serbs, who talk about their national trait of *inat*—malicious, perverse defiance, regardless of whether it brings catastrophic consequences. But Otpor also found, as politicians around the world do, that there were considerable advantages in being against something. Otpor didn't have to propose and defend solutions to Serbia's overwhelming problems—a task that would have necessarily alienated some potential supporters and muddied its clear, strong message.

More risky was the decision taken by Otpor organizers in October 1998 that they would have a collective leadership. Otpor would not exist to further any politician's career; instead, it existed to end one. Only one name was associated with Otpor: the enemy, Slobodan Milošević.

For a Serbian political group, this was truly revolutionary. Milošević and his wife, Mirjana Marković, had his-and-hers political parties that they ran as cults of personality. In the opposition, the Serbian Renewal Movement was completely centered on the figure of Vuk Drašković. The Democratic Party, while a real party with skilled politicians and a relatively deep bench, was in a more sophisticated way still an instrument for Zoran Djindjić. The Democratic Party's main campaign poster in the 1993 parliamentary elections, for example, was simply a photo of Djindjić with the slogan *Pošteno* ("Fair Deal") below it. In Serbia, a party was synonymous with its leader.

Otpor's decision to have no leader proved to be crucial. In Serbia, the head that sticks up gets cut off. Serbian politics was not a clash of ideas but a competition to discredit personalities. As the Democratic Party gained in strength, for example, the government never battled the party's pro-Europe ideology. Instead, the RTS nightly news simply took to calling Djindjić a CIA agent, traitor, drug trafficker, or criminal. When Djindjić went to Montenegro during the NATO bombing in the spring of 1999, after being warned there was a price on his head, the government assailed him as a coward and a traitor, and upon his return two months later arrested him for draft evasion. The campaign against Djindjić was quite effective, discrediting his party and eliminating him as a possible candidate against Milošević. Otpor's founders knew that if there was no face to Otpor's leadership, that removed a weapon the regime could use to destroy the movement.

Other politicians told Otpor's leaders they were kidding themselves—collective leadership couldn't last. Indeed, the group had serious divisions. Otpor's founders agreed on the need to overthrow Milošević and the importance of civil and human rights, such as a free press and checks on government, but they didn't agree on much more. Some, like Srdja Popović, were in political parties; others wanted nothing to do with them. Some people wanted Otpor to have a saint—literally a saint—as many organizations and political parties in Serbia did. Among others, Milja Jovanović, a committed atheist, opposed it. There was no agreement on what Serbia after Milošević might look like—Otpor even had some monarchists. "We never discussed what should be the economic system of post-Milošević Yugoslavia," said Jovan Ratković. "We knew such a discussion would split the movement."

The traditional politicians couldn't even understand why Otpor would *want* to be run by a collective. The whole point of politics, in their view, was to further your career—and people followed you in hopes that you would throw them patronage jobs or opportunities for corruption. The politicians were sure that some Otpor organizer would decide he wanted the spotlight. Even student leaders had big egos— maybe especially student leaders.

But it did last. Many of Otpor's founders said that the durability of the collective leadership was the aspect of the movement that surprised them the most.

Far from being anarchic, Otpor was meticulously and carefully organized. The eleven founders became a group of thirty or so in Belgrade, and others were in charge in cities and towns throughout Serbia. The Belgrade leadership, plus a few people from elsewhere, met constantly in ratty restaurants or cafés or just held ambulatory meetings in the street.

And while the organization was loose and people crossed lines, there were leaders in charge of different aspects: Ivan Marović handled the press and dreamed up actions and strategies. Milja Jovanović also talked to reporters and took charge of organizing in the universities. Nenad Konstantinović organized the network of activists around Serbia. Slobodan Djinović was Otpor's link to other civic groups; Ivan Andrić and Dejan Randjić did propaganda and marketing; Slobodan Homen, along with Konstantinović, met with foreign governments and scooped up money; Andreja Stamenković hid the money and doled it out; and Srdja Popović was in charge of recruiting and training volunteers.

If Otpor did have a most prominent face, it was that of Ivan Marović. A radical and a jester, highly charismatic and theatrical (and extremely disorganized), he invented the most outrageous actions and, along with Milja, was an early spokesperson. But as membership grew, Otpor trained dozens of activists to speak for the organization. Each held the job for less than two weeks—longer than that and the government would find ways to compromise the spokesperson. It didn't actually matter who spoke for Otpor, as the collective leadership always provided the spokespeople with the same simple, disciplined message, on the need for and inevitability of Milošević's removal. The message was unsophisticated enough that a seventeen-year-old could transmit it perfectly adequately. What was sophisticated, in fact, was the use of many different spokespeople, which made the movement look bigger, and the use of the least-threatening faces possible.

That Otpor was not a cult of personality also raised the movement's credibility with young people and all Serbs who were disillusioned with the opportunism and personal ambition of opposition political party leaders. Otpor was pushing a cause, not a person. It kept the movement untainted and helped Otpor volunteers to feel important. Every political party, of course, says to its volunteers: "This movement is you." The traditional parties were always nagging their youth leaders: "Look at Otpor! Why can't you get all those volunteers?" But the traditional parties meant that recruits were welcome to become cogs in their leaders' machines. They couldn't even grasp Otpor's organizing principle: that its day-to-day work was completely decentralized.

Early on, Otpor's leaders realized that to keep volunteers happy, they needed to feel responsible and important, that their work and achievement mattered. They also needed to be constantly busy, not sitting around and waiting for instructions from above. So while the central organization set overall strategy, each cluster decided how to carry it out and how best to use local talent. Volunteers were trained in Otpor methods and the principles of nonviolent struggle and then set loose to *be* the movement in their towns or neighborhoods. It was the starfish Randy Frazee had wanted for Willow Creek: an animal with no central brain; each finger contains the whole idea.

In Novi Sad, I met a young man named Nenad Šeguljev. A photographer by profession, Nenad was a rarity—he had been a politically active teenager before Otpor was created. Or he had tried, anyway. He went to the offices of the local branch of an opposition political party and volunteered his considerable energies. "But you needed 100 approvals to do something," he said. Whenever he suggested an activity, the party leaders told him, "We'll see, we'll see." The party was rigid and old-fashioned and hierarchical. Then he heard about Otpor. "Everything they forbade me to do was allowed in Otpor," he said. "Every action I could design or think of, I did." He became Novi Sad Otpor's most valuable utility man, spending "twenty-five hours a day" putting up Otpor's posters and stickers and running from the police.

Nenad, like everyone else in Otpor, had to follow only two rules. Every Otpor action had to be aimed at Milošević. And it had to be nonviolent. If someone is egging you on to violence, activists were told, that person is likely to be a police provocateur. Follow the two rules and anything was permissible. "Five kids from a high school would come in and tell us, 'We want to make Otpor in our school.' We said, 'Here's a computer; make a leaflet and we'll print it.' They were amazed someone would treat them like that," said Milja. Otpor would even teach the skills—Duda was running what he called the Otpor School of Design. One of the few leaflets that Otpor agreed to print in color was one that some high school students had designed with the green graphics from the *Matrix* movies.

You could write your own script for street theater, create whatever props you needed, and stage any action, no matter how goofy. You could design your own leaflet and propose designs for more expensive-to-print stickers and posters, which would receive serious consideration from the marketing team. You could put up stickers and posters wherever you wanted. You could recruit anyone you wanted and organize your high school the way you wanted. "If you were anti-Milošević and nonviolent, you could go naked with 'Otpor' painted on your chest and we wouldn't denounce you, we wouldn't say you weren't Otpor," said Milja. "Our job was to say yes," said Stanko Lazendić, one of Otpor's leaders in Novi Sad.

If you wanted to, you could become a hero. You could be an Otpor spokesperson and appear in all the opposition media, or you could risk your neck picking up boxes of fresh posters from secret printers and leaving them at midnight in clandestine drop spots indicated to you in code. You could wallpaper your neighborhood and run from the police, heart pounding. If you didn't run fast enough, then you would be arrested—but when you finally got out of the police station late at night, a crowd of supporters would be cheering you and you could get your picture in the paper for all your friends to see the next day. It was the closest anyone who wasn't interested in the Mafia could get to becoming James Bond.

"Let's say you are a kid in the countryside," said Vesna Dozet, Otpor's Belgrade office manager. "Your parents are unhappy, they have no work and no money, and they're getting drunk. Then you join Otpor. You are still some kid from nowhere but now they've given you a cell phone. It's your job to go to the bus station and give a code to the driver to pick up a package of posters from Belgrade. Then you spirit it away and give it to your friends, and they put up the posters during the night. Young people become Partisans. You were never a part of anything, and you feel all of a sudden that you're part of something."

RADE MILIĆ WAS TWENTY-ONE when he joined Otpor in 1999. He was an archaeology student at Belgrade University, tall, dark-haired, with a black beard and long hair he often wore in a ponytail. He was sweet and shy, with a bit of a lisp. Rade—pronounced "RAH-day"— did not start out as a hero. Yet he became, during the year of his involvement, a dedicated, full-time fighter for freedom—not fearless, but someone who could control his fear because he shared the risks with friends and had learned to regard himself as someone playing an important part in making his country better. Thousands and thousands of young Serbs made the same psychological journey. Their transformation is perhaps the clearest and most successful illustration of the possibilities of the social cure. It is useful to get to know Rade to see how it was done.

Rade had watched the student protests of the early 1990s avidly when he was barely a teenager, and in high school he joined the 1996 and 1997 student marches. Like most young people in Belgrade, he had been swept up in the protests' emotion and optimism, and he crashed hard when they failed. He felt betrayed by the opposition political parties. He was not finished with politics but was "looking for an organization that was not dirtied by 96/97," he said.

He didn't, however, join Otpor until a year after its founding. His first activity proved to be a dramatic one. On November 9, 1999, Otpor held a march—one of its few. Milošević was accusing Otpor members of being foot soldiers of the United States Army. Otpor wanted to demonstrate its patriotism, so it asked anyone who had served in a war to join its activists in marching on Parliament from the plaza of the university's philosophy faculty. As the columns of marchers approached the Parliament building, police descended and began to beat them with truncheons. Rade was not in the first rows, so he was unhurt, but he was shaken—and mad. About half the people beaten up were young women or girls, which made him particularly furious. "I felt that now is the moment—you're looking at something happening and you just want to join," he said. "You say to yourself: If not now, when?"

The next day, he went to Otpor headquarters on Knez Mihailova Street for an introductory talk, but he was disappointed. He tried to ask about what had happened to the victims, and the trainers kept telling him, "We'll talk about that later." As he was leaving, he ran into Ivan Marović. Ivan had noticed Rade's questions and answered them. Then he asked Rade if he wanted to join Otpor's press department. Rade was startled. "I had expected an organization that was already formed and developed," he said. Otpor was a year old—why were they still recruiting new people into important jobs? He was accustomed to more static organizations. The next day, he returned to Otpor's office to work and was assigned to collect press clippings. That week, he started his press training. Ivan and Vukašin Petrović taught Rade and about nine others how to write announcements and talk to the press about Otpor events. They simulated various Otpor actions and had the new trainees practice writing them up and answering questions about them. Then Ivan and Petrović made a schedule of times for the new recruits to take over the press desk.

A little over a week later, Rade had his trial by fire. He was nearly alone in the office (everyone else except the office secretary was out at an action) when someone called from the town of Smederevo. There had been an event that day called Stomp on the System. The idea—a rather silly one—was to toss posters of Milošević on the ground and step on them. Ivan had been one of fifteen people arrested.

The press machine had to go into motion. Rade tried to call Petrović to ask for advice, but he couldn't find him. So he took a deep breath, wrote up an announcement, and began calling a two-page list of friendly journalists and giving interviews about the arrest. Speed was key. His job was to spread the news as rapidly as he could, informing people who could gather outside the police station or call and pester the police. It was important for the police to know they were being watched.

As usual, the Otpor office radio was turned to B92, which carried one of Rade's first interviews. As Rade worked down his list, he heard himself on the radio. He wished he hadn't been working alone, but the accompaniment of his own voice gave him confidence—it was proof he was doing his job well. He concentrated on the job of getting Ivan and his colleagues out of jail as fast as possible. He was nervous. "On the other hand," he said, "you are taking part in something that's happening. When you are useful, you feel very proud. You are doing something against a big evil—somebody who ruined your childhood. I realized what it means to assume responsibility." He was conscious that in that moment he crossed a line, moving from observer to participant.

Late that night, all fifteen arrested were released. "It was a scary experience," Rade said. "I couldn't sleep that night. It was the first time I was working when someone was arrested, and the person was someone I had confidence in. I thought that mass arrests were starting." When he woke up, he went out to buy the newspapers and there was the story, with his name as the Otpor spokesman. He still has those newspapers.

"I told all of my friends that I was in the newspapers," he said. "They all wanted to join. It was seen as very brave at the time." Several more of his friends did join, along with his uncle, and he brought two school friends into Otpor's press department. After that, Otpor became his full-time job, and he abandoned his classes, going to the university only when Otpor had an event there.

Rade recalls that time with great nostalgia. "I was proud of myself, and I saw that something I was doing actually had an effect," he said. He felt like a member of a team and made new, strong friendships. Rade and his friends spent every day working together, and at night the same group would go to parties. "The atmosphere was very tense,

and the tenseness would be discharged through laughter. It was schizo-
phrenic," he said. "We managed to create an atmosphere where everything appeared like a game. That helped us to overcome the enormous
pressure that all of us felt. We had our own jokes, our own symbols, our
own words. There was a special atmosphere of closeness to people. I
might not see those people from Otpor now for three, four or five years,
but when we meet again, we still feel that closeness."

OVER AND OVER AGAIN, people connected with Otpor echoed Rade,
saying that it was the best time of their lives—with the telling exception
of Slobodan Homen, who spent those years on an airplane, wearing
a suit. For Homen, the best period was during the student protests of
1996–97. Evidently, discussing revolution with the American secretary
of state is not as intense an experience as carrying out that revolution
with your friends.

I recognized this feeling; it was what I had experienced, even as a
foreigner, during my four years in Chile. Even at the tamest protests,
ones the police left alone, there was a *mística*—a sense of mission and
purpose—I had rarely felt before. But when there was the certainty of
tear gas and the possibility of real violence, running through the streets
in a bonfire-lit night ahead of the police, the protests were thrilling.
Being part of a crowd somehow made us feel the danger was tolerable,
even desirable—it turned repression into a unifying force. It made us
feel brave and important, part of something larger than us, something
that mattered. It is no doubt the case in all such movements, but probably greater with Otpor, as the activists weren't simply interchangeable
parts in some politician's machine. They had a stronger sense that this
revolution was *theirs*, that the movement belonged not to one person but
to everyone. "We were so much alive," said Duda, the designer. "It was
living on the edge; there was risk and we were doing something big."

That feeling of safety in numbers was an illusion. To be effective,
Otpor needed to grow, but its leaders knew that, as it grew, it would
become more and more of a target for the regime. The possibility of
being arrested, beaten, or worse would vastly increase, so people would

stay home. The very repression a large movement would attract threatened to deplete Otpor of its numbers. For Otpor, the existence of risk was itself risky.

But Otpor realized that danger also carried tremendous advantages. If it were managed correctly, the whiff of danger could become a powerful lure for many young people. There were plenty of people who liked to see themselves and have others see them as daring—as long as they were well prepared and the risks could be kept predictable. It did not escape Otpor's leadership that brutal repression made for excellent publicity. Otpor knew just how the regime would react as it became more of a threat. It set out to turn that reaction to its benefit.

Chapter Nine

The Judo
of Fear

OTPOR'S PREDICTIONS OF A CRACKDOWN WERE proven correct. In the spring of 2000, as Otpor was passing the 20,000-member mark, clashes with the police, interrogations, and arrests were becoming daily events. At an April meeting at Nenad Konstantinović's house, Otpor's eleven top leaders agreed it was the last time they would all gather in one place. The chance of arrest was now too high.

Across Serbia, no activist was too marginal to attract police attention. Simply possessing handbills or stickers was enough to get a young person hauled into the police station for an afternoon of questioning. Arrest was a real possibility for any young person active in Otpor. Over the two years of its existence, there were at least 2,500 arrests of Otpor members—and the smaller the town, the greater the chance of arrest and the worse the treatment the police were likely to mete out. In May 2000, the average number of arrests of Otpor activists was more than seven per day.

The fear this provoked was potentially one of the most critical obstacles to Otpor's growth. And the organization's ability to take advantage of fear—through the use of the social cure—was perhaps its most creative and significant achievement.

Otpor's lead organizers always knew they had chosen a path strewn with land mines. Milošević did not use mass killings of the political opposition, but he used selective killings, and it was prudent to assume that some in Otpor's leadership would become targets. Several Otpor leaders were warned by people with good contacts in the security service that they were at risk. There were credible rumors of a hit list featuring the fifty top opposition leaders. People who saw it claimed that Srdja and Homen's names were on it, and it was likely that it also had the names of other Otpor founders. Nenad Konstantinović, Otpor's network organizer and Homen's partner in dealing with foreign countries, reported that someone had tampered with the car that he and Homen used to drive back and forth to Hungary for meetings with Western officials. A wheel fell off at high speed, nearly killing Konstantinović; when he took it to a mechanic, he found out that someone had loosened the screws. Others also had unpleasant experiences. Beatings and physical threats during arrests were common.

Milošević's legal system was also used to intimidate Otpor. Arrest, obviously, was a constant threat, but the perils went beyond arrest. In May 2000, the government accused Stanko Lazendić and Miloš Gagić, Otpor's leaders in Novi Sad, of being the intellectual authors of a local murder. The murder had apparently been the result of a personal dispute, but the government seized on the fact that the accused killer had some Otpor leaflets in his apartment—although by that time, it was the rare household in Serbia that did not. The next day, Milošević's spokesman called Otpor a "terrorist organization."

The larger menace for Otpor leaders was not the street policeman but the secret police. These men, closely tied to the regime, with plenty to lose if it fell, were not just simply going through the motions when they made arrests. They viewed Otpor as a personal threat. Ivan Marović was kidnapped several times by the secret police; once they told him they had a great dentist who could work on his teeth. The secret police kept trying to get Ivan Andrić to admit that he was buying guns for terrorist organizations. They seemed to be looking for confessions that would allow the government to "prove" Otpor's terrorism in a show trial.

Otpor organizers felt somewhat protected by the fact that none of them was the face of the movement—killing a few top leaders would not have stopped Otpor. They didn't employ bodyguards, whereas Djindjić and Drašković traveled in clouds of them. But they took other precautions. They knew their cell phones were tapped—some of them had been tapped continuously since the student-protest days—so they talked in code. "Milenko is listening," they would remind each other— "Milenko" being the generic name they assigned to the secret policeman who was always the third party on the call. Before going to meetings, they would take the batteries out of their phones so their locations could not be tracked. Most had escape plans—false passports stashed in safe places and escape routes to Bulgaria for those with money and connections, life on the run in the forest for the less fortunate. Most of Otpor's leaders had left their parents' homes and were in hiding, moving among different friends' apartments.

"For two months I had my lawyer on speed dial," Ivan Andrić said. When he was arrested, he merely had to hit the button, which he could do while the phone was in his pocket, and his lawyer could hear everything.

The perils faced by Otpor's politburo were not a surprise. They had early on decided the risks were worth taking. That they thought this way was one reason they were leaders of the movement. But they could not expect tens of thousands of recruits to hold the same view.

In a few places, it required tremendous courage to belong to Otpor, even as a foot soldier. The worst place was Požarevac, the hometown of Milošević and his wife, a town whose despot was the couple's wild, bleached-blond son, Marko. In May 2000, Marko's bodyguards beat up the town's main Otpor activists, injuring two of them severely and lightly injuring another. In an example of Milošević's justice, the Otpor activists were jailed for two months and one was charged with attempted murder. Otpor took a photo of the destroyed face of one of those injured, Radojko Luković, turned it into a poster with text that said, "This is the face of Serbia," and put it up all over the country.

Požarevac was the extreme. But from Otpor's very first action in 1998, which cost Teodora Tabacki and her colleagues ten days in jail, it was clear that even the everyday work of Otpor—holding street actions, spraying graffiti, and putting up posters—was risky. Students didn't have families to support or jobs they had to worry about losing. But I remember a veteran opposition leader in Chile telling me that he never got over the difficulty of persuading himself to go to each demonstration knowing he would be teargassed—and that was just tear gas. Signing up for Otpor meant pushing yourself to do the work despite knowing that arrest was a serious possibility. At best, that meant several hours of unpleasantness with the police. And at worst—well, who knew what the worst could be? Otpor's organizers knew that most young people would sympathize with its goals, but fear could keep them at home. Otpor could not become a mass movement unless it could solve this problem.

THE CHALLENGE OF PERSUADING foot soldiers to overcome fear was not a new one. Even institutions with the luxury of drafting their soldiers still must worry that when men are called on to put themselves in danger, they will decide to stay in the safety of the foxhole. And generals since time immemorial have found the same solution to this problem. Colonel William Darryl Henderson, who has taught military psychology at West Point, studied the North Vietnamese, Soviet, Israeli, and American armies in his book *Cohesion: The Human Element in Combat.* "The only force on the battlefield strong enough to make a soldier advance under fire is his loyalty to a small group and the group's expectation that he will advance," Henderson wrote. Concluding that men put themselves in danger mainly because their buddies expect them to, he explored how army policies create or undermine such cohesion.

This, of course, is classic social cure: men who did not enter the army with suicidal tendencies acquire a willingness to die for a cause (even a cause they may not particularly believe in) because they identify with a small group of their peers and wish the group to see them as courageous.

More extreme behavior change would be hard to find. Every successful army uses this technique, but no nonviolent political movement has employed it as consciously and overtly as Otpor.

Rade Milić went nearly a year without being arrested; his first arrest occurred on August 31, 2000. He was in the Otpor office and an Otpor courier had driven up to deliver boxes of *Reporter,* a magazine from the Serb Republic of Bosnia, banned in Serbia because of its criticism of Milošević. When Rade went downstairs to help him unload the boxes, the police were waiting. Along with two of the couriers, Rade was arrested. Ivan Marović came down from the office in an Otpor T-shirt and was promptly arrested as well. When the police weren't looking, Rade turned off his cell phone and clipped it on the back of his pants. The four detainees were driven to a police station. As they entered, a policeman pointed a Kalashnikov machine gun and said, "Be afraid, now I will kill you all." Another policeman also pulled out a gun, but then they put down their guns. The police chained the two couriers to the radiator and put Rade and Ivan in separate cells.

Rade's cell was filthy, with urine all over the floor. It had a lightbulb surrounded by a perforated metal sheet. The police hadn't found his phone, so the first thing he did when the door of his cell clanged shut was to call Radio Index and do a live-from-jail interview. (His mother kept the station on in her kitchen all day—that's how she found out about his arrest.) A while later, the police took Rade back upstairs and interrogated him. In a departure from the usual pattern, he was not asked to write a statement. (The standard statement written by arrested Otpor activists was "I have nothing to say.") They took mug shots and prints.

A policeman named Joca was constantly cursing Rade, calling him and his family traitors. When Rade was washing his hands after being fingerprinted, he dirtied the sink with fingerprint powder. Joca grabbed him by his ponytail and pushed his head into the sink. "Clean this, you motherfucker," he told Rade. As Joca bent over, his T-shirt rode up, revealing the cell phone. Joca froze for a moment and then began to scream. "What do you think we are, monkeys?" he yelled. The police took the phone. Rade was handcuffed, spread over a table, and beaten.

The police put him back in the cell while they debated what to do. After an hour or two, they brought him back up and began to interrogate him again. They asked the standard questions: Who are the leaders of Otpor? How many members are there? Who is financing you? Where do you get your materials? Rade answered with the standard responses: We don't have a leader. We get our financing from Serbians abroad, and from donations—it is not our fault if a million people each gave us a dinar. We get our materials from Knez Mihailova Street.

The police called in the four men one by one to write their statements, and then they were released. "When I came out, all these people had gathered at the door," Rade said. "There were about thirty of them in the street. They had waited eight or nine hours for us." The crowd had organized a party in front of the police station. They drew flowers on the sidewalk with chalk, played volleyball, picnicked. Reporters were there. The crowd clapped and cheered when Rade emerged.

"When I was down in the cell, I could hear their voices," Rade said. "It gave me a lot of encouragement to know people were outside—it was very important for us. I knew I wasn't alone, I had support. You hope they'll release you quicker." He went right back to the office to review the announcement about his release that his fellow press officers had written. The radio was on, as always, tuned to an opposition station. It was playing news of his release. "I wasn't really free until I heard it on the radio," he said.

Rade had changed. He had not joined Otpor feeling daring. He had lain awake at night worrying that mass arrests were starting. But as time went on, his relationship to fear had altered. "There was the constant pressure of fear, mixed with despair, anger, hopelessness— but also with pride and euphoria. I believe that those feelings made me stronger," he said. The fear did not limit him, because he was not alone. He had worked backstage at the Otpor nonconcert on New Year's Eve. That night, people had been afraid the government would try to provoke the crowd, to create an excuse for violence or arrests. But the press team stuck together, and that made Rade feel safe. And he could hold his fear in context. Risk was a choice he had made, a choice he owned. "It's uncomfortable to have handcuffs on, to be in a dirty cell with urine all over the floor," he said, "but there are moments in history when you can influence important events. I knew I was right, and they were not."

RADE MILIĆ DID NOT make this journey by himself. He was carefully shepherded by Otpor, which was deliberately structured to use peer pressure to turn ordinary, scared kids into superheroes. The crowd outside the police station during his arrest was not spontaneous. It was a key part of Plan B—as Otpor called its strategy for overcoming activists' fear and for helping them think of themselves not as victims of a ruthless dictatorship but as protagonists in the liberation of their country. In most movements, arrests discourage. But because of Plan B, each Otpor arrest became an opportunity to embarrass the government, to build public support for Otpor, and to provide those arrested with solidarity and social recognition for their commitment and courage.

Once it became clear that there was a pattern to the arrests, and that ordinary activists were not likely to be severely hurt or even kept overnight, Otpor realized that it could turn the arrests to the movement's advantage. When it was preparing activists to do actions, marches, or protests, Otpor also gave them a presentation aimed at demystifying arrest. The trainers told activists what arrest was like, the questions police would ask, and what answers had proven best at reducing the chance the police would respond violently. Otpor even made the answers into a leaflet, treating them as FAQs. Activists were assured that they would never be alone—if arrested, they could count on a crowd of friends, journalists, and lawyers outside. They were asked to sign powers of attorney, allowing Otpor's on-call lawyers to represent them.

Then, at each street action Otpor performed, one person would be designated as a reserve. The reserve's job was simple: stand back and not get arrested. If the police arrived, the reserve would call the Knez Mihailova office with information about who had been arrested and to which police station they were taken. At headquarters, Otpor activists would then assemble a traveling circus. They would call the list of independent journalists (that was Rade's job), call the lawyers, call the detainees' families, send a crowd of people to hang out on the pavement outside the station (including the journalists and lawyers), and get another few dozen people to call the police station to inquire about the physical health and legal status of the activists inside.

Ideally, the lawyers would arrive at the police station first, as their presence helped to prevent further arrests of those who gathered. (If members of the crowd were arrested, the process would start anew, now dubbed Plan C.) The crowd would then hang around until every detainee was free—sometimes two hours, sometimes ten. They would spend those hours in nonthreatening, nonviolent, and preferably noisy activities—singing songs, listening to music, playing volleyball or soccer. The press photographers were particularly important—when the police knew their detainees would be filmed for TV or have their pictures taken, they were less likely to beat them up.

Plan B improved the treatment of detainees and led to shorter detentions. It created a sense of solidarity, a sense that the movement took care of its people. It ensured that even though an action was interrupted by police, the outcome would be successful. In fact, arrests were *more* successful for Otpor—they were front-page news, so more people usually learned of them than would have learned of the action itself. And they embarrassed the regime more, making the government look silly and panicked for arresting young people who were doing nothing wrong.

Political movements must always worry that, after arrest, a detainee will choose to withdraw from the movement. But with Plan B, the opposite usually was true—arrests improved morale. "The arrested immediately become rock stars," said Siniša Šikman, who was responsible for distribution of Otpor materials. Best of all was to be arrested in front of your friends. "If a policeman comes to someone's high school and takes him out of class, the next morning all the girls want his phone number and our office is mobbed," he said.

Unlike the political parties, Otpor had never been permitted to register legally in Serbia—when it tried, the government rejected it as an "illegal terrorist organization." Otpor turned this apparent setback to its advantage. Legal organizations had to abide by a minimum age requirement. Illegal Otpor could have members younger than eighteen, and they made up a critical part of its troops. "The younger you were, the cooler it was," said Rade Milić. "In 2000, entire high school classes would come in to sign up. They were fearless—and we, as their trainers, weren't allowed to show any sign of weakness. For them, this was a big game, a competition around who would have the most arrests. When someone asks me who took down Milošević, I say, 'High school kids.'"

"It was uncool to say it, but my male friends were attracted to the fact that you could be arrested," said Jelena, who had been a high school Otpor activist. "My task was to give out leaflets and talk to people to get them to join. My friends would consider me brave, that I was standing up for something. You could be some kind of hero. It was appealing for teenagers *because* of the physical danger and the thing of being rebellious."

Very few of those arrested were women. This might have been because police, whose views reflected the cultural traditions of Serbian society, were far less likely to arrest a woman. Also, women tended not to go looking for trouble—when police approached, the women ran away from them, not toward them. Many young men, by contrast, competed to be arrested. Branko Ilić, who at nineteen became the chief of street actions for Otpor (he was the organization's true James Bond), was once arrested three times in one day.

In Novi Sad, Nenad Šeguljev and another young man, David Solar, kept a half-in-jest tally of who was ahead—every time David was arrested, Nenad would announce he was going back out to hang more posters to keep his numbers up. Nenad claimed he stopped counting at thirteen, but others in Novi Sad said that Nenad was arrested at least seventeen times. It got to the point, said Nenad, where anyone out walking with him was in danger of being arrested as well, just for accompanying him. The police knew Nenad so well that if they didn't see him for a while, upon his next arrest they would joke that they'd been worried about him. Eventually, he grew bored with being arrested and began to play games. Sometimes he'd write his statement in a child's handwriting. "Sometimes I'd on purpose stay a little longer in the police

station talking to the police inspectors, who were usually more intelligent," he said. "I was arguing with one policeman and he told me, 'I
never thought of that before,' and he asked me if there was a Web site
he could visit. It was a propaganda war even inside the police station."

THERE INDEED WAS A PROPAGANDA war going on for the minds of
the police. Winning over, or at least neutralizing, Serbia's police was a
chief Otpor goal, a way to pull out a key pillar of support for the regime.
Ivan Marović called each arrest an opportunity for communication
between Otpor and the police, a chance to tear just a little at the loyalty police felt to the regime. While in earlier eras of protest, marchers
often would insult the police or howl at them ("dog" is a common slang
term for police in Serbia), Otpor had a different strategy. When police
approached a march or action, Otpor's troops would begin to cheer,
"Blue guys! Blue guys!" It was the cheer used for the national soccer
team, which wore blue—as did the police. May 13 is Serbia's national
day of recognition for its security forces. In Novi Sad, Vlada Pavlov,
Otpor's coordinator for the province, put on a tie and, accompanied by
two women and a TV camera, knocked on the door of the police station with a dozen roses. The policeman who came to the door was the
same one who had recently arrested Pavlov. "Vlada, get lost," he said.
"No, no, I insist—it's your day," replied Pavlov sweetly. "Let's have a
drink!" All over Serbia that day, Otpor members, accompanied by their
mothers and younger siblings, were delivering homemade cookies to
their local police stations.

Such sly subversion had a double effect. It made the activists feel like
insiders, winking at fellow citizens who appreciated the prank. And it
confused the police, who were not immune to Otpor's tactics. "If the
joke is good, even the police get it," Ivan Marović said. "They use repression, but something in their mind tells them: 'That was really good.' At
the very end, it produces an effect crucial in nonviolent struggle"—it
diminishes their obedience to the regime.

The average policeman, in truth, was arresting Otpor activists only
because he was under orders. "The police felt silly," said Rade. "When

they appeared, we would run to be arrested. It was pointless." Nor did the police welcome the carnival outside the station that inevitably sprang up after an arrest. The Otpor party was noisy, journalists and lawyers were always inconvenient, the phones would be ringing off the hook inside. Arrests meant that the police would be unable to do their real work for the rest of the day. Since Otpor had chapters and actions all over Serbia, each town's local police were in charge of the arrests. Some police had siblings or children in Otpor, and many knew the students they were arresting. They understood that, despite the government's accusations, these students were unlikely to be terrorists and spies. Some police were impressed with the students' nonviolent discipline, as well as the fact that they were dedicated enough to be arrested again and again.

The police were aware that Otpor's activists usually hadn't even done anything illegal: hanging up posters, wearing Otpor buttons, or doing street theater was not, strictly speaking, against the law. Stanko Lazendić in Novi Sad said that police sometimes asked *him* why they were arresting him. And as the election approached, some asked him, "Will we be able to keep our jobs after you take over Serbia?"

Even many police were fed up with Milošević. "Police officers would complain to *us* about their salaries," said Slobodan Homen. "We'd get put in dark cells, and when we asked the police to turn on the light, they'd tell us there was no money for a lightbulb. If later you order these people to shoot us—well, don't count on it."

Otpor never could figure out the purpose of the arrests. They didn't produce information. The questions were always the same: Who is Otpor's leader? Where do you get your money? When the police files were opened after Milošević's fall, Otpor's organizers realized that the regime already knew the real answers—the phone taps had been very effective, but the intelligence service had been incapable of understanding and using what it had. It was too politicized, its chiefs chosen for their loyalty to Milošević or his wife. The political police's priority, for example, was to locate Otpor's supposed mother ship in Washington—a figment of their imagination. "They were completely incapable of understanding that a couple of kids were making them crazy," said Siniša Šikman. "They were persuaded there must be some higher intelligence at work."

"They would expect someone with social status to be a threat, but when it's someone just out of university, you dismiss that," said Ivan Marović. "We looked too silly."

Still, one puzzle for Otpor was that the government never sought to expose the connections the group *did* have to America. The regime knew potentially game-changing details—such as how the money coming from Washington was being laundered—but it never acted on the information. Nenad Konstantinović said that he learned from the police files that many of the activists in Otpor's network who handled money had said they had gotten it from him. "I was disappointed—I thought they would have been brave enough to say nothing," he laughed. But he was never arrested.

The arrests were likely a reflex, done out of arrogance: I'll show you for challenging me. But they failed to intimidate, and there were so many ways they were counterproductive. Arrest was not brutal enough to be a serious deterrent, but it was dramatic enough to make public heroes out of those detained. Government spokesmen on television were describing Otpor activists as terrorists, traitors, and spies, but the people arrested were neighborhood kids everyone knew. It robbed the regime of credibility. Each arrest that was publicized in the independent media exposed the government's paranoia and malice to more people. (The idiocy of the arrests was truly epic. At one point, police arrested seventeen Otpor activists in Novi Sad who were running an auction of locally donated toys. The auction was raising money to finance treatment for a twelve-year-old with leukemia.) All across Serbia, the families of those arrested were enraged, especially the detainees' grandparents—and older people had always been Milošević's base of support. It was a message to parents and grandparents, Homen said, "If I can be arrested at sixteen or seventeen, then what are you waiting for?"

The government had long labeled Otpor a CIA spy organization. When it upped the charges to terrorism, Otpor leaders were jubilant. On May 14, 2000, Srdja Popović was watching TV at home with his mother when Milošević's information minister called Otpor a "neofascistic organization in the tradition of the Red Brigades." Srdja picked up his cell phone and called a colleague. "How many recruitment forms do we have? We're going to need thousands!" Srdja shouted into the phone. Over the next week, he said, Otpor added "probably a few thousand" new members.

"We really milked it," said Milja Jovanović. As the accusations escalated—two days later, the government accused Otpor of planting bombs—the Otpor people responding to the government's charges were younger and younger. To defend itself from charges of terrorism, Otpor spoke through seventeen-year-old girls. "They were so completely awesome," Milja said. "Journalists loved them. Even if they were confused, they couldn't possibly be malevolent." The spokesperson on election day, the culmination of all Otpor's work, was a seventeen-year-old girl.

Otpor's strategy, effective as it was, implied turning idealistic young people into cannon fodder. And some of them were really, really young. One Otpor leader recounted to me how he sent out ten-year-old girls to put stickers on the windows of the fancy shops along Knez Mihailova Street near the office. The police weren't watching ten-year-olds, and the girls were thrilled at their adventure. They were not caught, but it was a disturbing concept.

Another example was the November 1999 march to the Parliament that had been Rade's introduction to Otpor. Otpor, tipped off that the police were planning to attack, did not choose to take another route. Instead, it made sure the journalists were alerted, and organizers deliberately put a Serbian Orthodox priest and young women in the front row. Even though the men in the second row tried to move the women aside at the last moment, the street was narrow and some couldn't get out of the way. Of the twenty-three people officially beaten up by the police, more than half were young women or girls. The priest was beaten as well. To Otpor's thinking, beatings were desirable—even more effective than arrests at showing Serbs the regime's true desperation and cruelty. Otpor suggested to its activists a slogan to repeat when they came out of jail: "Violence is the last refuge of the weak."

"The best strategy would have been the one they never used—to ignore us," said Jovan Ratković. If Otpor's troops had been free to mock

Milošević in the street and wallpaper Serbia with their posters, the movement might have lost its excitement and importance, and it would not have aroused the widespread outrage against the regime the arrests produced. On the other extreme, if the government had raised the stakes by ordering the police to murder just one young person in custody, it might have brought the flow of new activists to a halt. Instead of either course, the regime chose the middle ground, a knee-jerk, halfhearted attempt to intimidate Otpor. The movement turned that course greatly to its advantage. Zoran Djindjić used to say that each Otpor arrest gained a thousand votes for the opposition.

OTPOR'S STRATEGIES WERE DEVELOPED through trial and error— drawing on the group's experience of previous protests, the negative lessons offered by Serbia's political parties, an appreciation of modern marketing, an immersion in youth culture, a hardheaded analysis of the realities of Serbia, and a desire for a good time. But in the spring of 2000, the organizers of Otpor made a startling discovery: many of their ideas were part of an already-existing canon. A bible for nonviolent struggle had already been written by Gene Sharp, an American academic who had founded the Albert Einstein Institution in Boston to disseminate his theories. Sharp is the Clausewitz of nonviolence, someone who has analyzed its tactics and strategies as closely as if he were a general explaining how to fight a war, which in a sense he is. He had written several books, among them *From Dictatorship to Democracy*, *Gandhi as a Political Strategist*, and the three-volume *The Politics of Nonviolent Action*. A Belgrade group called Civic Initiatives had even translated the first of them into Serbian. But no one at Otpor had heard about it until they met Bob Helvey.

Helvey was a former army colonel, an American who had served two tours of duty in Vietnam and had been a defense attaché at the American Embassy in Burma, where he worked with the democratic opposition to the military dictatorship. He had taken an interest in Sharp's ideas and became the president of the Albert Einstein Institution. The International Republican Institute invited Helvey to Budapest. At the IRI's urging, about two dozen Otpor activists traveled to Budapest to hear him at the beginning of April 2000. Since most of the leadership was busy preparing for an upcoming political rally of the whole opposition, Otpor sent mostly foot soldiers, people who had been on the front lines and needed to have some fun in Budapest for a few days. Srdja was one of the few leaders who went.

The Otpor contingent was uncomfortable being lectured to by an American former military officer. They played games with him, spending the first part of the session trying to convince him that their movement was spontaneous and unorganized. "They were trying to bullshit me," Helvey said. At that point, Otpor had 20,000 active members, a clandestine national logistical network, and brand recognition rivaling Coca-Cola's. It was, in the regime's eyes, public enemy number one, or close to it. Helvey was impressed with their clear goals, their use of humor, their decision not to seek power for themselves, the way they made volunteers important, their exploitation of the media, and their strategies of cheering for the police and maintaining strict nonviolent discipline. On its own, Otpor had come to many of the same conclusions that Helvey was teaching. As Helvey listened to the Otpor members talk, however, he learned from them that they had hit a wall they couldn't scale. The movement could grow and grow, but the question was how to turn that growth into the fall of Milošević.

Helvey walked them through an analysis of how a regime stays in power—which, Sharp had written, was through the obedience of the people it governs. Without the consent of the governed, power disappears. The goal of a democracy movement should be to withdraw that consent. Helvey compared a government to a building held up by various pillars; it was the job of democracy activists to pull out the pillars. Otpor needed a strategic estimate of the pillars holding Milošević in power, and then a plan for pulling each pillar into the opposition camp.

These concepts were useful. "It helped us to understand why we were efficient in some things and not in others," Srdja said. "For example, we were doing well with the police. We fraternized a lot with the police. But we hadn't understood the role of the bureaucracy, or the army." The seminar also allowed Otpor to think more systematically about its actions and overall strategy. Otpor subsequently published a manual for its own recruits, with some of the parts adapted from the ideas of Sharp and Helvey. It also designed a weekend course for its members, bringing to Belgrade several hundred activists from various parts of Serbia, about seventy people at a time. Being able to systematize and teach Otpor's strategies to its members was a security measure as well. "It meant that the regime could arrest all eleven of us and still have the same outcome at the end of the day," Srdja said.

Helvey's seminar had given Otpor a psychological lift. It showed the members that they were part of a historical continuum, heirs to Gandhi, the American civil rights movement, and Poland's Solidarity. It took the ideas Otpor was already thinking about and handed them back to Otpor tied up neatly in a package.

When Otpor was a year old, in the fall of 1999, it still had only about 2,000 members. By late spring 2000, it had more than 20,000, and there was an Otpor chapter in every town in Serbia. By that summer, Otpor was paying the bills for 500 cell phones, Ivan Andrić said. On the day Milošević fell, it would have at least 70,000 members.

In the spring of 2000, however, the explosive growth of Otpor was the only good news for the anti-Milošević forces. The opposition political parties were, as always, divided and feuding. The government had cracked down on the independent media, levying larger and larger fines. At 2 a.m. on May 17, heavily armed police took over the offices of the TV station Studio B, the newspaper *Blic*, and Radio Index and B292 (B92 had changed its name after the government had taken over its frequency). That was the end of the most important opposition media in Belgrade. The opposition protests against the crackdown quickly petered out. A supposedly major protest rally against the takeover of Studio B drew only 15,000 people.

Milošević once again was feeling untouchable. Then he made an error of enormous consequence: although he still had a year left in his term as Yugoslav president, his overconfidence led him to call early elections, setting them for September 24, 2000.

■   ■   ■   ■

ANYONE WHO HAS LIVED under a dictatorship has to be very glad that dictators want legitimacy so badly that they like to hold elections. For a dictator, elections are often a mistake. They were a mistake for Augusto Pinochet in Chile and for Daniel Ortega in Nicaragua. And they were a mistake for Milošević. Dictators call elections because they think they will win them. This is what they hear from the people who surround them, people who hold on to their jobs precisely because they deliver only good news to the boss. Dictators typically are too arrogant to conduct public-opinion surveys. But if they do commission polls, these often will produce just what they want to hear: people who live under extremely repressive regimes are usually too afraid to say honestly that they are fed up. So dictators usually assume they are far more popular than they really are. They also assume that in the event they do not win the election, they can steal it. But this often fails. Elections provide a sharp focus for opposition organizing. They wake up the citizenry to the question of who runs the country. If it is clear that a leader has lost an election but refuses to acknowledge it, even people who lived passively under his thumb for many years tend to get motivated to act—a phenomenon seen recently with the protest movement in Iran born after the stolen elections of 2009.

This is what the opposition was hoping for in Serbia. In September 1999, the American National Democratic Institute (NDI) paid for a survey by Penn Schoen & Berland Associates, a firm that had done polling for President Bill Clinton. It was early yet—at that point, the opposition was thinking that elections were two years away, but it wanted to set a baseline and get information that would help choose the best strategy for defeating Milošević.

The good news that emerged from the NDI survey was that 70 percent of Serbs viewed Milošević unfavorably. He could be beaten—but only if the opposition could unite on a single candidate. That was the bad news—Milošević could be kept in power by the bickering and pettiness of the opposition.

The only important opposition leader who disagreed publicly with the idea of supporting a single candidate was Vuk Drašković, who eventually left the opposition coalition. Eighteen other party leaders united their parties in a group called the Democratic Opposition of Serbia (DOS). None of them dared disagree publicly with the idea of a single candidate, but privately, some were adding a qualifier: as long as I'm that candidate.

Otpor began a new campaign, one focused on the egos of a few men. "A third of our activity was blackmailing the opposition," said Srdja. Ivan Marović and Vlada Pavlov attended meetings of the DOS. At the same time, Otpor was putting public pressure on the parties to unite. Otpor activists in cities across Serbia warned that the organization would work on behalf of one candidate—"and treat any other candidates as agents of Milošević," as one activist put it.

In April 2000, the DOS held a rally; Otpor decided to hijack it. The day before, Vlada set out at the head of a column of several hundred people marching from Novi Sad to Belgrade—eighty-three kilometers. Eighteen hours later, the column, having gathered thousands of people, arrived at the rally in Belgrade, where Vlada climbed onto the stage. He pulled out an Otpor flag and challenged each of the politicians on stage to hold up the flag and pledge to back a single candidate. Some of the politicians enthusiastically held up the flag, Djindjić among them. Others, especially Drašković, looked at it as if it were radioactive. "Next time one of you betrays us, 100,000 of us will appear at your door," Vlada warned them. "Symbolically, Otpor brought them together," said Sonja Licht, at the time the director of George Soros's Open Society Institute in Belgrade, and a godmother to much of the opposition.

Otpor's strategy worked. The politicians knew that unity was the only way to win, but that had long been true—and it hadn't kept the opposition united. This time, however, the politicians knew that breaking ranks would end their political careers. That was in part due to Otpor. The only one who didn't grasp this was Drašković, who put up his own candidate. The rest of the DOS agreed to unite on one candidate. But who? In the NDI poll, this interesting question was included: For whom would you never vote? It turned out that none of the most prominent leaders could be elected—each was hated by too large a percentage of the electorate. Djindjić's negative rating almost matched Milošević's.

The best possibility seemed to be Vojislav Koštunica, the leader of a minor opposition party. Very few people knew of him—which meant that very few disliked him. He had a negative rating of 29 percent and a favorable rating of 49 percent. A professor of constitutional law, he had recently translated the *Federalist Papers* into Serbian. But he admired the West much more in theory than in practice; he was as hostile to Washington and Europe as he was toward Milošević—a useful stance in a country that had just been bombed by NATO. He had never been a Communist. Although a democrat, he was a Serb nationalist, with a history of writings that gave intellectual cover to Serb adventurism. (Unfortunately, this also seemed to be part of the reason he was popular.) Another attraction was his reputation as incorruptible. He lived modestly and drove an old, beat-up Yugo. This allowed the opposition to put up billboards with a pair of eyes and the slogan "Who can look you in the eye? Koštunica."

There remained, however, two important question marks. One was Koštunica himself. He was shy, private, and hesitant, his demeanor heavy with doubts. He always appeared tired and he didn't seem to want to be president very much. If the average Serb voter was at bottom undecided about whether he could bring himself to vote for Koštunica, the candidate seemed to reflect him perfectly.

Almost as important was whether Djindjić would accept a background role. Djindjić was not plagued by existential doubt; he felt entitled to be the candidate. In some ways, he was entitled to feel entitled. He was clearly first among equals in the DOS—by far the most capable politician. He had built the largest and best-organized political party in the DOS, the only one that was a real party.

Djindjić was furious at the poll data—so much so that, according to Douglas Schoen, he boycotted the pollster's presentation of the results. But Djindjić understood its implications, and there were other factors that made his decision an easy one. The job Koštunica would run for, president of Yugoslavia, was only important because Milošević held it. Yugoslavia was an illusion, a country of two wildly unequal parts taped together. Once Milošević had departed, the real power would be wielded by the prime minister of Serbia. That post would go to the head of the largest group in Parliament and was not chosen by the electorate, so popularity among ordinary Serbs was not a requirement. Djindjić understood this, too.

Djindjić also knew that winning the election was not the most difficult task ahead. Koštunica would certainly win—possibly in the first round. But if no one got a majority (besides Drašković's candidate, the ultranationalist Radical Party also had one), then he would win in the runoff.

The real problem would come afterward: getting Milošević to respect the results. Djindjić, like Otpor, subscribed to the theory of removing the pillars of the government. After Milošević's election loss, the only pillar that would matter would be the security forces. The challenge would be to persuade the men running the army, the police, and Milošević's special military units to defy the orders they would receive to assassinate opposition figures, shoot at protesters, and carry out mass arrests in order to steal the election.

Djindjić felt—rightly—that he was the best person to persuade the security forces. Some were his "friends in hell"—his web of shadowy connections could now prove useful. Also, he was going to be the one wielding power after the opposition won, which meant he could make credible promises or threats to these men. So, with Koštunica as the candidate, Djindjić took command of the campaign. It was the chess game he had been preparing for all his life.

Otpor's relationships with the politicians in the DOS were not warm. Otpor had spent its time criticizing their fecklessness, feuding with them, and browbeating them into unity. Otpor saw this as tough love; the party leaders mainly saw it as disloyalty. Of all the opposition leaders, only Djindjić understood what Otpor was trying to do and grasped its value, several people said. "Though, of course, he didn't like that he couldn't control it," Jovan Ratković added. Koštunica, in particular, was appalled by Otpor's tone of insolence and its ties to Washington. "They knew, although we denied it, where we got our money," Milja said. "Koštunica hated our guts. He told me to my face that I'm a traitor for taking American money."

"And where does yours come from?" Milja challenged him.

"Domestic sources," he said.

"Criminal domestic enterprises—that's who has money here," she said.

Even as Koštunica was denouncing money from Washington, his campaign, like Otpor, was dependent on it. Djindjić had no problem with taking Washington's money for the campaign. He had very little problem with money from anywhere, as long as it allowed him to do what he thought he needed to do. At that point, Washington was providing a lot of money to the anti-Milošević movement—by the reckoning of one U.S. official, perhaps just over $20 million in U.S. government money in the year 2000. It was doled out through groups such as the National Democratic Institute, the International Republican Institute, the National Endowment for Democracy, and Freedom House. There was also some financing from the Open Society Institute and European institutes and governments. A lot of it went to buy equipment for the independent media. Washington, as well as European governments, also financed several extensive get-out-the-vote campaigns, a massive program of election monitors, and assembly of a parallel vote count—and helped to fund Koštunica's campaign.

THE CAMPAIGN BEGAN IN EARNEST in the summer of 2000. By July 27, the day Milošević announced he was holding early elections, Otpor had been preparing for months. Back in late 1999, Otpor had realized that it could supply the opposition with a crucial advantage: Serbia's youth. Otpor's polls showed that the youth vote would tip 90 percent against Milošević. The problem was that in Serbia, as in most countries, young people didn't like to vote. Previous elections had seen a youth turnout of five or ten percentage points below the national average of 56 percent. So Otpor drew up plans for a campaign to get young people to the polls.

To do that, Otpor had to branch out from the fist logo. The brand developed around the fist had attracted a lot of attention and tens of thousands of volunteers, but now those numbers needed to rise into the millions, capturing people too cautious and traditional to be attracted by the fist's irreverent and even aggressive symbolilsm. Otpor created a separate campaign with a separate brand, called *Vreme Je*—"It's Time." It was softer and more feminine than the fist. It said nothing about Milošević but simply aimed at increasing voter turnout, especially among young people, and it was ostensibly nonpartisan (although there was no mystery about the political preferences of Serbia's youth). Vreme Je's logo—a clock with hands at five minutes to midnight—was printed in a colorful, almost childlike hand.

Vreme Je had no public connection to Otpor, but it was thoroughly an Otpor product—run, in fact, by three of Otpor's top leaders: Slobodan Djinović, Dejan Randjić, and Ivan Andrić. It had some 15,000 volunteers and was just one of several get-out-the-vote campaigns organized by Serbian groups. The Serbs received important guidance from Slovakia, which had just ousted an autocrat, Vladimír Mečiar, in a campaign where a high turnout among young people had been key. The Slovaks had mobilized young voters in part through a series of concerts, in a campaign called *Rock Volieb*, or "Rock the Vote." The Serbs adopted the tactic—B292's network sponsored a series of rock concerts in twenty-five cities aimed at stimulating excitement about the election. Serbian civic groups also learned from their counterparts in Croatia, who had established a nonpartisan citizen-participation group that had successfully prevented electoral fraud in January 2000 by establishing a nationwide network of election monitors. In Serbia, a civic group called the Center for Free Elections and Democracy trained 21,000 election monitors.

The plan was to have monitors at every polling station in Serbia to make sure the votes were counted accurately. The opposition also established several overlapping systems to centralize that information instantly, so it could count the votes itself. Djindjić wanted to announce the totals before the government could give its own—surely falsified—version. If Milošević was going to steal the election, he would at least not do it unnoticed.

The fist was still in business, however. Otpor needed a new slogan for the election campaign. Some of the leadership met at Srdja's parents' apartment—they were away—to devise one. They found it when

Slobodan Milivojević, an Otpor leader from Kruševac, simply blurted out what was on his mind: "*Gotov je*" ("He's finished").

It was too blunt for the lawyers in the group. "Do you want to get us all killed?" asked Slobodan Homen. But "He's Finished" became the perfect slogan. It was simple, easy to remember, and expressed the most important thought Serbs needed to hear for the election: the inevitability of Milošević's defeat. It turned the election into a victory lap—the slogan was so insolently confident that it didn't even need to say who "he" was.

The NDI poll had revealed that while 70 percent of Serbs wanted Milošević to leave, 64 percent of Serbs thought it was impossible. Only 16 percent felt it could happen. A lot of people would vote against the regime only if they thought they were on the winning side. This was an old problem; Drašković and Djindjić, campaigning, would often hear people say, "I'll vote for you once you're in power." In a country where people were accustomed to following instructions from a leader, the only way to create a bandwagon against him was to give the impression that one was already rolling.

By this time, Otpor no longer had to pretend to be a mass movement. The Gotov Je campaign, run by Srdja, eventually had some 25,000 volunteers. Otpor printed 1.2 million stickers with "Gotov Je" next to the fist or Milošević's face. The stickers could simply be slapped on top of any existing Milošević campaign poster, instantly turning it into an opposition message. Duda's poster showed the back of Milošević, walking away, with "Gotov Je" on the bottom.

Otpor's main audience was the Serbian voter, but it had a secondary target that was almost as important: Milošević's security forces. The goal was to convince them that Milošević's defeat was certain. If the average Serbian voter *liked* to back the winner, the army, police, and secret police *needed* to. Their careers depended on latching on to those in power, and they worried about losing their jobs—or swinging from a lamppost—if they guessed wrong. This thinking was articulated by, among others, a secret policeman who detained Rade Milić in April 2000. "If you were stronger, we'd be on your side," he told Rade. "But we still don't have that estimate."

On election day, turnout among under-thirty voters was 86 percent—astronomical, higher than even the overall turnout of around 74 percent, itself very impressive. (In the United States, turnout of under thirty voters has never gone higher than 56 percent, even when Barack Obama was elected.)

The opposition's vote count showed that Koštunica won in the first round, with 51.8 percent of the vote. And, as everyone had expected, the government disagreed. It announced that Koštunica had garnered more votes than Milošević but had fallen short of a majority, so a second round of voting would be necessary. Milošević was buying time.

The opposition's response was defiance. "We won outright and there will be no second round," Koštunica announced. The campaign gave Milošević a deadline: Step down by October 5 at 3 p.m. Milošević had eleven days.

Otpor played a role in forcing Milošević to meet that deadline. Perhaps most important was the model of nonviolence it had provided. Any aggression by the opposition in the days after the election would have been used as a pretext for a crackdown by the regime. If some protester had shot at the police, Milošević would have responded instantly with mass arrests or worse; there were those credible rumors of a list of fifty top opposition figures marked for assassination. Otpor's lack of aggression against the police was also important: it showed the police that the opposition would treat them humanely, thus loosening police loyalty to the regime. Absolute nonviolent discipline was crucial, and Serbia had learned it from Otpor.

Otpor's other contribution was in helping to create a national show of insubordination. Djindjić's job now was to convince the security forces that to support Milošević was to be on the losing side. The pillars of Milošević's regime needed to smell his blood. Djindjić set the long deadline to give them time to get a good whiff. He called a national strike to demonstrate that the opposition could shut down the country. Plans were drawn up to have opposition convoys arriving in Belgrade from every region on October 5, deadline day. Each convoy would have a different objective for securing control: the airport, RTS, the Parliament. Otpor's job on October 5 would be to retake from the regime B92's radio transmitters and switch on transmitters for the debut of TV B92. The field general was Branko Ilić, Otpor's chief of street actions, who was turning twenty-one that day.

Ordinary people were assigned in teams to go to police stations and military barracks and barricade the security forces inside—not with guns and threats but with flowers and kisses. They would be firm but friendly.

If needed, however, there would be more than flowers and kisses. Otpor had done its part to spark a mass movement against Milošević. Now the fate of Serbia was in the hands of a few men. What would determine it was power politics, played out in secret deals with violent people, a conversation conducted in the language long familiar to Serbian politicians.

On September 26, two days after the stolen election, the DOS leaders agreed that they would respond to Milošević with whatever level of force was used against them. "If he fires, we will fire," was the official position. The decision was unanimous, because Koštunica, who had reservations about the plan, had left the meeting before the vote. The opposition needed weapons, so it procured a truckload of them and recruited task forces of well-armed former police and soldiers.

After dark on Armageddon Eve, October 4, a tense Djindjić went to meet with Milorad Ulemek, known as Legija. He was the head of Milošević's Red Beret special forces, the regime's most ruthless and elite fighting unit. Milošević called on Legija and his men to do his most violent jobs. Legija carried out assassinations of Milošević's political opponents—including an attempt on Drašković—and ran a death squad during the Kosovo War. In return for these favors, Milošević gave Legija free rein for criminal activity.

Legija had requested the meeting and had asked Djindjić to show up alone. Djindjić knew that he was at the top of the government's hit list, and that if Milošević were to kill him, Legija would be the man to do it. But he went; only he could pull out this particular pillar. He did not wear a flak jacket—there was no point. Djindjić climbed into Legija's armored Jeep and the two men drove around. When he returned to the campaign headquarters, Djindjić told a colleague that Legija had said his men would not use violence as long as the protesters did not. Djindjić was relieved: "It's all over," he said. No one will ever know what Djindjić promised Legija in return, but it was likely the assurance that the new government, like the old one, would not touch him.

The next day, Legija kept his word. The police and the army built the barricades they were ordered to build, but when the opposition told them to step away, they did. The opposition convoys swept aside the barricades with bulldozers. At least half a million people amassed in front of Parliament on October 5. By the end of the day in this violent country, power changed hands with only two deaths: one due to a heart attack, one a vehicular accident. That evening, President-elect Vojislav Koštunica addressed the crowd. "Good evening, liberated Serbia," his speech began.

THAT MOMENT WAS THE high point; what has followed in Serbia is a lesson in the limits of revolution. Euphoria turned to disillusion. It is a phenomenon seen everywhere, from post-apartheid South Africa to post-Communist Eastern Europe to post–military-dictatorship El Salvador. People's hopes for change tend to be impossibly high. They blame their troubles on the people at the top, not realizing that the system is much more difficult to vanquish than the men who ran it. Being against Milošević was clear and simple: Serbs could blame Milošević for everything. After he fell, the country would no longer fight war after war. It was now a free country. But Serbia was still desperately poor, with few jobs, still controlled by criminal gangs. Only now there was no hope of solving those problems by getting rid of Milošević.

Two months after Koštunica's inauguration, the opposition overwhelmingly won parliamentary elections and Zoran Djindjić became prime minister of Serbia in January 2001. On April 1, he had Milošević arrested and turned over to the International Criminal Tribunal for the former Yugolslavia in The Hague. (Milošević died there on March 11, 2006.) To the outside world, which rewarded Serbia with desperately needed foreign aid, it was a sign of how much had changed. But there were two signs of how little had changed. Djindjić conducted the arrest when Koštunica, who vehemently opposed it, was out of the country. And the arrest party was led by Legija, now very much Djindjić's man.

Djindjić, to his credit, eventually broke with Legija; it cost him his life. A little over two years into his tenure, Djindjić was preparing to move against Legija and other underworld figures. He had recently survived an assassination attempt when a truck plowed into his motorcade. Publicly, he dismissed it as "careless driving," but he had been telling people there would be other attempts. "Anyone who thinks that they will stop the implementation of reforms and the rule of law by eliminating me is seriously mistaken," he said in a speech two weeks before he died. On March 12, 2003, just after noon, he was shot by a sniper while heading into the main government building. Legija was convicted of organizing the assassination and sentenced to forty years in prison. There he remains, having lost his last appeal.

Otpor's fortunes became another study in disenchantment. The election of Koštunica created a dilemma for Otpor: Now what? Until that point, the movement had made perhaps not a single serious misstep. Afterward, very little went right. Otpor's leaders decided to keep the organization going and turn it into a watchdog group to remind Serbia's politicians not to start acting like Milošević. Otpor's campaign right after the fall of Milošević—"It's Not Time to Relax Yet!"—helped raise youth turnout for the parliamentary elections in December 2000. And Otpor's "He Is Guilty" campaign provided crucial backing for Djindjić's arrest and extradition of Milošević.

Many Otpor members did not like what the organization had become, and felt betrayed. The secret was out about Otpor's Washington financing, too, and it met with widespread fury. Some of the members had gone into politics: Srdja Popović won a parliamentary seat on the Democratic Party slate and Ivan Andrić on the slate of Civic Alliance. To some Otpor members, this seemed a breach of the group's implicit promise that it would not be a vehicle for personal advancement. These issues tainted Otpor; many of its members no longer felt the movement was theirs.

It was inevitable that Otpor could not continue to command a national army of eager volunteers. So much had changed since the early days. The movement had maintained a single focus—the fall of Milošević—and he had fallen. The new government was made up of Otpor allies, and many people felt that Otpor should simply support it. Most Otpor members were tired of politics and wanted to go back and finish school and live a normal life. The more ambitious ones were sought after by dozens of new civil-society organizations, for which money was now pouring in from abroad. Or they could even go into government. Very few people from the original Otpor group remained.

The work of Otpor had also been transformed. Its social-cure strategies vanished. Since protests and street actions were now legal, no longer a way to be cool and daring, they lost their romance and young people lost interest. The job of motivating people to overthrow Milošević—a message simple, unwavering, and massive popular— now had to be diluted and made nuanced. Otpor could make stickers warning the politicians they were being watched—but that didn't give members any specific tasks. Nor was it clear what Otpor wanted from politicians. Its members did not agree on policy—and Serbia was not seeking advice on governing from kids who had dropped out of college. Most important, Otpor failed because everything was failing in Serbia. The habits learned under dictatorship, the country's multiple crises, and the hold of organized crime were too much. A government watchdog armed only with moral rectitude and spectacular graphic design was no match.

Otpor's final demise was painful. By 2003, the Democratic Opposition of Serbia had splintered. Fighting between Djindjić and Koštunica had consumed much of the government's energy while Djindjić had been alive, and it continued among the parties after his death. Once again, Otpor offered itself as an alternative for Serbs disillusioned with political parties.

Under the slogan "Otpor! Freedom, Solidarity, Justice," Otpor put up a slate of candidates for parliamentary elections in December 2003. Otpor ran on the platform of building lasting political institutions to make a real break with the past, and emphasizing competence over political loyalty. These were fine ideas—just what Serbia needed— but they were not vote-getters. Otpor received less than half the votes needed to meet the threshold for parliamentary representation. It collected fewer votes than the Otpor of 2000 had members.

The campaign compounded Otpor's problems with a series of tactical errors. The party entered the campaign just one month before the vote. There was no time for step-by-step organizing. Instead of doing the daily work of recruiting, training, and using volunteers, Otpor the political party relied on brand recognition alone for votes. And that brand was muddied by a message that was anything but clear, emotionally resonant, and motivating. Otpor had abandoned the social-cure strategy that brought it such success. This time, it had little to distinguish itself from the rest. It became just one more party. In 2004, Otpor formally merged into the Democratic Party.

Sitting in his parliamentary office on a dark evening in the middle of a snowstorm in 2009, Ivan Andrić told me a story: A foreigner he met during the Otpor years asked him a rhetorical question: Why did so many of the astronauts go on to become alcoholics or drug addicts? "Because the greatest thing in their lives happened in their early twenties," Andrić was told. The man meant it as a caution—don't let that happen to kids of fifteen, sixteen, seventeen.

It did happen, of course, just as it did to many of the protesters in Chile. People who survive on adrenaline will crash when the protests stop. After Milošević's fall, the cartoonist Corax did a drawing in the newspaper *Danas* of the Otpor fist slouched in an armchair in front of a TV, remote in hand.

Some of those who lived on adrenaline will find another drug. But even for those who stay active in politics, the disillusion can be profound. Slobodan Homen is now deputy minister of justice. Ivan Andrić and Nenad Konstantinović are in Parliament. Jovan Ratković is a foreign-policy adviser to President Boris Tadić, and Dejan Randjić is in the Belgrade city assembly. The frustrations and corruptions and ugliness of political life in Serbia are overwhelming. There is no more romance. "If I had been aware of what we'd have to do after October 5, I would have left," said Ivan Andrić ruefully.

■   ■   ■   ■

SERBIA HAS NOT YET become, as Koštunica used to promise, a "boring country." But this does not in any way discredit the work of those who overthrew Milošević. The Serbian revolution became known as the Bulldozer Revolution, after the convoys of October 5, 2000. But what seemed to some in the outside world like a one-day uprising was no such thing. It owed its success to the integrity of Vojislav Koštunica, the strategic dexterity of Zoran Djindjić, the hard work of thousands of Serbs who guarded people's precious votes on election day, the groups that trained them, the courage of the independent journalists, and money from Washington and Europe. But the groundwork had been laid by Otpor, using the social cure to crack the initial and most difficult problem of any democratic revolution: overcoming apathy and fear.

This was valuable knowledge, and it was not long before others wanted it. In late 2002, the Open Society Institute (OSI) called to say that an organization of young people in the former Soviet republic of Georgia was asking for help from the Serbs. The country's president, Eduard Shevardnadze, was not as repressive as Milošević, but he was moving in that direction. There were elections coming up, and many in Georgia worried that they would be stolen. OSI paid for a visit to Tbilisi, Georgia, by Slobodan Djinović of Otpor and Marko Blagojević, who was the leader of the Center for Free Elections and Democracy, along with Sonja Licht of OSI's Belgrade office.

The back-and-forth began. A group of Georgians visited Serbia. Djinović went back to Georgia, staying for nearly a month. The Georgians began a youth movement called *Kmara!*—which means "Enough!" Kmara's logo was a near-exact copy of the Otpor fist. The Georgians chose it in part because they liked it and in part to scare the government, which was well aware of what had happened to Milošević. The activists' T-shirt featured a fist with "Kmara!—Because I Love Georgia" underneath.

Like Otpor, Kmara started out with a group that could fit comfortably in a van. For their first action, in April 2003, they bought paint—this took all their combined funds; Serbia was rich compared to Georgia—and drove around Tbilisi at night scrawling "Kmara!"

alongside major thoroughfares. Even Shevardnadze noticed; he commented on it the next day.

Kmara then adapted more of Otpor's tactics—the street actions, the humor and irreverence, the careful planning, use of the available media, the roses and sandwiches for the police. In November 2003, there were elections, which Shevardnadze stole. As in Belgrade, crowds marched on Parliament three weeks later. There was even a "Gotov Je" flag visible in the throng—in Serbian. By that evening, Shevardnadze was out.

That uprising was dubbed the Rose Revolution, as protesters carried roses when they confronted Shevardnadze's troops. It changed Georgia, and it spread like influenza to democracy activists nearby. The next in what became known as the Color Revolutions was the Orange Revolution, in Ukraine. On March 21, 2004, the first day of spring, Ukrainians all over the country awoke to find their cities plastered with stickers. They were black and white, with the word *Pora*—"It's Time" (*Vreme Je* in Serbian). Ukrainians didn't know what it meant, but the sudden appearance of thousands of stickers was mysterious and significant. Who were these people?

This was a strategy—surprise, shock, secrecy—taken directly from the early days of Otpor. The year before, Siniša Šikman had gone to Ukraine, along with Stanko Lazendić and Aleksandar Marić of Novi Sad. (Marić formed another group, the Center for Nonviolent Resistance, which has since become a more traditional civic organization.) Young Ukrainians had visited Novi Sad. Otpor was a frequent presence in Ukraine until Marić eventually was kicked out. Once again, history repeated itself. On January 26, 2005, the opposition's presidential candidate, Viktor Yushchenko, was inaugurated as president of Ukraine. (He was not reelected in 2010. Feuding between the former opposition leaders led to the restoration of the presidency of Viktor Yanukovych, the man the Orange Revolution had ousted.)

Otpor's transformation into a band of itinerant revolutionaries began in 2003. A group of political activists from Zimbabwe asked for Otpor's expertise, and Srdja and Slobodan Djinović flew to South Africa to lead a workshop. In Cape Town, the two of them mused for the first time about starting an organization to advise democracy movements. The next year, they formally registered the group, calling it CANVAS—the Center for Applied NonViolent Action and Strategies. It grew to include Ivan Marović, Siniša, and at times other Otpor leaders; later they hired a few other former democracy activists from the Philippines, South Africa, Lebanon, Georgia, and Ukraine. CANVAS's logo—designed by Duda—of course included the fist, but it was superimposed on a triangle of three arrows: the international symbol for recycling. CANVAS would try to recycle Otpor's strategies around the world.

Otpor's success was beginning to reverberate internationally. CANVAS set to work distilling its teachings into materials people anywhere could use. It created a training manual (strikingly designed, of course, and available in five languages—including Farsi) and a Web site. Ivan Marović, a lifelong fan of video and computer games, spent several years in Washington working on two versions of a computer game designed to teach the strategies of nonviolent change. The company behind the game is York Zimmerman, which has made films about nonviolent revolution, including one about Otpor.

Players of the game in its first edition, called A *Force More Powerful*, can choose from various scenarios—force a dictator to hold free elections, fight corruption, repel foreign occupation, or win minority rights. The player makes strategic decisions about how to form alliances, recruit members, use resources, and pull out the government's pillars of support. The gamer then must deal with the consequences—say, if the government responds by shooting activists and the movement's level of enthusiasm plummets. Or if the player stages an ill-planned march and someone in the movement uses violence, he or she must watch as police support dries up. Players can download the game, use it on nearly any computer, and easily translate it into any language and alphabet. A new version, called *People Power*, was released in late 2010.

By 2010, CANVAS, with Srdja as executive director, had conducted workshops for activists from fifty countries, including Zimbabwe, Iran, Belarus, Venezuela, Nigeria, Iraq, Egypt, Lebanon, Burma, and even North Korea. The group has a standard three- to five-day workshop and a five- to seven-day advanced one. The workshops are in English and often involve bringing activists out of their own country—the Zimbabweans went to Cape Town, for example. Some have been paid for by Western pro-democracy groups. But not always—Djinović is now a mogul, CEO of a telecommunications and Internet company, Orion Telekom. He subsidizes CANVAS's headquarters operation in his company complex and has financed about half of its workshops.

Many people now advise would-be democracy movements, but CANVAS offers something different. The CANVAS trainer is not some highly paid American consultant in a nice suit but rather a young person in a T-shirt and jeans who has lived through hyperinflation and electrical cuts and corrupt police and TV news shows that lied even about the weather. He or she may also have dodged American bombs—a useful political credential in some places. And none of those other buttoned-down trainers have overthrown a dictator. CANVAS's trainers have a swagger, a kind of cowboy charisma. They inspire panic in repressive governments, who sometimes react as if the Serbs were teaching black magic. "They think we are carrying a revolution in our suitcases," said Srdja. In several countries, including Iran, democracy activists who have attended CANVAS workshops have been arrested afterward.

Most democracy consultants work with political parties; CANVAS prefers more unusual partners. "We've worked in some countries with opposition parties," Ivan Marović said, "but we like youth groups more. They are much more efficient at organizing political pressure."

Most important, what CANVAS teaches is something that other groups do not. Plenty of organizations that help parties or civic groups build their capacities will teach them how to write a press release, keep track of money, manage a supply chain, or run a parallel vote count. CANVAS focuses, instead, on how to get inside people's heads—how to turn a vanload of disaffected people into a mass political movement. It shows small groups of activists how to define their vision inclusively, in ways that unite people, with an eye to draining support from the regime. For example, it stresses that democracy groups need to know what the police officer wants his future to be, because they are going to need him to join the movement. CANVAS emphasizes the need for meticulous planning—forget about the romantic idea that if people have a grievance against the government, they will erupt spontaneously. And it teaches budding movements to forgo mass demonstrations in favor of growing step-by-step, with social-cure tactics. CANVAS teaches the use of branding, humor, dilemma actions, and techniques for turning fear to advantage. It shows groups how to make people want to take part, by structuring the movement so that your members can see themselves, and be seen by others, as creative, clued in, valuable, and heroic.

Not every organization that seeks CANVAS training wants to overthrow a government. Ivan Marović worked with *Mjaft!* (Enough!) in Albania, a group formed by a handful of students active in many issues—especially fighting corruption and promoting better government. It calls itself the largest organization in Albania. Mjaft's real goal is to create a civil society in a country where one is conspicuously missing, overcome apathy, and make protest cool. In Nigeria, Ghana, Maldives, Colombia, Guatemala, Sierra Leone, and elsewhere, CANVAS has worked with anticorruption, good-government, anticrime, and environmental groups.

Otpor's story greatly expands the scope of the social cure. A casual examination of the idea of behavior change through peer pressure might suggest that it is applicable only to personal problems. Serbia's experience is spectacularly the opposite. It shows that while the social cure can help people to conquer their personal demons, it can also mobilize them to act in the grandest dramas of our time. Where there was only atomization and apathy, fatalism and fear, the social cure in Serbia created a movement of citizens. That movement transformed the way people thought about the government and their own role in political life. And it helped to bring down the regime and establish democracy—however imperfect—in a country that had never known it. The social cure's ability to mobilize citizens is a powerful tool. The story of Slobodan Milošević's fall only hints at where it can take us.

Chapter Ten

Next

THIS BOOK IS THE HISTORY OF AN IDEA, ONE CREATED over and over again by pioneers in various fields. Together, their stories show how the social cure works: what kinds of problems are susceptible; which part of each problem is vulnerable; what steps to take first, and after that, and after that; what tools to use; which outside resources are necessary; and how to defend the idea when the problem fights back. The resourceful entrepreneurs described in this book had no blueprint for using the social cure—but they have helped to write one.

The social cure no longer is a strategy that would-be entrepreneurs must stumble onto. People wrestling with an important issue can now sit down and think through whether a join-the-club solution might help. We can ask ourselves: Is this a problem where it might be possible and fruitful to provide people with a new peer group that can encourage them to think of themselves in a new way?

To begin, it is useful to do a thought experiment. Let us

look at a few ways one might go about applying a join-the-club solution to a new problem.

One avenue is to begin with the stories in this book. They vary in every possible way. They use the social cure for both intimate personal problems and sweeping political dramas, among teens and adults, poor and rich, in South Africa and South Carolina, Serbia and suburbia. Each example is different in the way it introduces people to a new peer group and the mechanism through which that peer group brings about identity change. They differ in the essence of the change they seek.

One characteristic they have in common, however, is that each of these cases is part of a family: other problems share enough DNA to be able to use the social cure in a similar way. The most direct way to expand the social cure to new problems is to look for those related to ones we already know.

The logical place to begin is with the most personal set of issues, those that deal with temptation. The behavior change necessary in these cases is a shift from present to future orientation: the ability to postpone pleasure today in order to be healthier (or happier) tomorrow. Different groups achieve this through different kinds of identity change: loveLife, for example, uses peers to help South African youth think of themselves as people with a future, people with a reason to say no to risky sex. The Rage and SWAT antismoking groups offer teenagers clubs that allow them to see themselves as rebellious and cool. Alcoholics Anonymous creates a peer group that holds a member accountable for changing from a deceitful drinker into a respectful and honest citizen, and it gives the satisfaction of helping others to do the same.

Risky sex, smoking, and drinking are not isolated behaviors. Plenty of other temptations can be addressed with the same forms of the social cure. Some already are—there are "Anonymous"-branded twelve-step support groups for compulsive eaters, compulsive gamblers, drug users, and debtors. These groups, however, offer a particular kind of rehabilitation, one that depends on making amends to others, trusting in a Creator, and changing many aspects of one's personality. They are not for everyone. While Alcoholics Anonymous is widespread, with two million members worldwide, its kin are much less so.

The *essence* of an AA group, however—a small group of people who gather regularly with the common goal of overcoming a personal addiction or temptation—might be adapted to almost every kind of important personal problems of the "I'll-be-sorry-later" type. One test is whether the problem could be on your list of New Year's resolutions—such as to spend less, go to church more, become a vegetarian, be faithful to your spouse, give more to charity, reduce your carbon footprint, stop yelling at your kids, or exercise five times a week. With any such personal-behavior goal, your chance of success greatly increases if you use the social cure.

Of all our personal struggles with temptation, diet and exercise are by far the most widespread. They are everybody's New Year's resolutions. Yet while AA is the first response for dealing with the daily struggles of a drinking problem—so much so that people only believe you're serious if you join AA—very few people think of joining a group to lose weight. When they do, it is often in the form of corporate-sponsored meetings at Weight Watchers. There are strong indications, however, that the social cure can be a powerful factor for weight control. It's intuitive that having friends who drink contributes to an alcohol problem, but it seems that something similar is true for overeating. Nicholas Christakis, a professor of medicine and medical sociology at Harvard, and James Fowler, a political science professor at the University of California, San Diego, looked at happiness, health, and weight patterns in a well-established social network of 5,000 people. They found that weight is socially contagious. If your friends are overweight, you are also likely to be overweight, even controlling for other factors. The contagion also works in the other direction; people with thin friends are more likely to be thin. Oddly, the connection also skipped a link—in the study, participants were significantly more likely to gain weight if a friend of a friend did, even if the friend who connected them gained no weight at all.

Association, of course, doesn't mean causality. Theoretically, the phenomenon could be sparked by people seeking out fat friends because they are already fat, or the opening of a Pizza Hut in the neighborhood that all the friends go to. Christakis and Fowler did find proofs of causality, but these have been challenged by other researchers. Even some of these researchers, however, say that although the authors may not yet have convincing evidence of causality, they still believe it is true.

Christakis and Fowler's explanation for the social contagion of weight is peer pressure. Having a friend who is heavy affects your own views about what normal weight is. That gives you permission to gain weight, and you, in turn, give permission to other friends. Having overweight friends releases you from accountability, a social norm you then pass on to others. The authors believe that the viral nature of these behaviors likely stems from the evolutionary advantage of tight social connections.

Research on diets and groups tends to bear out the importance of a social network on weight. Studies show that Weight Watchers' biggest asset is its group meetings—they help participants stick to the plan. Other research shows that people who diet or exercise in groups, or even with a partner or spouse, keep it up longer and lose more weight.

This is the theory behind the Triwomen group. In late January 2010, about ninety women met one evening at the YMCA in Scotch Plains, New Jersey. All were interested in competing in a triathlon—a race involving running, biking, and swimming—sponsored by the women's apparelmaker Danskin. They listened to three speakers, all triathletes who had completed the race in 2009. One was Peggy Brown, a forty-seven-year-old middle-school earth sciences teacher and mother of three in Scotch Plains. She weighed 240 pounds.

The meeting was the idea of Amy Carow, who also lives in Scotch Plains. She is a competitive swimmer and all-around athlete whose mission is to get the women in her community to exercise. She structures the program around the Danskin Triathlon, held in Sandy Hook, New Jersey, each September. Although it takes only six weeks to train for a beginner's triathlon of this type—a half-mile swim, three-mile run, and 12.5-mile bike ride—Carow starts in January. She knows that some of the women have never been on a bike, or are afraid to put their heads in the water.

Carow knew that, as an athlete and race veteran, she was the right person to provide advice on how to train for the race and a structure for getting in shape. But she was not the right person to inspire women who viewed a three-mile run as being on the same order of difficulty as a moon landing. For that, Carow turned to people like Brown.

When a fellow teacher at her school invited Brown to train for the race the year before, she had not exercised in twelve years. She had spent those years attending to her children and her husband, never finding the time to do things for herself. Her family was shocked that she was trying and skeptical it would happen. "Let us know if you make it," they said. But she did make it. Brown finished the 2009 triathlon in the bottom 3 percent—but she finished.

She was, in other words, the perfect speaker for motivating the women who most desperately needed to start exercising. Brown gave a funny, self-deprecating speech about her triathlon adventure—talking about her fears of jellyfish and spandex and the fact that she walked instead of running at the I Hate Running Club training sessions every Sunday. She also spoke about how she had set a goal of finishing the race—and, with the help of the group, she achieved it. After the meeting, people came up to her and said, "If you can do this, I can do this," she told me later.

Brown succeeded because of the group. On Saturday mornings, she would ride her bike alone. She did all her other workouts—three a week at first, then four, then five, then six—with fellow Triwomen. "I would have made a date to go swim at 8:30 at night," she said. "I was tired, it was cold out, I worked all day. But I had to go because Bonnie was going." She went with other rookie Triwomen to buy a bike and to get new running shoes. She went to the meetings to learn about training strategy.

A healthy-living social cure does not have to be done under the umbrella of a corporation. All it requires is a group of neighbors who meet to exercise or to weigh each other, offer support, and hold each other accountable. But do-it-yourself groups of friends do pose one danger: they can quickly degenerate into permission-giving. If everyone clucks sympathetically when a member returns from a vacation five pounds heavier, the social norm of the group has shifted and has now become a force for weight gain, much worse than no group at all:

even my weight loss group says it's okay. Sympathetic understanding is counterproductive; what's needed is ruthlessness.

No one would claim that weight loss is straightforward, but adapting the social cure to weight loss is. Christakis and Fowler's study also offers other fruitful avenues for social-cure solutions, as they found that the chance that you smoke or drink and your level of happiness were also linked to those of your friends, and friends of friends.

PERSONAL STRUGGLES WITH TEMPTATION are not the only candidates for a broader application of the social cure. Many of the other join-the-club strategies used by the innovators described in this book can also be applied more widely.

One such social cure is DOTS—the strategy of having a neighbor, family member, or health worker observe as tuberculosis patients take their medicine. DOTS greatly increases the chance that patients will take their pills correctly and complete their course of treatment. As we saw in chapter 6, DOTS has slowed the development of strains of TB resistant to antibiotics and has limited the disease's spread.

DOTS works by boosting adherence. People do not want to disappoint their pill partner. Very often that partner is someone who has already had tuberculosis, or has other things in common with the patient, and can provide crucial encouragement and incentive to restore a patient's will to get better.

We already know that the DOTS model can help with other diseases. The use of *accompagnateurs* is now widespread in AIDS programs in Haiti and Africa, and has shown success with hard-to-treat patients in Boston.

The possibilities for a DOTS model should not be limited to communicable diseases in poor countries or among the poverty-stricken in the United States. Since adherence is an enormous problem for all diseases everywhere, DOTS can be a solution. If it is not necessary or feasible to provide a patient with daily in-person encouragement, then a weekly visit or meeting might be enough. The peer can be a community health worker with a similar background or a more direct peer—a fellow patient. In chapter 6, we saw that pilot programs using both have been successful in the United States, showing they can help people of all social classes to manage chronic diseases. They deserve to be expanded.

DOTS is also a microversion of the small-group social cures that could prove effective for all those New-Year's-resolution–style personal struggles. A DOTS strategy is more adaptable and easier to follow than going to a formal meeting. Your impatience with your young children may not rise to a level of toxicity where you will actually go to meetings about it (a high threshold for anyone with young children), but it could certainly help if you and another parent would agree to call each other when you are about to explode. Students who resolve to double the amount of time they spend studying don't have time to go to meetings, which are not necessary anyway—they just have to find someone else with the same goal and study together. If you wanted to cut down on your family's consumption of fast food, you could get together with one or two like-minded people each weekend and spend a few hours preparing three different big pots of food to split. You would end up with meals for three days, an enjoyable afternoon, many new chili recipes—and a positive new identity as a person in control of your family's eating.

Any problem that requires consistent adherence—which a good proportion of life does—can benefit from this kind of social cure. Since there is ample evidence that the greater impact comes when you help others rather than when they help you, the benefits are likely to be notable.

The calculus clubs described in chapter 5 are another join-the-club strategy that could be broadened effectively. It is helpful to look again at the essence of this social cure: Students are trying to master a challenging subject. Whether or not they succeed depends on more than their previous preparation and talent. Their learning is also impeded by a reluctance to risk asking questions, low math confidence, and lack of context. Faced with a problem they can't solve, they don't know whether their own skills are deficient or the problem is exceptionally difficult. Students in typical classes also don't have the benefit of being forced to think through a solution thoroughly enough to be able to teach it to someone else. They must also overcome the perception that it's not cool to be interested in math or spend a lot of time on it. Small-group learning, in which students help each other solve advanced-calculus problems, helps knock over all these barriers.

The description of the hurdles in the way of calculus success could also apply to many other learning situations—perhaps most of them. Other college courses that require mastery of tough skills are obvious candidates: there could be organic-chemistry clubs (a few universities have these) and Arabic-language clubs. But there's no reason that small-group study should be limited to college students. At the other extreme, even five-year-olds learning to read deal with problems of self-confidence and worry about looking dumb and uncool in front of the class. They suffer from overcrowded classrooms where high student-to-teacher ratios condemn them to be passive listeners. Kindergarteners are not going to meet after school for study dates, but it could be a useful part of every reading lesson in school to have children sit in groups of three or four and help each other read.

The Jamkhed-program model described in chapter 6 could also be applied to many more problems than village health. Many of the reasons people cannot escape poverty in the developing world share a common root: the services enjoyed by middle-class people in big cities are not available to village-dwellers in remote areas. In the majority of poor countries, rural people don't have medical care, decent schools, training in the most modern practices in agriculture or other livelihoods, access to credit and safe savings, or many other advantages their fellow citizens in towns and cities enjoy.

Let us examine the essence of this social cure. When Raj and Mabelle Arole set up the Jamkhed program, they were trying to solve the problem of a lack of health care in rural villages. Professionals—doctors and nurses—were of little help. They wouldn't come to villages, their unfamiliarity with local customs led to a lack of trust among villagers, they did not prioritize working with the people who needed them most, and they used a health-care model that emphasized expensive cures—a system that did not help people take responsibility for their own well-being through preventive health care.

The Aroles solved the problem by gathering members of exactly the group they wanted to reach and training them in the skills most needed to improve village health. The illiterate village women easily learned the material and skills. Helping them acquire the necessary persistence and confidence was more difficult, however. For that, the Aroles turned to the social cure.

Poor countries are in desperate need of low-cost rural health care. This is especially true in English-speaking poor countries, where nurses and doctors are being poached to fill vacancies in Britain's National Health Service and rural areas of the United States, Australia, and Canada. The numbers are staggering. About one in five African-born physicians were working in a wealthy country in 2000—each doctor representing several hundred thousand dollars in medical aid Africa sends to Britain, Canada, or the United States.

Those who stay in Africa, moreover, remain in cities. Health conditions in rural areas are worsening. Tuberculosis is rising, in some places AIDS is widespread, and climate-change–induced drought has increased malnutrition and water scarcity, leading to serious illness. Someone needs to be addressing public health—and in the countryside, it isn't going to be doctors or nurses. The world urgently needs many more Jamkheds.

Health care is not the only service in scarce supply in the world's villages. Uneducated farmers could be trained as agricultural extension agents. The men in the village can learn to plant drought-resistant corn just as their wives learned to purify drinking water. Women with a little education, just a step ahead of their students, can teach middle school and high school in communities where students have no other possibility of education beyond primary school. This is especially useful for educating girls, whose parents may not be willing to risk their safety and the family's honor by sending them on a long walk to a school in another village. Villagers can also help each other to get loans and small-business training; through the microcredit movement, they are doing just that.

The same women who are trained as health workers could also become counselors and social workers. Jamkhed's health workers not only have replaced old ideas about health care with more modern ones, they also have brought a measure of organization and income to village women and shattered traditional notions of caste. They could also help their villages to overcome attitudes tolerating domestic violence, female genital mutilation, abuse of brides, and family preference for sons so overwhelming that millions of families abort female fetuses or kill daughters through deliberate neglect. And perhaps the greatest contribution any man could make to his village in most of the world would be to start a chapter of Alcoholics Anonymous. As the success of Jamkhed shows, the social cure is a tool that can help villagers not only to get services but also to change cultural practices that have kept them in poverty.

THE STORIES IN THIS book are by no means a complete catalog of the different ways to use the social cure. They have not included, until this final chapter, a group of problems for which the social cure of a good peer group should be an obvious solution: problems caused by a bad peer group. There are situations where the footprint of a bad peer group is instantly recognizable—for example, a young person's choice to join a gang or become a criminal.

When bad peers lead people into trouble, it should be the case that good peers can lead them out again. Delinquency and gang membership are so strongly peer-related that you might reasonably expect the social cure to be widely used to help young people avoid them, but this is not so—in large part because nothing is. Prisoners and gang members are outcasts; spending money on their problems has little political support.

Like any other program, the social cure depends on the abilities of its advocates to amass and sustain the necessary money, support, and other resources. Sometimes, no matter how well the social cure works, those resources are absent. Antismoking programs need constant vigilance, because tobacco companies are always trying to block their funding or substitute ineffective strategies for effective ones. For the calculus clubs, the enemy is neglect—they require champions in influential university positions, and these have been scarce.

Even so, these programs have the advantage of widespread popular support. Most people do care about preventing smoking and increasing minority success in college, whereas they tend to revile or ignore former prisoners and youth who live in gang-ridden neighborhoods. When politicians deal with such people—and that is not often—they usually have designed policies primarily to give voters the emotional satisfaction of harshly penalizing bad behavior.

The treatment of prisoners upon release is proof that policies toward offenders are designed for maximum punishment, even if that means minimum crime prevention. The usual package granted to someone released from prison after serving time for a felony is $90 (if that), a bus ticket, and the considerable stigma that follows an ex-offender. Since prisoners are often incarcerated far away from their families, and states charge astronomical rates for prison-originated phone calls, prisoners often lose touch with their loved ones and may not have anyone to take them in when they get home. They tend to arrive in their home cities with no plans other than—worrisomely—those hatched with fellow prisoners. They have few prospects for jobs or housing. Since they likely had no drug treatment in prison, some will still crave a fix, which costs money. It is little wonder that some of them fall back into crime within hours of their release.

Prisoners returning to the outside world need many things: stable housing, drug treatment, job training, GED (high school equivalency) classes, parenting and anger-management lessons. But even the handful of people who do worry about ex-offenders rarely mention what may be the most crucial need of all: a better class of friends. Former prisoners go back to their old neighborhoods and meet up with their old gangs or new people of the only type they may be comfortable with—criminals. They need to stop hanging out with associates who tempt them with stories of easy money or drug-filled nights. They need to start hanging out with people who consider the consequences of their actions, who value legitimate jobs, sobriety, and family—people who attend their AA meetings and GED classes, who are trying to rebuild their lives.

In the West Harlem neighborhood of Upper Manhattan, there is a large and beautiful Gothic-style building overlooking the Hudson River. Formally called the Fortune Academy but known as the Castle, it is owned by the Fortune Society, a group dedicated to helping returning prisoners succeed with starting new lives. Staffed largely with former offenders, Fortune helps about 4,000 newly released prisoners each year with job training and placement, drug treatment, classes in cooking and anger management and parenting, and GED classes. But about 300 people a year get something more: a bed in the Castle and the chance to start a productive and law-abiding life in the company of sixty-one other people trying to do the same.

The Castle has single rooms for those residents who earn them; the rest have roommates. It serves meals and has staff on duty around the clock. It has a computer lab, a laundry, and a cafeteria. Residents are required to go to counseling or classes. Every Thursday night at six, the Castle has a group meeting of all its residents. At one recent meeting, people spoke about the successes of their week. One woman talked about her job as a janitor at a shelter for women. "It's a safe place, and clean—that's because of me," she said with pride. One man reported attending a speech by a political candidate. Another said he had opened a bank account for the first time in his life. One man announced that the Castle's chorus was rehearsing and was open to new members. The residents applauded each other fervently.

A very different community for former prisoners is Delancey Street, in San Francisco. People arrive at Delancey Street when they have hit bottom. Often they have been in prison, have histories of drug and alcohol addiction and no skills, are unable to read, and are unfamiliar with ways of responding to the world except through violence. They live at Delancey Street for an average of four years. Each resident is required to get at least a high school equivalency diploma and learn several marketable job skills, such as furnituremaking, sales, or accounting. The organization is run entirely by its residents, who teach each other—there is no paid staff. Teaching others is part of the rehabilitation process. The residence is financed in part by private donations, but the majority of its financing comes from the businesses the residents run, such as restaurants, event planning, a corporate car service, a moving company, and a framing shop. All money earned goes to the collective, which pays all the residents' expenses.

Both Fortune and Delancey rely heavily on the social cure. A person emerging from prison is surrounded by a community of people who support him, hold him accountable, teach him skills, and model good behavior. Many of the men and women in these programs come to think of themselves as productive members of society for the first time in their lives, and it may also be the first time they ever feel competent at anything besides lawbreaking.

The Delancey Street residence, which began in 1971, has never been formally evaluated, but there is no question that it is phenomenally successful. It has helped more than 14,000 people graduate from prison into constructive lives. Carol Kizziah, who manages Delancey's efforts to apply its lessons elsewhere, says that the organization estimates that 75 percent of its alumni go on to productive lives. (For former prisoners who don't go to Delancey, only 25 to 40 percent manage to avoid rearrest.) Since it costs taxpayers nothing, from a government's point of view it could very well be the most cost-effective social program ever devised. The program has established similar Delancey Street communities in Los Angeles, New Mexico, North Carolina, and upstate New York. Outsiders have replicated the Delancey Street model in about five other places.

While some other Fortune Society programs have been researched and found to be effective (a program that provides alternatives to incarceration, for example), there has been no study of its Castle, which began in 2002. Nevertheless, the Castle often is cited by criminal-justice experts as a model for helping ex-offenders. It seems intuitive that it works. But one possible reason that the Castle seems so impressive is that most of those I saw at the Castle were in their thirties or older—an age where people are leaving crime on their own, finally ready to accept some responsibility, aware they are not immortal, and looking for a stable family life. Crime is a young person's game. No doubt the vast majority of those at the Castle will successfully turn around their lives, but that is a much more difficult proposition for a twenty-three-year-old.

Delancey Street and the Castle attract streams of visitors from around the globe (British prime minister Tony Blair visited Delancey Street) and are universally applauded. Yet, nearly forty years after Delancey Street's founding, it had been replicated in only a handful of places—half of them by Delancey Street itself—and the Castle has never been replicated. Neither program has been formally studied—for example, comparing the fates of former residents with matched pairs who did not go into the program. That these programs remain lonely outposts is symptomatic of a serious problem in criminal justice: powerful people do not care enough about it to spend money.

Numerous academic studies show that peer pressure is a major contributor to youth criminality. It has been demonstrated over and over that hanging around with delinquent friends encourages young people to think of themselves as delinquents, and it puts them in a world where criminal behavior is easy to engage in and is rewarded by peers.

One particularly intriguing study from Ohio State University found that the effect of antisocial friendship groups was so powerful that it *completely* explained the fact that black and Hispanic youth are more likely to be involved in criminal behavior than other youth, after controlling for other factors. A black or Hispanic youth is more likely to commit a crime than a similar white or Asian youth because his peer group is more likely to be a delinquent one.

Peer pressure has always been studied as a negative factor—the impact of antisocial peers. What has hardly been studied at all is the impact of *pro*social peers on *anti*social people. Can a new, prosocial peer group turn around someone who is antisocial? It *seems* that it should work. We have anecdotal evidence that it works, but we don't really know—and it is not safe simply to assume the inverse of the research on antisocial peer groups. Experts with whom I spoke did not know of studies focusing on whether programs that promote prosocial contacts work.

Little that has to do with criminality has been well researched, and what research there is often gets ignored. Even though it is obvious that the way society treats prisoners contributes to their rapid return to criminality, politicians have been loath to spend the money to help prisoners reintegrate into society. They have tended to believe that voters will only support punishment. It is difficult to obtain financing for analyses; understandably, the few organizations that will spend money to help ex-prisoners prefer to finance programs, not studies. Politicians might think it makes no sense to spend money to evaluate the Castle if there is no chance that anyone would try to replicate it.

Today, however, all this may be changing. It is becoming possible to imagine good, wide-scale programs, including the social cure, to prevent recidivism. Prisoner reentry into society is a hot topic in the field of corrections (albeit still invisible to the rest of the world), in large part because so many prisoners are being released. America's incarceration rates are astronomically high by world standards, and virtually everyone in prison will get out at some point. The political situation also has changed. The crime rate has dropped, which means that voters are less panicked about crime and more willing to get past the emotional satisfaction of harsh measures and examine what works. Perhaps more important, states are in budget crises, and prisons are hugely expensive. Many states are looking for ways to let prisoners out—and they can't afford to see them return.

These changes have produced a shift away from ideology and toward science and "what works." There may be a new interest in the utility of peer groups. "We never understood how to deal with peer associations," said Christopher Lowenkamp, director of the Center for Criminal Justice Research at the University of Cincinnati. "We never cracked that nut correctly. The interest is still there, and it's coming around full circle. Reentry is the thing right now, and trying to figure out how the heck we manage a million offenders coming back to the community."

WHILE THE FIELD OF PRISONER reentry looks at how to help people getting out of jail lead productive lives, another group needs similar help—young people who have not yet become criminals but are at risk of doing so.

Gangs tempt in many ways; they offer physical protection (often illusory), respect, and the chance to make fast money. But the most important reason people join gangs is that their friends do. We know this is true. The question that matters for preventing crime is the reverse: Can peer-pressure–based programs help young people avoid or exit gangs and criminality?

The anecdotal evidence is overwhelming that it can help. Dozens of programs throughout the United States attempt to use forms of the social cure with young people to help them avoid gangs, get out of gangs, or just avoid falling into crime. A few are run by cities, such as midnight basketball leagues. According to the Association of Midnight Basketball Leagues, these peaked at about fifty U.S. cities in the early part of the 2000s, but more than half have subsequently lost their funding. Some antigang programs are run by nongovernmental groups. In 1998, Delancey Street opened the Life Learning Academy, for San Francisco–area children who were not in school—they were on the streets instead, most involved in drugs and gangs. Most had no functional parents. They couldn't read. They were enrolled in school but never went.

At the Life Learning Academy, school runs twelve hours a day. Students are picked up by Delancey drivers at their homes at 8 a.m. and returned at 10 p.m. The school uses Delancey's each-one-teach-one model, with strong emphasis on group work and peer support. Students tutor each other and enforce the rules at the school, participating in the Student Mediation Council. The San Francisco mayor's office did an evaluation that tracked students over three years, finding the program to be "profoundly effective." Its graduation rate is more than 90 percent—for students who were considered unteachable. More than 40 percent of graduates have gone on to college.

The Life Learning Academy costs $12,000 per student per year, but it is cost-effective even without factoring in the crimes these students might have committed if they had not changed their lives. If they were not at the school, most of them would be in detention or a group home, at triple the price.

Another notable success took place in Benning Terrace, a neighborhood of housing projects in Washington, DC. In 1997, Benning Terrace had been suffering a gang war that had killed fifty-three people in two years. To avoid getting shot, residents headed into their apartments sometimes as early as 3 p.m. The police didn't go near Benning Terrace. Postal workers left the mail for the entire neighborhood in a heap at the entrance. The complex was so hellish that the DC Housing Authority had decided to tear it down.

All that changed after Darryl Hall was killed in early 1997. He was abducted in broad daylight and killed execution-style, his body found a few days later; he was twelve. This got people's attention, including that of the Alliance of Concerned Men, a new organization of older ex-convicts and former drug addicts who had remade their lives. The Alliance members went to Benning Terrace and invited the gang leaders to a series of meetings at the office of the Center for Neighborhood Enterprise, a nongovernmental group with experience in reducing violence. One of the Alliance's men, who worked at a car dealership, borrowed two vans—one for each gang—to take them to the meeting.

Robert Woodson, leader of the Center for Neighborhood Enterprise, wrote that at the first meeting, the gang members were wary, looking around for an ambush. The adults asked the young men to set the rules for the meeting. "They agreed that there would be no cursing or personal attacks. The "n" word was not to be used. They would take turns speaking, and everyone would get a chance to speak. They would not interrupt each other," Woodson wrote. The adults asked how the problem had started. No one knew. Midway through the meeting, it became evident to the adults that neither gang had sent its true leader, so they asked the members present to come again.

At the next meeting, the two leaders, Wayne Lee and Derrick Ross— Woodson testified before Congress that police considered Ross "one of the seven most dangerous men in Washington"—were part of the group. The adults reminded them that when they themselves were young, before the cycle of killing started, they had played outside; didn't they want that for their younger siblings? Since many of the gang members maintained that they had gone into gang life to protect their families from violence, the argument had weight. Woodson wrote: "Wayne Lee then came around the table and shook hands with Derrick Ross. It was a most dramatic and moving moment for us. They then told us that we didn't need two vans to bring them for the meetings. They would all come together in one van. We had the beginnings of a truce. We celebrated by taking them to Phillips Restaurant on Washington's Southwest waterfront. To our amazement, we found that many of them had never seen the Potomac River, even though they had lived all their lives in DC."

After the truce was announced, the director of the DC Housing Authority agreed to put on hold the plans to tear down Benning Terrace. He went to talk to the gang members and ended up hiring them to remove the graffiti and do apartment repairs. The gang members, on their own initiative, spent part of their first paychecks to build and equip a basketball court for younger children. They held four barbecues and bought the food themselves. Then they gave their new group a name— Concerned Brothers and Sisters of Benning Terrace.

The Housing Authority jobs paid $6.50 an hour—minimum wage at the time. The conventional wisdom was that kids like these would not give up the easy money of crime for a minimum-wage job. But 100 people were hired, and another 100 signed up on the waiting list for jobs. Woodson wrote that when the Housing Authority's maintenance director, Bill Knox, was driving around the complex with Derrick Ross, he asked Ross what he wanted to do with his life. "Landscaping," Ross replied. Knox said he nearly ran off the road. But then he added planting grass and gardens to the new employees' work plans.

Some of the men, including Ross, ended up in permanent jobs with the Housing Authority. Some started a construction company. Wayne Lee opened a convenience store near Benning Terrace. Many of the former gang members still volunteer after work with an organization called Benning Terrace Youth Opportunities. About twenty-five volunteers from the community meet in the afternoons to work with about 265 children aged seven to seventeen. They coach football and basketball and conduct group workshops to teach such skills as controlling anger and dealing with the bureaucracy of a legal life. Charles Penny, one of the original gang members, said that the children are required to attend tutoring and homework programs and do chores at home. "We check that you are respecting your mom," he said. The kids get a reward for "doing those positive things throughout the year and staying around positive people." The reward used to be a trip to Orlando, Florida, but money got tight, so it is now more likely a trip to Atlantic City to see a professional fight.

The truce in Benning Terrace held for thirteen years; there was no gang-related killing until 2010. There have been other kinds of violence, however, including murders, and the neighborhood is once again seeing gang crime. When the Housing Authority official who had worked with Benning Terrace left his position, the jobs and other support from the city for the former gang members dried up. Only the volunteer efforts of the former gang members go on.

What worked—at least for a while—in Benning Terrace? In part it was the mentorship of the Alliance of Concerned Men, people with credibility because they had been there. In part it was the offer of jobs. But it was also the fact that the gangs suddenly became a different kind of peer group. The gangs had provided a place to belong, a substitute family, a way to be someone special, to win respect. What the gang had become still gave young men those things—but no longer through intimidation and violence. Now the way to be a big man was to coach football or contribute a paycheck to build a kids' basketball court. The way to be a big man was to be applauded by your neighbors and looked up to by children for putting food on the table. The big man was the one who *didn't* pull out a weapon and break the truce.

This was peer pressure sponsored by three different organizations, one of them the DC Housing Authority. But such peer pressure can also be informal and cost-free. One example comes from Sampson Davis, George Jenkins, and Rameck Hunt—three black men who grew up in dangerous Newark neighborhoods in the 1980s, at the height of the crack epidemic. Two of them had spent time in juvenile detention. There were no doctors in their neighborhoods, so they had no role models, but the three boys made an agreement with each other in high school that they would stay in school, attend college, and go on to medical school.

In their much-celebrated book, *The Pact*, the three tell how they saved each other. "We knew we'd never survive if we went after it alone," they wrote. "And so we made a pact: we'd help one another through, no matter what. . . . We provided one another with a kind of positive peer pressure. From the moment we made our pact, the competition was on. When one of us finished his college application, the other two rushed to send theirs out . . . each of us felt pressured to perform well because we knew our friends would excel and we didn't want to embarrass ourselves or lag behind. When one of us made an A on a test, the others strived to make A's, too." Davis, Jenkins, and Hunt became, respectively, an emergency-room physician, a dentist, and an internist.

The stories of the three doctors and of Benning Terrace are not unique. They are repeated in many places around the United States, but they are seldom evaluated or done on a large scale. They remain scattered, isolated, and vulnerable to shifts in the political and financial winds.

THE WRONG PEER GROUP can drag a person into criminal behavior, and it is likely that the right peer group can pull him out again. These facts are significant in themselves, pointing to new join-the-club strategies for the prevention of common crime. But they also raise a tantalizing question even more ambitious in scope: Could the social cure be of use in combating global terrorism?

At first glance, this would seem to be a considerable leap. It is one thing to take a program that can help people resist the temptations of alcohol and adapt it to chocolate cake. It is quite another to take midnight basketball and use it to fight Al Qaeda. But Marc Sageman, for one, would see some sense in the possibility. Sageman, the psychiatrist and former CIA officer who worked with the Afghan mujahideen, has written two books on the subject of who becomes a terrorist, how, and why. His work relies on a database he created; by the time of his second book, it contained data on more than 500 known Islamic terrorists. Much of his information comes from trial documents; transcript of wiretaps, testimony, evidence from captured documents or computer hard drives. To a lesser extent, he relies on media accounts.

Sageman's views are controversial. (Most of the controversy revolves around a different part of his argument, not one relevant for thinking about the social cure.) He is challenging the conventional wisdom on a subject of enormous importance—one where a lot of money is also at stake—but people take his views very seriously. He has consulted on counterterrorism with the New York City Police Department and virtually every U.S. government agency that works on the issue. His books have changed the way people think about terrorism.

The gist of Sageman's argument is that the major terrorist threat today is not a powerful, centrally controlled Al Qaeda that brainwashes and recruits young radical Muslims from around the world. Rather, the vast majority of terror attacks in the West come from small groups of disaffected young men, cut off from their roots, who initially have nothing to do with Al Qaeda. He argues that Al Qaeda does not recruit these men into terrorism—they recruit themselves. Once they are committed to violent extremism, they contact Al Qaeda or another group, or simply take it upon themselves to act. (Al Qaeda's challenge, writes Sageman, is not to find willing terrorists but to sort through the volunteers to choose ones who are competent and trustworthy.) A terrorist's radicalization comes not from any outside brainwashing but from inside his own group, from peer pressure. The men move more and more to the extreme because of the escalating radicalization of their ever-tightening social circle.

For an example of peer-pressure–driven radicalization, Sageman offers the most spectacular case, that of the 9/11 plotters. The nucleus of the group consisted of men who lived in Hamburg, Germany, in a middle-class expatriate student community. There was a militant study group at Al Quds Mosque in Hamburg, and in 1996 three students at the Technical University of Hamburg-Harburg joined it, including Mohamed Atta, who would become the leader of the plot. Several other Muslim immigrants studying at the university became friends with the group. Two of them were already friends from their childhoods in Marrakech, Morocco. One had an apartment in the student housing complex, which became the group's hangout. Later the men began to go to the apartment shared by Atta and two others, which they named "House of the Supporters," the same name as Al Qaeda's guesthouse in Pakistan.

Wiretaps show that, over two years, their conversations gradually became more and more radical. The men sought to impress each other with the extremism of their views. Talk was increasingly focused on the evils of the United States and world Jewry. Their entertainment, according to Sageman, was watching battlefield videos and singing songs about martyrdom. Finally, they made contact with a man in Germany who was the brother-in-law of one of Osama bin Laden's chief aides.

The men of the Hamburg terror cell had several attributes shared by most Islamic terrorists, wrote Sageman. First, they were outsiders in the society they lived in. Sageman found that 70 percent of the men in his database were expatriates when they became radicalized. Especially vulnerable to the message of violence were sons of mildly religious upper-middle-class families from the Middle East or North Africa who were sent to universities in Western Europe, where they felt homesick and lonely. Another 8 percent were sons or grandsons of Muslim immigrants in Europe. These young men often were raised in completely secular households, but they felt marginalized and discriminated against—the unemployment rate for young Muslim men in Europe is double or triple that of their non-Muslim peers. Many of these men dropped out of high school and joined gangs; after about a decade of gang life, they turned to radical Islam.

One particularly interesting point is Sageman's explanation for why there has been far more Islamic terrorist activity—successful or not—in Europe than in the United States. He attributes this in large part to the fact that Muslims in the United States are more assimilated, face far less discrimination, and think of themselves as part of the world around them more than do Muslims in Europe.

The effect of being away from home—and living in a totally different culture—is profound. The most common route to terrorism, Sageman wrote, was this: A man moved from Morocco or Egypt to London or Hamburg. He looked up friends from his hometown and joined their social circles. If he did not have connections from home, he looked for companionship at the local mosque, or, if he were a student, at the university's Muslim student organization. He found himself in a group of young men who were angry and alienated. It is the anger that matters—terrorists tend to know little about Islam and are motivated by a sense of injustice, not religious fervor. If there were a local extremist mosque, then the transition to the use of violence would be smoother. But listening to the preaching of violence was not a necessary part of radicalization. Many, many young Muslim men are angry—over the war in Iraq, Israeli treatment of the Palestinians, the West's failure to stop Milošević's genocide in Bosnia, their own harassment by the police. Only a tiny minority of them would be susceptible to the argument that these abuses mean that they are in a war with nonbelievers and Islam permits them to respond with violence. But only a tiny minority is needed to create great havoc. If one man in the group began to take this view seriously, it soon spread to the others.

Since these men tended not to have jobs, they had a lot of time to hang out. They formed a tight clique, egging each other on to more and more radical views. If they tried to impress their increasingly extremist beliefs on other kinds of friends, those friends began to avoid them, which meant their social circle became smaller and smaller, eventually reduced solely to others interested in terrorism. Each tried to out-tough the others by being the most radical, the most willing to embrace violence.

This is likely why so many become radicalized in places where they are outsiders. Back home, surrounded by family, the outside world would have intervened and it would have been impossible to live in a radical cocoon. They would have to live by social norms larger than those of just their clique.

In the clique, however, the idea of using violence easily became attractive. From wiretaps, we know that the 9/11 men didn't focus on the fact that they were going to kill. Rather, they focused on their own willingness to die. They saw themselves as heroes, sacrificing their lives to bring more attention to the misdeeds of the west and more justice to the world.

"As new born-again novices," Sageman wrote of the men joining, "they constantly proselytized their beliefs and enthusiasm for the fight. They wanted to impress their friends. In a sense, it was a constant, mutual self-recruiting atmosphere. . . . The mutual group reinforcement also allows them to leave behind traditional societal morality for a more local morality, preached by the group. . . . Cliques do not start out as terrorist groups. They evolve in that direction as their mutual relationships deepen, in a spiral of greater loyalty, mutual devotion, self-sacrifice and intimacy." Eventually, a member of the group finds some link to Al Qaeda or another terrorist organization, or the group decides to act on its own.

With increasing military pressure on Al Qaeda, and growing surveillance of the frequent hangouts of budding terrorists, the movement is being fragmented and pushed underground. Some young and angry Muslims who would have been hanging out at a mosque now find the same ever-escalating group dynamic in Internet chat rooms. Clearly, people have turned to violence this way, but the pro-terror social norm is probably less intense over the Internet than face-to-face.

The friendship factor explains one of the great puzzles about suicide bombers: the free-rider problem. The rational way to react to a group-suicide project is to hang back in safety and let others take the risk. But the tightness of the clique is similar to that of a foxhole; you get someone to carry out a suicide bombing the same way you get him to charge up Hamburger Hill. People in the clique are loyal to their buddies and want to be heroes in their friends' eyes. Even if a man began to have doubts about the use of violence, his loyalty to the others would make it very difficult to abandon them. The group gives courage. Even leaving aside the logistics, it is very hard to muster the will to go through with a terror plot alone, but the mutual encouragement of the group and men's loyalty to it effectively creates that will.

A similar group dynamic is also the driving force behind other terrorist groups and extremist cults. Studies of people who joined Reverend Sun Myung Moon's Unification Church or Germany's Baader-Meinhof Gang—a leftist terrorist group active in the 1970s—found that, as with Islamic radicals, the social bonds come first, leading people into the ideology. The radicalization is a product of the gradual tightening of that social circle as all moderate voices depart. At that point, the group pressure crushes doubts and prevents people from turning away. Sageman named the phenomenon after a term the Canadian police used to label a Montreal Islamic terror cell: bunch of guys, or BOG. It is the bunch-of-guys theory of terrorism.

Marc Sageman argues—convincingly, to a lot of people who know terrorism close up—that negative peer pressure is extremely important in driving young Muslim men to become suicide bombers. The question is whether the reverse is also true. Can positive peer pressure provide a way to divert young men from the path of terror?

If they were gang members, the social-cure solution would be straightforward. It would start with people who grew up in the same gang-permeated environment. They would perhaps be former gang members—people who have street credibility and understand these men and their world completely. They could start groups (or perhaps turn around existing groups) to offer young people what they look for in a gang, but in a healthier way: the tight clique of peers, the sense of belonging, the chance to be admired and respected, to be a "big man."

As Sageman's research showed, young Islamic violent extremists have much in common with gang members. Like gang members, they have grievances, and they excuse their criminal behavior as a justified response to an unfair world. As with gangs, what turns a marginalized, angry young person (there are many) into a member of a terrorist group (there are few) is being drawn by friends into a clique with its own insular social norms. The right clique might be able to keep that from happening.

To try to apply the antigang model to Islamic terrorism initially seems naïve in the extreme, but that is only because we are accustomed to thinking about the behavior of Islamic terrorists as extraterrestrial. On the contrary, suicide bombers do not live outside the rules of human behavior; they respond to group dynamics the way others do. This is what the social cure could attack. It cannot attempt to take away their grievances. Many millions of Muslims have grievances against the West, and it is naïve to imagine that we can change this. But a new peer group might break the last link in the chain that turns grievances into terror—to prevent an angry young man from becoming a violent one.

It is easy for Westerners to picture a social cure to turn people away from gangs, as gang culture is not incomprehensible to the average American or Briton the way radical Islamic culture is. But there is an influential group of people who understand perfectly the inner life of future suicide bombers. These are fellow fundamentalist Muslims.

ABDUL HAQQ BAKER, born Anthony Baker, is a Londoner. His father was from Nigeria, his mother from Guyana. He grew up a Christian and converted to Islam in 1990. Three years later, he became chairman of the Brixton Mosque and Cultural Center. The mosque sits one block off a shopping street in an ethnically and racially mixed neighborhood of South London. It consists of two connected brick townhouses with a green door; inside is a large hall, sparely adorned. More than half the worshippers here are converts, like Baker, and like its imam, Omar Urquhart.

For an unassuming building, the Brixton Mosque has had a remarkable impact on global events. Britain has the West's largest concentration of Al Qaeda supporters, and the head of MI5, the internal security service, has said that the government is aware of 2,000 radicalized Muslims in Britain who might be involved in terrorism—undoubtedly a low estimate. London is home to some poison-spewing mosques, which is one reason it produces a healthy percentage of the world's known Islamic terrorists and has acquired the nickname "Londonistan." The most infamous extremist preacher is the former imam of Finsbury Park Mosque, Abu Hamza, a man with one eye and steel hooks for hands, who preached that the killing of nonbelievers was justified. Police had linked the mosque (now called the North London Central Mosque) to dozens of terror plots. In 2006, he was convicted of soliciting murder and stirring up racial hatred and sentenced to seven years in prison. When he finishes serving his sentence, he is due to be extradited to the United States for trial on charges of financing terrorism and setting up a terrorist training camp, among other accusations.

Another influential voice of terrorism is Abdullah el-Faisal, who was the imam at Brixton Mosque in the early 1990s. Although he did not preach violence when he was there, he later began to tell his students that they were permitted to kill and rob nonbelievers and even to use nuclear weapons against countries such as India. He was arrested and served four years for soliciting murder and inciting racial hatred, after which he was deported to his native Jamaica.

To outsiders, the Brixton Mosque could seem to be fertile soil for the cultivation of terrorism. It is Salafist. *Salaf* means predecessor, and Salafism is a fundamentalist branch of Sunni Islam that advocates a return to the righteousness of the time of the Prophet and the generations that immediately followed him. (The form of Salafism best known to Americans is the Wahhabism of Saudi Arabia.) Salafis believe that a return to the literal reading of the Koran is necessary to be able to live as the companions to the Prophet did. Salafis reject Western ideologies and advocate a strict constructionist form of Sharia, or Islamic law.

The rigid fundamentalism of Salafism, and the tendency of Salafist communities to reject secular practices and isolate themselves from the West, has led some scholars to associate the ideology with violent extremism. Sageman referred to terrorism today as "global Salafi jihad," but this idea is disputed by other scholars and experts on Islamic terror. Some terrorists share fundamentalist views with Salafis, but the vast majority of Salafis, like Baker and his colleagues at Brixton Mosque, are nonviolent and, indeed, nonpolitical—they are concerned with the practices of their own community, not with the wider world.

The Brixton Mosque's community of worshippers is young, with an average age of thirty. Some have recently emerged from prison, which in Britain has often been a school for radicalization. A majority are converts, and some of the rest are immigrants. Many of the worshippers have experienced discrimination not just as Muslims but also as black people. As would be expected with a socially conservative community, some of the mosque's values are not those of the liberal West; many women wear a full *niqab* and *abaya*, showing the world only their eyes. The mosque became known worldwide because two infamous terrorists worshipped there prior to their radicalization: Zacarias Moussaoui, the would-be twentieth hijacker in the 9/11 plot, and Richard Reid, the so-called shoe bomber.

If Abdul Haqq Baker were a supporter of terrorism, he would be one of the world's most dangerous men. Instead, some of Britain's frontline experts on Islamic radicalism consider him to be one of the most effective and important voices for preventing young men from falling into terrorism. "The Brixton Mosque is not a center of violent extremism—it is a center of resistance to violent extremism," said Robert Lambert, a longtime counterterror Special Branch operative at London's Metropolitan Police Service. Lambert was the cofounder of the Muslim Contact Unit, which works with Muslim groups throughout the city to prevent terrorism.

The mosque has been involved in a low-intensity ideological guerrilla war with the violent extremists. If the calling of Abu Hamza and Abdullah el-Faisal is to turn young men into guided missiles, Baker's mission is to turn them off that path. The mosque condemns criminality, condemns the idea that Islam is at war with the West, and attacks the extremist preachers by name.

Baker is now a trustee of the mosque, no longer chairman. He has turned his energies toward setting up an organization called STREET—Strategy to Reach, Empower and Educate Teenagers. STREET does traditional antigang work: the sports, the trips, the place to hang out, the links to school and jobs. The men who work there and interact with youth are themselves mostly Muslim converts, mostly Salafi, some of them veterans of gang life or prison. But to the antigang work STREET adds something else: the staff counters the violent extremists' propaganda. The youth workers talk to young men who have been radicalized in prison or around Brixton to offer a different understanding of Islam. Some of those staff had once been attracted to extremism themselves, and nearly all of them share their clients' histories and their grievances about the West's treatment of Muslims.

Baker, the mosque, and STREET are trying to deradicalize fragile and potentially explosive young men while standing in the line of direct fire from two opposing camps. Some in Britain see him as an ideological ally of the violent extremists, and the extremists in turn threaten him and accuse him of spying for the government. Neither is true.

The issue for political conservatives in Britain is that while the community of the Brixton Mosque is nonviolent (something no one disputes), it is nonetheless Salafist. The debate at the national level in Britain concerns whether its theology alone should discredit it as a partner in the fight against terrorism. Some influential commentators believe that it should—that the Salafist ideology makes Baker, the Brixton Mosque, and STREET necessarily a part of the support structure of terror. "The central theoretical flaw in PVE (the government program Preventing Violent Extremism) is that it accepts the premise that non-violent extremists can be made to act as bulwarks against violent extremists," the influential conservative think tank Policy Exchange wrote in a 2009 report entitled "Choosing Our Friends Wisely." The report specifically cited work with Baker and the Brixton Mosque as one of the big mistakes of Britain's counterterror strategy.

The right-wing journalist Melanie Phillips, author of the book *Londonistan,* wrote that "the government had failed to grasp that the core problem is actually religious/ideological extremism which produces a continuum of divisive, antisocial or threatening views which provides the sea in which violence swims." She specifically criticized the borough of Lambeth, where Brixton is located, for "partnering a hard-line Salafist from Brixton Mosque in the belief that this constitutes the best antidote to violent extremism."

Another criticism came from the Quilliam Foundation, a group established by two men who had belonged to the radical (but non-violent) political Islamist group Hizb ut-Tahrir. Both left the group, renounced radicalism, and now run the foundation, which is financed largely by the British government. "It doesn't surprise me if STREET does good work," said Ghaffar Hussain, the head of outreach and training for Quilliam. But he still considered it an inappropriate partner for government counterterror work—because of its theology, not its politics. "The Brixton Mosque subscribes to an austere, conservative Saudi brand of Islam," he said. "Without that ideology, you can't promote terrorist acts."

At the same time, the extremists warn that Baker's work in partnership with the police and the government is betrayal and that Baker is a spy. El-Faisal demonstrated a particular animus toward the mosque that expelled him and toward Baker, whom he counted as his top pupil before Baker's departure from his study group when el-Faisal turned to violence. In 1993, el-Faisal tried to take over the mosque with his followers—Baker cut the electricity to shut off el-Faisal's microphone, and the standoff eventually ended without violence. In his preaching, el-Faisal has counted the Salafis of Brixton Mosque as being among the nonbelievers, labeling them legitimate targets for violence. There is a chilling tape on a violent extremist Web site of a phone conversation in which one worshipper at Brixton Mosque complains to a mosque official that Baker had called the police on him. (Baker said that he had not.) What consequences, the Web site asks ominously, should Baker suffer for his betrayal of a Muslim brother? Another Web site refers to Brixton Mosque as the "Brixton synagogue." Some of the men on STREET's staff have received threats, which have been serious enough in Baker's case that he moved his family to Saudi Arabia, where he now lives most of the time—he works as the director of a language institute and goes back and forth to London. It is telling when someone feels safer from extremist violence in Jeddah than in London. What Baker is doing requires subtlety and deftness and is fraught with danger. It is very much like disarming a bomb.

ALTHOUGH THE TERRORISTS REID and Moussaoui were early worshippers at Brixton Mosque, they did not become radicalized there. Reid left in 1998, and Moussaoui was actually kicked out in 1997 because he was starting to exhibit aggressive and extremist views. Both then dropped out of sight. Moussaoui surfaced at his arrest, and Reid became a household name when he failed in his attempt to blow up the airplane on which he was a passenger.

Baker knew both men. He testified during the sentencing portion of Moussaoui's trial in federal court in Washington, asking the jury to spare him a death sentence in order not to give him the martyrdom he craved.

Brixton Mosque did not turn Reid and Moussaoui into suicide bombers, but it failed to prevent them from falling into violence. The mosque could control what went on behind its doors, but it could not prevent young men from hearing a message of violence even a few blocks away, Baker said. He could see people like Moussaoui falling under the sway of violent extremism, but he didn't have the resources to do anything about it, as their relationship had been completely centered on the mosque. It was a potentially dangerous gap. So, after sixteen years as chairman of the mosque, with his thoughts focused by earning a PhD from the University of Exeter (his dissertation was titled "Countering Terrorism in the UK: A Convert Community's Perspective"), Baker left to start STREET. "When Moussaoui left the mosque environment, there was no way to determine where he was, where he'd gone," he said. "There was no conventional organization to pick up the pieces outside the mosque. We needed some sort of entity that Muslims who do not attend mosques want to attend."

STREET is a drop-in center in Brixton aimed at young Muslim men and women, mostly seventeen to twenty-eight. In 2009, some 4,600 young people came in, and Baker expected that in 2010 the total would hit 5,000. About 70 percent of the clients are converts, and about a quarter of the clients have immigrated to London from other countries.

Baker would not allow me to visit STREET or talk to its clients or the youth workers. His explanation was that the clients—and even the staff—are highly suspicious of the media and would be angered or feel they were being taken advantage of by the presence of a reporter. It was also possibly unhelpful that I am female, American, and Jewish, but I had the impression that these factors didn't matter as much; STREET rarely grants interviews to anyone. So this description of STREET's work is based on published reports; interviews with Baker and Tharik Hussain, who is head of its Deconstruct Program, aimed at countering extremist propaganda; interviews Hussain conducted on my behalf with STREET's staff; and my interviews with people in official Britain who work with STREET in police, probation, and local government. Because I have not been able to visit STREET and it is difficult to measure the program's success, I am treating STREET as a possible social-cure success, not as a proven example.

STREET offers the atmosphere of an urban youth club. Men can play video games, watch documentaries, and hang out. (A few women on the staff run programs for women during certain hours.) Activities include boxing, martial arts, and a soccer league—the London equivalent of midnight basketball. The men have gone on camping trips. There are referrals to high school classes and job training. STREET bought a mannequin, and staffers use it to show what knives and guns can do to the human body. Baker wanted the idea of death to hit home, to be something men could feel in their gut, so the clients go to the local Muslim cemetery to attend funerals. During one, the men performing the funeral invited the STREET group to help carry the dead person.

The traditional antigang work is a response to an issue that far outranks terrorism for STREET's members. For the men who walk through the door, gang violence and dead-end lives are their own problems; terrorism is someone else's. But because STREET works on the issues that matter to the community—and did that work first—it has more credibility when it talks to its members about terrorism.

About 60 percent of the men who come into STREET have been involved with the criminal-justice system at some point—for either terror-related or ordinary crimes. (About the same proportion come from single-parent families.) STREET has a contract with the London probation system to provide mentors for young Muslims coming out of prison. Simon Cornwall, a senior probation officer with the Central Extremism Unit, said that STREET has taken half a dozen men on probation for terrorist offenses. His office is planning to begin send-ing more people to STREET, including Muslim offenders serving sentences for common crimes who also expressed support for vio-lent extremism. He said that he hoped that over the course of a year, STREET could grow to be able to take thirty-five of these men at any given time.

STREET's budget is about US$540,000 per year and comes largely from the British government—from its contract to work with criminal offenders on probation, national counterterrorism programs, and a few local initiatives. Some of the young people at STREET object to this. Baker's argument to them is that the government money is merely supporting his programs, which began before official funding did. He also says: Take advantage of it. We are doing work important to the community. We can help you get into school and find a job. "Think intelligently," he tells them. "You've got your own colleagues working as a communicative and social bridge between Islam, the government and wider society, empowering you."

Baker must also deal with the accusation that because he works in partnership with the government and the police, he is a spy. He said his policy is this: Even a young man who embraces extremist beliefs will not be reported to the police while STREET is able to work with him. If he begins to show signs that he is definitely aspiring to violent extremism and STREET cannot prevent him from going down this path, then STREET will contact the police. Baker maintains that he has not yet had to do this.

Some of the men come in to play soccer or video games or find a job or take computer classes, or they come because they would have to go back to prison if they didn't. Many simply come because their friends do. No one who knocks on the door of STREET does so in order to be turned away from violent extremism. But Islam—a different Islam from the kind the terrorists profess—is a pervasive presence. Most of the men who come in have only a very basic knowledge of the tenets of Islam. STREET offers theology classes, but it sees most activities as opportunities to teach about Islam. Mixed into the soccer league, for example, are talks about Islamic concepts of leadership and fair play.

The part of STREET most directly related to preventing terrorism is the refutation of violent extremism. This is not deemed necessary for everyone at STREET, but twenty to thirty young men a month get some sort of antiviolence Islamic counseling, and five to ten each month get a more intense version. "One of the main things they want to know is what is wrong with Osama's rhetoric of retaliating in the way he says," said Baker. "In view of the perceived oppression of the Muslim world, the heavyhandedness and double standards of the West and of America in particular, why isn't the only way to fight back with suicide bombing? Why not consider Osama a hero?"

The temptation for Westerners—after we get over our dismay about what is at the top of the FAQs among the Muslim youth of South London—is to react by dismissing the grievances: to try to convince the questioner that reports of oppression of Muslims are greatly exaggerated.

However meritorious the argument, it is unlikely to be a successful line of response. Millions and millions of Muslims share the grievances of these men: prosecution of the war in Iraq despite the failure to find the advertised weapons of mass destruction, displacement of the Palestinians, the abuses of Abu Ghraib and Guantanamo Prisons, the banning of head coverings in France and of minarets in Switzerland.

Convincing the men of Brixton that their grievances are wrong is a fool's errand—one that would likely serve only to diminish the questioner's confidence and trust in the interlocutor. It might also be difficult to find any suitable interlocutor who would disagree with theses complaints. "We do agree in many instances," said Baker, "but the marked difference is what the religion says about how to respond—how to articulate our grievances."

This is the key. Millions of people hold these grievances yet do not become suicide bombers. The challenge is to convince a young man to join them.

This work begins with daily discussion groups to debate news relating to gangs, extremism, or instances of what the men would see as anti-Muslim policy. Typical subjects have been the video made by Dutch politician Geert Wilders, in which he calls Islam "a retarded culture"; the arrest of the American woman known as "Jihad Jane"; and the French prohibition of head coverings. These sessions offer a way for the men to be listened to and for discussion to be conducted in a group where the social norm is one of finding peaceful ways to respond—quite different from what they would get on the street.

If a young man talks about an extremist video or document he has seen, STREET's staff forwards the material to the Deconstruct team. They use an approach developed by Tharik Hussain, a teacher of media studies at a London college, in his University of London master's thesis analyzing the construction of one particular Al Qaeda video. Hussain is not a Salafi himself, but he thinks STREET, because of its ideology, can make the most effective use of his techniques. The approach combines media theory with theology. Staff members watch or read the material with the client who cited it, point out the propaganda techniques, and show him what Islam really says about the subject. By exposing the way the argument was constructed, Hussain's idea is not only to rob that particular video of credibility but also to enable clients to deconstruct such material in the future or at least question its validity. The strategy also shows the men how they are being manipulated, which no one likes—shades of Florida's "truth" campaign. STREET hopes eventually to develop Hussain's techniques into a formal course.

STREET's Web site shows how some of the men responded, using what they learned in the Deconstruct workshops to make their own videos to counter the extremist narrative. The cognitive-dissonance theorists would applaud. Such projects not only teach important skills, they encourage the men to invest themselves in the antiextremist message.

In late 2009, when a young Muslim man in South London was murdered, the family of the victim asked STREET to bring its members to the burial ground. Four hundred people turned up, many in tears. "There was impact in seeing one of their own colleagues dead and preparing him for burial," Baker said. STREET obtained the family's permission to tape the funeral, and some of the men made an arty video (visible on STREET's Web site) called *Taking a Life*, which also employs—disapprovingly—graphic footage from the London Underground security cameras of trains blowing up during the bombing of July 7, 2005. In the video, young STREET men condemn terrorism as hateful in the sight of Allah and warn that terror kills innocent people. And they give arguments that might carry more weight with STREET's audience: that terror causes people to judge all Muslims based on their appearance and causes society to introduce draconian laws.

Most of the men come in to STREET with only a basic knowledge of Islam and few critical-thinking skills. Baker said that when they first did a pilot group, one of the men was quite shocked when he was shown Islam's condemnations of violence. "I wish we were aware of this before," he had told Baker. The man said that he and his friends had attended study sessions with Abu Hamza and his followers, and they usually had left those sessions crying over the injustices against Muslims and wanting to take revenge. "We were told we don't need to travel abroad—best to sit tight and inflict maximum damage with minimum input," he told Baker.

"*Maximum damage with minimum input,*" said Baker. "I will never forget those words."

Baker said that one argument that carried a lot of weight with converts should have been obvious but apparently was not: that the infidels the extremists consider legitimate targets include their own parents and siblings. "When extremists talk about killing disbelievers, they are always pointing to the heads of government or areas of decadence," he said. "They don't point out to these men that this group includes your family. When we point out that according to the extremist rhetoric it is permissible to kill your family, you see they are very taken aback."

It stretches credulity that such basic information could be effective. Very powerful forces are needed to entice a young man to give up his life and kill innocent people. Countering those forces would seem to require sophisticated rhetoric and thinking. Apparently it does not. As is always true with the social cure, the information itself counts less than who delivers it, and how. The reason that very basic antiviolence messages can work is that, for most of STREET's clients, this is the first time they have ever heard them from people they trust. When they think of the government, it is in terms of conspiracy theories. When they think of the police, it is in terms of the 1993 murder of Stephen Lawrence, an eighteen-year-old black man stabbed to death while waiting for a bus in South London. The subsequent police inspection was so badly handled that it provoked a famous report accusing the police of "institutional racism." No one was ever convicted. Messages from officialdom are at best dismissed and at worst serve to confirm the rightness of a radical path.

The questions that these men bring with them to STREET are ones they cannot ask anywhere else. Most mosques seldom if ever touch these issues. "These are issues the entire community is petrified of addressing," said Tharik Hussain. "They can't go to the local mosque and question what is jihad about? The local mosques don't want this associated with them, and if they're going to start questioning, people become suspicious immediately."

STREET's motto is: "For you, from people like you." The members of the staff have lives very similar to those of the clients—indeed, several of them have been clients.

"The emotion comes first," Baker said. "If they cannot relate to you, if your lifestyle doesn't resonate, they will not accept anything from you. But they see we're prepared to walk and talk with them. They see that the individual in front of them talking to them and providing a counternarrative is from a similar background, is as robust in his beliefs. They see it's okay to belong to society, okay to be angry and upset. But how we contextualize and understand that religiously and how we engage with it becomes very powerful. The emotional and group idea is inextricably linked to them coming away from violent extremism."

It is easy to imagine that STREET can turn young men off the path of violent extremism, but it is hard to prove. For Baker and his staff, the usual difficulty of proving a negative—i.e., terrorist incidents averted—is compounded by their reluctance to talk about specific cases, a discussion they argue would not sit well with their clients. Baker said that dozens of men who came to STREET as gang members are now in school or jobs instead, some of them volunteering at STREET and teaching others about the fallacies of violent extremism. He said that other men had come in to STREET talking about committing murders and were dissuaded by STREET's explanation of what Islam says about criminality and the killing of innocents.

He will not offer details, but he is not alone in claiming that STREET is working. In 2009, the program won a London award for most innovative project to prevent violent extremism. "The feedback that we get from offenders and probation officers is that STREET is very successful," said Simon Cornwall, the probation officer. "I see change in people over a period of time—they have more of an insight into themselves as individuals." As an example, he cited one man who "now has a different ability to voice his grievances—before, he was using anger to express disagreement with the government about policy. Now he is able to see that he can use the regular channels other people use." The local Lambeth public-security official also considered STREET to be effective. Security officials in Vancouver, Los Angeles, and parts of the United Kingdom have contacted Baker to learn more about the

STREET model, with an eye to starting something similar in their own communities.

If all this sounds familiar, it should. Jonathan Githens-Mazer, a senior lecturer in politics at the University of Exeter who studies British Muslims, has interviewed young Muslims flirting with violent extremism. He grew up in Baltimore and remembers the Police Athletic League programs and other antigang initiatives of his youth. "No one would question that former gang members are the people most effective at designing ways to turn young people away from gangs," he said. "They've been there. They know how the teenagers feel, what they are looking for. They have credibility. It is worth trying to apply the same idea to fighting terror."

Githens-Mazer said the reasons that young Muslims fall in with terror groups are sometimes sadly trivial. "What comes out when you interview is that sometimes kids get on the path not because they have a particularly deeply felt grievance, it's that they have no cash in their pocket," he said. "So someone from STREET says, 'Let's order pizza and watch a DVD next weekend,' and 'Have you ever been out of London? Let's go camping out of London.' These are sixteen- and seventeen-year-olds who have left school. They have really limited worldviews. There are a lot of parallels with gang violence and the drug culture. Street credibility matters—having people who directly know from that experience matters."

There are many parallels between falling into gang life and falling into terrorism. A young radical often will have done both. Many of the STREET clients have criminal backgrounds—in part because it is an official destination for recently released prisoners, and in part because the neighborhood has a lot of gangs, so many of these men are simply coming home. Baker said that men from three different gangs attend STREET's programs. Richard Reid showed up at Brixton Mosque right out of prison, his belongings still in a prison box.

For some, the cause of radical Islam is a natural progression from their criminal gang—indeed, one reason they are attracted to Islamic extremism is the justification it provides for criminal behavior. They are told that their robberies and muggings are suddenly praiseworthy, even noble, part of a fight against the oppressor. "You have guys that feel like they have no other option." said Githens-Mazer. "They think, 'I've always been a soldier and I don't know how to live a normal life. What am I supposed to do now? If I can't be violent in this way I'll be violent in that way.'"

STREET IS NOT THE ONLY program of its kind. In the East London neighborhood of Waltham Forest, three British brothers of Pakistani descent, Hanif, Imtiaz, and Abad Qadir, along with Mike Jervis, a black Londoner of Caribbean descent, run an organization called the Active Change Foundation. Hanif Qadir, a gang member in his youth, became a successful businessman, owner of an auto workshop so prosperous that he drove a Rolls-Royce. After the American invasion of Afghanistan in 2001, he and his family gave money to charities in Afghanistan. As he followed what was going on, he became angrier and angrier at the American soldiers. "There was blatant disregard for innocent civilians," he said. "I felt the Americans and British were committing atrocities." In December 2002, he made a will, left his wife and children, and bought a ticket to Pakistan—one way—to join the fight.

Going through the mountains into Afghanistan, he encountered a truck full of people coming from the other direction. A young boy in a bloodstained robe and bleeding from the head, who looked to be twelve or thirteen—about the same age as Qadir's son—shouted to Qadir's truck to turn back. When they stopped, the boy told them his story. He and his fellow recruits had been told to go to the front lines and run in a certain direction to be met by other soldiers. They had no arms or training, and, as they were running, bombs were raining on them from aircraft. Many were killed, and the rest piled into the truck to return to Pakistan. They had been used—sent to draw fire and be killed. "They were all Pakistani, and my parents come from Pakistan," said Qadir, who was horrified; all his romantic images suddenly collapsed.

He began to think about his own son and quickly returned to London. A few days later, the son of a close friend was killed in a gang fight in their neighborhood. Qadir decided that his real struggle was not in Afghanistan but in London: to do something to oppose local violence and turn young people away from what he calls the "false blandishments" of the terrorists. Meanwhile, a war was brewing in his neighborhood. A few Muslim boys had mugged an elderly black woman, and threats and counterthreats were rising between the Asian Muslims and the blacks. Jervis, a youth worker and a leader of the local Afro-Caribbean community, proposed to the Qadirs that he would talk to the black community if they could talk to the Muslim community— together they might be able to defuse tensions. They were successful. The Qadirs and Jervis then realized that they worked well together, so in 2003 they established the Active Change Foundation in a gym owned by Imtiaz Qadir.

The foundation still has the gym—with fitness training, boxing, and judo—but it also runs classes in leadership training, conflict and crisis management, arbitration, and public speaking. It has the usual links to schools and job training and it has outreach workers, some of whom patrol the neighborhood on bikes. Some are former gang members. One is on probation after having served a sentence for a terror-related offense. That young man, said Hanif Qadir, was furious when he was released from prison and sent to Active Change; he wanted nothing to do with any group that worked alongside government. But Qadir said that as the young man hung out at the center, he watched as it dealt with such community problems as domestic violence, gang rapes, and gang violence. He began volunteering as an outreach worker and once intervened to prevent a local young girl from being gang-raped. "He's quite a success story," said Simon Cornwall. "He's able to go to others and say, 'I understand why you're angry.' He can articulate that he's gone through the same process."

"The Active Change Foundation does very good youth outreach work," said Robert Lambert, the former counterterror policeman. "They will be attacked, no doubt, as being wrongly in partnership with state authorities, but that doesn't totally diminish their street credibility. What they share with Brixton is a high level of street credibility."

"People think religion is driving them," Hanif Qadir said. "Based on our experience, it's not religion. It's rebellion and the perception that the West is against their faith. Most of the kids don't know much about their faith. They're looking for a cause, something to belong to—and they find it fighting the aggressor known as the West."

Active Change differs from STREET in a few ways. One is that it invests a lot of effort in improving relations between young people and the police—for example, holding regular pool tournaments between the two groups. The camping and hiking outings are also used for this purpose. In 2009, seventeen young Muslim women went camping—accompanied by three female police officers. The other major difference is that Active Change is more Islamically diverse. The neighborhood has Muslims from Pakistan, Somalia, Algeria, Bangladesh, and other countries, along with converts, and everyone's Islam takes a different form. Active Change has had deradicalization counselors from various Muslim strains. That has saved it from the controversy that has dogged STREET because of its Salafist views, but that is practically the only problem Active Change doesn't have. The foundation lives from hand to mouth, starting and stopping programs as its financing dictates. It is constantly battling with radical extremist groups who try to hijack its meetings, and with older, sleepier leaders of local mosques who would rather just ignore the whole problem.

And both Jervis and Hanif Qadir complain that Active Change, while celebrated by national politicians and often visited by counter-terrorism officials from abroad, gets little support from local authorities. Jervis said the local borough government won't even talk to the group. "At the local level, they are too fluffy," said Qadir. "Violent extremism is something they don't even want to talk about. They want to promote community cohesion and diversity and multicultural fairs and Islam Awareness Weeks. They've been doing this for thirty or forty years and it hasn't changed an ounce. This is not going to tackle violent extremism.

"When we have an individual we are trying to change, we need local government to sit with us and put services and safeguards around that individual. That individual believes that the government is anti-Muslim and anti–young person. We need to demonstrate exactly the opposite. Local governments call that too risky, but this is a risky business."

■   ■   ■   ■

STREET'S POLITICAL PROBLEMS ARE different from those of its cousins in the social-cure family. While antigang and prisoner-reentry programs like Benning Terrace and the Fortune Academy's Castle are desperate for money and attention, there is plenty of both for antiterrorism efforts. Britain, however, is not at all sure that it should be spending any of it on STREET.

Counterterrorism, of course, is a highly political and politicized subject, even more in Britain than in the United States, as there are many more Muslims who are supporters of violent extremism in Britain than in America. As Marc Sageman wrote, Muslims in America are far more prosperous and assimilated than in Britain, and America is not the destination of choice for young Middle Eastern or North African men who leave their homes to study abroad. The United States has not had to face on a large scale the challenge of widespread radicalization of young Muslim men. In Britain, this is a challenge crucial to the country's security—and that of the United States. So even more than the post-9/11 the debate in the United States about loss of civil liberties, there is fierce argument in Britain about the proper response to homegrown terror. Should even peaceful speech be banned if it supports the narrative that the United States is an enemy of Islam? Should police be able to stop and search young men for "Breathing while Muslim"—and does doing so contribute to radicalization? How can the British government work with Muslim groups to deradicalize young people in a way that allows those groups to maintain credibility with the people they try to affect?

The question of relevance to the social cure is the distinction that has come to be known by the shorthand of "Good Muslim/Bad Muslim." Britain has been moving toward a strategy of fighting terror that relies heavily on Muslim community organizations: only the community can set nonviolent social norms for its members, and only community members know whom they must reach. This is widely accepted. But the question of what groups are appropriate partners in the community has been the subject of much controversy. Fundamentalist or liberal? Assimilated or anti-Western?

Just as with crime, the debate is highly partisan and emotion reigns. Politicians feel that voters demand they take a hard-line stance on terror even if such positions can be counterproductive; it is a mystery how Switzerland's ban on minarets could possibly be helpful in diminishing terrorism, but voters passed it overwhelmingly anyway. Since there is no evidence about what works in fighting terrorism, there is little to counter the weight of public passion.

The decisions facing British policymakers in some ways echo those of the last time Britain faced a terrorist threat—from the Irish Republican Army (IRA). In fact, when the Metropolitan Police Service set up the Muslim Contact Unit in 2002, Robert Lambert was consciously trying to avoid repeating the mistakes police had made when dealing with the IRA. Lambert had been a counterterror policeman then, and he had seen how indiscriminate repression of Irish Catholics had helped drive up IRA recruitment and made Irish Catholics unwilling to cooperate with the police.

The Muslim Contact Unit's officers—never more than seven or eight—were placed in Muslim neighborhoods of London, especially in communities where imams preach a more radical form of Islam. In the traditional approach, police would have tried to recruit informants while carrying out searches and letting the community know it was being watched—to create a looming, somewhat menacing presence. The Muslim Contact Unit was different. Its officers were open about their counterterrorism mission, but they tried to do the equivalent of community policing: get out of the car, treat people respectfully, get to know the neighborhoods. They attended conferences held by local Muslim groups, gatherings in people's homes, even weddings and funerals. They helped with local problems. Muslims could go to the officers they knew in the Contact Unit to complain about police mistreatment. They could get help writing funding proposals for local counterterror projects or briefs arguing that certain fundamentalist but nonviolent Muslim clerics should be allowed to visit and preach in Britain. The Contact Unit helped Muslim groups obtain permits for political rallies—even those in opposition to British foreign policy or the war in Iraq.

The Muslim Contact Unit's biggest achievement was wrestling

control of the Finsbury Park Mosque away from Abu Hamza. Another group of worshippers at the mosque was affiliated with the Muslim Brotherhood—a fundamentalist, hardline Islamist group, but one that is Al Qaeda's sworn enemy. Lambert helped them engineer a takeover of the mosque, pushing out Abu Hamza in 2005. Today, Lambert praises it as a model mosque.

Before the Muslim Contact Unit began, the police looked at Brixton Mosque with suspicion. When Abdullah el-Faisal was recruiting men in Brixton to the cause of Islamic radicalism and was trying to take over Brixton Mosque in 1993, the police called on Baker to ask whether el-Faisal had any association with Brixton Mosque. The answer was no, said Baker. When the police asked why not, Baker replied that it was because el-Faisal was preaching violent extremism.

The local police dismissed the conflict between the mosque and el-Faisal as a territorial dispute between two Muslim leaders and decided not to get involved. The police didn't know enough to distinguish between the two. Lambert today expresses astonishment that the police force could have hung the Brixton Mosque out alone against el-Faisal. "It is remarkable they achieved as much success as they did with no support whatsoever," he said. "We found strength and bravery in the management of Brixton Mosque. They literally fought off Abdullah el-Faisal. They were very strong and cohesive and had done great work. They did a great service standing up to these people."

When the Muslim Contact Unit began, relations quickly improved. "The MCU was pioneering," said Baker. "There wasn't much trust in the beginning, and it was very difficult for them and very difficult for us. But they were prepared to take risks in engaging Muslim communities, and they've been very successful."

From the beginning, however, the idea of working alongside people like Baker attracted criticism. Some of it was sheer ignorance—unwillingness to believe that a Salafi mosque is not proviolence. But most of those objecting understood the antiviolence stance of the Brixton Mosque yet still believed that Baker should not be a partner in counterterror work.

The most serious argument is made by the conservative think tank Policy Exchange and the Quilliam Foundation. They ask a reasonable question: Why should the British government give money and support to groups that share much of the ideology of suicide bombers? Policy Exchange argues that government money should go only to moderate Muslim groups that share Western values, which does not include Salafists. "Typically, Salafists advocate one of the most austere and literalist forms of Islam and a range of values that are not always compatible with liberal democracy," says its report "Choosing Our Friends Wisely."

Maajid Nawaz, the director of Quilliam, argues that the most important work in fighting terror is to counter the violent extremists' narrative: the story that America and Britain are at war with Islam—and that, in a state of war, any kind of violence is Islamically permissible. For Quilliam and Policy Exchange, extremist views—even nonviolent ones—contribute to this narrative.

"This is a long-term problem," said Ghaffar Hussain, Quilliam's head of outreach. "It's not a long-term strategy to take a very negative image of the West and replace it with a slightly less negative image of the West. There are people who embrace the narrative, people who are sympathetic to it, and people who are religiously extreme but not politically extreme. They are all inappropriate partners. It's not enough to say, 'Well, I oppose terrorism but I still embrace a harsh Islam.' The theology of the Saudis has to be challenged. You have one side that promotes a medieval interpretation of Sharia as state law, and the other side wants to embrace modern political ideas. Ultimately, what it comes down to is that we should be empowering the right side of that debate. It's offensive to me to say, 'This is as good as Muslims get,'" he said. "It is the racism of lower expectations to work with extremists rather than people who promote democracy and tolerance. These people exist. Why not work with them?"

Nawaz's former codirector at Quilliam, Ed Husain, has gone farther—he believes that religiously extremist views and terror are essentially one and the same, and that the government should be watching and targeting Muslims who have radical views even if they do not advocate violence. "Wherever they encounter people who articulate extremist views that provide the mood music to which suicide bombers dance, they should not only be challenged in a civic way but handed over and alerted to the local authorities," he said.

These arguments essentially divide Britain's Muslim community into "Good Muslim" and "Bad Muslim." They have had some sway with the British government even under Labor. By early 2010, the government was getting nervous about some of its partnerships and was taking some actions that pulled back to a more traditional line in both policing and counterterrorism work. The Muslim Contact Unit, for example, no longer has autonomy. Robert Lambert retired in 2008, and members of the unit now spend most of their time advising local police. The effects of this advice vary. Baker said that in Lambeth, relations with police have worsened.

Hazel Blears, then Britain's minister for communities, said in February 2009 that even if a group does not espouse violence, engagement must be limited if the group has "equivocal attitudes on core values such as democracy, freedom of speech or respect towards women." The election of a Conservative government in May 2010 made it likely Britain would become even less willing to work with fundamentalist Muslim groups.*

By the typology of Policy Exchange and Quilliam, Brixton Mosque and STREET are clearly "Bad Muslim." The mosque practices a strict, fundamentalist Islam that has strong links to the official ideology of Saudi Arabia; the women are covered; the people have many grievances against British foreign policy and global treatment of Muslims. A second look at the mosque and STREET, however, illustrates the danger of such broad judgments. "Social conservatism is not a crime," Baker said. Orthodox Jews, he added, are not criticized for being isolationist

---

*Indeed, the Conservative–Lib Dem coalition government did cut off STREET's funding. In February 2011, Prime Minister David Cameron gave a speech arguing that the roots of terrorism lay in nonviolent extremism, and announced that no public money would go to what the government considered to be nonviolent extremist groups—STREET among them. As of June 2011, STREET was down to a four-person staff. In a letter to the government, Baker noted that the suspect in a March shooting that left a five-year-old girl paralyzed was a man whom probation officials had sought to refer to STREET when he got out of prison, as STREET had worked successfully with other members of his gang before. STREET had to decline—the group no longer had the personnel. "There are very few entities engaged in this 'hard end' work", Baker wrote. So when these men get out of prison, where are you going to put them?

and confined to their own community. He noted that, in particular, the Brixton Mosque—heavily populated by converts—does not share some of the cultural practices widespread in other places, such as honor killings, female genital mutilation, and forced marriage. However members of Brixton Mosque choose to dress and behave, there is no evidence they seek to impose those ideas on others. Those in official Britain who work with the mosque—in the borough government, the police, and the probation office—consider it a positive force in the community that works well with other groups. Nor does the mosque's preaching or STREET's work contribute to the poisonous narrative of war with the West that Maajid Nawaz decries. Just the opposite. One piece of evidence comes from perhaps the single most unlikely visitor imaginable, Carie Lemack, a young American Jewish woman whose mother, Judy Larocque, died on a plane on 9/11. Lemack was cofounder of a group called Families of September 11 that works to support families of the victims of terror attacks and campaigns for effective policies to fight terrorism.

In 2008, Abdul Haqq Baker invited Lemack to Brixton, along with John Falding, a Briton who lost his partner during the London bombings of July 7, 2005. The three toured local schools—from the primary school run by the mosque to a rough local high school—to talk about tolerance and terror. At the elementary school, Baker had the children draw pictures of their recent vacations and talk about their hopes for the future. Then he, Lemack, and Falding talked about the same subject. Baker then pointed out to the children that even though they were very different, they all had the same hopes and dreams. Lemack gave out "Families of September 11" bracelets. At the high school, Lemack answered more pointed questions from students, such as: "What do you say about the fact that the United States invaded Iraq under the guise of finding weapons of mass destruction, but they were never found?"

"I'm not here to defend the U.S. government one way or the other," Lemack responded. "It may have been wrong. I'm here to make sure that what happened to my mother doesn't happen again. That's a completely separate thing. At least we can talk about it and try to resolve it instead of using violence."

Baker then made his point: There are many reasons for anger and resentment—but not for violence. "Criminality is not permitted in Islam," Baker told the students.

Lemack considers Baker a friend and ally. "My goal and the goal of Abdul Haqq and the STREET team are roughly the same—to provide a counternarrative," she said. "It takes a lot of courage to acknowledge there are these radical or extremist elements out there and confront them and their ideology head on. He's gone out on a limb. He engages with them and says, 'Here's what they may not have been telling you.'"

QUILLIAM IS RIGHT IN one sense—it is crucial to fight the narrative, to refute unreasonable grievances, to change the social norm among Muslims so that the idea of war with the West is no longer accepted. But this is, as Ghaffar Hussain says, a long-term goal. And it leaves us with a short-term problem: What do you do with young men today who are future suicide bombers? Quilliam argues that moderate Muslim groups can challenge these people. "Anybody who knows their stuff can challenge them," Hussain said. "They may not like the person, may not be thinking he's credible, but if he's making an argument, they have to respond to it." This is naïve. The "Good Muslim" groups can talk forever at these men, but they won't listen. To the question of why the British government should be giving taxpayer money to support the work of Muslims who share much of the ideology of the terrorists, there is an answer: because they are ones who can do something about terrorism.

Simon Cornwall compares it to the work he used to do with drug users. "The best drug counselors are ex-users," he said. "You want to put someone in who can show they've dealt with their grievances in a positive, proactive way—'I'm now in employment, I'm in the community.' You want the mentor to mirror the offenders. You want the offenders to say, 'I want to be like that.'"

The personal journey of Maajid Nawaz, Quilliam's director, is evidence for this argument. He was a member of Hizb ut-Tahrir, a group that, while nonviolent, shares the narrative of war with the West. On the American television show *60 Minutes*, he talked about the first moment of his turn away from radicalism: It came when he was in jail in Egypt, sharing a cell with the two men who had killed Egyptian president Anwar Sadat in 1981. They had renounced violence, and they convinced him that terror today has more to do with fascism than with Islam. If he had heard that argument from a moderate Muslim—the people Quilliam believes should be the British government's sole partner on counterterror work—it would have had no effect. But he heard it from two men who had spent two decades in prison for assassinating the president of Egypt for negotiating with Israel. Their hardline credentials gave their arguments weight with him; he considered them his ideological peers. Quilliam has no use for street cred, but it was street cred that sparked the deradicalization of Maajid Nawaz.

It is not easy for us Westerners to put ourselves in the shoes of a potential suicide bomber, but it does not take much imagination to understand the best way to convince an angry young Muslim tough in South London to turn away from religious violence. It takes someone who shares his life story, shares his hardline views, and shares his grievances, but believes that the correct response is peaceful—in other words, people who are, as much as possible, his peers. Identity, not information, is what matters. "The government has to become comfortable working with uncomfortable bedfellows like ourselves," said Abdul Haqq Baker. He is right.

The idea of a social cure for terrorism is improbable from the outside: How can human connection transform men who do not value human life? But at least some people who understand terrorism find it is reasonable that young men flirting with religious extremism could turn away if they were given a different group to belong to, one that shatters the social norms of the terrorists and offers a way into a productive life. If STREET loses its financing from a Conservative government and cannot replace it, then it will have been a short-lived experiment. That would be a shame. It may not be obvious that a social cure for terrorism is possible, but few would question that it is necessary.

EACH SOCIAL-CURE STORY IN this book is a member of a family; each particular variation of a join-the-club solution can be used to address not just one problem but others that share its genetic matter. The family with the most cousins—the social-cure approach with the potential to attack the widest variety of problems—is the variation employed in Serbia. The essence of what Otpor did was to fight fatalism, atomization, and passivity. Most citizens of Serbia thought of themselves as powerless victims of dictatorship. But Otpor used the social cure to make political activism attractive, to provide a way for people to be involved in something creative, important, hip, and courageous— and to be seen by their peers as all those things. Otpor did not produce democracy, it produced protagonists. And these protagonists, in turn, were a key part of the creation of democracy in Serbia.

Protagonists can also produce other good things—an end to foreign occupation, cleaner government, less crime, better policies. But as Otpor's failure to thrive in a more-or-less-democratic Serbia illustrates, these tactics do not work in every circumstance. There are some situations where Otpor-style social-cure tactics have a better likelihood of success, some conditions that lend themselves more readily than others to the creation of a mass movement of protagonists who can change their nation. To understand what these are, it is helpful first to look at the activities of CANVAS—the nonviolent strategy group formed by Srdja Popović, Slobodan Djinović, Ivan Marović, and other Otpor leaders to teach their tactics to other movements around the world. Today, the former Otpor leaders who work in CANVAS are trying to apply Otpor's strategies to as wide a spectrum of problems as possible.

The most obvious transfer of Otpor's strategies would be to use them to try to bring democracy to other dictatorships or near-dictatorships. It has worked—first in Georgia and Ukraine, where Otpor activists were a constant presence and local activists directly adapted Serbia's tactics. Later Otpor helped bring about other revolutions: in Lebanon, CANVAS advised students carrying out what came to be known as the Cedar Revolution—the movement after the 2005 assassination of opposition leader Rafiq Hariri that forced Syria to end its occupation of Lebanon. In the island nation of Maldives, CANVAS trainers worked with a movement in 2008 that unseated Maumoon Abdul Gayoom, who had ruled the country for thirty years and had never permitted multiparty elections.

CANVAS's track record, particularly its roles in the Rose Revolution in Georgia and the Orange Revolution in Ukraine, has terrified repressive governments. The group has become nearly synonymous with what has become known as the Color Revolutions—the student-led mass uprisings that have led to democratization in some autocratic countries and have made considerable trouble for authoritarian leaders in others. CANVAS is in part a victim of its own success, as democracy activists who attend its workshops run the risk of being arrested. After a 2005 workshop in Dubai for Iranian activists, several of the participants were arrested. CANVAS's partners in a few other countries have been arrested as well. Authoritarian leaders, afraid of their own people, like to blame outside influences for political dissidence, even if two young Serbs in jeans and T-shirts cannot possibly be a bogeyman in the same category as the CIA. Among the ways Hugo Chávez has found to pass his many hours on Venezuela's national television is to warn viewers to beware of Otpor. Noting the similarities between Otpor's fist and the fist of Venezuela's Otpor-trained movement, he warned of a "form of a soft coup."

Even though CANVAS has worked with activists in some fifty countries, it cannot point to fifty revolutions. It would hardly be fair to blame this on CANVAS; obviously, there are many more factors that decide whether a nonviolent revolution succeeds or fails than whether Otpor's leaders have trained their activists. CANVAS may not always be training the group best placed to get something moving, or the people at the workshop might be too low-level to influence a movement's strategy. In some countries, CANVAS has worked with organizations that seek not to change their government but to accomplish other goals—fight corruption or protect the environment, for example. In other countries, dictatorship remains but democracy movements may have grown larger and stronger because of their workshops with CANVAS. And a few countries whose activists Otpor has trained, such as Belarus and North Korea, are simply a long way away from democratization—perhaps too far to benefit from anything CANVAS teaches.

The fact that revolutions have occurred using Otpor-style tactics in some countries and not others leads to the question of whether these strategies work better under certain conditions. Georgia and Ukraine, after all, had much in common with Serbia. Perhaps the conditions in those countries were particularly propitious—the "sweet spot" for using the social cure to build a citizens' movement. If so, it is useful to think through what that "sweet spot" might be. One clue comes from looking at how Otpor was able to manage fear. The state policy of mass arrest worked greatly to Otpor's advantage. It was a lure for young people, who wanted the social advantages of being daring and rebellious. But— and this was important—it could work because everyone knew that the police were just going through the motions.

What if the consequences had been more serious? If Serbia had been like Iran, where ordinary protesters risked being shot by the police, dissidents were being raped in prison, and courts were meting out the death penalty to opposition supporters, it is likely that many fewer people would have come out to protest. (That Iran could have any protests at all under those conditions speaks volumes about the bravery of Iranians.)

By the standards of global dictatorship, repression inside Serbia was light. There were independent media, even television, which gave Otpor a way to get its message out to the public every day. There were opposition political parties that held power in the major cities. Printers were willing to make posters and T-shirts. Otpor's money men could go to Budapest or Vienna and return with cash. At election time, the people's will was defended by election observers and a parallel vote count.

It seems possible that advice from a country like Serbia would have little relevance in Burma, where the regime was capable of killing perhaps 3,000 unarmed, peaceful protesters over four days in August 1988. Or in Iran, which has no opposition media at all, and where the 2009 presidential election was run and overseen by progovernment institutions, no independent election monitors were allowed, and many opposition poll-watchers were turned away. In China and Vietnam, rolling out a barrel plastered with the dictator's picture would get you years in prison.

When CANVAS works with the opposition in Burma or Belarus,

countries where citizens have virtually no civil rights, what can it hope to achieve? Those countries have none of the advantages Otpor enjoyed in Serbia. Srdja Popović had an answer for that. "Serbia *built* those advantages," he said. "Political space is never granted. It is always conquered. It is definitely easier to work in a wider environment than a narrow one. It was definitely easier to work in Serbia in 1998 than it would be in, say, Iran. But the question is: How do you get to that point?"

There had been several elections under Milošević, he pointed out. But before 2000, the opposition never had people at polling stations to observe the counting of votes. It forced Milošević to permit that. Before 1996, there were no cities in opposition hands, and no independent media. The opposition won those elections, and when Milošević stole those victories, the opposition defended them by marching in the dead of winter for months on end. The opposition forced Milošević to recognize that he had lost control of Serbia's municipalities—and, with them, the local TV stations. In 1991, the regime responded to protests by rolling out tanks into the streets; eight years later, Otpor members were punished with largely token arrests. That was not generosity on Milošević's part. It was the result of the opposition *forcing* him to calculate that Serbs would not stand for more.

"The first rule of nonviolent conflict," said Srdja, "is that the skills and energy you bring into the conflict are more important than the conditions on the battlefield." In other words, he felt, if you are organized and determined and take the right steps, you can gradually win the conditions you need for defeating a dictator.

This might be true some of the time, but not always. The harsher the repression, the less likely it was for people to have the energy and skills necessary to overthrow it. After decades in captivity, the instinct for freedom can dim and the talents needed to win it can shrivel. There will always be some who resist—and they count among the world's hardiest and freest souls—but the great majority of people living in a place like Belarus or Burma will grow accustomed to listening only to the voice coming out of the loudspeaker. The one in their head fades to a whisper.

People's efforts to free themselves, moreover, are only one factor in whether or not a dictatorship falls. Democracy is not always the product of an inexorable march. Time can bring a desert for the growth of freedom, or it can bring a gust of wind that can blow over a tyrant—and everything in between. Sometimes it is absurd and random. A citizen movement of Serbs felled Milošević. Croatians got rid of their own autocratic nationalist a few months earlier—it was not a popular groundswell that toppled Franjo Tudjman, however, but stomach cancer.

This is not an argument for fatalism. The Serbs, unfortunately, cannot carry revolution in their suitcases. A nonviolent revolution must have majority support to be successful, and so must be indigenous. But mass movements do not emerge spontaneously. Over the life of every dictatorship, there are events, shocks to the system, that democracy campaigners can take advantage of: the government fails to help people during a natural disaster such as a cyclone or earthquake, it removes food subsidies or oil subsidies, it disgraces itself during a war, it shoots a beloved opposition figure, it steals an election, international forces suddenly remove the dictatorship's external support. Such events intensify grievances, raise them above background noise, and make them a focus for citizens. What CANVAS does, better than anyone else, is help dissidents understand how to motivate people to take advantage of grievances—how to convert them into a mass movement, and how to convert that mass movement into political change.

Dictatorship is far more than a switch with two positions. If a social movement cannot topple a dictator but can at least create more freedoms, it can still be useful. And the manner of his fall also matters. Governments swept into office by popular democracy movements tend to be better regimes than those that arrive in power through violence or outside intervention. Even if some deus ex machina fells a dictator, the freer his nation is at that moment, the more democratic a future government is likely to be.

Not every dictatorship, moreover, is Burma or North Korea. Medium-level repression and semiautocracy are more common than absolute tyranny. In both of the dictatorships under which I lived—Chile under Pinochet and Nicaragua under the Sandinistas—there were opposition political parties and some independent media (Pinochet had softened considerably from the terrifying early years). When there were elections, the opposition was able to have poll-watchers and a parallel vote count to detect fraud. A quick survey of the world map ten years after Otpor turns up perhaps two dozen countries in similar positions, including Russia, Zimbabwe, Venezuela, and Cambodia, just to name a few.

Could there have been an Otpor in Chile in the 1980s? I think the answer is yes, and it might have sped the return of democracy. The opposition in Chile had some advantages Otpor didn't have, including a strongly ingrained culture of political involvement and a belief that politics mattered. Chileans were not passive and fatalistic, but they were afraid, unfocused, and cynical about their opposition. With good reason—the opposition seemed terminally divided and had no real strategy for restoring democracy.

The opposition in Chile could have profitably borrowed several moves from Otpor. The most basic was, as the Albert Einstein Institution's Bob Helvey counseled, to develop a strategy. No one had identified the pillars of Pinochet's regime and mapped out how to pull them out from under him. Just the opposite: Pinochet had been able to keep the security forces and much of the middle class in his camp by painting the opposition as violent and unpredictable. In his propaganda, an opposition victory would bring Communist dictatorship. The propaganda worked because there was a tiny, violent guerilla group, and Chileans had strong memories of the chaos during the years of Socialist president Salvador Allende. The opposition needed to show that, in fact, it was peaceful and strongly committed to order and prosperity. To do this, it could have used Otpor's social-cure strategies. The Chilean opposition would have greatly benefited from a plan to gradually build a national force of young, nonviolent activists. It could have used humor and insolence to make political activity attractive to them. It could have adapted Otpor's Plan B—its strategy for making those arrested feel like heroes—to turn fear to its advantage. And this force, in turn, could have reassured Pinochet's supporters and torn them away from the regime.

Pinochet eventually fell, as did Milošević and the Sandinistas, because he lost an election. This is what overturning a dictator often requires, but perhaps if the opposition had used more effective methods, that election might have happened earlier.

■ ■ ■ ■ ■

THERE ARE OTHER FORMS of repression that a join-the-club strategy can fight. Hondurans opposed to the June 2009 military ouster of the president could have used it. The social cure can help drive out foreign occupiers, as it did in Lebanon with Otpor's help. Even Poland's Solidarity, the mother of modern civic movements, employed a form of the social cure in its struggle to free Poland from Soviet Communism. It started as a shipyard strike in support of a fired worker and became a national labor movement, but ten million Poles eventually joined Solidarity—a quarter of the population. Many people joined because it was what everyone else was doing. Life under Communism was very boring and Solidarity was exciting. It was the best place to meet girls. Even members of Poland's Communist Party politburo and a member of the party's central committee joined Solidarity—clearly, membership was not an expression of opposition to Communism. For many people, it was simply fashionable.

The social cure as people's movement requires at least some liberties to be able to work. Masses of people will not get involved if activism is life-threatening or if communication is suppressed to the point where no one can find out about your events. But there is also a flip side to the limits of the social cure—it may also be harder to use if times are not harsh enough, as Otpor's fortunes show.

Many people in Serbia during the fight against Milošević wondered why he didn't simply ignore Otpor. If the government had stripped Otpor of its forbidden allure and deprived members of the chance to be James Bond, perhaps young people would have lost interest. And if it hadn't made arrests, it would not have driven all those grandmothers out of Milošević's camp. Srdja had an answer to this question, too: Otpor wouldn't have *let* Milošević ignore it. "We could become as irritating as we needed to be," he said. If offering Milošević's face on a barrel to whack didn't summon the police, putting the face of his much thinner-skinned wife on the other side might have. If that hadn't worked, well, Otpor's members were creative and the possibilities were endless—one can always find ways to get arrested. Moreover, by using dilemma actions, Otpor had made *not* arresting its actors costly to the government as well. Allowing people to whack the barrel unmolested would have given tacit permission to a whole new spectrum of freedoms. In a sense, Otpor was one giant dilemma action: it forced Milošević either to reveal his brutality by repressing it or to expand the scope of liberties in Serbia.

For Otpor, arrests were invaluable, but they worked only as long as they punished actions that the public perceived as legitimate. Masses of people will not become hooligans—they will only agree to be arrested for activities they know should not be punished. That is the only way to convert arrests into public sympathy.

This strategy can work in a democratic society from time to time. Civil rights and peace movements rely on arrests to generate public support and raise participants' levels of adrenaline. Examples are the suffragette campaign in Britain in the early 1900s and the civil rights movement and anti–Vietnam War protests in the United States. Here's why they worked: These were issues that directly affected large swaths of society; the injustice was visible and present; the case for change was anchored in a strong moral argument; and campaigners sought simple-to-grasp (if not necessarily simple-to-implement) policy change by the government—votes for women, an end to Jim Crow laws, a pullout from Vietnam. These campaigns had narratives that were clear, strong, and personal. They hit you in the gut.

It's not often that situations lending themselves to civil disobedience and mass arrest arise. If the social cure is to be useful in democratic societies—say, to persuade Mexico to reduce corruption or Washington to do something about climate change or Darfur—then it must have tactics other than mass arrests to mobilize people.

Often the obstacle to using an Otpor-style social cure to effect political change in a democracy is that the policies people want changed do not affect them personally. While the issue of genocide in Darfur is life-or-death for the people of that region, it is not life-or-death for antigenocide activists in America. (If there had been no draft, it is likely that protests against the Vietnam War would have remained isolated and small.) Many people care about Darfur; perhaps they care a lot.

But the social cure works best when the issue is of such overwhelming importance that people will put in a great deal of time—a very high bar in places where the norm is to solve problems by writing a check instead of going to meetings. "Busy people don't have a problem getting to their AA group," said Bill Donahue of Willow Creek Community Church—but they can have a problem getting to the event for Darfur.

The hurdle for mobilizing people can also be that the harm being protested is not yet visible. Al Gore has called for civil disobedience to prevent the construction of new coal plants that do not have carbon-capture mechanisms. It is easy to imagine this happening in the rapidly drowning Maldives or drought-stricken Ethiopia—or it would be if they had coal—but not in America, where the ill effects of global warming are still largely hidden.

Some campaigns, moreover, do not lend themselves to a simple narrative. Corruption, for example, is a huge political issue, one that routinely topples governments. But it is difficult to motivate people to invest the time for repeated protests and take the risks of getting arrested in order to push the government to do—what, exactly? Fighting corruption is much more complex than the passage of a few new laws. Nor is it just an issue for the government; it requires change on the part of numerous groups in society. The narrative is too messy to lend itself to heroic protest based on mass arrest.

The question, then, is whether there are other variations on the social cure that use peer pressure to effect change in a democratic society—ones that do not depend on being arrested and don't even require people to spend lots of time at events. Can there be social change in five minutes a day? The answer is yes. Mass movements need not involve bringing people into the street to protest. In wealthy countries, people buy things, and those buying decisions can be the basis for an effective political or social movement. The boycott of table grapes in support of the United Farm Workers (UFW), and the boycott of Nestlé over the company's efforts to push baby-formula sales in countries where breast-feeding was crucial, are two examples of effective mass movements that relied on changing people's buying decisions.

Altering what people consume can be very effective, and peer pressure can help. As every advertiser knows, what our peers are doing greatly influences our buying decisions. This factor is most powerful if the product is on display to the world—one reason why cars are the ultimate identity purchase. But peer pressure can also affect decisions about what's in your fruit bowl. For it to influence consumption of more hidden items, there must be a way for people to know what others are buying, and to put their own choices on display. The UFW sent such a signal with bumper stickers and buttons. A particularly iconic one had a black eagle on a red background encircled by "Boycott Grapes, Viva la Causa." At some universities, that button seemed to be on every backpack.

Peers can even affect your electric bill. Robert Cialdini, the psychologist and marketing expert, found an ingenious way to put into your calculus information about what your peers are doing. He is chief scientist at a company called OPOWER, which makes software that measures electrical use by neighborhood. In 2008, Sacramento consumers began receiving an extra bit of information along with their electric bills: how their consumption compared with that of their neighbors with houses of similar size, age, and heating type. The report tells you, for example, if you are doing 19 percent better or 50 percent worse than your peers, and it compares you with your most efficient neighbors. If you are doing better than the rest, you receive a smiley face or two, a rating of "good" or "great," and some reassurance: "You should feel good about your energy efficiency and the savings this means for you."

Not above average? You don't get a frowny face, but you are told how much your profligacy costs you in dollars, and "This means you have a great opportunity to save energy and money in the future." Some reports also provide specific others-do-this tips, such as: "Most people in your area keep their air conditioning at 78 degrees." A Yale Law School study found that households typically reduce their energy consumption an average of 2 percent within three months of receiving their first reports, and the decrease is sustained over time. In another study, households consuming the most energy reduced their consumption by 7 percent, compared with similar households that did not get the special bills. Since the enhancements to the electric bills are virtually free, this is one of the most cost-effective ways to reduce energy consumption. The idea is now spreading to other cities, and a water-use component is due to be added.

There are other possible uses for the OPOWER model. Ian Ayres, a professor at Yale Law School who conducted one of the studies of OPOWER and who writes and blogs about behavioral economics, suggests that schools send reports to parents comparing their children's absences with those of other kids. Businesses could tell employees who are not taking advantage of their 401(k) plans how much their peers are saving. Instead of the "It's time to come in for your cleaning" postcard from your dentist, the postcard could inform laggards how often other people have their teeth cleaned. With almost everything that people need to be nagged about, the nagging is much more effective if it comes with information about what others are doing.

What OPOWER does is not a social cure. It seems unlikely that a smiley face on your electric bill will change the way you think of yourself. OPOWER does not try to change your identity in order to get you to use less electricity—Cialdini calls it "peer proof" instead of "peer pressure"—but its success demonstrates that once people know the social norm, they will take steps to abide by it.

Even in wealthy democracies, the social cure can be a way to make changes in society. For young people, rebellion itself can still be the draw. In Florida and South Carolina, the teen antitobacco groups were not risking arrest when they made prank phone calls or staged a sit-in in the smoking section at Shoney's—but these activities were fun, cool, and anti-authority. And they were aimed at widespread social change, not just at improving individual behavior.

The Obama presidential campaign had some aspects of a social cure. Obama's intellect and temperament made him an extraordinary candidate, but his race made him an identity-changing phenomenon. He made black people feel good about themselves, and he also made white people feel good about themselves—they could feel enlightened for supporting him. The more of themselves they invested in getting him elected, the more positive their view of themselves could be.

The campaign had a record number of volunteers; it ran the largest field operation in American history. The volunteer network was decentralized. Campaign workers could download lists of phone numbers in crucial states and could make the calls from their own homes at their own pace. When they finished their list, they would log in their results to the campaign's computers, to build a database for election-day get-out-the-vote efforts. But many chose to work with others, and the glow they felt from being at the local headquarters on a weekend with a crowd of fellow volunteers kept people coming back. As with Otpor, there was useful work for volunteers with minimal direction from campaign central, and they did it partly because it made them feel like an important part of something.

THE APPLICATION OF THE social cure to most political problems in a democratic society is a challenge. We know that, in the right conditions, the social cure can draw people into activism, and their activism can then create social change. But it would seem that many places are too comfortable for those conditions to be met. In a democracy, the social cure must overcome our busyness and our discomfort with participating in public life. It has to surmount certain obstacles: noble defiance of the law is not a practical lure, and the problems to be solved may be either not overwhelming or not ours. It is hard to create a convincing, strong message when the issue is complex and a change in governmental policy may be only part of what's needed.

Yet it is possible to envision how the join-the-club strategies that Otpor employed to create mass activism could be useful in a democracy. As a thought exercise, let us try to design a social cure to attack one of the most complex and difficult problems imaginable: corruption in Mexico.

Mexico is a middle-income country and a democracy. Although Mexico has long been a symbol of corruption, it actually ranks almost exactly at the middle on the global index of perception of corruption compiled by Transparency International—tied for eighty-ninth of 180 countries. (That in itself indicates how badly off half the world is.)

The popular perception is that corruption is impossible to clean up—that a corrupt country will only get worse—but many countries have seen dramatic victories against corruption. In his fascinating book *Controlling Corruption*, Robert Klitgaard shows that when the political will is strong enough, countries have successfully reduced corruption. Australia, now one of the world's cleanest nations, was a longtime Wild West of lawlessness. Singapore, now a model of probity, was awash in corruption in the 1950s. Bolivia is one of the world's most corrupt nations, but for a time a reformist mayor gave residents of its biggest city, La Paz, a reprieve. Ferdinand Marcos, of all people, cleaned up the tax bureau in the Philippines for a few years. (It is amusing to recall that he declared martial law in 1972 in part to combat corruption.)

Mexico is not part of Klitgaard's book, but it, too, has positive examples. One is the successful reform of its customs department. It is useful to take a closer look at how Mexico did this.

Mexico City's airport is where the highest-value merchandise enters the country. It sets the image for international business. Yet the customs area at the airport in 1989 was a medieval bedlam. There was no registry of what entered. There were no lights. There was no security, no fence around the customs pen—anyone could come in and cart away valuables. The warehouse was filled with a jumble of abandoned merchandise that had been looted. Boxes of radioactive substances clearly marked "Refrigerate" sat out in the sun. Getting an item through customs took sixteen steps—hence sixteen opportunities for someone to solicit a bribe. If this seems like a system designed to produce the maximum amount of corruption, it was.

Mexico changed the system by following one simple principle: Reduce the opportunities for illegal acts. That meant such simple changes as keeping good records of what came in and went out and putting up a fence so people couldn't commit outright theft. It meant cutting the number of steps necessary to get import permits, reducing human discretion for those steps, and narrowing the scope of goods on which duty had to be paid.

Mexico did all this. The airport changed to the same system that most developed countries use: major shipments were handled by licensed customs brokers, who inventoried merchandise and calculated the correct duty. After the duty was paid, the merchandise passed through a random customs stoplight. (Mexico instituted a similar system for incoming travelers.) Ten percent of the merchandise got a red light and was inspected; there were steep penalties for lying. The sixteen steps became three steps, and a process of importation that previously had taken as long as a month was reduced to ten minutes. From one month to the next, officially collected duties jumped by 30 percent.

In addition to raising revenue and increasing the flow of goods, the reforms also curtailed corruption. The red light reduced the ability of inspectors to choose targets and took away a major source of bribes. The smaller the role for officials to make choices about who paid and who didn't, the less the corruption.

"It's not that I'm an administrative genius," said Francisco Gil Díaz, then an assistant secretary of the treasury, who led the reforms. "These changes were simply logical." A first-year business student could have designed a clean system, but customs had been structured to serve the interests of the powerful. Customs officials had deliberately designed a system that was so complex that importers would pay large bribes to avoid it. Officials liked the system because it produced graft; big importers liked it because whatever bribe they paid, it was still less than what they legally owed the state. Officials would look the other way when importers brought in anything they wanted, duty free.

What changed? It was not that Mexico suddenly realized that it needed to design pocketless uniforms for customs officials. What happened was the North American Free Trade Agreement (NAFTA) was being negotiated. Gil Díaz was able to break the customs Mafia because the Mexican government and powerful businessmen needed to clean up customs in order to get a trade deal they craved. Absent NAFTA, the government wouldn't have given customs a second look.

The point of this story is that it is easy to fight corruption when people want to do it. The hard part is getting them to want to. Ordinary citizens—the same ones who complain about everyday corruption—are also full participants in it. When processing birth certificates or driver's licenses, officials rarely solicit bribes. Instead, they work so slowly, sloppily, and arbitrarily that people see no hope of getting the services to which they are entitled without offering a tip, *pa'el refresco* (literally, "for a soda").

When I lived in Mexico City, my husband and I bought a used car. To transfer the registration to our name took five trips to government offices over the course of months. When we tried to get a birth certificate for one of our Mexico-born daughters, we went to the civil registry in our district. Dozens of people, most carrying infants, sat on precarious stacks of cardboard boxes in two tiny rooms filled with trash. There was no attempt to help people figure out where to start, no sign on the wall listing required documents, no take-a-number. One official told us we could not register the baby without producing the birth certificates of her grandparents; at the next desk, we were told we could. (In a neighboring registry, an official had offered to do it for a large bribe.) We followed our doctor's recommendation to hire a helper who knew the system, so at least we were mostly finished in one morning. An acquaintance who went alone needed four trips.

I was not the only fed-up resident of Mexico City. Everyone complained about corruption, all the time. But when bribery is the only way to get services without taking a week off from work, people bribe; the social norm is to pay up. Corruption is a problem that brings to life nonviolence guru Gene Sharp's mantra: Power resides in the consent given by people in society. Corruption requires even more than people's consent; it can survive only if people are active participants. But if the population has given its consent to corruption, it can also withdraw it. Corruption in Mexico is a problem susceptible to a join-the-club assault.

Two different levels of social cure are necessary: internal and external. The government would use the internal strategy in the government offices it wished to reform. As we have seen, it is not difficult to create an administrative system that lessens corruption. But organizations have their own internal social norms. If those norms favor corruption, they can sabotage the implementation of even well-designed reforms. Hence the need for an internal social cure, to create peer pressure for honesty.

Let's say Mexico was trying to reduce corruption in the awarding of contracts to build highways and roads. Mexico currently has a transparent online system of bidding for government contracts, but corrupt officials and contractors keep finding ways around it. A possible social cure would be to divide the procurement officers into groups. The government has to devise a way to measure honesty, perhaps through an audit of contracts. At the end of the year, the group with the highest honesty score—assuming it passed a certain threshold—would get a 100 percent salary bonus and public recognition. (The awards themselves have their downsides. While everyone appreciates public acknowledgment, if the organization's social norm favors corruption, receiving awards for honesty can make you an outcast.) The group with the lowest percentage—assuming, again, that it fell below a certain threshold—would be fired. Perhaps the rewards could be even higher if many groups did well. This produces a system where the members of each group push each other to behave honestly.

Some people in both groups will be unfairly rewarded or unfairly punished, lifted up or dragged down by the behavior of their colleagues. One solution is to review carefully the winners and losers and make exceptions if there is widespread agreement that they are warranted. It is also important to ensure that the audit itself is honest and not corrupt. And there must be a way to measure behavior and detect corruption. This is not a trivial problem. With tasks such as awarding procurement contracts, determining whether workers have been honest is relatively easy. When the issue is corrupt policing, it is very hard to spot.

To encourage the government to institute anticorruption reforms to begin with, a wider front for a social cure is necessary: a mass movement of Mexicans ready to turn their grievances about constant corruption into action.

Such a movement might borrow liberally from Otpor. It would lack Otpor's attraction of danger (as long as it stayed away from drug corruption), but it could try to lure members by forming a group that is hip, witty, and rude to authority figures. Its stickers could read, "I Don't Pay" or "Mexico Is Not Corrupt." Everything Otpor did to Milošević, the *Yo No Pago* movement could do to corruption. Students would be the natural constituency. The organizers could build their movement with street actions. They could ask people to whack a barrel plastered with images of their most infamously corrupt politicians, sell government contracts for play money on the street, or set up a candid camera to catch people on videotape bribing a fake policeman—or a real one. They could stage a "Marathon of Corruption" in honor of the governor and unsuccessful presidential candidate, Roberto Madrazo, who was disqualified from the Berlin Marathon for cheating. The group could, with great fanfare, present the relevant authorities with a book of ideas for designing an honest bureaucracy—all written by high school students. Activists could visit the halls where construction licenses and birth certificates are doled out, passing out buttons and stickers and soliciting signatures on a "No Pago" pledge. They could give flowers and "Mexico Is Not Corrupt" buttons to bureaucrats and police. Activists could provide "*Hago Patria*" (roughly translated, "I do my patriotic duty") buttons and bumper stickers to citizens who could prove they paid taxes—starting with the coolest actors and sports stars. They could ambush important public officials and candidates and—cameras rolling—demand they commit to taking certain anticorruption steps, just as Otpor publicly wrested unity pledges out of the Serbian political opposition.

The public actions would stress humor and puckishness. As with Otpor, they would try to create a bandwagon even before they had numbers. But if the movement did grow, it could use those numbers to hold public actions all over Mexico, targeting local officials and offices known for corruption. There could be a chapter just for police, and one for government bureaucrats.

There are endless variations on this theme. All are useful if they contribute to creating a social movement that can be a source of political pressure on the government to make and sustain reforms, and to establishing a new social norm that gets people to look at corruption and their own participation in it in a different way—to rebrand themselves: "I Don't Pay."

This is all speculation, of course. A real social cure for Mexican corruption would have to be designed by the people who would carry it out, after analyzing the problem and the resources and strengths of the organizers. The point here is to show how the social cure might be employed to lure people into activism that could create new social norms for change in a democratic society. Mexico is not sui generis and neither is corruption. Similar strategies might work to defy organized crime, prevent water and air pollution, or shrink a carbon footprint.

A FEW YEARS AGO, if anyone had asked me about the transformational ability of positive peer pressure, I would have thought of Alcoholics Anonymous, and maybe nothing else. Now I see the possibilities everywhere. The moment that really drove its power home to me, however, came during a 2008 visit to India, when I met Sarubai Salve. I was researching an article for *National Geographic* magazine about community health workers, not looking for join-the-club stories. But it was a revelation to watch this steely, competent, authoritative woman—without a doubt the most respected person in her village— and to realize how she became who she is.

As described in chapter 6, Sarubai was a village health worker in the Jamkhed program. When I met her, she was fifty-six and had been a village health worker for twenty-three years. She was thin, with long hair streaked with gray, and wore steel-rimmed aviator glasses. She was from Jawalke, the same village as Babai Sathe; she had trained Babai and they worked together. Sarubai had been married at the age of two and a half, to an eighteen-year-old man. Before she entered the Jamkhed program, she cleaned her hair with mud because she did not have soap, and she owned only one sari—when she laundered it, she had to stay in the river until it dried. She owned a pair of sandals, but as a Dalit, she could not wear them in Jawalke. Her early life, as with the vast majority of women like her, was devoid of any expectation that anything would or should be different.

But because of Jamkhed, everything *was* different. By the standards of her village, which were the only ones she knew, Sarubai was prosperous. She sold bangles and earrings as she did her medical rounds, and she invested those profits in other businesses. She owned a flour mill and a Jeep that she rents out. She had two houses—with real walls and cement floors—and, she said proudly, "fifteen saris, and enough food and oil and soap."

More important to Sarubai was this: There was no one in Jawalke whom she had not saved in some way, large or small. Along with Babai, she delivered her neighbors' babies and cured their fevers. She taught them why and how to keep their water clean and what to feed a child. She banished superstitions. She had led a village project to build an eight-kilometer road so that Jawalke could have bus service for the first time. She convinced villagers to plant 125,000 trees. She organized the women, helped them start businesses, and broke the caste system. Despite the fact that these extra activities brought her no income, she spent a good part of each day on them. When I met her, she was preparing to teach a class on hypertension and was in the middle of a campaign to collect a rupee from every family to pay a high school teacher, so Jawalke's girls could go beyond seventh grade.

"A year ago I had major intestinal surgery, and I took the time to look at my life," said Sarubai. "They used to treat me like an animal because I am a Dalit. But my life has brought me so much more than I expected. Because of Jamkhed, I have respect and knowledge. I have prestige—people call me doctor." She has enjoyed a privilege available to only very few in a place where people are consumed by the struggle to exist: she has been able to live a life full of the satisfactions of being useful.

Of all the transformations in this book, that of Sarubai and some of her companions at Jamkhed seems to me the most profound: to go from looking only at the ground to a life so big that its main fulfillment has come from being a benefactor to others. Sarubai had not left her village, but she had moved to a different universe. What wrought this change was her fellowship with her sister village-health workers.

If a new peer group could do this, what could it not do? It is logical, really, that peer pressure can get us out of so many bad situations, because peer pressure is one important reason we get into them. If you knock on doors in housing projects in poor neighborhoods of American cities and ask mothers and grandmothers what they most fear, chances are they will say it is peer pressure. "My son is a good boy," the mother will tell you, "but he runs with a bad crowd."

Peer pressure helps fill prisons. It keeps emergency rooms busy treating high school kids who can't tell a friend he is too drunk to drive and young men who must maintain the respect of their group by answering every perceived slight with violence. Peer pressure crowds bankruptcy courts with people who did nothing wrong except want to buy what others had. The smoker dying of lung cancer at seventy-five—sixty years after smoking his first cigarette—has something in common with a woman dying of AIDS at twenty-five. In a sense, they are both dying of peer pressure.

We are all good boys at risk of the bad crowd. Peer pressure is a mighty and terrible force—so powerful that, for the vast majority of people, the best antidote to it is more peer pressure. There are many different stories of salvation in this book: of people weighing babies together, doing math problems, playing soccer, making prank phone calls, getting arrested, and sharing a potluck supper. Indeed, a lifeline can take infinite forms. What matters is that at the other end, someone's hand is there.

Acknowledgments

WRITING ABOUT THE USES of peer pressure is obviously a team project, and the most important members of the team are the innovators profiled in this book. I am grateful for their creativity and daring, their clarity of thought and firmness of purpose, and their patience in explaining their work to me. A few of my subjects, such as Raj and Mabelle Arole, Abdul Haqq Baker, and the Otpor gang, assumed considerable risk or hardship in service of their vision, and they have my special admiration.

Some people who do not figure in these pages (or only briefly) helped me by reading parts of the manuscript: Elisabeth Malkin, Jennifer Stephen, Paul Rosenberg, Ritta Rosenberg, and Rob Varenik. David Bornstein was a source of always-fruitful ideas and inspiring conversations.

A few of the stories in this book were published in different form in magazines. The *New York Times Magazine* published my articles about corruption in Mexico on August 10, 2003; about South Africa's AIDS-prevention efforts on August 6, 2006; and about the travails of girls in India on August 23, 2009. *National Geographic* published my story on the Aroles and their village health workers in Jamkhed in its December 2008 issue. I am grateful to the *Times* and the *Geographic* for allowing me to adapt those works for this book, and for the guidance of my magazine editors: Paul Tough and James Ryerson at the *New York Times Magazine*, and Barbara Paulsen at *National Geographic*.

Bob Weil, my editor at W. W. Norton, has been all I could wish for; I see what the fuss is about. His assistants, Lucas Wittmann and Philip Marino, have given thoughtful help as well. Emily Brady stepped in to aid in fact-checking and assembling reference materials, and saved me from a number of mistakes.

I owe special thanks to my agent, Gail Ross, and her colleague Howard Yoon. They journeyed outside the mapped terrain of agentry into inspiration, editing, guidance, nudging and hand-holding. There is no one in my professional life to whom I have been attached for so many years as Gail, and this has been my good fortune.

This book is in part an argument for the importance of social support, so I would like to thank mine. The following people contributed to this book by giving me technical advice, creative suggestions, a listening ear, a few hours to work child-free, or a well-timed round of beer or ice-cream cones: Barbara Becker, Patti Cohen, Maggie Fishman, Angela Gutierrez, Nancy Horowitz, Anna Husarska, Calla Jo, Corinna Lindenberg, Amanda de Matto, Pam Pedersen, Audrey Pierson, Lisa Polen, Lynda Richardson, Emily Russell, Noah Schwartzberg, Sara Silver, John Thomas, and Sylvia Weiner.

Finally, I am grateful to Rob, endlessly. And to my girls, who provide my personal ongoing master class in the power of peer pressure—and also in the lesson that there are more important things to do than write about it.

[Notes]

INTRODUCTION

xi **most influential church** churchrelevance.com, "Top Churches to Watch in America," January 1, 2010, http://churchrelevance.com/resources/top-churches-in-america/.

xvii **$35 million per day** Federal Trade Commission, "Federal Trade Commission Cigarette Report for 2006," issued 2009, http://ftc.gov/os/2009/08/090812cigarettereport.pdf.

One   Turning Positive

1 **better than even chance of dying of AIDS** Tina Rosenberg, "When a Pill Is Not Enough," *New York Times Magazine*, August 6, 2006.

4 **Mbeki knew no one who had died of AIDS** *Washington Post*, September 25, 2003.

10 **AIDS prevalence among pregnant teens** National Department of Health, "2008 National Antenatal Sentinel HIV & Syphilis Prevalence Survey," *South Africa Report*, September 2009, http://www.doh.gov.za/docs/reports/2009/nassps/results_a.pdf.

11 **survey of fifteen- to twenty-four-year-olds** Audrey E. Pettifor et al., "Young People's Sexual Health in South Africa: HIV Prevalence and Sexual Behaviors from a Nationally Representative Household Survey." *AIDS* 19, no. 14 (2005): 1525–34.

11 **KwaZulu-Natal study of loveLife** loveLife, *"Melmoth Report: An Assessment of Effects Associated with loveLife's Intervention*, 2007, http://www.lovelife.org.za/corporate/research/.

11 2007 prenatal AIDS prevalence rates National Department of Health, "2008 National Antenatal Sentinel HIV & Syphilis Prevalence Survey."

11 new infections among teenagers plummeted O. Shisana, et al., *South African National HIV Prevalence, Incidence, Behaviour and Communication Survey, 2008: A Turning Tide Among Teenagers?* (Cape Town: HSRC Press, 2009).

12 60 percent drop in new infections Gus Cairns, "Overall HIV Prevalence Stabilises at 11% in South Africa, with Decreases in Younger Age Groups," *Aidsmap News,* February 18, 2010, http://www.aidsmap.com/en/news/C5BD4E85-066F-4FF6-AA43-17149503CAED.asp.

12 Botswana and Namibia Namibia prenatal clinic surveys of women fifteen to twenty-five showed a 21 percent decline in new infections between 2002 and 2008. Botswana has no comparable new-infection figures over time, but the AIDS prevalence rate among fifteen- to nineteen-year-old women (the age at which it most closely approximates the new infection rate) fell by 30 percent between 2001 and 2007, with almost all of the decline coming before 2005. See http://www.hiv.gov.bw/uploads/SENTINELL_SURVAEILLENCE_07_%20technical_report.pdf.

12 condom use higher among young people Shisana, South African National HIV Prevalence, Incidence, Behaviour and Communication Survey.

13 loveLife's reach Ibid.

13 risks of leaving school David Harrison, Linda Richter, and Chris Desmond, "Changing Perception of Opportunity: The link between structural and behaviour change interventions for HIV prevention" (Johannesburg, unpublished, 2009).

13 Limpopo school-leavers J. R. Hargreaves, et al., "The Association Between School Attendance, HIV Infection and Sexual Behaviour Among Young People in Rural South Africa," *Journal of Epidemiology and Community Health* 62 (2008):113–19.

Two   **The Empire of Irrationality**

22 *The Ego and Its Defenses* Henry P. Laughlin, *The Ego and Its Defenses* (New York: Meredith Corporation, 1970), 7.

23 doomsday cult Leon Festinger et al., *When Prophecy Fails: A Social and Psychological Study of a Modern Group That Predicted the Destruction of the World* (Minneapolis: University of Minnesota Press, 1956).

24 Elliot Aronson Carol Tavris and Elliot Aronson, *Mistakes Were Made (but not by* me)(Orlando, FL: Harcourt, 2007).

25 catharsis study Michael Kahn, "The Physiology of Catharsis," *Journal of Personality and Social Psychology* 3 (1966): 278–86.

26 nicotine addiction This is a good synthesis: http://www.ehealthmd.com/library/smoking/smo_whatis.html.

26 addiction's genetic component Nora D. Volkow, "What Do We Know About

Drug Addiction?" *American Journal of Psychiatry* 162 (August 2005): 1401–2.

26 children of alcoholics "Children of Alcoholics," American Academy of Childhood and Adolescent Psychiatry Web site, http://aacap.org/page.ww?name =Children+of+Alcoholics&section=Facts+for+Families.

26 alcoholism among adopted children D. W. Goodwin et al., "Drinking Problems in Adopted and Nonadopted Sons of Alcoholics. *Archives of General Psychiatry* 31 (1974): 164–69.

26 child molester with a brain tumor BBC News World Edition, "Brain Tumor 'Caused Paedophilia,'" http://news.bbc.co.uk/2/hi/health/2345971.stm.

26 Ramachandran Sandra Blakeslee, "Scientist at Work: Vilayanur Ramachandran: Figuring Out the Brain from Its Acts of Denial," *New York Times*, January 23, 1996, Science section.

27 Trivers on irrationality Robert Trivers, "A Full-Force Storm with Gale Winds Blowing," October 14, 2004, Edge Foundation, Inc., http://www.edge.org/3rd_ culture/trivers04/trivers04_index.html.

28 Trivers on self-deception Robert Trivers, "The Elements of a Scientific Theory of Self-Deception," *Annals of The New York Academy of Sciences* 907 (2000): 114–31, http://www.ncbi.nlm.nih.gov/pubmed/10818624.

28 Wobegon academics Ibid.

29 industry of selling food to children http://www.newscientist.com/article/ dn12431-fast-food-branding-makes-children-prefer-happy-meals.html.

29 preschoolers swayed by McDonald's wrappers Thomas N. Robinson et al., "Effects of Fast Food Branding on Young Children's Taste Preferences," *Pediatrics & Adolescent Medicine* 161 (2007): 792–97.

29 commercials and obesity Shin-Yi Chou et al., "Fast Food Restaurant Advertising on Television and Its Influence on Childhood Obesity," *Journal of Law and Economics* 51 (2008): 599–618.

31 tobacco-company antismoking ads Melanie Wakefield et al., "Effect of Televised, Tobacco Company–Funded Smoking Prevention Advertising on Youth Smoking–Related Beliefs, Intentions, and Behavior," *American Journal of Public Health* 96 (2006): 2154–60.

31 Asch experiments Solomon Asch, "Studies of Independence and Conformity: A Minority of One Against a Unanimous Majority," *Psychological Monographs* 70 (1956).

32 Milgram on obedience Stanley Milgram, "Behavioral Study of Obedience," *The Journal of Abnormal and Social Psychology* 67 (1963): 371–78.

32 Milgram variations Stanley Milgram, Obedience to Authority: An Experimental View (New York: HarperCollins, 1974).

34 Zimbardo's car Philip Zimbardo, "The Human Choice: Individuation, Reason, and Order Versus Deindividuation, Impulse, and Chaos," *Nebraska Symposium on Motivation* 17 (1969): 237–307.

34 Allegory of the Cave Plato, *The Republic* (New York: Penguin Classics, 2007), 240–48.

40 discrimination against Indian girls Tina Rosenberg, "The Daughter Deficit," *New York Times Magazine*, August 23, 2009.

41 infant mortality rates in India R. Khanna et. al., "Community Based Retrospective Study of Sex in Infant Mortality in India," *British Medical Journal* 327 (July 19, 2003): 126.

Three   Righteous Rebels

44 patient-adherence statistics Allan Showalter, "Prevalence and Incidence of Patient Noncompliance," *Align Map*, http://alignmap.com/noncompliance-fact-fiction/prevalence/.

46 MADD print ad http://www.madd.org/getdoc/e1c8e7ed-72c1-4e11-9686-55f01180228f/LikeFather_LikeSon2_Eng.aspx.

47 Cialdini petrified-wood study Robert B. Cialdini, "Crafting Normative Messages to Protect the Environment," *Current Directions in Psychological Science 12* (2003): 105–9.

48 Albarracin study Dolores Albarracin et al., "A Test of Major Assumptions About Behavior Change: A Comprehensive Look at the Effects of Passive and Active HIV-Prevention Interventions Since the Beginning of the Epidemic," *Psychological Bulletin* 131 (2005): 856–97.

57 Gladwell on teen smoking Malcolm Gladwell. *The Tipping Point: How Little Things Can Make a Big Difference* (New York: Little, Brown, 2000), 220.

57 Monitoring the Future study "Monitoring the Future: Cigarettes: Trends in 30-Day Use, Risk, Disapproval, and Availability, Grades 8, 10, 12," University of Michigan, 2009, http://www.monitoringthefuture.org/data/09data/cfig09_1.pdf.

57 despair about teen smoking John Schwartz, "Officials Seek a Path to Cut into Haze of Youth Smoking; The Bottom Line: No One Knows What Works," *Washington Post*, November 2, 1997, Section A.

58 Joe Camel known to kids Paul M. Fischer et al., "Brand Logo Recognition by Children Aged 3 to 6 Years: Mickey Mouse and Old Joe the Camel," *Journal of the American Medical Association* 22 (1991): 3145–48.

58 girls' susceptibility to cigarette ads John P. Pierce et al., "Smoking Initiation by Adolescent Girls, 1944 through 1988: An Association with Targeted Advertising," *Journal of the American Medical Association* 271 (1994): 608–11.

58 teen preference for advertised brands Centers for Disease Control and Prevention, "Changes in the Cigarette Brand Preference of Adolescent Smokers, U.S. 1989–1993," *Morbidity and Morality Report* 43 (August 19, 1994): 577–81.

59 just under half will be hooked "Selected Cigarette Smoking Initiation and Quitting Behaviors Among High School Students—United States, 1997," *Morbidity and Mortality Weekly Report* 47, no. 19 (May 22, 1998): 386–89, http://www.cdc.gov/mmwr/preview/mmwrhtml/00052816.htm.

59 the young initiate smoking U.S. Department of Health and Human Services. "Preventing Tobacco Use Among Young People: A Report of the Surgeon General," National Center for Chronic Disease Prevention and Health Promotion, Office on Smoking and Health, 1994, http://profiles.nlm.nih.gov/NN/B/C/F/T/_/nnbcft .pdf.

59 Iowa billboards Iowa Department of Justice, "Tobacco Billboards Come Down—Pro-Health Messages Go Up," April 23, 1999, http://www.iowa.gov/ government/ag/latest_news/releases/tob_billboards.html.

59 Pam Laffin "Obituaries in the News," *Washington Post*, November 3, 2000.

59 Illinois billboards Illinois Department of Public Health, Anti-Tobacco Campaign, 1999, http://www.idph.state.il.us/tobacco/billboards.htm.

60 Arizona campaign Schwartz, "Officials Seek a Path to Cut into Haze of Youth Smoking; The Bottom Line: No One Knows What Works."

62 California rejects tobacco taxes Stanton A. Glantz and Edith D. Balbach, *Tobacco War: Inside the California Battles* (Berkeley: University of California Press, 2000).

Four   Corporate Tools

64 California ad-campaign contract Stanton A. Glantz and Edith D. Balbach, *Tobacco War: Inside the California Battles* (Berkeley: University of California Press, 2000), 149.

65 "Industry Spokesman" text Paul Keye, e-mail message to author, April 21, 2010.

65 "We used to pick it" Glantz and Balbach, *Tobacco War*, 130.

66 smoking prevalence dropped dramatically John P. Pierce et al., "Tobacco Use in California: An Evaluation of the Tobacco Control Program, 1989–1993," (University of California, San Diego, 1994): 60, http://libraries.ucsd.edu/ssds/ pub/CTS/cpc00003/finalrpt1993.pdf.

66 California media campaign effective M. C. Farrelly et al., "Youth Tobacco Prevention Mass Media Campaigns: Past, Present and Future Directions," *Tobacco Control* 12, Supp.1 (2003): i35–i47 http://www.ncbi.nlm.nih.gov/pmc/ articles/PMC1766092/pdf/v012p00i35.pdf.

66 Glantz on Florida's success Mary Ellen Klas, "Florida's Anti-Smoking Plan Has California Roots," Cox News Service, *The Tuscaloosa News*, March 21, 1999, http://news.google.com/newspapers?nid=1817&dat=19990321&id=88k dAAAAIBAJ&sjid=VqYEAAAAIBAJ&pg=6814,3155460.

67 Florida's settlement with tobacco companies Andrew Holtz, "Turning the Rebellion: How Florida Is Trying to Incite Teens Against Tobacco," *The Holtz Report*, 1999, http://holtzreport.com/FL_paper.htm.

68 tobacco-industry internal memos Campaign for Tobacco-Free Kids,

"Tobacco Company Quotes on Marketing to Kids," May 14, 2001, http://www
.tobaccofreekids.org/research/factsheets/pdf/0114.pdf.

72 message and messenger University of Miami, "Youth Tobacco Prevention
in Florida: An Independent Evaluation of the Florida Tobacco Pilot Program,"
prepared for the Florida Department of Health, December 15, 1999, http://www
.doh.state.fl.us/DISEASE_CTRL/EPI/Smoking/reports/eval.pdf.

74 drop in teen smoking Florida Department of Health, "Youth Tobacco Survey
(FYTS)," 2000, http://www.doh.state.fl.us/disease_ctrl/epi/FYTS/vol3rep_1
.pdf.

74 Ed Trapido on Florida's effectiveness Klas, "Florida's Anti-Smoking Plan Has
California Roots."

74 Florida's drop in teen smoking slowed Florida Department of Health, "Youth
Tobacco Survey (FYTS)," 2009, http://www.doh.state.fl.us/disease_ctrl/epi/
Chronic_Disease/FYTS/2009_FYTS.html.

75 teen beliefs and smoking rates Jeff Niederdeppe, Matthew Farrelly, and
M. Lyndon Havilland, "Confirming 'truth': More Evidence of a Successful Tobacco
Countermarketing Campaign in Florida," *American Journal of Public Health* 94,
no. 2 (2004): 255, http://ajph.aphapublications.org/cgi/reprint/94/2/255.

76 texting and smoking Anne Charlton and Clive Bates, "Decline in Teenage
Smoking with Rise in Mobile Phone Ownership: Hypothesis," *British Medical
Journal* 321 (November 2000): 1155.

76 national drop in teen smoking "Monitoring the Future: Cigarettes: Trends in
30-Day Use, Risk, Disapproval, and Availability, Grades 8, 10, 12," University of
Michigan, 2009, http://www.monitoringthefuture.org/data/09data/cfig09_1.pdf.

77 New York teen-smoking rates Youth Risk Behavior Surveillance System
(YRBSS), "Youth Online: Comprehensive Results, New York," National Center
for Chronic Disease Prevention and Health Promotion (2008), http://apps
.nccd.cdc.gov/yrbss/CompTableoneLoc.asp?X=1&Loc=NY&Year1=1997&Y
ear2=2007.

77 squandering of antismoking money Campaign for Tobacco-Free Kids, "A
Broken Promise to Our Children: The 1998 State Tobacco Settlement 11 Years
Later," 2009, http://tobaccofreekids.org/reports/settlements/FY2010/State%20
Settlement%20Full%20Report%20FY%202010.pdf.

78 if states spent what the CDC recommended J. A. Tauras et al., "State Tobacco
Control Spending and Youth Smoking," *American Journal of Public Health* 95,
no. 2 (2005): 338–44.

78 themes permitted in the Master Settlement Agreement National Association
of Attorneys General, "The Master Settlement Agreement," http://www.naag
.org/backpages/naag/tobacco/msa/msa-pdf/MSA%20with%20Sig%20Pages%20
and%20Exhibits.pdf/file_view.

79 decline in state funding Campaign for Tobacco-Free Kids, "State Cigarette
Excise Tax Rates & Rankings," 2010, http://www.tobaccofreekids.org/research/
factsheets/pdf/0097.pdf.

79 drop in teen smoking ends http://www.cdc.gov/healthyyouth/yrbs/pdf/yrbs07_us_tobacco_use_trend.pdf.

80 face-to-face programs can work R. Campbell et al., "An Informal School-based Peer-led Intervention for Smoking Prevention in Adolescence (ASSIST): A Cluster Randomised Trial," *The Lancet* 371, no. 9624 (2008): 1595–1602, http://www.thelancet.com/journals/lancet/article/PIIS01406736%2808%29606923/abstract.

82 South Carolina smoking rising again Centers for Disease Control, *Morbidity and Mortality Weekly Report*, June 4, 2010, http://www.cdc.gov/mmwr/pdf/ss/ss5905.pdf, table 29.

88 sponsorship and sobriety Two studies about this phenomenon in twelve-step groups are Byron L. Crape et al., "Effects of Sponsorship in 12-Step Treatment of Injection Drug Users," *Drug and Alcohol Dependence* 65 (2002): 291–301; and Sarah E. Zemore et al., "In 12-step Groups, Helping Helps the Helper," *Addiction* 99, no. 8 (2004); 1015–23. And for the same thing with former prisoners in mentor relationships, see Thomas P. LeBel, "An Examination of the Impact of Formerly Incarcerated Persons Helping Others," *Journal of Offender Rehabilitation* 46, no. 1–2 (2007): 1–24, http://www.jjay.cuny.edu/centersInstitutes/pri/events/41808Examination_FormerlyIncarcerated/Impact%20of%20Formerly%20Incarcerated%20Persons%20Helping%20Others.pdf.

90 Harley-Davidson success Fact Sheet, Harley-Davidson, Inc., http://investor.harley-davidson.com.factsheet.cfm.

93 suicide and contagion James A. Mercy et al., "Is Suicide Contagious? A Study of the Relation Between Exposure to the Suicidal Behavior of Others and Nearly Lethal Suicide Attempts," *American Journal of Epidemiology* 154 (2000): 120–27.

93 Internet radicalization Marc Sageman, *Leaderless Jihad: Terror Networks in the Twenty-First Century* (Philadelphia: University of Pennsylvania Press, 2008), 109.

94 terrorist chat rooms Ibid., 114–23.

94 Internet buddies and health Stanford Professor Emerita Kate Lorig has conducted numerous studies on this issue. See Kate Lorig et al., "Community-Based Peer-Led Diabetes Self-Management: A Randomized Trial," *Diabetes Educator* 35 (2009): 641–51; K. Lorig et al., "The Internet-Based Arthritis Self-Management Program: A One-Year Randomized Trial for Patients with Arthritis or Fibromyalgia," *Arthritis and Rheumatism* 59 (2008): 1009–17; K. Lorig et al., "The Expert Patients Programme Online: A One-Year Study of an Internet-Based Self-Management Programme for People with Long-Term Conditions," *Chronic Illness* 4 (2008): 247–56; K. Lorig et al., "Internet-Based Chronic Disease Self-Management: A Randomized Trial," *Medical Care* 44 (2006): 694–71; K. Lorig et al., "Can a Back Pain E-Mail Discussion Group Improve Health Status and Lower Health Care Costs? A Randomized Study," *Archives of Internal Medicine* 162 (2002): 792–96.

95 Internet buddies and depression Thomas K. Houston et al., "Internet Support Groups for Depression: A 1-Year Prospective Cohort Study," *American Journal of Psychiatry* 159 (2002): 2062–68, http://ajp.psychiatryonline.org/cgi/reprint/159/12/2062.

Five   The Calculus Club

100 minority students' calculus scores Most of the facts about minorities studying calculus at Berkeley and descriptions of Treisman's program come from interviewing him and from several descriptions of his program. They are: Robert E. Fullilove and Philip Uri Treisman, "Mathematics Achievement Among African-American Undergraduates at the University of California, Berkeley: An Evaluation of the Mathematics Workshop Program," *Journal of Negro Education* 59, no. 3 (1990): 463–78. This paper contains detailed data about the program's impact on the calculus grades achieved by black students at Berkeley. Also see a speech given by Treisman, "Teaching Mathematics to a Changing Population: The Professional Development Program at the University of California, Berkeley," reprinted in *Mathematicians and Education Reform: Proceedings of the July 6–8, 1988, Workshop,* Conference Board of the Mathematical Sciences, American Mathematical Society. Another useful speech by Treisman, "Academic Perestroika: Teaching, Learning and the Faculty's Role in Turbulent Times," was delivered March 8, 1990, at California State University, San Bernardino, http://www2.ed.gov/about/offices/list/ope/fipse/perestroika.html. More concise is a paper available from Treisman's office at the Charles Dana Center, University of Texas, Austin: "University of California–Berkeley: The Professional Development Program." There are other resources on the Internet that offer descriptions of Treisman's work and its impact.

100 average calculus grade for black students Jerome Dancis, "Alternate Learning Environment Helps Students Excel in Calculus: A Pedagogical Analysis." Unpublished. http://www-users.math.umd.edu/~jnd/Treisman.txt.

105 Emerging Scholars results at Berkeley The data in these paragraphs and those that follow are from Robert E. Fullilove and Philip Uri Treisman. "Mathematics Achievement Among African-American Undergraduates at the University of California, Berkeley: An Evaluation of the Mathematics Workshop Program."

106 Rose Asera research Rose Asera, "The Math Workshop: A Description," speech reprinted in *Mathematicians and Education Reform: Proceedings of the July 6–8, 1998, Workshop*, Conference Board of the Mathematical Sciences, American Mathematical Society.

108 importance of academic friends Susan Elaine Moreno, "Keeping the Door Open: Latino and African American Friendships as a Resource for University Mathematics Achievement" (PhD diss., The University of Texas at Austin, 2000).

109 **National Bureau of Economic Research paper** Eric P. Bettinger and Bridget Terry Long, "Addressing the Needs of Underprepared Students in Higher Education: Does College Remediation Work?" National Bureau of Economic Research Working Paper no. 11325, May 2005, http://www.nber.org/papers/w11325.

110 **failures of pre-calculus at Berkeley** Treisman, "Academic Perestroika: Teaching, Learning and the Faculty's Role in Turbulent Times."

110 **"stereotype threat"** The Web site www.reducingstereotypethreat.org has a thorough bibliography of studies and interesting discussions of the subject.

110 **Steele and Aronson study** Claude M. Steele and Joshua Aronson, "Stereotype Threat and the Intellectual Test Performance of African Americans," *Journal of Personality and Social Psychology* 69 (1995): 797–811.

111 **Asian women study** Margaret Shih et al., "Stereotype Susceptibility: Identity Salience and Shifts in Quantitative Performance," *Psychological Science* 10 (1999): 80–83.

111 **Rigorous calculus test study** Catherine Good, Joshua Aronson, and Jayne Ann Harder, "Problems in the Pipeline: Stereotype Threat and Women's Achievement in High-Level Math Courses," *Journal of Applied Developmental Psychology* 29 (2008): 17–28.

112 **Obama effect** David M. Marx et al., "The 'Obama Effect': How a Salient Role-Model Reduces Race-Based Performance Differences," *Journal of Experimental Social Psychology* 45 (2009): 953–56.

113 **Berkeley matching study** Steven Chin et al., "Evaluation of a Program to Help Minority Students Succeed at College Math," presentation to the Mathematics Association of America, January 2008.

Six   Angels of Change

125 **microcredit's effects** Evaluating the impact of microcredit has proven much more difficult than people think, in part because it is hard to recruit a control group. Studies of its effects reach a broad range of conclusions. The one most proponents cite is a 2005 study of microcredit in Bangladesh by Shahidur R. Khandker, lead economist in the World Bank Institute's Poverty Reduction and Economic Management Division: Shahidur Khandker, "Microfinance and Poverty: Evidence Using Panel Data from Bangladesh," *The World Bank Economic Review* (2005), http://www.microfinancegateway.org/gm/document-1.9.25680/34361_file_01 .pdf. That study found that microcredit accounted for 40 percent of the entire reduction in moderate poverty in rural Bangladesh—and that it had an even greater impact on extremely poor borrowers than on moderately poor ones. The study found that microcredit raises an entire village's standard of living—even nonborrowers' lives improve. Subsequent studies have found different effects, and more research is needed. Some have not confirmed the World Bank's finding that microcredit lifts the poor out of poverty. Others found that microcredit helps the poor, but not in the way people expect. For example, it solves a cash-flow problem that can devastate families without savings, helping them survive illness or drought. It is certain, however, that poor people place a high value on microcredit. When a new microbanking program arrives in a village, it is usually mobbed—no advertising needed. For a brief discussion of the state of the evidence, see http://www.cgap.org/p/site/c/template.rc/1.26.11415/.

127 Grameen Bank www.grameen.com (note, please, that it is .com, not .org).

131 transformation of Jamkhed Information on the Jamkhed program comes from interviews and from the Aroles' well-written and detailed book: *Jamkhed: A Comprehensive Rural Health Project* (London: Macmillan Education Ltd., 1994). It is available for purchase from the organization by contacting crhp@jamkhed .org, or, in America, from Alex Kaysin at alex@jamkhed.org. For a shorter story about Jamkhed with wonderful photos by Lynn Johnson, see Tina Rosenberg, "Necessary Angels," *National Geographic*, December 2008.

142 India's health statistics www.jamkhed.org.

147 each man's corn as it ripens David Hume, *A Treatise of Human Nature* (New York: Oxford University Press, 2000), 322.

150 XDR-TB *Multidrug and Extensively Drug-Resistant TB (M/XDR-TB): 2010 Global Report on Surveillance and Response*, World Health Organization, 2010, http://whqlibdoc.who.int/publications/2010/9789241599191_eng.pdf.

150 TB in Ukraine World Health Organization, *Treating Tuberculosis in Ukraine*, WHO Web site, www.who.int/features/2004/tb_ukraine/en/.

151 China and tuberculosis The story of China's turnaround on tuberculosis comes from Ruth Levine, "Millions Saved: Proven Success in Global Health," 2004, available for download from the Center for Global Development at http://www.cgdev.org/section/initiatives/_active/millionssaved.

151 AIDS patients in Boston Partners In Health USA/Pact: http://www.pih.org/where/USA/USA.html.

154 patient adherence www.alignmap.com.

155 peer programs for chronic diseases Michele Heisler, "Building Peer Support Programs to Manage Chronic Disease: Seven Models for Success," California HealthCare Foundation, 2006, http://www.familydocs.org/files/Building%20Peer%20Support%20Programs%20CHCF.pdf.

156 benefits to the sponsors See note for "sponsorship and sobriety" in chapter 4.

Seven   A Problem That Has No Name

162 number of megachurches Scott Thumma, Dave Travis, and Warren Bird, *Megachurches Today, 2005 Summary of Research Findings*, Hartford Institute for Religion Research Web site, http://www.hirr.hartsem.edu/megachurch/megas today2005_summaryreport.html.

164 Drucker's three classic questions Peter F. Drucker, *The Practice of Management* (New York: Harper & Row, 1954).

164 Drucker cites Willow Creek Peter F. Drucker, "What Business Can Learn From Nonprofits," *Harvard Business Review* 67 (1989): 88–93.

167 Willow Creek's expansion of small groups When Jim Mellado, now president of the Willow Creek Association, was a student at Harvard Business School, he prepared a series of papers as a case study of Willow Creek's use of business principles to further members' spiritual development. See James Mellado, MBA 1991, Harvard Business School. Case Study: HBS case 9-691-102, rev. February 23, 1999. "Willow Creek Community Church" (A). Also: Willow Creek Community Church (B): "Cracks in the Foundation." HBS case 9-899-123, January 21, 1999. Also: Willow Creek Community Church (C): "Rebuilding the Foundation." HBS case 9-899-124, April 15, 1999.

167 small groups appeared to be a success For a discussion of how Willow Creek fits in with previous megachurches, see Michael S. Hamilton, "Willow Creek's Place in History," *Christianity Today* (November 13, 2000): 62–68.

167 congregational survey "Small Groups at Willow Creek: Analysis of the 2004 Congregation Survey" (unpublished working document of Willow Creek Community Church).

168 small-group leaders survey Results from the Congregation Survey and Group Life Assessment were summarized in "A Future for Community at Willow Creek: Purpose and Impact Beyond Small Groups" (unpublished working document of Willow Creek Community Church, 2005).

169 Reveal Web site http://www.revealnow.com.

171 *Sharing the Journey* Robert Wuthnow, *Sharing the Journey: Support Groups and America's New Quest for Community* (New York: The Free Press, 1994), 6.

176 "get on my camel and go to Bethany" Peter J. Mundey, "The Neo-Parish: Reconstructing Social Space at Willow Creek Community Church" (unpublished senior thesis, Princeton Theological Seminary, 2007).

176 "A modern-day prison" Randy Frazee, *The Connecting Church: Beyond Small Groups to Authentic Community* (Grand Rapids, MI: Zondervan, 2001), 111.

177 *Feminine Mystique* Betty Friedan, *The Feminine Mystique* (New York: W. W. Norton, 1963).

178 *Habits of the Heart* Robert N. Bellah et al., *Habits of the Heart: Individualism and Commitment in American Life* (Berkeley: University of California Press, 1985).

178 *Bowling Alone* Robert D. Putnam, *Bowling Alone: The Collapse and Revival of American Community* (New York: Simon & Schuster, 2000).

178 reasons for the decline in community Ibid.

180 growth of nonprofit sector Amy Blackwood et al., *The Nonprofit Almanac 2008* (Washington, DC: Urban Institute Press, 2008).

181 the happiness paradox There has been much writing lately on the "happiness paradox." Here is the original paper: Richard Easterlin, "Does Economic Growth Improve the Human Lot? Some Empirical Evidence," *Nations and Households in Economic Growth* (New York: Academic Press, 1974), 89–124, http://graphics8 .nytimes.com/images/2008/04/16/business/Easterlin1974.pdf.

181 lottery winners Philip Brickman et al., "Lottery Winners and Accident Victims: Is Happiness Relative?" *Journal of Personality and Social Psychology* 36 (1978): 917–27.

181 activities that make us happy Stephen Bezruchka, "Health, Happiness, Inequality, and Hierarchy," PowerPoint presentation. University of Washington (2009), slides 7–8. http://courses.washington.edu/hserv482/docs/Hserv482-04-Happiness.ppt.

181 don't commute David Halpern, *The Hidden Wealth of Nations* (Cambridge, UK: Polity Press, 2009).

181 the "We Generation" Northwestern Mutual Newsroom Press Release, "New Research on America's Millennials Finds Their Mood 'Eager but Anxious'," July 21, 2004, Northwestern Mutual Life Insurance Company, http://www.northwest ernmutualnews.com/article_display.cfm?article_id=1111.

182 *New Urban News* www.newurbannews.com.

183 EPA study Gabriel Nelson, "'Smart Growth' Taking Hold in U.S. Cities, Study Says," *New York Times*, March 24, 2010.

183 paying more for walkability Christopher B. Leinberger, *The Option of Urbanism: Investing in a New American Dream* (Washington, DC: Island Press, 2009), 97–98.

183 home buyers looking for community Nigel F. Maynard, "Hear Them Roar," *Builder* (July 2009).

183 Orenco Station Robert Steuteville, "New Urban Community Promotes Social Networks and Walking," *New Urban News* 14 (2009).

185 "ambassadors for Christianity" Peter J. Mundey. "The 'Neo-Parish': Willow Creek's Middle Ground Between Small Groups and Mega Worship" (unpublished master's thesis, University of Notre Dame, 2009), 42.

187 "replacing 'small groups' with 'community'" Mundey, "The Neo-Parish, Reconstructing Social Space at Willow Creek Community Church," 14.

203 Hybels on transforming communities David D. Kirkpatrick, "The Evangelical Crackup," *New York Times Magazine*, October 28, 2007.

204 Hybels as possible Democratic Convention speaker Amy Sullivan, *The Party Faithful: How and Why Democrats Are Closing the God Gap* (New York: Scribner, 2008), 134.

204 Hybels critical of evangelical leadership Kirkpatrick, "The Evangelical Crackup."

Eight   The Party

212 "we were completely insane" Most of the information about Otpor comes from interviews I conducted with sixteen Otpor leaders and members from 2007 to 2010 in Belgrade, Novi Sad, New York, and other cities, some on multiple occasions.

213 Chile opposition to Pinochet An expanded essay on the anti-Pinochet movement in Chile can be found in Tina Rosenberg, *Children of Cain: Violence and the Violent in Latin America* (New York: William Morrow, 1991).

216 earlier Serbian protests An excellent analysis of various protest movements is Olena Nikolayenko, "The Learning Curve: Student Protests in Serbia 1991–2000," (paper prepared for Eleventh Annual Graduate Workshop, Kokkalis Program, Harvard University, 2009), http://www.hks.harvard.edu/kokkalis/gsw/2009/Leadership/Nikolayenko%20Paper.pdf.

216 occupation of Belgrade University Another useful account of the 1992 protests can be found in Mirjana Prosic-Dvornic, "Enough! Student Protest '92," *Anthropology of East Europe Review* 11 (1993): 108–16, http://condor.depaul.edu/~rrotenbe/aeer/aeer11_1/prosic-dvornic.html.

216 municipal-election victories "Serbia Opposition Claims Municipal Vote Victory," *New York Times*, November 19, 1996, http://www.nytimes.com/1996/11/19/world/serbia-opposition-claims-municipal-vote-victory.html?pagewanted=1.

217 wild Drašković Dusko Doder and Louise Branson, *Milosevic Portrait of a Tyrant* (New York: Free Press, 1999).

218 Djindjić's friends in heaven and hell Ian Traynor and Dejan Anastasijević, "Death of a Balkan Hero," *The Observer*, March 16, 2003.

218 William Montgomery on Djindjić William Montgomery, "Memories of Zoran Djindjić," B92 Radio, *Opinions,* March 14, 2005, http://www.b92.net/feedback/misljenja/press/djindjic.php.

225 Otpor's first action For this and other important facts and dates, refer to *Chronology of Events: A Brief History of Otpor*, CANVAS, Belgrade, and to CANVAS's legacy Web site: http://www.canvasopedia.org/legacy/content/serbian_case/intro.htm.

225 leaflet message Matthew Collin, *The Time of the Rebels: Youth Resistance Movements and 21st Century Revolutions* (London: Serpent's Tail, 2007), 11.

226 Tabacki interview "Graffiti Is the Only Means of Protest Left," *Danas*, November 14, 1998.

227 depleted uranium shells *Depleted Uranium in Serbia and Montenegro*, United Nations Environment Programme, 2002, http://postconflict.unep.ch/publications/duserbiamont.pdf.

227 civilian deaths in bombing "Civilian Deaths in the NATO Air Campaign," *Human Rights Watch* 12 (February 2000).

237 **heating-oil program** Philip Shenon, "U.S. Backs European Effort to Send Heating Oil to Serbs," *New York Times*, November 2, 1999.
245 **Smederevo arrests** List of Arrested Activists (unpublished Otpor internal document, Belgrade, 2000).

Nine   The Judo of Fear

249 **daily arrests** "Spotlight on Police Crackdown on Otpor," Humanitarian Law Center, Belgrade, 2000.
251 **escape plans** Matthew Collin, *The Time of the Rebels: Youth Resistance Movements and 21st Century Revolutions* (London: Serpent's Tail, 2007), 54.
252 **battlefield cohesion** Wm. Darryl Henderson, *Cohesion: The Human Element in Combat* (Washington, DC: National Defense University Press, 1985), 22–23.
255 **Plan B** Zorana Smiljanić, "Plan B: Using Secondary Protests to Undermine Repression," *New Tactics in Human Rights,* 2003, http://www.newtactics.org/en/PlanB.
262 **Djindjić on the value of Otpor arrests** He is interviewed in Brian Lapping, *The Fall of Milosevic,* BBC documentary, 2003 (DVD).
266 **Otpor threatens opposition** Richard Boudreaux, "Light Touch to Deadly Serious Struggle," *Los Angeles Times,* May 12, 2000.
267 **Djindjić angry at poll** Douglas E. Schoen, *The Power of the Vote: Electing Presidents, Overthrowing Dictators, and Promoting Democracy Around the World* (New York: William Morrow, 2007), 136.
270 **Serbia's election monitors** Joerg Forbrig and Pavol Demeš, eds., *Reclaiming Democracy: Civil Society and Electoral Change in Central and Eastern Europe* (Slovak Republic: The German Marshall Fund of the United States, 2007), 84.
272 **youth turnout** *Exit 2000 Pre-elections Campaigns of NGOs in Serbia*, Non-governmental Organizations for Democratic and Fair Elections, Belgrade, 2001, http://www.centaronline.org/postavljen/60/izlazeng.pdf.
273 **DOS leaders decide to fight back** Dragan Bujosevic and Ivan Radovanovic, *The Fall of Milosevic: The October 5th Revolution* (New York: Palgrave Macmillan, 2003), 29.
275 **Legija exhausts his appeals** "Serbia's Top Court Confirms Maximum Sentences for Milosevic Aides," *Deutsche Welle,* December 25, 2009, http://www.dw-world.de/dw/article/0,,5057281,00.html.
275 **Otpor's mistakes after Milošević's fall** A good analysis of Otpor post-October 5 is Stef Arens, "In the Wake of Authoritarianism" (master's thesis, Utrecht University, 2008).
278 **Otpor goes international** Some of the information about the Georgian and Ukrainian youth movements comes from Collin, *Time of the Rebels.*
280 **CANVAS organization** The Web site is www.canvasopedia.org, but more

information about Otpor is in the "Serbian case" section of CANVAS's old Web site: http://www.canvasopedia.org/legacy/content/serbian_case/intro.htm.
280 computer game *A Force More Powerful: The Game of Nonviolent Strategy.* York Zimmerman Inc., International Center on Nonviolent Conflict and BreakAway Ltd., 2005–6.
282 Albanians Mjaft! movement, www.mjaft.org.

Ten Next

285 Christakis and Fowler study Nicholas A. Christakis and James H. Fowler, "The Spread of Obesity in a Large Social Network over 32 Years," *New England Journal of Medicine* 357 (2007): 370–79.
285 association doesn't mean causality Clive Thompson, "Are Your Friends Making You Fat?" *New York Times Magazine,* September 10, 2009.
286 studies showing groups help diet adherence J. Poulter et al., "Evaluation of Referral to Weight Watchers," *International Journal of Obesity* 31, suppl. 1 (2007): S110; L. Zukley et al., "Regular Meeting Attendance as Part of a Comprehensive Weight-Loss Program Decreases Insulin Resistance and Body Weight," Obesity 14, suppl. (2006): A252; L. Zukley et al., "Regular Attendance Enhances Results in a Comprehensive Weight-Loss Program," *Diabetes* 55, suppl. 1 (2006): A518.
291 African health diaspora Michael A. Clemens and Gunilla Pettersson, "New Data on African Health Professionals Abroad," *Human Resources for Health* 6 (2008): 1.
296 Ohio State study Dana L. Haynie and Danielle C. Payne, "Race, Friendship Networks and Violent Delinquency, *Criminology* 44 (2006): 775–805.
298 Life Learning Academy evaluation http://www.delanccystreetfoundation .org/circle_rep_lla_accomp.php.
299 Benning Terrace meetings Robert L. Woodson, unpublished manuscript, available from the Center for Neighborhood Enterprise, http://www.cneonline .org/pages/homepage.
299 Derrick Ross http://commdocs.house.gov/committees/judiciary/hju62441 .000/hju62441_0f.htm.
301 *The Pact* Drs. Sampson Davis, George Jenkins, and Rameck Hunt, *The Pact* (New York: Riverhead Books, 2002), 2.
303 radicalization of the 9/11 plotters Marc Sageman, *Understanding Terror Networks* (Philadelphia: University of Pennsylvania Press, 2004).
308 radicalized Muslims in Britain Con Coughlin, "British Al-Qaeda Hub 'Is Biggest in West,'" *Daily Telegraph,* January 15, 2010.
310 STREET www.streetonline.org.
311 critique of working with STREET Shiraz Maher and Martyn Frampton,

"Choosing Our Friends Wisely: Criteria for Engagement with Muslim Groups," Policy Exchange, London 2009.

311 **"the sea in which violence swims"** Melanie Phillips, "Persistently Validating Extremism," *Spectator*, March 11, 2009.

311 **Quilliam Foundation** www.quilliamfoundation.org.

313 **Baker PhD dissertation** Abdul-Haqq Baker, "Countering Terrorism in the UK: A Convert Community's Perspective" (unpublished PhD diss., University of Exeter, 2009).

319 **award for STREET** Christopher Warren, "Award for STREET Project," *Streatham Guardian*, February 23, 2009.

321 **Active Change Foundation** www.activechangefoundation.org.

327 **"mood music to which suicide bombers dance"** http://www.guardian.co.uk/politics/video/2009/oct/16/prevent-spying-muslims-mi5.

328 **Hazel Blears** http://www.communities.gov.uk/speeches/corporate/many voices.

331 **Maajid Nawaz's deradicalization** "The Narrative," *60 Minutes*, April 25, 2010.

341 **peers and your electric bill** http://www.opower.com/Products/Home EnergyReport.aspx.

341 **effectiveness of OPOWER** Ian Ayres et al., "Evidence from Two Large Field Experiments that Peer Comparison Feedback Can Reduce Residential Energy Usage" (unpublished working paper, 2009, available at http://papers.ssrn.com/sol3/papers.cfm?abstract_id=1434950. Ayres's blog on behavioral economics is also fun to read: http://islandia.law.yale.edu/ayers/indexhome.htm.

343 **Mexico is middlingly corrupt** "Corruption Perceptions Index 2009," Transparency International, available at http://www.transparency.org/policy_research/surveys_indices/cpi/2009/cpi_2009_table.

344 **defeating corruption** Robert E. Klitgaard, *Controlling Corruption* (Berkeley: University of California Press, 1988).

344 **customs bedlam** Tina Rosenberg, "The Taint of the Greased Palm," *New York Times Magazine*, August 10, 2003.

348 **Berlin Marathon** James C. McKinley, Jr., "For Mexicans, Little Surprise Over Madrazo's Shortcut," *New York Times*, October 10, 2007.

Bibliography

Books

Ackerman, Peter, and Christopher Kruegler, *Strategic Nonviolent Conflict: The Dynamics of People Power in the Twentieth Century*. Westport, CT. Praeger Publishers, 1994.

Arole, Mabelle, and Rajanikant Arole. *Jamkhed: A Comprehensive Rural Health Project*. London: Macmillan Education Ltd., 1994.

Bellah, Robert N., Richard Madsen, William M. Sullivan, Ann Swidler, and Steven M. Tipton. *Habits of the Heart: Individualism and Commitment in American Life*. Berkeley: University of California Press, 1985.

Bujosevic, Dragan, and Ivan Radovanovic. *The Fall of Milosevic: The October 5th Revolution*. New York: Palgrave Macmillan, 2003.

CANVAS. *Strategic Nonviolent Agenda Students Book*. Belgrade: Center for Applied NonViolent Action and Strategies, 2005–2006.

Collin, Matthew. *The Time of the Rebels: Youth Resistance Movements and 21st Century Revolutions*. London: Serpent's Tail, 2007.

Davis, Sampson, George Jenkins, and Rameck Hunt. *The Pact: Three Young Men Make a Promise and Fulfill a Dream*. New York: Riverhead Books, 2002.

Doder, Dusko and Louise Branson. *Milosevic: Portrait of a Tyrant*. New York: Free Press, 1999.

Donahue, Bill, and Russ Robinson. *Building a Church of Small Groups: A Place Where Nobody Stands Alone*. Grand Rapids, MI: Zondervan, 2001.

Festinger, Leon, Henry W. Riecken, and Stanley Schachter. *When Prophecy Fails: A Social and Psychological Study of a Modern Group That Predicted the Destruction of the World*. Minneapolis: University of Minnesota Press, 1956.

Forbrig, Joerg, and Pavol Demeš, eds. *Reclaiming Democracy: Civil Society and Electoral Change in Central and Eastern Europe*. Slovak Republic: The German Marshall Fund of the United States, 2007.

Frazee, Randy. *Making Room for Life: Trading Chaotic Lifestyles for Connected Relationships*. Grand Rapids, MI: Zondervan, 2003.

———. *The Connecting Church: Beyond Small Groups to Authentic Community*. Grand Rapids, MI: Zondervan, 2001.

Friedan, Betty. *The Feminine Mystique*. New York: W. W. Norton, 1963.

Gladwell, Malcolm. *The Tipping Point: How Little Things Can Make a Big Difference*. New York: Little, Brown, 2000.

Glantz, Stanton A., and Edith D. Balbach. *Tobacco War: Inside the California Battles*. Berkeley: University of California Press, 2000.

Harris, Judith Rich. *The Nurture Assumption: Why Children Turn Out the Way They Do*. New York: Touchstone, 1998.

Helvey, Robert L. *On Strategic Nonviolent Conflict: Thinking About the Fundamentals*. Boston: The Albert Einstein Institution, 2004.

Henderson, Wm. Darryl. *Cohesion: The Human Element in Combat*. Washington, DC: National Defense University Press, 1985.

Klitgaard, Robert E. *Controlling Corruption*. Berkeley: University of California Press, 1988.

Laughlin, Henry P. *The Ego and Its Defenses*. New York: Meredith Corporation, 1970.

Milgram, Stanley. *Obedience to Authority: An Experimental View*. New York: HarperCollins, 1974.

Plato. *The Republic*. New York: Penguin Classics, 2007.

Popović, Srdja, Andrej Milivojević, and Slobodan Djinović. *Nonviolent Struggle: 50 Crucial Points*. Belgrade: Center for Applied NonViolent Action and Strategies, 2006.

Putnam, Robert D. *Bowling Alone: The Collapse and Revival of American Community*. New York: Simon & Schuster, 2000.

Sageman, Marc. *Leaderless Jihad: Terror Networks in the Twenty-First Century*. Philadelphia: University of Pennsylvania Press, 2008.

———. *Understanding Terror Networks*. Philadelphia: University of Pennsylvania Press, 2004.

Schock, Kurt. *Unarmed Insurrections: People Power Movements in Nondemocracies*. Minneapolis: University of Minnesota Press, 2005.

Schoen, Douglas E. *The Power of the Vote: Electing Presidents, Overthrowing Dictators, and Promoting Democracy Around the World*. New York: William Morrow, 2007.

Sharp, Gene. *Waging Nonviolent Struggle: 20th Century Practice and 21st Century Potential*. Boston: Extending Horizons Books, 2005.

———. *From Dictatorship to Democracy: A Conceptual Framework for Liberation.* Boston: Albert Einstein Institution, 1993.

———. *Gandhi as a Political Strategist, with Essays on Ethics and Politics.* Manchester, NH: Porter Sargent Publishers, 1979.

———. *The Politics of Nonviolent Action.* Manchester, NH: Porter Sargent Publishers, 1973.

Shisana, O., T. Rehle, L. C. Simbayi, K. Zuma, S. Jooste, V. Pillay-van-Wyk, N. Mbelle, J. Van Zyl, W. Parker, N. P. Zungu, S. Pezi, and the SABSSM III Implementation Team. *South African National HIV Prevalence, Incidence, Behaviour and Communication Survey, 2008: A Turning Tide Among Teenagers?* Cape Town: HSRC Press, 2009.

Tavris, Carol, and Elliot Aronson. *Mistakes Were Made (but not by me).* Orlando, FL: Harcourt, 2007.

Teerlink, Rich, and Lee Ozley. *More Than a Motorcycle: The Leadership Journey at Harley-Davidson.* Boston: Harvard Business School Press, 2000.

Wuthnow, Robert. *Sharing the Journey: Support Groups and America's New Quest for Community.* New York: The Free Press, 1994.

———. ed. *"I Come Away Stronger": How Small Groups are Shaping American Religion.* Grand Rapids, MI: William B. Eerdmans Publishing Company, 1994.

Journal Articles

Albarracin, Dolores, Jeffrey Gillette, Allison Earl, Laura Glasman, Marta Durantini, and Moon-Ho Ho. "A Test of Major Assumptions About Behavior Change: A Comprehensive Look at the Effects of Passive and Active HIV-Prevention Interventions Since the Beginning of the Epidemic." *Psychological Bulletin* 131 (2005): 856–97.

Asch, Solomon, "Studies of Independence and Conformity: A Minority of One Against a Unanimous Majority." *Psychological Monographs* 70 (1956).

Centers for Disease Control and Prevention, "Changes in the Cigarette Brand Preference of Adolescent Smokers, U.S. 1989–1993." *Morbidity and Morality Report* 43 (August 19, 1994): 577–81.

Chou, Shin-Yi, Inas Rashad, and Michael Grossman. "Fast Food Restaurant Advertising on Television and Its Influence on Childhood Obesity." *Journal of Law and Economics* 51 (2008): 599–618.

Christakis, Nicholas, and James H. Fowler. "The Spread of Obesity in a Large Social Network over 32 Years." *New England Journal of Medicine* 357 (2007): 370–79.

Crape, Byron L., Carl A. Latkin, Alexandra S. Laris, and Amy R. Knowlton.

"Effects of Sponsorship in 12-Step Treatment of Injection Drug Users." *Drug and Alcohol Dependence* 65 (2002): 291–301.

Dansinger, Michael L., J. A. Gleason, J. L. Griffith, H. P. Selker, and E. J. Schaefer. "Comparison of the Atkins, Ornish, Weight Watchers, and Zone Diets for Weight Loss and Heart Disease Risk Reduction," *Journal of the American Medical Association* 293 (2005): 43–53.

Fischer, Paul M., Meyer P. Schwartz, John W. Richards, Jr., Adam O. Goldstein, and Tina H. Rojas. "Brand Logo Recognition by Children Aged 3 to 6 Years: Mickey Mouse and Old Joe the Camel." *Journal of the American Medical Association* 22 (1991): 3145–48.

Fullilove, Robert E., and Philip Uri Treisman. "Mathematics Achievement Among African-American Undergraduates at the University of California, Berkeley: An Evaluation of the Mathematics Workshop Program." *Journal of Negro Education* 59 (1990): 463–78.

Good, Catherine, Joshua Aronson, and Jayne Ann Harder. "Problems in the Pipeline: Stereotype Threat and Women's Achievement in High-Level Math Courses." *Journal of Applied Developmental Psychology* 29 (2008): 17–28.

Haynie, Dana L., and Danielle C. Payne, "Race, Friendship Networks and Violent Delinquency." *Criminology* 44 (2006): 775–805.

Kahn, Michael. "The Physiology of Catharsis." *Journal of Personality and Social Psychology* 3 (1966): 278–86.

Lorig, Kate, Philip L. Ritter, Frank J. Villa, and Jean Armas. "Community-Based Peer-Led Diabetes Self-Management: A Randomized Trial." *Diabetes Educator* 35 (2009): 641–51.

Lorig, Kate, Philip L. Ritter, Diana D. Laurent, and Kathryn Plant. "The Internet-Based Arthritis Self-Management Program: A One-Year Randomized Trial for Patients with Arthritis or Fibromyalgia." *Arthritis and Rheumatism* 59 (2008): 1009–17.

Lorig, Kate, Philip L. Ritter, Ayesha Dost, Kathryn Plant, Diana D. Laurent, and Ian McNeil. "The Expert Patients Programme Online: A One-Year Study of an Internet-Based Self-Management Programme for People with Long-Term Conditions." *Chronic Illness* 4 (2008): 247–56.

Lorig, Kate, Philip L. Ritter, Diana D. Laurent, and Kathryn Plant. "Internet-Based Chronic Disease Self-Management: A Randomized Trial." *Medical Care* 44 (2006): 694–71.

Lorig, Kate, Diana D. Lauren, Richard A. Deyo, Margaret E. Marnell, Marian A. Minor, Philip L. Ritter. "Can a Back Pain E-Mail Discussion Group Improve Health Status and Lower Health Care Costs? A Randomized Study." *Archives of Internal Medicine* 162 (2002): 792–96.

Mann, Vera, Alex Eble, Chris Frost, Ramaswamy Premkumar, and Peter Boone. "Retrospective Comparative Evaluation of the Lasting Impact of a Community-Based Primary Health Care Programme on Under-5 Mortality in Villages Around Tamkhed, India." *Bulletin of the World Health Organization* 88 (2010) 727–36.

Marx, David M., Ray Friedman, and Sei Jin Ko. "The 'Obama Effect': How a Salient Role-Model Reduces Race-Based Performance Differences." *Journal of Experimental Social Psychology* 45 (2009): 953–56.

Milgram, Stanley. "Behavioral Study of Obedience." *The Journal of Abnormal and Social Psychology* 67 (1963): 371–78.

Pettifor, Audrey E. Helen V. Rees, Immo Kleinschmidt, Annie E. Steffenson, Catherine MacPhail, Lindiwe Hlongwa-Madikizela, Kerry Vermaak, Nancy S. Padian. "Young People's Sexual Health in South Africa: HIV Prevalence and Sexual Behaviors from a Nationally Representative Household Survey." *AIDS* 19, no. 14 (2005): 1525–34.

Pierce, John P., Lora Lee, and Elizabeth A. Gilpin. "Smoking Initiation by Adolescent Girls, 1944 through 1988: An Association with Targeted Advertising." *Journal of the American Medical Association* 271 (1994): 608–11.

Poulter, L., and P. Hunt, "Evaluation of Referral to Weight Watchers." International *Journal of Obesity* 31, suppl. 1 (2007): S110.

Prosic-Dvornic, Mirjana. "Enough! Student Protest '92." *Anthropology of East Europe Review* 11 (1993), http://condor.depaul.edu/~rrotenbe/aeer/aeer11_1/prosic-dvornic.html.

Robinson, Thomas N., Dina L. G. Borzekowski, Donna M. Matheson, and Helena C. Kraemer. "Effects of Fast Food Branding on Young Children's Taste Preferences." *Pediatrics & Adolescent Medicine* 161 (2007): 792–97.

Shih, Margaret, Todd L. Pittinsky, and Nalini Ambady, "Stereotype Susceptibility: Identity Salience and Shifts in Quantitative Performance," *Psychological Science* 10 (1999): 80–83.

Steele, Claude M., and Joshua Aronson. "Stereotype Threat and the Intellectual Test Performance of African Americans." Journal of Personality and Social *Psychology* 69 (1995): 797–811.

Trivers, Robert. "The Elements of a Scientific Theory of Self-Deception." *Annals of the New York Academy of Sciences* 907 (2000): 114–31.

Wakefield, Melanie, Yvonne Terry-McElrath, Sherry Emery, Henry Saffer, Frank J. Chaloupka, Glen Szczypka, Brian Flay, Patrick M. O'Malley, and Lloyd D. Johnston. "Effect of Televised, Tobacco Company–Funded Smoking Prevention Advertising on Youth Smoking–Related Beliefs, Intentions, and Behavior." *American Journal of Public Health* 96 (2006): 2154–60.

Zimbardo, Philip. "The Human Choice: Individuation, Reason, and Order Versus Deindividuation, Impulse, and Chaos." *Nebraska Symposium on Motivation* 17 (1969): 237–307.

Zukley, L., V. Nguyen, A. Summers, M. Paul, J. Brosnahan, R. Alvarado, J. Lowndes, N. Meade, D. Knapp, T. J. Angelopoulos, and J. M. Rippe. "Regular Meeting Attendance as Part of a Comprehensive Weight-Loss Program Decreases Insulin Resistance and Body Weight." *Obesity* 14 (2006): A252.

Zukley, L., J. Lowndes, V. Nguyen, T. Angelopoulos, and J. M. Rippe. "Regular Attendance Enhances Results in a Comprehensive Weight-Loss Program." *Diabetes* 55, suppl. 1 (2006): A518.

Magazine and Newspaper Articles

Gillmor, Verla. "Community Is Their Middle Name." *Christianity Today*, November 13, 2000.

Hamilton, Michael S. "Willow Creek's Place in History." *Christianity Today*, November 13, 2000.

Rosenberg, Tina. "The Taint of the Greased Palm," *New York Times Magazine*, August 10, 2003.

Rosenberg, Tina. "When a Pill Is Not Enough." *New York Times Magazine*, August 6, 2006.

Rosenberg, Tina. "Necessary Angels." *National Geographic*, December 2008.

Thompson, Clive. "Are Your Friends Making You Fat?" *New York Times Magazine*, September 10, 2009.

Winner, Lauren F. "The Man Behind the Megachurch." *Christianity Today*, November 13, 2000.

Online Articles and Other Sources

Campaign for Tobacco-Free Kids. "A Broken Promise to Our Children: The 1998 State Tobacco Settlement 11 Years Later," 2009, http://www.tobacco-freekids.org/reports/settlements/FY2010/State%20Settlement%20Full%20Report%20FY%202010.pdf.

———"State Cigarette Excise Tax Rates & Rankings" (2010), http://www.tobaccofreekids.org/research/factsheets/pdf/0097.pdf.

loveLife. Melmoth Report: An Assessment of Effects Associated with loveLife's Intervention. 2007, http://www.lovelife.org.za/corporate/research/.

National Association of Attorneys General. "The Master Settlement Agreement," http://www.naag.org/backpages/naag/tobacco/msa/msa-pdf/MSA%20with%20Sig%20Pages%20and%20Exhibits.pdf/file_view.

"2008 National Antenatal Sentinel HIV & Syphilis Prevalence Survey." South Africa Report. National Department of Health. September 2009, http://www.info.gov.za/view/DownloadFileAction?id=109007.

U.S. Department of Health and Human Services. "Preventing Tobacco Use Among Young People: A Report of the Surgeon General." National Center for Chronic Disease Prevention and Health Promotion, Office on Smoking and Health, 1994, http://profiles.nlm.nih.gov/NN/B/C/F/T/_/nnbcft.pdf.

University of Miami. "Youth Tobacco Prevention in Florida: An Independent Evaluation of the Florida Tobacco Pilot Program." Prepared for the Florida Department of Health, December 15, 1999, http://www.doh.state.fl.us/DISEASE_CTRL/EPI/Smoking/reports/eval.pdf.

PowerPoint Programs, Unpublished
Academic Papers, DVDs, etc.

Arens, Stef. "In the Wake of Authoritarianism." Unpublished master's thesis, Utrecht University, 2008.

A Force More Powerful. DVD. Dir. Steve York. York Zimmerman Inc., 2000.

A Force More Powerful: The Game of Nonviolent Strategy. York Zimmerman Inc. International Center on Nonviolent Conflict and BreakAway Ltd. 2005–2006. Computer game.

Ayres, Ian, Sophie Raseman, and Alice Shih. "Evidence from Two Large Field Experiments that Peer Comparison Feedback Can Reduce Residential Energy Usage." Unpublished working paper, 2009, http://papers.ssrn.com/sol3/papers.cfm?abstract_id=1434950.

Baker, Abdul-Haqq. "Countering Terrorism in the UK: A Convert Community's Perspective." Unpublished PhD diss., University of Exeter, 2009.

Bettinger, Eric P., and Bridget Terry Long. "Addressing the Needs of Underprepared Students in Higher Education: Does College Remediation Work?" National Bureau of Economic Research Working Paper no. 11325, May 2005, http://www.nber.org/papers/w11325.

Bezruchka, Stephen. "Health, Happiness, Inequality and Hierarchy." University of Washington, 2009. http://courses.washington.edu/hserv482/docs/Hserv482-04-Happiness.ppt.

Bringing Down a Dictator. DVD. Directed by Steve York. York Zimmerman Inc., 2001.

Harrison, David, Linda Richter, and Chris Desmond, "Changing Perception of Opportunity: The link between structural and behaviour change interventions for HIV prevention." Unpublished, Johannesburg, 2009.

Heisler, Michele. "Building Peer Support Programs to Manage Chronic Disease: Seven Models for Success." California HealthCare Foundation, 2006, http://www.familydocs.org/files/Building%20Peer%20Support%20Programs%20CHCF.pdf.

Levine, Ruth. "Millions Saved: Proven Success in Global Health." Center for Global Development, 2004, http://www.cgdev.org/section/initiatives/_active/millionssaved.

Maher, Shiraz, et al. "Choosing Our Friends Wisely: Criteria for Engagement with Muslim Groups." Policy Exchange, London, 2009.

Mellado, James. MBA 1991. Harvard Business School. Case Study. HBS case 9-691-102, rev. February 23, 1999. "Willow Creek Community Church" (A). Willow Creek Community Church (B): "Cracks in the Foundation." HBS case 9-899-123, January 21, 1999. Willow Creek Community Church (C): "Rebuilding Foundation." HBS case 9-899-124, April 15, 1999.

Moreno, Susan Elaine. "Keeping the Door Open: Latino and African American

Friendships as a Resource for University Mathematics Achievement," PhD diss., The University of Texas at Austin, 2000.

Mundey, Peter J. "The Neo-Parish: Reconstructing Social Space at Willow Creek Community Church." Unpublished senior thesis, Princeton Theological Seminary, 2007.

———. "The 'Neo-Parish': Willow Creek's Middle Ground Between Small Groups and Mega Worship." Unpublished master's thesis, University of Notre Dame, 2009.

Nikolayenko, Olena. "The Learning Curve: Student Protests in Serbia 1999–2000." Paper prepared for Eleventh Annual Graduate Workshop, Kokkalis Program, Harvard University (2009), http://www.hks.harvard.edu/kokka lis/gsw/2009/Leadership/Nikolayenko%20Paper.pdf.

Pierce, John P. "Tobacco Use in California: An Evaluation of the Tobacco Control Program, 1989–1993." California Department of Health Services Report, 1994: 60, http://libraries.ucsd.edu/ssds/pub/CTS/cpc00003/final rpt1993.pdf.

"Small Groups at Willow Creek: Analysis of the 2004 Congregation Survey." PowerPoint presentation slides.

"Spotlight On Police Crackdown on Otpor," Humanitarian Law Center Belgrade, 2000.

Treisman, Philip Uri. "A Study of Mathematics Performance of Black Students at the University of California, Berkeley." *Issues in Mathematics Education: Mathematicians and Education Reform*. Proceedings of the July 6–8, 1988, Workshop, Conference Board of the Mathematical Sciences, American Mathematical Society.

———. "Academic Perestroika: Teaching, Learning, and the Faculty's Role in Turbulent Times." Lecture given on March 8, 1990, at California State University, San Bernardino. Transcript edited for publication by Joel Nossoff.

Web Sites

The Albert Einstein Institution: www.aeinstein.org

Active Change Foundation: www.activechangefoundation.org

Alcoholics Anonymous: www.aa.org

Align Map www.alignmap.com

Alliance of Concerned Men: www.allianceofconcernedmen.com

American Legacy Foundation: www.legacyforhealth.org

Campaign for Tobacco-Free Kids: www.tobaccofreekids.org

CANVAS: www.canvasopedia.org and www.canvasopedia.org/legacy

Delancey Street: www.delanceystreetfoundation.org

The Fortune Society: www.fortunesociety.org

Grameen Bank: www.grameen.com
Harley Owners Group: www.harley-davidson.com
Jamkhed: www.jamkhed.org
Kiva: www.kiva.org
loveLife: www.lovelife.org.za
Mjaft!: www.mjaft.org
New Urban News: www.newurbannews.com
OPOWER: www.opower.com
Partners in Health: www.pih.org
PEERtrainer: www.peertrainer.com
The Quilliam Foundation: www.quilliamfoundation.org
Rage Against the Haze: www.facebook.com/RAGESC
Reducing Stereotype Threat: www.reducingstereotypethreat.org
Reveal: www.rcvcalnow.com
STREET: www.streetonline.org
SWAT: www.swatfl.org
Transparency International: www.transparency.org
Truth: www.thetruth.com
Willow Creek Community Church: www.willowcreek.org
World Bank Consultative Group to Assist the Poor: www.cgap.org

Index

abortion, 204
  selective, 40–41, 130, 292
Abu Hamza, 308, 310, 317, 325–26
Acción International, 127
accountability, 95, 161, 171, 175, 194,
  195–96, 286, 295
Active Change Foundation, 321–23
ACT UP!, 4
Adams, Tom, 67, 72
addictions, 151–53, 162
  cigarette, 58–59, 65–66
  drug, 24, 220, 277, 293, 299, 330
  genetic predisposition to, 26
advertising and marketing, xxii, 2, 5,
  6, 29–31, 41, 44, 48–50, 51, 63–90,
  224, 234–35
  antidrug, 63–64
  counterproductive, social norms in,
   46–48, 60–61
  credibility in, 49–50, 60
  experiential, 83, 88–90
  face-to-face, 55–56, 80, 81, 89
  identity, 85–87
  junk-food, 29–30
  public service, 47–48
  Sprite, xix, 5, 7
  techniques of, 83–90
  tobacco industry, 29, 30–31, 50,
   58–59, 61, 64–66, 68, 77, 88
  word-of-mouth, 83, 86–88
  see also antismoking programs,
   advertising of; billboards

affirmative action, 101, 113, 116–21
Afghanistan, 321–22
  mujahideen of, 93, 302
African American college students, xvii,
  xxiii, 97–123
  reasons for failures of, 97, 100–104,
   112–13, 121
  solitary study habits of, 102–4, 106–
   7, 113, 121–23
  stereotype threat and, 110–12
  see also Emerging Scholars program
African Americans, 46, 65
  of Salem Baptist Church, 203–4
  youth criminality of, 296
Agency for International Development,
  Office of Transition Initiatives
  (OTI) of, 236–37
Agincourt, Battle of, xxi–xxii
AIDS, 1–20, 36, 204
  ABC message for, 8
  access to services for, 45, 46
  antiretroviral treatment of, 12,
   15–16, 18–19, 44, 45–46, 138,
   151–52, 157, 288
  circumcision as protective factor in,
   3, 10, 16
  monogamy and, 1
  patient adherence to treatment of,
   44, 45–46, 288
  red ribbon symbol of, 2, 3, 5
  safe sex and, xvii, xix, 1, 2, 6–7, 8,
   9–10, 11–12, 43, 44

AIDS (*continued*)
  tuberculosis and, 149
  see also HIV virus; South Africa,
    AIDS in
AIDS prevention programs, 2, 4, 5, 6–7,
    48, 58
  see also loveLife
Albania, 220, 227, 228, 232
  Mjaft! in, 282
Albarracin, Dolores, 48
Albert Einstein Institution, 262, 337
Albright, Madeleine, 236–37, 238, 239
Alcoholics Anonymous (AA), xxi,
    88, 121, 122, 152–53, 154, 162,
    284–85, 292
alcoholism, 26, 46, 122, 152, 220, 277
Allende, Salvador, 337
Alliance of Concerned Men, 299–300,
    301
Al Qaeda, 302–3, 306, 308, 316, 326
Al Quds Mosque, 303
American Cancer Society, 77
American Journal of Epidemiology, 93
American Journal of Public Health,
    31, 78
American Legacy Foundation, 76
  Lorillard lawsuit against, 78–79
American Neurological Association, 26
Amte, Leelabai, 141, 142–45
amygdala, 25
Andrić, Ivan, 212, 241, 264
  on Milošević's hit list, 228
  parliamentary seat won by, 275, 277
  secret police and, 250–51
  Vreme Je campaign run by, 270
Angelus Temple, 162
anger, 300
  Muslim, 304–5, 307, 319, 329–30,
    331
  venting of, 25
anosognosia, 26–27
antiretroviral drugs, 12, 15–16, 18–19,
    44, 45–46, 138, 151–52, 157, 288
antismoking programs, xvii, 48, 50–62,
    63–83, 292, 342
  beliefs linked to smoking rates in, 75
  of California, 30–31, 61, 62, 64–66,
    68, 80–81
  marijuana in, 49

Master Settlement Agreement money
    in, 54, 55, 74, 76, 77, 78, 82–83
  public health officials and, 60–62,
    64, 83
  school power groups and, 80–81
  see also cigarettes; Florida,
    antismoking program of; Rage
    Against the Haze
antismoking programs, advertising of,
    55–56, 58, 59–62, 64–75, 76
  in branding, 67, 70, 84
  cessation, 67–68
  children-designed, 60–61
  credibility of, 49, 60
  "Dog Walker" ad in, 79
  "I Care" campaign of, 74–75
  ineffective, health effects in, 48, 50,
    59–60, 61–62, 64, 65, 67, 69, 74–75,
    77, 78, 82, 83
  romantic rejection strategy in, 67
  teen-designed campaign in, 69–71
  tobacco companies as targets of,
    50–57, 65–66, 68, 69–75, 81
Appel, Gene, 172
Arizona:
  antismoking program of, 60, 61
  Petrified Forest National Park of,
    47
Arizona State University, 47
Arkan, 224
Arlington, Tex., 171–77
Armendariz, Efraim, 118
Arole, Raj and Mabelle, xxiii, 131–38,
    141, 144, 290–91
Arole, Shobha, xvi, 136
Aronson, Elliot, 24
Aronson, Joshua, 110–12
Asch, Solomon, 31–32
Asera, Rose, 106
Asian college students, 101, 102–4, 105,
    109, 111, 113, 119, 122
Association of Independent Electronic
    Media, 225–26
Association of Midnight Basketball
    Leagues, 298
astronauts, 277
Atta, Mohamed, 303–4
Auch, Tim and Michele, xii–xiii, xiv,
    192–200

Australia, 344
authority, obedience to, 32–33
Ayers, Emily, 53, 57
Ayres, Ian, 342

Baader-Meinhof Gang, 306
Baker, Abdul Haqq (Anthony), 308–21,
    326, 328–30, 331
Bal, Dileep, 64
Baldwin, Wis., 201
Bangladesh, 126–29, 149, 154, 323,
    363n–64n
banking industry, 127–30
Bauer, Ursula, 72
Beach, Nancy, 203–4, 206
beggars, no-interest loans for, 127
Behforouz, Heidi, 152
Belarus, 280, 333, 334–35
Belgrade University, xvii, xxii, 216,
    218–19, 225, 236, 244
Bellah, Robert N., 178
Benning Terrace, 298–301, 324
Benning Terrace Youth Opportunities,
    300–301
Berlin Marathon, 348
Berrizbeitia, Ana, 108
Bettinger, Eric P., 109, 112
bhishi scheme, 145
billboards, 2, 9, 59, 70, 267
    "AIDS Kills," 48
    loveLife, 6, 14, 30
bin Laden, Osama, 304, 315
Blagojević, Marko, 278
Blair, Tony, 296
Blears, Hazel, 328
Blic, 225, 233–34, 264
Bloomberg, Michael, 76
BOG (bunch-of-guys) theory of
    terrorism, 306
Boldt, Ryan, xi, 170, 189–90, 195, 201–
    2, 205–6, 210
Bolivia, 344
Borate, Nandabai Kantilal, 146
Bosnia, 216, 218, 227, 238, 253, 305
Boston, Mass., 288
    Partners in Health in, 151–52,
    156–57
Boston University, 33
Botswana, 3, 12

Bowling Alone: The Collapse and
    Revival of American Community
    (Putnam), 178–79
boycotts, 340–41
Boy Scouts of America, 69
brain, 25–27
    abnormal sexual behavior and, 26
    maturation of, 25
    serotonin levels of, 26
    social functioning and, 31
Brains on Fire advertising agency, 55,
    56, 82
branding, 29, 62, 63, 83
    in antismoking advertising, 67, 70,
    84
    cult, 89–90
    of loveLife, 5, 6, 14, 84–85
    of Otpor, 223–24, 263, 269–70, 277,
    282
    self-, xviii–xix
    typography style in, 70, 84
Branigan, Laura, 8
Branson, Richard, 9
Brixton Mosque and Cultural Center,
    308–21, 326, 328–29, 331; see also
    STREET
broken window theory, 34
Brown, Peggy, 286–87
Brunel, Frederic, 33
Bulldozer Revolution, 274, 278
Burma, 262, 280, 334–35
Bush, Jeb, 73, 74

calculus clubs, xxiii, 96, 97–123, 135,
    153–54, 289–90, 292–93
    see also Emerging Scholars program
calculus jokes, 108
California, 3, 34, 63, 69
    antismoking programs of, 30–31, 61,
    62, 64–66, 68, 80–81
    Health Services Department of, 64,
    68
    "industry manipulation" ad theme
    of, 65–66, 68, 70, 71
    Latino Health Access of, 156
    Proposition 99 of, 64
    Proposition 209 of, 119
California, University of, at Berkeley,
    xxiii, 98, 100–104, 121–22

California, University of, at Berkeley
(*continued*)
affirmative action at, 113, 116,
119–20
remediation at, 110
California, University of, at Los
Angeles, 109
California, University of, at San Diego,
26, 80–81, 285
California, University of, at San
Francisco, 64
Calingaert, Daniel, 237–38
Camel cigarettes, 30–31, 58, 68, 84
Campaign for Tobacco-Free Kids, 80
Canada, 306
CANVAS (Center for Applied
NonViolent Action and Strategies),
278–82, 332–36
teachings of, 281–82
trainers of, 281
workshops of, 280–81
Carnegie Foundation for the
Advancement of Teaching, 106
Carow, Amy, 286–87
Cary-Grove Neighborhood Life, 207
catalysts, 130–47
catharsis, 25
Cave, Plato's Allegory of, 34–35
Ceca, 224
Cedar Revolution, 332
Center for Criminal Justice Research,
297
Center for Free Elections and
Democracy, 270, 278
Center for Neighborhood Enterprise,
299
Center for Nonviolent Resistance, 279
Centers for Disease Control and
Prevention (CDC), 46, 54, 58, 60,
62, 67–68, 78, 82
Century City, Calif., 63
Cevallos, Albert, 236–37
Chávez, Hugo, 333
Chicago Marathon, 205
childhood obesity, 29–30
state campaigns against, 77
child molestation, 26
children, 39, 78, 148, 183, 289
antismoking ads designed by, 60–61

Joe Camel as appealing to, 58
marketing food to, 29–30
Chile, 213–16, 220, 247, 252, 265, 277,
336, 337
Chiles, Lawton, 67, 68, 73
Chin, Steven, 119–20
China, 149, 151
Chinese Americans, 102–4, 122
"Choosing Our Friends Wisely" (Policy
Exchange), 311, 327
Christakis, Nicholas, 285–86, 288
Church, Geno, 55, 82
churches, 159–210
fellowship of, 165
reasons for nonattendance at, 163
small groups in, 160–61, 165–66,
171–77
traditional neighborhood, 159, 165
see also Willow Creek Community
Church
Cialdini, Robert, 33–34, 47–48, 76–77,
341–42
cigarettes, 43, 48, 50–62, 63–83
addiction to, 58–59, 65–66
advertising of, 29, 30–31, 50, 58–59,
61, 64–66, 68, 77, 88
identity marketing of, 85, 86
menthol, 65
prices of, 79
state taxes on, 54, 62, 64, 66, 76, 78,
79, 81
urea in, 79
warnings on packs of, 67
"women's," 58
see also antismoking programs;
smoking; tobacco companies
Cincinnati, University of, 297
circumcision, 3, 10, 16
City University of New York, 113
Civic Initiatives, 262
clenched fist logo, 222–23, 225–26, 232,
234–35, 269–70, 271, 277, 278, 280,
333
Cleveland Veterans Affairs Medical
Center, 155–56
Clinton, Bill, 204, 265
cognitive dissonance, 23–25, 88, 317
*Cohesion: The Human Element in
Combat* (Henderson), 252

Color Revolutions, 278–79, 333
Columbia University, 110
community, 89, 157–58, 159–210, 292–97
    accountability in, 161, 171, 175, 194, 195–96
    biblical mandates for, 176, 188, 200
    characteristics of, 175
    churches as, 159, 160–62, 165; see also Willow Creek Community Church
    conflicts in, 196
    decline of, 177–84
    Internet in, 180, 181
    New Urban suburbs as, 182–84
    openness in, 195, 196–97, 199–200
    proximity as, 172, 175, 176–77
    recent emphasis on, 181–84
    risking speaking out in, 196–97
    spiritual transformation in, 195–200, 209–10
    time pressures and, 178, 179–80, 189–90, 191–92
    unwanted associations included in, 190–91
community colleges, 109–10
community health workers, 156, 288–89
    see also Jamkhed village-health-worker program
compulsive gambling, 26
computer games, 280
condoms, xix, 1, 2, 8, 9–10, 11, 12–13, 33, 43, 45, 48
Connecting Church, The (Frazee), 171, 175
consumer-generated media, 87–88
Controlling Corruption (Klitgaard), 344
coolness factor, 6, 71, 76, 78–79, 80–81, 84–87, 290, 342
    of Otpor, 223–24, 229, 256–58, 260, 276
Corax, 277
Cornwall, Simon, 314, 319, 322, 330
corruption, 339, 340, 343–49
Cozza, Matt, 87
Crawford, Jaron, 107
crime, criminal behaviors, 26, 40, 330
    bad peer groups in, 292–302

declining rate of, 34, 297
    Islamic extremist justification of, 307, 320–21
    neighborhood's influence on, 34
    organized, 218, 223–24, 244, 269, 274, 276
    see also gang membership; prisoner reentry into society
Crispin Porter + Bogusky, 67, 69, 71, 72, 76, 84, 86
Croatia, 216, 227, 270, 336
cult brands, 89–90
cults, 8
    doomsday, 23–24
cults of personality, 239–40, 242
Ćuruvija, Slavko, 226, 227–28

Dalit (Untouchable) caste, xiv–xvii, 36–42, 126, 130, 131, 133, 135–36, 137, 139–40, 142, 146–47
Danas, 226
    Corax cartoon in, 277
Daniels, David, 175–76, 191
Dannelly, Joe, 52–53, 55, 56
Danskin Triathlon, 286–87
Darfur, 339–40
Davis, Sampson, 301–2
Dawkins, Richard, 27
Deconstruct Program, 313, 316–17
defense mechanisms, ego, 22–26, 27, 35
Delancey Street program, 294–96, 298
Delaware, 79
democracy movements, xvii–xviii, xix, 211–48, 263, 278–82, 332–39
    in Burma, 262
    in Chile, 213–16, 220
    Color Revolutions of, 278–79, 333
    planning of, 216, 217
    see also CANVAS; Otpor
Democratic Convention (2004), 204
denial, xviii, 22–23, 46
    physiological roots of, 26–27
depleted uranium, 227
depression, 152, 220
Deukmejian, George, 64
diabetes, 46, 142, 152, 155–56
dialysis patients, 156
DiCaprio, Leonardo, 67

dictatorships, 211–48, 249–82, 332–37
  in Chile, 213–16, 220, 249, 252, 265,
    277, 336, 337
  consent of the governed needed by,
    263
  elections held by, 265
  see also Serbia
dilemma actions, 230–31, 282, 338–39
displacement, 22
Djindjić, Zoran, 216–18, 219, 221, 228,
    229, 262, 271, 278
  assassination of, 217, 275, 276
  DOS and, 266, 267–69
  government campaign against, 240
  Milošević arrested by, 274–75
  parallel vote count established by,
    270, 272
  personality cult of, 240
  personality of, 217–18
  as prime minister, 267–68, 274–75
  security forces targeted by, 268,
    272–74
  U.S. funding accepted by, 269
Djinović, Slobodan, 222, 241, 278
  in CANVAS, 279–80, 281, 332
  telecommunications company of,
    281
  Vreme Je campaign run by, 270
Dlamini, Gugu, 4, 35
Dnevni Telegraf, 226, 227–28
"Dog Walker" antismoking
    advertisement, 79
Donahue, Bill, 163–64, 167, 171–72,
    188, 191–92, 340
doomsday cult, 23–24
dopamine agonists, 26
Dorrah, George, 54
DOS (Democratic Opposition of
    Serbia), 265–69, 270, 273
DOTS (directly observed treatment,
    short-course), 150–52, 155, 213,
    288–89
Dozet, Vesna, 244
Drašković, Vuk, 216–17, 218, 219, 225,
    228, 240, 265–66, 268, 271, 273
Drucker, Peter, 164–65, 185
drug addiction, 24, 220, 277, 293, 299,
    330
drug resistance, 44, 150

drugs:
  antiretroviral, 12, 15–16, 18–19, 44,
    45–46, 138, 151–52, 157
  dopamine agonists, 26
  nevirapine, 23, 45, 46
  patient adherence to regimens of, see
    patient adherence
Duck Soup, 32
Dunn, Sue, 206–9, 210

economic factors, 10, 37, 130, 215, 220,
    227
Ego and Its Defenses, The (Laughlin),
    22
ego defenses, 22–26, 27, 35
  maturation and, 25
Egypt, 280, 330–31
Eichmann, Adolf, 32
electric bills, 341–42
"Elements of a Scientific Theory of Self-
    Deception, The" (Trivers), 28
el-Faisal, Abdullah, 308–9, 310, 311–12,
    326
El Salvador, 274
Emerging Scholars program, 97–123,
    153–54, 289–90
  academic friendships developed in,
    104, 107–8
  affirmative action and, 101, 113,
    116–21
  costs of, 114, 115
  dearth of, 114–16
  discussion sections of, 98–99, 104–8
  math SAT scores and, 100, 101, 105,
    113, 120
  number of, 114
  obstacles to, 114–16
  remediation vs., see remediation
  rural students in, 114, 116, 118–19
  student assistants of, 98, 106, 114
  study habits and, 102–4, 106–7, 114,
    121–23, 132, 135
  teaching assistants in, 98–99, 104–5,
    106, 107, 114
  traditional discussion sections vs.,
    98, 103, 106, 113–14
  value of, 113–14, 115, 120–21
  women in, 108, 114, 116
endorphins, 25

Environmental Protection Agency, U.S., 183
ethnic cleansing, 227
European Union, 218
Eve cigarettes, 58
evolutionary psychology, 27–28, 31
exclusivity, 235
Exeter, University of, 313, 320
experiential marketing, 83, 88–90
exurbia, 182–83

face-to-face marketing, 55–56, 80, 81, 89
fair-trade goods, 206
Falding, John, 329
Families of September 11, 329
fear, overcoming of, 212, 222, 232, 247–48, 249–62, 278, 282, 334
fear-based strategies, xix, xxi, 2, 19–20, 48–49, 59–60
Feed My Starving Children, 205–6
female genital mutilation, 33, 35–36, 292, 329
Feminine Mystique, The (Friedan), 177
Festinger, Leon, 23–24
Finsbury Park Mosque, 308, 325–26
Florida, antismoking program of, xxiii, 66, 75, 76, 77, 84, 114, 342
    advertising in, 67–71; see also "truth" antismoking campaign
    budget of, 66–67, 68, 74
    smoking-related lawsuit filed in, 66–67, 68
    state Health Department and, 68–69, 72–73, 74–75
    state legislature and, 73–74
    success of, 73–74
    SWAT groups in, 71–73, 74, 81, 92
    Teen Tobacco Summit in, 69, 71–72
Florida, University of, 48
Force More Powerful, A, 280
Fortune Society, Castle of, 293–97, 298, 324
Fowler, James, 285–86, 288
France, head coverings banned in, 316
Frazee, Randy, xxii, 171–77, 184, 185–86, 187, 189, 191, 192, 194, 200, 207, 209–10, 242

Frazee, Rozanne, 173, 174
Freedom House, 237, 269
Friedan, Betty, 177
"fried-egg" advertisement, 63–64
Friedman, Ray, 112
Friedman, Thomas L., 37, 180
friendships, 169, 171, 176–77, 199
    academic, 104, 107–8
From Dictatorship to Democracy (Sharp), 262

Gaffney, S.C., 51–54
Gagić, Miloš, 250
Gándara, Patricia, 109–10
Gandhi, Indira, 40
Gandhi, Mohandas, 224, 264
Gandhi as a Political Strategist (Sharp), 262
gang membership, 153, 154, 292–93, 297–302, 324
    Muslim, 304, 307–8, 319, 320, 321–22
Gayoom, Maumoon Abdul, 332–33
Geib, Matt, 52–53, 55, 56
Geis, Betty, 208–9
Geldon, Todd, 98–99, 105, 106, 107
generational change, 178–81
genetics, xx, 26, 28, 31, 102
Georgia, 278–79, 280, 332, 333, 334
Germany, 181, 303–4
    Baader-Meinhof Gang of, 306
Gil Díaz, Francisco, 345
GIO Global Intelligence, 87
Gite, Sakubai, 134
Githens-Mazer, Jonathan, 320–21
Gladwell, Malcolm, 34, 57
Glantz, Stanton, 64, 66, 74, 75, 80, 82
GlaxoSmithKline, 18
global warming, 340
Gómez, Concha, 106–7
Gonzales, Luis, 53, 55, 57
Gore, Al, 340
Gotov Je campaign, 270–71, 279
Graduate Record Exam, 111–12
Grameen Bank, 127–29
grapes, boycott of, 340, 341
gratification, delayed, 29, 43
groundBREAKERS, 7–10, 88
groups, see peer groups

group suicide, 92–93
Grutter v. Bollinger, 117

Habermas, Jürgen, 217
Habits of the Heart: Individualism and
*   Commitment in American Life*
*   (Bellah et al.), 178
Hahn, Sue, 114
Hall, Darryl, 299
Hamburg, Germany, 303–4
happiness, 181, 183, 285, 288
Hariri, Rafiq, 332
Harley-Davidson motorcycles, 89–90
Harris, Judith Rich, xx
Harris Interactive, 181–82
Harrison, David, xx, 6, 11, 13–14
Harry's Bar and American Grill, 63
Harvard Business Review, 164–65
Harvard University, 25, 285
Hawaii, 82
Hawkins, Greg, 187
Heinz ketchup, 87–88
Heisler, Michele, 155–56
Helvey, Bob, 262–64, 337
Hemingway, Ernest, 63
Henderson, William Darryl, 252
Henkin, Leon, 101
Henry V (Shakespeare), xxi–xxii
Hicks, Jeff, 67
Hill, Richard, 115
Hinduism, 36
HIV virus, 2, 6–7, 8, 9, 11, 13–14, 16,
    18, 83–84, 149
    contagion of, 4
    education on, 5
    in pregnant women, 10, 11, 23, 35,
    46
    sexual transmission of, 1, 2, 6–7
    see also AIDS
Hizb ut-Tahrir, 311, 330
HOG (Harley Owners Group), 89–90
Homen, Slobodan, 221, 229–30, 241,
    247, 259, 260, 271
    on Milošević's hit list, 250
    political office of, 277
    in U.S., 236–37, 239
homophobia, 22
homosexuality, 4, 22
Honduras, 338

Hopwood, Cheryl J., 116, 117, 118
house-builders, reciprocal, 148
How the Mind Works (Pinker), 27
Human Rights Watch, 227
Hume, David, 147–48
Hungary, 250, 262–64
Hunt, Rameck, 301–2
Husain, Ed, 327–28
Hussain, Ghaffar, 311, 327, 330
Hussain, Tharik, 313, 316–17, 318
Hybels, Bill, xii, 160, 162–65, 168–69,
    172, 185, 203–4, 206
    marketing techniques used by,
    164–65
    political views of, 204–5
    sermons of, 164, 204
Hybels, Lynne, 204
hypnotic suggestion, 22

"I Care" advertising campaign, 74–75
identity marketing, 85–87
Ilić, Branko, 257, 273
Illinois, 59, 60
    see also Willow Creek Community
    Church
Illinois, University of, 48
impulsivity, 26
India, xiv–xvii, xxiii, 130–47, 290–92,
    308, 349–50
    arranged marriages in, 37–39, 133–
    34, 143
    caste system of, xvi, xix, 36–42, 126,
    130, 131, 132, 133, 134, 135–36,
    137, 139–40, 142, 146–47, 292
    doctors in, 131–32, 140, 144, 290
    DOTS tuberculosis treatment in, 150
    dowries in, 41, 130, 137, 144
    harmful superstitions in, 41–42, 132,
    138–39, 142, 143
    leprosy in, 134, 138, 142, 143–44
    selective abortion in, 40–41, 130,
    292
    see also Jamkhed village-health-
    worker program
"industry manipulation" advertising
    theme, 64–66, 68, 70, 71, 74, 75,
    81
"Industry Spokesman" advertisement,
    65

Influence: Science and Practice
    (Cialdini), 34
information-based strategies, xix, xxi,
    2, 6–7, 8, 14, 19–20, 21, 44, 48,
    49 50, 83, 229, 239
internalization of risk, 6–7
International Criminal Tribunal, 274
International Imitation Hemingway
    ("Bad Hemingway") Competition,
    63
International Republican Institute
    (IRI), 237–38, 262–64, 269
Internet, 55–56, 85, 90–96, 179, 180, 181
    "buddy" groups on, 94–95, 156
    chat rooms of, 92–95
    Islamic terrorists on, 93–94, 306
Iowa, 59
    Just Eliminate Lies in, 82
Iran, 265, 280, 281, 333, 335
Iraq, 280
Iraq War, 204, 226, 305, 316, 329
Irish Republican Army (IRA), 325
"Iron Eyes Cody" advertisement, 47–48
irrationality, 21–42
    advertising and, 29–31
    culture in, 31–32, 121–22
    obedience to authority in, 32–33
    peer pressure in, 31–36
    see also self-deception
Islamic terrorists, 302–31
    BOG theory of, 306
    in Europe vs. U.S., 304, 324
    heroic self-image of, 305–6
    in Internet chat rooms, 93–94, 306
    in London, 304, 308–9
    9/11 plotters, 303–4, 305–6, 309,
        312–13, 324, 329
    self-radicalization of, 303–8
    see also London, England,
        counterterrorist efforts in;
        Muslims; suicide bombers
Israel, 305, 331
Ivan, Cris, 54

Jacobs, Jane, 176
James, Quentin, 53–54, 56–57
Jamkhed village-health-worker
    program, xiv, xv–xvii, xix, xxiii,
    37–39, 42, 130–47, 290–92, 349–50

    achievements of, 131, 141–42, 143,
        147
    auxiliary nurses in, 132–33, 290
    caste and, 132, 134, 135–36, 137,
        139–40, 142, 146–47
    compensatory business loans in, 131,
        136, 140–41, 145, 146, 147
    daily rounds of, 142–45
    diseases treated by, 131, 132, 138–39,
        142, 143–44
    doctors vs., 131–32, 135, 290
    establishment of, 131–38
    illiterate women recruited for, 133–
        35, 143, 291
    mobile teams' support of, 140
    preventive measures taught by, 131,
        132, 133, 134–35, 137, 139–40, 145
    respect earned by, 138–41
    self-confidence instilled by, 135–36,
        139, 141
    shared fellowship in, 138, 141
    soak pits project of, 142, 146
    superstitions countered by, 132,
        138–39, 142, 143
    taboos broken by, 144–45
    toilets project of, 131, 142, 146
    training of, 135–38
    tree plantings project of, 142, 145–46
    weekly discussions held by, 137–38,
        142, 145
    women's groups organized by,
        145–47
Japan, 92–93
Jelena (student activist), 224, 235, 257
Jenkins, George, 301–2
Jervis, Mike, 321–23
Jews, 328–29
    minyan of, 165
Joe Camel advertisements, 30, 58
Johns Hopkins University, 131
    Bloomberg School of Public Health
        of, 29
    Center for Civil Society Studies of,
        180
joint liability, 128–29
*Journal of Experimental Social
    Psychology*, 112
*Journal of Personality and Social
    Psychology*, 110–11

Journal of the American Medical Association, 58
Jovanović, Milja, 220, 221, 223, 224, 226, 230, 235, 240, 241, 243, 261, 268–69
Just Eliminate Lies, 82

Kadam, Lalenbai, xvi, 39, 41, 42, 130, 132, 135–36, 137
Kahn, Michael, 25
Kaiser Family Foundation, 3
Kamble, Alka Gokul, 147
Karadžić, Radovan, 218
Kean University, 114
Keye, Paul, 61, 62, 63–66, 68
Keye/Donna/Pearlstein, 64–66
Khatun, Sufia, 126–27
Kizer, Ken, 64
Kizziah, Carol, 295
Klitgaard, Robert, 344
Kmara youth movement, 278–79
Knox, Bill, 300
Konstantinović, Nenad, 236–37, 241, 249, 250, 260, 277
Koran, 309
Kosovo War, 220, 223, 227, 228, 232, 238, 273
Koštunica, Vojislav, 267–69, 272, 273, 274, 275, 276, 278
Kumbhar, Tukaram, 143–44

Laffin, Pam, 59, 60
Laibach Slovenian band, 224
Lambert, Robert, 310, 322, 325–26, 328
Larocque, Judy, 329
Laster, Hannah, 108
Latino college students, xvii, xxiii, 97–123
    see also Emerging Scholars program
Latinos, xxiii, 46, 156
    youth criminality of, 296
Laughlin, Henry P., 22
Lawrence, Stephen, 318
Lazendić, Stanko, 243, 250, 259, 279
Leaderless Jihad (Sageman), 93–94
Lebanon, 280, 338
    Cedar Revolution in, 332
Lee, Wayne, 299–300
Lemack, Carie, 329–30

leprosy, 134, 138, 142, 143–44
Lescano, Danny, 110
Lesotho, 3
Leswifi, Tebatso Klass, 8
Lewis and Clark College, 183–84
Licht, Sonja, 266, 278
lie-detector tests, 25
Life Learning Academy, 298
littering, 47–48
London, England, counterterrorist efforts in, 307–31
    Active Change Foundation in, 321–23
    Brixton Mosque and Cultural Center in, 308–21, 326, 328–29, 331; *see also* STREET
    countering Islamist narrative in, 327–28, 329, 330
    Deconstruct Program in, 313, 316–17
    Finsbury Park Mosque and, 308, 325–26
    "Good Muslim/Bad Muslim" in, 324–29, 330
    political conservatives' view of, 310–11, 326–29, 331
    street credibility in, 307, 330–31
    2005 bombing and, 317, 329
London, England, Metropolitan Police Service of, 311–12, 315, 318, 323, 329
    Central Extremism Unit of, 314
    IRA and, 325
    Muslim Contact Unit of, 310, 325–26, 328
Londonistan (Phillips), 311
London School of Hygiene and Tropical Medicine, 142
Long, Bridget Terry, 109, 112
Lorig, Kate, 94
Lorillard, 30
    American Legacy Foundation sued by, 78–79
Lossau, Matt, xi, 206
loveLife, xviii–xix, xx, xxii, 2–14, 30, 70, 83–85, 91, 284
    adult response to, 6
    billboards of, 6, 14, 30
    branding of, 5, 6, 14, 84–85
    coolness factor in, 6, 84–85

effectiveness of, 10–14
groundBREAKERS of, 7–10, 88
inception of, 3–5
lecture-hall strategy vs., 5, 8, 46, 49, 52
media campaign of, 5, 6, 14
naming of, 5
Orange Farm center of, 7
reach of, 13
at Serokolo High School, 8
size of, 10–11
Lowenkamp, Christopher, 297
Lucky Strike cigarettes, 70
Lukovi , Radojko, 251–52

MacAdam, Stephen, 106
Madrazo, Roberto, 348
Maguma, Sylvia, 16
Maine, University of, 115
Making Room for Life (Frazee), 171
Maldives, 282, 332–33, 340
Mandela, Nelson, 1–2, 4
Marcos, Ferdinand, 344
Marić, Aleksandar, 279
marijuana smoking, 49
marketing, *see* advertising and marketing
Marković, Mirjana, 240, 251, 259, 338
Marlboro cigarettes, 30, 58, 84
Marlboro Man, 70
Marović, Ivan, xvii–xviii, xxii–xxiii, 216, 219, 233, 245, 258, 260
    arrests of, 245–46, 253
    in CANVAS, 280, 281, 282, 332
    DOS and, 266
    secret police and, 250
    street actions staged by, 230–32, 241
Martin, Dorothy, 23–24
Marx Brothers, 32
Massachusetts, 59
Massachusetts Institute of Technology (MIT), 176–77
Master Settlement Agreement, 54–55, 68, 74, 76, 77, 78, 82–83
mathematics, teaching of, xvii, xxiii, 97–123
    see also Emerging Scholars program; remediation
Matić, Veran, 228

maturity, emotional, 25
Mbeki, Thabo, 4, 12, 15–16
McCluney, Brandon, 52–53
McDermott, Cheryl, 209
McMahon, Ed, 183
McPherson, Aimee Semple, 162
Mečiar, Vladimir, 270
Medicaid, 67
Meeks, James, 203–4
megachurches, 159–60, 165–66
    number of, 162
    sustainability of, 177
    see also Willow Creek Community Church
Mellado, Jim, 202–3
Mendoza, Daniel, 99
Mexico, 148
    corruption in, 339, 343–49
Mexico City, Mexico, Zona Rosa of, 33, 36
Mhaula, Grace, 17–19
Miami, University of, 74
Michigan, University of, 155
    annual "Monitoring the Future" study of, 57–58
Michigan State University, 115
microcredit movement, 125–30, 213, 291, 363n–64n
    first documented instance of, 127
    joint liability in, 128–29
    repayment rates of, 127, 128–29, 149
    see also small-business loans
microfinance, 127
midnight basketball leagues, 298, 302, 313–14
Milgram, Stanley, 32–33
Milić, Rade, 244–47, 257, 258–59, 261, 271
    arrest of, 253–55
military policy, xvii, xxi–xxii, 252–53, 306
Milivojević, Slobodan, 270–71
Milošević, Marko, 251–52
Milošević, Slobodan, xvii–xviii, xxii–xxiii, 129, 211–48, 249–75, 332–39
    arrest of, 274–75
    death of, 274
    early elections called by, 264, 265–69
    ethnic cleansing by, 227

fall of, 212, 238, 263–64, 272–74, 275, 276, 277, 278, 337
hit list of, 227–28, 250, 272, 273
hometown of, 251–52
independent media crackdown of, 264
nationalism of, 212, 218, 221, 227
nationalistic wars of, 216, 220, 223, 227–28, 229, 232, 273, 274, 305
1996 local elections annulled by, 216–19
people killed by, 212, 218, 227, 250, 273
personality cult of, 240
political methods of, 216, 220
Red Beret special forces of, 273–74
stealing election attempted by, 270, 272, 273
universities controlled by, 220, 221–22
violent repression by, 216, 335
see also Otpor; Serbia
mining industry, 4
minority college students, xvii, xxiii, 97–123
reasons for failures of, 97, 99–104, 121
see also Emerging Scholars program; remediation
Mississippi, smoking-related lawsuits filed by, 67, 68
Mitchell, Peter, 68–69, 71, 72–73
Mjaft! campaign, 282
Molotsi, Pauline, 23, 46
"Monitoring the Future" study, 57–58
Montana, 82
Montenegro, 227, 228, 240
Montgomery, William, 218
Monty Python, 229–30
Moon, Reverend Sun Myung, 306
mopane worm, 16
Moral Animal, The (Wright), 27
Morales, Dan, 116
Moreno, Susan Elaine, 108
Moss, Tim and Beth, xiii, 192–200
Mothers Against Drunk Driving, 46
Moussaoui, Zacarias, 309, 312–13
mpintshis, 7
Mundey, Peter J., 185

Muslim Brotherhood, 326
Muslims, 227, 302–331
anger of, 304–5, 307, 319, 329–30, 331
fundamentalist, 308–21, 326, 328–29
gang membership of, 304, 307–8, 319, 320, 321–22
grievances of, 307, 310, 315–16, 319, 328, 330
Salafist, 309, 310–11, 323, 326–27
Sharia of, 309, 327
Sunni, 309
in U.S., 304, 324
women, 309, 313, 323, 328, 329
see also Islamic terrorists

NAFTA (North American Free Trade Agreement), 345
Namibia, 12
NASHI (National Adolescent Sexual Health Initiative), 5, 8
National Bureau of Economic Research, 109
National Democratic Institute (NDI) poll, 265, 266–67, 269, 271
National Endowment for Democracy, 269
National Geographic, 349
National Kidney Foundation, 156
Native Americans, 47–48
NATO, 212, 226–28, 231, 236, 238, 240, 267
natural selection, 27
Nawaz, Maajid, 327, 329, 330–31
Nelson, Debra, 207–8
Nestlé, boycott of, 340
networking, 103, 112
nevirapine, 23, 45, 46
New Jersey, 59, 301–2
REBEL in, 81
Newport cigarettes, 58, 78–79, 84
New Urbanism, 182–84
New Urban News, 182
New Year's resolutions, 285, 289
New York, 76–77, 295
antismoking program of, 76
cigarette tax of, 54
Reality Check in, 77, 81–82

New York, N.Y., 35
 antismoking program of, 76–77, 80
 declining crime rate in, 34
 Fortune Society's Castle in, 293–97,
  324
 Police Department of,
  counterterrorism and, 303
New York Times, 37, 203, 204
New York University, 110
Nicaragua, 213, 265, 336
Nigeria, 280, 282
nonviolent resistance, *see* Otpor
Northbrook, Mr. (pseudonym), 188–89,
 191
North Carolina, 75
 TRU in, 82
North Carolina, University of, 14
North Dakota, 82
North Korea, 280, 333
Northwestern Mutual, 181–82
Notre Dame University, 185
'N Sync, 71
Nurture Assumption, The (Harris),
 xx
Nwokedi, Judi, 3, 4–5, 46, 49, 52, 88

Oak Hills Church, 200
Obama, Barack, 54, 87, 112, 182, 272
 presidential campaign of, 180,
  342–43
obesity, childhood, 29–30, 77
O'Brien, James, 238, 239
Ohio State University, 296
oil and gas, 177, 183, 237
Open Society Institute (OSI), 266, 269,
 278
OPOWER, 341–42
oral-rehydration salts, 132, 145
Orange Revolution, 279, 333
Oregonians Against the Blank Check,
 78
Orenco Station, Ore., 183–84
Origins of Virtue, The (Ridley), 27
Orion Telekom, 281
Ortega, Daniel, 265
Otpor, xvii–xviii, xix, 211–48, 249–82,
 332–39, 343, 347
 as band of itinerant revolutionaries,
  278–82; *see also* CANVAS

black T-shirt of, 229, 231–32, 235–
 36, 237, 253
branding of, 223–24, 263, 269–70,
 277, 282
camaraderie created by, 229–30,
 246–47
clenched fist logo of, 222–23, 225–
 26, 232, 234–35, 269–70, 271, 277,
 278, 280, 333
collective leadership of, 239–42, 249,
 250–51, 263, 264, 270–71, 280, 332
computer games based on strategies
 of, 280
coolness factor in, 223–24, 229,
 256–58, 260, 276
corporate marketing assistance of,
 234–35
decentralization of, 232, 241, 242,
 259, 264
demise of, 276–77
dilemma actions of, 230–31, 282,
 338–39
disillusionment stage of, 274–77
divisions within, 240–41
DOS and, 266–69
escape plans of, 251
exclusivity exploited by, 235
failed protests previous to, 216–20,
 221–22, 225, 226, 244, 247, 251
fear overcome by, 212, 222, 232,
 247–48, 249–62, 278, 282, 334
financing of, 233, 234, 235–39, 241,
 260, 268–69, 334
first actions of, 225–26, 252
foreign involvement with, 241, 250
founders of, 212, 216, 220–24, 225,
 227–28, 229–30, 240–41
front-page stories achieved by, 226,
 231, 233–34, 256
Gotov Je campaign of, 270–71, 279
graffiti of, 225, 233, 234, 252
humor and ridicule employed by,
 223, 229–32, 239, 256, 258, 263,
 279, 282
as illegal organization, 256–57
illusion of size created by, 225–26,
 233–34, 239, 242
information-based strategy eschewed
 by, 229

Otpor (*continued*)
  leaflets of, 225–26, 243, 250, 255, 257
  legal system used against, 250
  marches eschewed by, 230, 232
  meaning of term, 212, 222, 235
  membership of, 212, 226, 230, 232,
    249, 261, 263, 264, 271
  mission of, 212, 224, 239, 243, 275,
    276
  Monty Python as patron saint of,
    229–30
  as nationwide organization, 228,
    229–39
  NATO bombing and, 226–28
  New Year's Eve 2000 street action
    of, 232, 254
  nonviolence model of, 212, 222, 242,
    243, 258, 262, 272
  nonviolent discipline of, 259, 263,
    272–74
  November 1999 march to Parliament
    of, 245, 261
  oil barrel action of, 230, 231, 338–39
  paid professionals in, 237
  personal transformation in, 244–47,
    254–55
  pessimistic thinking changed by,
    212, 223
  pillars of regime targeted by, 258–
    60, 263–64, 268, 272–73, 280
  planning of, 212, 216, 224–25, 229–
    36, 279, 281–82
  as political party, 276–77
  posters of, 233, 234–35, 237, 238,
    243, 251–52, 259, 271
  press department of, 233–34, 241,
    245–47, 253–55
  recruitment by, 226, 233, 241, 243,
    245, 257, 261
  regime's epithets for, 235, 238, 245,
    250, 256–57, 259, 260–61
  reporters and photographers called
    by, 230–31, 233–34, 246, 253,
    255–56, 261
  rock music of, 224
  security forces targeted by, 268, 271,
    272–74
  Sharp's nonviolence theories noted
    by, 262–64

  slogans of, 234–35, 239, 261, 270–71,
    276
  spokespeople for, 241–42, 243, 246,
    261
  stickers of, 233, 234, 237, 238, 243,
    261, 271
  theatrical street actions of, 230–34,
    241, 243, 245–46, 252, 254, 255–
    56, 257, 259, 273, 276, 279, 338–39
  training manual of, 264
  two rules of, 243
  underground image of, 222, 225, 234
  U.S. government support of, 236–39,
    260, 268–69, 275
  volunteers in, 233, 237, 242–47,
    251–52, 256–57, 261, 263, 264, 271,
    275
  Vreme Je campaign of, 269–70, 279
  women in, 221, 224, 245, 257, 261
  youth vote mustered by, 269–72, 275
  Yugoslav Partisans as model for,
    222–23, 244
  see also Milošević, Slobodan; Serbia
Otpor, police involvement with, 222,
    230–31, 245, 249–62, 272–74, 334
  apparent pointlessness of, 259–60
  arrests in, 212, 225, 226, 230, 231,
    234, 243–44, 245–46, 249, 250–52,
    253–56, 257–59, 264, 335, 338–39
  beatings in, 212, 226, 245, 250,
    251–52, 253–54, 256, 261
  cell phones tapped in, 251, 259–60
  cheering for police in, 258, 263
  as coolness factor, 256–58
  counterproductiveness of, 260
  interrogations in, 253, 254, 259
  jail conditions in, 253, 254–55
  lawyers and, 255, 256, 271
  morale improved by, 256–57
  noisy supporters outside police
    stations in, 243–44, 246, 254,
    255–56, 259
  number of arrests in, 249
  Plan B of, 255–56, 337
  police files in, 259–60
  secret police in, 250–51, 271
  statements given in, 253, 254, 257
  widespread outrage produced by,
    260, 261–62

winning over policemen in, 257–59,
263, 279, 281

Pacharne, Savita Baba, 143
Pact, The (Davis, Jenkins, and Hunt),
301–2
PACT (Prevention and Access to Care
and Treatment) program, 151–52,
156–57
Pakistan, 93, 303, 321–22, 323
Pantego Bible Church, 171–77
parents, xx, 148
of minority college students, 97, 101,
102
teen smoking and, 30–31
Parkinson's disease, 26
Partnership for a Drug-Free America,
64
Partners in Health, 151–52, 156–57
Patel, Kishan, 99
patient adherence, 44–46, 149–57
to antiretroviral drug treatment, 44,
45–46, 151–52, 157, 288
cost savings and, 156–57
in curing tuberculosis, 149–51, 154
doctors and, 154–56
DOTS in, 150–52, 155, 213, 288–89
drug-resistant bacteria and, 44, 150
ineffective programs for, 150, 155
Pavlov, Vlada, 258, 266
peer groups, 31–42, 50–51, 102–4,
121–23, 147–48
antisocial, 296
bad, 292–302
defying expectations of, 35
happiness increased by joining of,
181, 183
identification with, xviii, xx, 33, 121,
148, 153, 239, 252–53, 284
independent-sector, 180
networking of, 103, 112
reciprocal house-builders as, 148
school power, 80–81
social norms of, *see* social norms
support, 95, 152–53, 154, 156,
284–85
see also Willow Creek Community
Church, neighborhood-based
(Table) groups of

peer pressure, xix–xxiv, 31–36, 46–48,
60–61, 72–73, 80–81, 83–90, 122–
23, 252–53, 282, 340–43
antigang, 301–2
in consumerism, 340–41
to defy authority, 32–33
in microcredit, 128–29
negative, 92–94, 307
negative connotations of, xx–xxi
radicalization by, 303–8
in Rage Against the Haze, 56–57
as resource, 147–57
in village life, 128–29, 148–49, 154
in weight control, 286–88
in youth criminality, 296
Peixoto, Tatiana, 98–99
Penn Schoen & Berland Associates, 265,
266–67
Penny, Charles, 300–301
People Power computer game, 280
Perez, Jared, 69, 70, 71, 73, 92
Pešić, Vesna, 216
Petrified Forest National Park, 47
Petrović, Nenad "Duda," 223, 230,
234–35, 243, 247, 271, 280
Petrović, Vakašin, 221, 245, 246
Pettifor, Audrey, 14
Philip Morris, 30, 70
Philippines, 280, 344
Phillips, Bradley, 53
Phillips, Melanie, 311
"Physiology of Catharsis, The" (Kahn),
25
Pierce, John, 30–31, 80–81
Pinker, Steven, 27
Pinochet, Augusto, 213–16, 265, 336, 337
Piot, Peter, 46
Plato, 34–35
Policy Exchange, 311, 326–27, 328
Politics of Nonviolent Action, The
(Sharp), 262
Popović, Srdja, 220–22, 223, 224, 232,
233, 235, 236, 240, 241, 260–61,
270–71, 335, 338–39
arrest of, 226
in CANVAS, 279–80, 281, 332
on Milošević's hit list, 228, 250
parliamentary seat won by, 275
on Sharp's ideas, 263–64

Portland, Ore., 183–84
poverty, 125–49, 199, 204, 205, 206,
    213, 274, 290–92
    in Chile, 214
    doctors and, 131–32
    happiness and, 181
    reasons for, 126
    social capital of, 147–49, 152
    village peer pressure and, 128–29
    see also India; microcredit
        movement
Požarevac, Serbia, 251–52
prefrontal cortex, 25
Preventing Violent Extremism (PVE),
    311
Princeton University, 165, 171
prisoner reentry into society, 43, 153,
    154, 156, 206, 292–97, 309, 314,
    315, 320
    programs for, 293–97, 324
"Programmed" advertisement, 65
public health, xviii, xix, 52, 64, 83, 131,
    291
    counterproductive methods of,
        46–50, 60–62, 83
    DOTS in, 151
    in India, *see* Jamkhed village-health-
        worker program
public service advertisements, 47–48
Putnam, Robert, 178–79

Qadir, Hanif, Imtiaz, and Abad,
    312–23
Quilliam Foundation, 311, 326–28,
    330–31

Radio B92 (B292), 225, 228, 246, 264,
    270, 272–73
Radio Index, 253, 264
Radio Television Serbia (RTS), 221,
    227, 228, 231, 240, 272
Rage Against the Haze, 51–57, 71, 77,
    79–83, 92, 235
    adult dislike of, 55
    budget of, 54–55
    face-to-face marketing of, 55–56, 81
    at high school football games, 51–54,
        56, 57
    illusion of size projected by, 81

peer pressure in, 56–57
    TV commercials for, 56
Rage Against the Machine, 224
Ralph Lauren Polo advertisements, 85
Ramachandran, Vilayanur, 26–27
Randjić, Dejan, 241, 270, 277
rationalization, 22
Ratković, Jovan, 225, 234, 240–41,
    261–62, 268, 277
reACT! Against Corporate Tobacco, 82
reaction formation, 22, 35
Reagan administration, 215
Reality Check, 77, 81–82
REBEL (Reaching Everyone By
    Exposing Lies), 81
Recife, Brazil, 127
recycling, logo of, 280
Red Queen, The (Ridley), 27
Reefer Madness, 49
regression, 22
Reid, Richard, 309, 312, 320
remediation, 108–13
    in community colleges, 109–10
    standards for, 109
    stereotype threat and, 110–12, 113
    success determinants vs., 112–13
Reporter, 253
repression, 22
Reproductive Health and HIV Research
    Unit study, 11, 14
reproductive success, 28
Republic (Plato), 34, 35
"Rescued" (Mellado), 202–3
Ridley, Matt, 27
Riordan, Meg, 80
risk, internalization of, 6–7
risk-taking behavior, xxi, 9, 13–15, 26
R. J. Reynolds Tobacco, 30, 56, 58, 68,
    78
Robinson, Russ, 166, 167, 189
Rock Volieb ("Rock the Vote") Slovak
    campaign, 270
Rose Revolution, 278–79, 333
Ross, Derrick, 299–300
RTI International, 75
Rutgers University, 27, 113

Sadafule, Surekha, 37–39, 42, 130, 132,
    138, 140

Sadat, Anwar, 331
Saddleback Church, 204
safe sex, xvii, xix, 1, 2, 6–7, 8, 9–10,
    11–12, 43, 44
Sageman, Mark, 93–94, 302–7, 309, 324
Salafism, 309, 310–11, 323, 326–27
Salamon, Lester, 180
Salem Baptist Church, 203–4
Salve, Sarubai, 138–40, 146–47, 349–50
San Antonio, Tex., 200
Sánchez, Raul, 98–99, 106, 107
Sandanistas, 213, 336
Sanford, Mark, 79
San Francisco, Calif., 64
    Delancey Street program in, 294–96,
    298
sangomas, 16–19, 138
Sarafina II, 2
Sathe, Babai, xiv–xvii, xxiii, 37, 39, 40,
    42, 130, 132, 138, 146–47, 349, 350
SAT test scores, 100, 101, 105, 109, 113,
    116, 120
Saudi Arabia, 309, 311, 312, 327, 328
Schoen, Douglas, 267
Schweitzer, April, 80
Scotch Plains, N.J., 286–87
Šeguljev, Nenad, 242–43, 257–58
self-concepts, 24
self-deception, 14–15, 21–28
    brain and, 25–27
    cognitive dissonance in, 23–25, 88,
        317
    ego defenses in, 22–26
    evolutionary psychology and, 27–28
    genetic factors in, 26, 28
    justifications in, 22, 23–25, 27
    selective, 28
    self-justifying information sought in,
        24–25
self-esteem, inflation of, 28
self-interest, 43–45, 148
Selfish Gene, The (Dawkins), 27
Seoul, South Korea, 162
September, 11, 2001, terrorist attacks,
    303–4, 305–6, 309, 312–13, 324,
    329
Serbia, xvii–xviii, xix, 211–48, 249–82,
    332–39
    Bulldozer Revolution of, 274, 278

calendar of, 232
disillusionment stage of, 274–77
economy of, 220, 227
Greater Serbia concept of, 217
historic grievances against neighbors
    of, 227, 229
inat as national trait of, 239
insular political culture of, 228
legal system of, 250
national day of recognition for
    security forces of, 258
nationalism in, 224
national strike called in, 272
NATO bombing of, 226–28, 231,
    236, 238, 240, 267
NDI poll of, 265, 266–67, 271
1996 local elections in, 216–19
organized crime in, 218, 223–24,
    244, 269, 274, 276
political parties of, 217, 218, 222,
    224, 229, 231–32, 237–38, 239–40,
    275
prime minister of, 267–68, 274–75
sardonic humor in culture of, 229–30
security forces of, 263, 268, 271,
    272–74
small-town TV stations in, 234, 335
turbo-folk music of, 224
university students in, 218–19, 220,
    226
    see also Milošević, Slobodan; Otpor
Serbia, political opposition in, 216–20,
    221–22, 237–38, 244, 262, 263,
    265–74
cities and towns controlled by, 216–
    19, 220, 225, 234, 237, 335
as cults of personality, 239–40, 242
DOS coalition of, 265–69, 270, 273
independent media in, 220, 225, 226,
    227–28, 231, 233, 243, 255–56,
    260, 263, 264, 269, 335
infighting of, 217, 220, 221, 238, 264,
    276
Milošević's selective killing of, 250,
    273
U.S. government support of, 237, 269
Zajedno coalition of, 216–19, 220
Serbia, 2000 elections of, 237, 261, 264,
    265–74, 275, 278

Serbia, 2000 elections of (*continued*)
DOS coalition in, 265–69, 273
Milošević's attempted stealing of, 270, 272, 273
October 5 enforcement convoys of, 272–73, 274, 278
parallel vote count of, 270, 272, 335
youth vote in, 269–72
Sernovitz, Andy, 86–87, 88, 90
serotonin, 26
Shakespeare, William, xxi–xxii
Sharia, 309, 327
Sharing the Journey (Wuthnow), 170–71
Sharp, Gene, 262–64, 346
Shevardnadze, Eduard, 278–79
Showalter, Allan, 154–55, 156
Sibaca, Sibu, 8–10
Siberia, 71–72
Šikman, Siniša, 256, 259–60, 279, 280
Silva Thin cigarettes, 58
Simonelli, Lucia, 108
simultaneous relationships, pattern of, 4
Sinclair, Michael, 3
Singapore, 344
Singleton, Mike, 208–9, 210
Slovakia, 270
Slovenia, 216, 224, 227
small-business loans, xv, xvi, 126–29, 131, 136, 140–41, 146, 147, 149, 154
bhishi scheme in, 145
see also microcredit movement
Smart Growth, 182–84
smoke-free areas, 76, 81
smoking, 14–15, 21–22, 24, 29, 30–31, 43, 45, 48–62, 63–83
death and, 21, 43, 59, 60, 64, 70, 75
genetic factors in, 26
illnesses related to, 59, 67
marijuana, 49
prevalence of, 57–58, 59, 64, 66, 73–75, 76, 79–81, 82
secondhand smoke from, 65
see also antismoking programs; cigarettes; tobacco companies
social contagion, 285–86
of suicide, 93

social cure, xvii, xix–xxiv, 20, 21, 22, 29, 66, 83–90, 140, 165, 167, 188, 191, 192, 195, 331
in antismoking campaigns, 50–62, 73, 77, 78–79, 81
behavior change and, 43–50, 100, 121
catalysts of, 130–47
consumer-generated media for, 87–88
Emerging Scholars program and, 98, 100–105, 113, 120, 121–23
first step in, 187
hard-sell issues addressed by, 83
helping others as benefit of, 88, 156, 289
identity marketing for, 85–86
as indirect solution, 129
military uses of, xvii, xxi–xxii, 252–53, 306
Otpor and, 212–13, 229, 239, 244, 250, 276, 278
problems susceptible to, 121, 125–30, 147–58, 161, 282, 283–351
showing up in, 83–84
two conditions needed for, 153–54
for Western middle-class people, 154–58
social isolation, 35, 36, 157–58
social norms, xx, 33–42, 76, 305, 316, 342, 346, 348–49
antismoking, 76–77
in counterproductive advertising, 46–48, 60–61
in India, 36–42
nonviolent, 324
permission-giving and, 287–88
pro-suicide, 93
pro-terror, 306, 307, 330, 331
social psychology, 31–33
Sociobiology (Wilson), 27
Solar, David, 257
Soros, George, 266
South Africa, 1–19, 274, 279–80
apartheid in, 1, 3–4, 5, 18
education in, 7–8
KwaZulu-Natal province of, 11
sangomas of, 16–19, 138
sex as taboo subject in, 4
XDR-TB in, 150

South Africa, AIDS in, xviii–xix, xxii,
   1–19
   antiretroviral treatments of, 12,
      15–16, 18–19, 45–46, 138
   deaths from, 4, 12, 16, 18, 19
   magic cures for, 16–17
   mopane worm as cure for, 16
   in newborns, 23, 35
   of pregnant women, 10, 11, 23, 35,
      46
   prevention program for, see loveLife
   rates of, 1, 2–3, 10–14
   school as protective factor in, 13–14
   sex with virgin as cure for, 16
   simultaneous relationships pattern
      in, 4
   stigma of, 4, 16, 17, 35, 46
   as taboo subject, 4
South Carolina, 51–57, 79–83, 92, 342
   antismoking programs neglected by,
      54–55
   cigarette taxes in, 54, 76, 79
   Health and Environmental Control
      Department of, 55
   high school football in, 51–54
   motto of, 54
   teen smoking decline in, 79–81
   see also Rage Against the Haze
South Carolina Physicians Care
   Charity, 55
Soviet Union, 56, 149, 150, 278, 338
Speer, Natasha, 115–16
Sprite advertising campaign, xix, 5, 7
Stamenković, Andreja, 228, 241
Stanford University, 34
starfish strategy, 185–86, 242
State, 54–55
State Department, U.S., 236–37, 238,
   239
Steele, Claude, 110–12
Stephen, Jennifer, 87
stereotype threat, 110–12, 113
Steuteville, Rob, 182
STREET (Strategy to Reach, Empower
   and Educate Teenagers), 310–11,
   312–21, 322–23, 324, 328–29, 330
   activities of, 313–14
   budget of, 314–15
   clientele of, 313

   effectiveness of, 319–20
   motto of, 318–19
   questions brought to, 318
   street credibility of, 314, 318–19,
      320, 321, 331
   violent extremism refuted by, 310,
      315–19
   Web site of, 317
stroke, left-brain vs. right-brain, 26–27
Studio B TV, 225, 264
study, small-group, 289–90
   see also Emerging Scholars program
suburbia, 36, 161, 162, 165–66, 172–73,
   176–84
   Smart Growth design of, 182–84
suicide, group, 92–93
suicide bombers, 306–8, 309, 312, 315–
   16, 327–28, 330, 331
   free-rider problem of, 306
   negative peer pressure in, 307
Sunni Muslims, 309
support groups, 95, 152–53, 154, 156,
   284–85
Supreme Court, U.S., 117
Surgeon General's Report on Smoking
   and Health, 59, 61
Swarthmore College, 31
SWAT (Students Working Against
   Tobacco), 71–73, 74, 81, 92
Swaziland, 3
Switzerland, minarets banned in, 316, 325

Tabacki, Teodora, 226, 252
Table groups, see Willow Creek
   Community Church,
   neighborhood-based (Table)
   groups of
Tadić, Boris, 232, 277
Talmud, 165
teenagers, xvii–xix, xxi, xxii, 2–14, 46,
   152, 153
   bad judgment in, 25
   fashions of, 33
   fear as ineffective deterrent of,
      48–49, 59–60
   and internalization of risk, 6–7
   obesity rate of, 29–30
   smoking by, 29, 30–31, 43, 57–62;
      see also antismoking programs

teenagers (*continued*)
 suicides of, 93
 see also South Africa, AIDS in
Teen Tobacco Summit, 69, 71–72
televangelists, 162
television, 6, 14
 community time reduced by, 178
 global popular culture on, 5
 obesity rate linked to, 29–30
television commercials, 14, 47–48, 56,
 65, 69–73, 75, 79, 81, 85, 87, 88
"tells," 28
Tembisa, South Africa, 17–19
temptation, 284–88
Texas, University of, at Austin, 98–99,
 106–8, 113, 114
 affirmative action at, 116–19, 120–21
thrill-seeking, 26
Thun, Michael, 77–78
Tipping Point, The (Gladwell), 34, 57
Titanic, 67
tobacco companies, xvii, 50–62, 63–83,
 292
 advertising of, 29, 30–31, 50, 58–59,
  61, 64–66, 68, 77, 88
 Congressional testimony of, 68
 experiential marketing by, 88–89
 internal documents of, 54, 56, 57, 68,
  69, 70
 international, 71–72
 lawsuits against, 30–31, 58, 66–67,
  68
 lawsuits filed by, 78–79
 litigiousness of, 79
 lobbying of, 73, 77–78
 Master Settlement Agreement with,
  54–55, 68, 74, 76, 77, 78, 82–83
 as target of antismoking campaigns,
  50–57, 65–66, 68, 69–75, 81
 see also cigarettes; smoking
Tocqueville, Alexis de, 178
Transparency International, 343
Trapido, Ed, 74
Treisman, Uri, xxiii, 97–98, 100–105,
 106, 110, 113, 117–18, 120, 121–23,
 127–28, 132
triathlon race, 286–87
Trivers, Robert, 27–28
Triwomen group, 286–87

TRU (Tobacco Reality Unfiltered), 82
"truth" antismoking campaign, 69–75,
 76, 78–79, 81, 92, 317
 branding of, 70, 84
 budget of, 74, 75
 prank phone calls in, 70, 73
 teen-designed ads for, 69–71
Tshabalala-Msimang, Manto, 12
tuberculosis, xvii, 138, 142, 143, 213
 cure of, 149–51, 154, 288–89
 XDR-TB, 150
Tudjman, Franjo, 336
turbo-folk music, 224
Tuscaloosa News, 74
TV Guide awards, 48
twins, studies of, 26

Ukraine, 150–51, 280, 332, 334
 Orange Revolution in, 279, 333
Ulemek, Milorad "Legija," 273–74, 275
"Unchurched Harry," xii, 160, 163, 185,
 201
unconscious mind, 22
Unification Church, 306
United Farm Workers (UFW), 340, 341
United Nations, 228
 AIDS agency of, 46
 Environment Programme of, 227
universities, 97–123
 affirmative action in, 101, 113,
  116–21
 SAT test scores and, 100, 101, 105,
  109, 113, 116, 120
 success determinants for, 100, 101,
  112–13, 120–21
 see also Emerging Scholars program
Untouchable (Dalit) caste, xiv–xvii,
 36–42, 126, 130, 131, 133, 135–36,
 137, 139–40, 142, 146–47
Urban Land Institute, 183
Urošević, Jelena, 221
Urquhart, Omar, 308

value, consumer-added, 87, 88
Vanderbilt University, 112
Vaudrey, Scott, 190, 201
Venezuela, 280, 333, 337
Vietnam War, 339
Virginia, University of, 26

Virginia Slims cigarettes, 58
Vreme Je campaign, 269–70, 279

Wahhabism, 309
Wahrman, Harlan, 181–82
Warren, Rick and Kay, 204
Washington Post, 4, 57–58
We Generation, 181–82
weight control, 95, 285–88
Weight Watchers, 95, 285, 286
"What Business Can Learn from
    Nonprofits" (Drucker), 164–65
Whistling Vivaldi (Steele), 110
Wiebler, Peter, 237
Wilders, Geert, 316
Williams, Bradley, 57
Willow Creek Association, 160, 168–69,
    171 72, 186, 202
Willow Creek Community Church, xi–
    xiv, 159–77, 184–210, 211, 242, 340
    Advocate for Global Engagement of,
        204
    anniversary celebrations of, 203
    annual food challenge of, 199, 206
    anonymity as founding mission of,
        160, 163–64, 165, 172, 184, 201,
        203
    area pastors of, 170, 201, 206, 207
    committed believers at, 164, 168,
        169–71
    diversity of, 203–4
    food for Zimbabwe orphans project
        of, 190, 205–6
    gym of, 186
    local service projects of, 203, 205,
        207–9
    market surveys conducted by, 163,
        164–65, 167–69
    McHenry County satellite church of,
        203, 206–10
    midweek service for committed
        believers of, 164, 169, 186, 187
    music of, 164
    naming of, 164
    political issues and, 204–5
    "Reveal" survey of, 167–69, 170, 171
    seekers as target audience of, xii,
        160, 163–64, 169, 184, 185, 201,
        202–3
    spiritual growth issue of, 161, 168–
        69, 170, 176, 177, 195–200, 208
    taped sermons of, 164
    theatrical weekend services of, 162,
        164, 167, 169, 192, 202
    2005 Christmas services canceled by,
        184
    "Walking with God" curriculum of,
        166
Willow Creek Community Church,
    neighborhood-based (Table)
    groups of, xi–xii, xiii–xiv, xix,
        xxii, 166–77, 184–210
    affinity-based groups vs., 160–61,
        167, 169–70, 176–77, 184, 185, 188,
        194, 200–201
    challenges to, 187–92
    conventional small groups vs., xii–
        xiii, 160–62, 166–71, 184, 186, 188,
        194, 207
    as evangelistic agents, 185–86
    rewards of, 192–200
    see also community
Wilson, E. O., 27
Winston cigarettes, 30, 56
Wisconsin, University of, 106, 113
Witwatersrand, University of,
    Reproductive Health and HIV
    Research Unit of, 11, 14
Wolfe, Chuck, 68–69, 76
women:
    discrimination against, xix, 37–42,
        130
    in Emerging Scholars program, 108,
        114, 116
    in India, *see* India; Jamkhed village-
        health-worker program
    Muslim, 309, 313, 323, 328, 329
    in Otpor, 221, 224, 245, 257, 261
    pregnant HIV-positive, 10, 11, 23,
        35, 46
    small-business loans to, 126–28, 131,
        136, 140–41, 145, 146, 147, 149, 154
    stereotype threat and, 111, 112
"women's" cigarettes, 58
Woodson, Robert, 299–300
word-of-mouth marketing, 83, 86–88
World Is Flat, The (Friedman), 37
World Vision, 205

World War II, 177, 178–79, 231–32
    Yugoslav Partisans in, 222–23, 244
Wright, Robert, 27
Wuthnow, Robert, 165, 170–71, 175
Wyatt, Lisa, 117

XDR-TB (extreme drug-resistant
    tuberculosis), 150

Yale University, 32
    Law School of, 341–42
Yanukovych, Viktor, 279
Yoido Full Gospel Church, 162
Yonamine, Doug, xi–xiii, xvii, 169–71,
    186–88

Yonamine, Jen Tweedie, xi, 186–88
York Zimmerman, 280
YouTube, 87
Yugoslavia, xvii–xviii, 129, 211–48
    see also Serbia
Yugoslav Partisans, 222–23, 244
Yunus, Muhammad, 126–29
Yushchenko, Viktor, 279

Zajedno coalition, 216–19
Zimbabwe, 10, 190, 205–6, 279, 280,
    337
Zimbardo, Philip, 34
Ziqubu, Vusi, 19
Zuma, Jacob, 16

[About the Author]

TINA ROSENBERG IS THE AUTHOR OF *CHILDREN OF CAIN: VIOLENCE and the Violent in Latin America* and *The Haunted Land: Facing Europe's Ghosts After Communism*, which won the Pulitzer Prize and the National Book Award. She was the first freelance journalist to receive a MacArthur Fellowship. She is a contributing writer for the *New York Times Magazine*, was an editorial writer for the *Times*, and writes an online column, Fixes, for the *Times*. Her work has also appeared in *The New Yorker*, *Rolling Stone*, *The Atlantic* and many other publications. She lives in New York City with her family.